LITERACY PORTFOLIOS IN ACTION

Sheila W. Valencia
University of Washington, Seattle

This book was written by Sheila W. Valencia in collaboration with the following elementary school teachers from the Bellevue Public Schools: Lynn Beebe, Sue Bradley, Robin Carnahan, Marla English, Nancy Place, and Phyllis Richardson. Each of these teachers not only wrote a chapter but helped conceptualize the book and contributed ideas, examples and experiences about literacy learning, instruction, and portfolios to every chapter.

Harcourt Brace College Publishers

Fort Worth   Philadelphia   San Diego   New York   Orlando   Austin   San Antonio
Toronto   Montreal   London   Sydney   Tokyo

Publisher:	Earl McPeek
Acquisitions Editor:	Jo-Anne Weaver
Product Manager:	Don Grainger
Developmental Editor:	Tracy Napper
Project Editor:	Laura Miley
Art Director:	Don Fujimoto
Production Manager:	Andrea A. Johnson

DEDICATION

For our colleagues on the Bellevue Literacy Portfolio Project
and the students of Bellevue Public Schools.

ISBN: 0-15-505139-3
Library of Congress Catalog Card Number: 97-71347

Address for orders:
Harcourt Brace College Publishers
6277 Sea Harbor Drive
Orlando, FL 32887-6777
1-800-782-4479

Address for editorial correspondence:
Harcourt Brace & Company
301 Commerce Street, Suite 3700
Fort Worth, Texas 76102

Web site address:
http://www.hbcollege.com

Printed in the United States of America

7 8 9 0 1 2 3 4 5 6 039 9 8 7 6 5 4 3 2 1

PREFACE

I first began working with Bellevue teachers in 1989, as they were reconceptualizing their student learning outcomes for literacy. As with other curriculum development projects, it quickly became apparent to teachers and administrators that the content and form of their assessments had to change as well. Classroom-based portfolios became our focus. A year later, we began a long-term collaboration to design and implement classroom assessments that would help us document student progress on the learning outcomes, and that would also help us improve teaching and learning. When we began this process, none of us could have imagined that it would last seven years, and none of us would have predicted that we would write this book. Now, after seven years of problem-solving, conducting action research, collecting data, and actually implementing portfolios, we are ready to share our work with teachers and administrators who want to change the face of literacy assessment and instruction.

The concepts and strategies contained in these pages have stood the test of time and of experimentation by many teachers working at many grade levels with students from diverse backgrounds. Our intention is not to provide a formula or prescription for how portfolios should look or how they should be implemented and used, but rather to take you through a process of thinking about how to put portfolios into action. We hope to raise issues and offer ideas for your consideration; ultimately, the decisions to make are yours and they must fit with your goals for student learning, your particular students, your teaching style, and your purposes for keeping portfolios. Our aim is to foster good instruction—to view portfolios as an instructional tool as well as an assessment tool. In the end, it is good instruction that improves student achievement, not simply good assessment.

This portfolio book is different from many other portfolio books in two important ways. First, we systematically present a way of *thinking* about portfolios. We model, if you will, a process for making decisions about the type of portfolio, what to place in it, how to structure interactions with it, and how to use it to evaluate student progress and report to others. In other words, rather than simply providing ideas, we provide a problem-solving approach that teachers can use to make their own decisions. We do this by describing the rationale and thinking behind what we do as we present examples from our own classrooms and our students.

Second, we emphasize *using* portfolios rather than simply collecting student work. The premise of this book is that if literacy portfolios are to achieve their intended benefits, then they must be used by teachers and students as instructional tools as well as assessment tools. *Using* portfolios in this way requires that teachers and students understand the reading and writing processes, be able to interpret student literacy work samples and portfolio artifacts, and apply that knowledge to improve instruction and learning. In this book we use actual student portfolio artifacts to discuss student performance and instructional considerations. We also help readers understand how to use portfolios by providing suggestions for making portfolios an integral part of instructional lessons and for helping students learn how to engage in self-reflection and self-assessment.

Literacy Portfolios in Action is intended for new and experienced teachers in grades K–8; we assume that readers have a basic understanding of literacy learning and instruction. It can be used as a supplementary text in literacy courses, it can stand alone as a text for literacy assessment courses and professional development experiences, or it can be used as an individual professional resource. The chapters are clustered into three sections. The first section (chapters 1 and 2) provides the conceptual framework for understanding classroom-based assessment and portfolios. In this section several different portfolio models are presented. It is important to read this section before reading any of the other chapters because terms used throughout the book are introduced and explained here. Section 2 (chapters 3–8) dives into the heart of using portfolios including logistics of setting up and managing portfolios, in-depth analysis of reading and writing artifacts, issues of growth, and the role of self-reflection and self-evaluation for students and teachers. Section 3 (chapters 9 and 10) addresses using portfolios to communicate with outside audiences, both parents concerned with individual children and administrators concerned with large-scale portfolio evaluation. Each of the ten chapters begins with an overview and a quote from a student, teacher, or parent involved in the portfolio process. Research background, conceptual frameworks, practical suggestions, and dilemmas are woven throughout each chapter.

I am indebted to several colleagues and friends who, over many years, have helped me think about portfolios and ultimately supported the writing of this book. First and foremost are my co-authors Nancy Place, Lynn Beebe, Sue Bradley, Robin Carnahan, Marla English, and Phyllis Richardson. This remarkable group of teachers has done the hard work of implementing portfolios and they have generously shared their classrooms, their thinking, and their successes and failures in the most collaborative and intellectually stimulating context I have even experienced. A special group of colleagues, Karen Wixson and Freddy Hiebert (University of Michigan), Marge Lipson (University of Vermont), Kathy Au (University of Hawaii), Taffy Raphael (Oakland University) and David Pearson (Michigan State University) have been constant companions as I have conceptualized, debated, and researched the quagmire of literacy assessment. They also provided the needed encouragement to write this book and helpful feedback on the chapters. A special thanks to Walter Parker for his tireless interest and support throughout the two years this book has been in progress.

I also want to thank the people at Harcourt Brace who were patient during the long manuscript production and quick to respond to my concerns. Jo-Anne Weaver, the acquisitions editor, supported my vision for this book and stood by until we were ready to write. Tracy Napper carefully watched over the content and production. And Laura Miley's careful attention to the manuscript preserved the integrity of the ideas and of teachers' voices. She juggled art, text, timelines, and budgets with grace and attention to detail.

Finally, I want to thank the students, teachers and administrators of Bellevue Public Schools who have become my lifeline to daily school life and my inspiration. They have taught me more than they will ever know.

SWV
8/97

ABOUT THE AUTHORS

Bottom row (left to right): Phyllis Richardson, Lynn Beebe, Sue Bradley. Top row (left to right): Robin Carnahan, Sheila Valencia, Marla English, Nancy Place

Phyllis Richardson is in her eighth year of teaching at Newport Heights Elementary, in Bellevue, Washington. She enjoys a multiage classroom of seven- and eight-year-olds. Phyllis has presented workshops statewide and nationally about the importance of involving parents in portfolio assessment. She recently completed her Masters of Language Arts.

Lynn Beebe has been a classroom teacher for 24 years, having taught preschool through post grad students. She currently teaches a multiage primary classroom of six- to nine-year-olds in Bellevue where her interests center around investigating children's thinking, portfolio-based assessment, and creating a democratic classroom. She has been a member of the Four Seasons National Faculty, worked with the New Standards Project, and has presented workshops locally and nationally on multiage classrooms and portfolio assessment.

Sue Bradley has been teaching in a multiage, third–fifth grade combination classroom for the last eight years at Ardmore Elementary, Bellevue, Washington. Sue has made several presentations about the project at state and national conferences and she has worked on Washington State's Learning Goals for Reading and The New Standards Project in language arts.

Robin Carnahan teaches a multiage class of second and third graders at Eastgate Elementary School in Bellevue. She has taught both regular education and special education classes in California and Washington. She has been associated with the Bellevue Literacy Assessment Committee since its formation has been the building portfolio leader for her school.

Sheila Valencia is Associate Professor of Education at the University of Washington, Seattle. Her teaching and research are focused on literacy instruction and assessment, with a special emphasis on classroom-based assessment and professional development. Sheila has served on several national and statewide assessment task forces and has worked with numerous school districts to develop classroom-based assessment systems. She has published articles in *Educational Assessment, Reading Research Quarterly, The Reading Teacher, Language Arts, The Journal of Reading Behavior,* and *Applied Measurement in Education.*

Marla Rae English has been a multiage primary teacher for eight years at Woodridge Elementary School in Bellevue, Washington. Her classroom is composed of six-, seven-, eight-, and nine-year-olds. In 28 years of teaching, her assignments have included high school, preschool, and self-contained special education for severely/profoundly handicapped students. She was a five year participant in the Four Season Alternative Assessment group, Member of the Four Season National, a participant in the New Standard Literacy Portfolio Project.

Nancy Place has been a curriculum specialist in Bellevue Public Schools for the past 10 years. Currently a Reading Recovery teacher and District Language Arts Specialist, she directs the Bellevue Literacy Portfolio Project with Sheila. She has been a leader in the New Standards Portfolio Project and has presented papers and workshops on portfolios at state and national conferences. Prior to working in Bellevue, Nancy was a classroom teacher and college instructor in Asia and the Southwest, and was on the faculty of Pacific Oaks College in Pasadena, CA.

TABLE OF CONTENTS

PART 1

Definitions, Principles, and Decisions

chapter 1

Why Portfolios?
Assessment Principles and a Portfolio Definition

SHEILA W. VALENCIA

We begin this chapter with six principles for sound classroom assessment. Using these principles as a backdrop, we then provide a working definition of portfolios. These principles and the definition provide a framework to help you design, implement, and reflect on your own classroom portfolios as they evolve.

The essential benefit of portfolios lies in the shifting of the paradigms of teaching and learning. Portfolios are a shared process. The tendency in the past has been to look at teaching and learning in isolation from each other—"I teach; you learn"—when, in fact, the two cannot and should not be isolated from each other.   *L. G., intermediate teacher*

My "awakenings" about assessment can be traced back to three professional experiences. The first insight occurred in 1972, my initial year of teaching. I had been hired in October to teach a new "overflow" class in a large inner-city school in Brooklyn, New York. The other five sixth-grade classes had more than 40 students each, so they decided to form a new class—mine. The reading levels of my 35 students ranged from preprimer to ninth grade. I was overwhelmed, scared, excited. I talked with my more experienced colleagues, watched them carefully, and took notes on what they taught, how they taught, and how they managed their classrooms.

In November, the assistant principal visited each of the sixth-grade teachers, handed us a shrink-wrapped package of standardized reading tests, and said, "Lock these in your closet; keep them safe. We're going to administer them in January, after the Christmas break." I dutifully placed them into my personal locked closet and forgot about them. A few weeks later I noticed an odd coincidence—lists of vocabulary words began to

1

appear in all the sixth-grade classrooms. And the words on these lists were remarkably similar. It didn't take long for me to catch on. I went to my closet, tore open the test packet, and found the words I suspected I would find. "So," I thought to myself, "these are the words sixth graders should be learning. I guess I'd better teach them." And so I proceeded to introduce lists of words and have students look up definitions and use the words in sentences. Of course, my best efforts didn't necessarily result in student success when January testing came around. Although Roseanne breezed through the test in 40 minutes, Daryl decided, after looking at the first couple of words and their five multiple choice definitions, that he was too sick to take the test, and Javier, my primer-to-second-grade-level success story, put his head down after 15 minutes of desperate effort. It's hard to imagine that those word meanings, my vocabulary "instruction," or that assessment experience was ever useful or informative for the students; it certainly wasn't for me.

My second insight happened 15 years later in the Midwest while I was a researcher at the University of Illinois. My colleagues and I arranged a meeting with a local school principal to discuss a reading comprehension study we hoped to do. The meeting went well. We settled on logistics, then we asked for permission to use the results of a standardized test the district had given several months before. The principal shared the summary test results with us, proudly indicating that students were at the 60th percentile in reading, although none of us was sure exactly what students had read or done to score at the 60th percentile. He graciously agreed to allow us access to student test data and showed us the sealed pack that had just arrived. We thanked him and made arrangements to return six weeks later to begin the study and to record the standardized test information.

Six weeks later, we returned and asked the school secretary for the test scores. She led us into the principal's office and located the test results still in the same sealed package and still on the corner of the principal's desk. We opened the package, recorded the results, placed them back onto the desk, and got on with our study, fairly certain that the test results would remain in the very same spot for a long time to come. By the time we finished our work in the school, it had been more than four months since the students had taken the test, and still no results had been shared with teachers, parents, or students.

My third insight happened more recently. I was visiting several classrooms in which children were keeping and using portfolios. As I entered one classroom I noticed a large cardboard box filled with tagboard folders— the portfolios. Each was brightly decorated by these third- and fourth-grade students. As the children entered the class that morning, several made a beeline for their portfolios, entering work they had completed the day before or had brought from home. But the students weren't particularly efficient about filing the work; they lingered, looking through some of their older pieces, sharing with other students who were nearby.

I eavesdropped, startled at the level of "good talk" that quickly emerged. One young man and his friend congratulated each other on the "cool" *Star*

Wars story they had just completed, including very detailed drawings of the final battle. They debated how to put a copy of the story into both of their portfolios. Together they laughed at how "bad" their stories had been at the beginning of the year—no excitement in them. At the same time, a fifth-grade girl looked through her folder, searching for the poem she had written earlier in the year so she could revise it to give to her mom as a birthday present. It wasn't quite as good as she remembered. She decided that she would need to work on a new poem. Another youngster couldn't find his portfolio; he had refiled it alphabetically, but it wasn't there. It was on the teacher's desk. The teacher had been working with it before school as she was preparing for parent conferences and writing her progress report. The teacher explained that she wasn't finished using the portfolio, but she invited the youngster to take it off her desk and return it when he was finished using it.

Taken together, these three experiences highlight some of the problems of past assessments and some of the possibilities of more recent assessment efforts. The first experience demonstrates vividly what happens when assessment drives curriculum and leads to inappropriate outcomes, teaching, and learning. It's not that my colleagues or I wanted to cheat; I honestly believe we were trying to make good decisions about what we should be teaching. We inferred that if it was on the test, it must be worthwhile to teach, both in content and in form. Unfortunately, this was a bad inference. In contrast, the second experience demonstrates what happens when assessment has *no* influence on curriculum, instruction, or assessment of students' learning. Time, money, and effort are wasted. Both are extremes—perhaps brought on by overemphasis on testing that is outside daily classroom life, perhaps brought on by placing assessment into "others' hands" rather than into the hands of teachers and students, perhaps brought on by an overconcern with numbers and achievement rather than growth. The third experience is a bright light in this darkness. It represents how assessment can become seamlessly integrated into classroom life. Using classroom work in students' portfolios, teachers and students shared the assessment process and valued the information they derived as they stepped back to look thoughtfully at where they had been and where they needed to go next.

Fortunately, we can learn from all these experiences. As educators, policy makers, and test publishers reconceptualize assessment, they will try to do better. And, as teachers, inside our own classrooms, we, too, will try to do better. Although we still have a long way to go, we have made great strides in our understanding of what good assessment should look like.

New Insights

One of the most important insights of the past ten years has been that assessments must tap the literacy of thoughtfulness—the thinking curriculum (Brown, 1991; Resnick & Resnick, 1992; Shepard, 1989). We are seeing a dramatic shift in *what* is assessed as well as in *how* it is assessed (Linn,

1994; Mitchell, 1992; Shepard, 1995). Instead of answering multiple choice questions aimed at discrete reading and writing skills, or literal questions about simple reading selections, students are asked to use literacy to engage in complex and challenging tasks. Many new standardized reading and writing tests, for example, require students to read texts similar to those they would read in real books and to write about what they have read (e.g., Garcia & Verville, 1994; Valencia, Pearson, Peters, & Wixson, 1989). Other assessments require students to work collaboratively in their classrooms over several days to perform tasks such as reading about a topic and writing a research report, building a model, or carrying out a science experiment (e.g., Kapinus, Collier, & Kruglanski, 1994; National Council on Education and the Economy, 1996; Shavelson, Baxter, & Pine, 1992; Weiss, 1994). And other new forms of assessment, such as portfolios, rely on classroom-based evidence of student progress produced during the natural flow of ongoing learning (Valencia & Calfee, 1991; Wolf, 1989).

A second important insight acknowledges that a single assessment cannot meet the needs of different audiences who are interested in assessment results (Cole, 1988; Farr, 1992; Shepard, 1989; NCEST (The National Council on Educational Standards and Testing), 1992; Valencia & Pearson, 1987). My experiences in New York and the Midwest are glaring examples of how large-scale, standardized assessments didn't meet the needs of teachers or students. These tests didn't provide the kind of ongoing, specific feedback and opportunity for reflection that is essential to improve teaching and learning. However, you should not infer from these examples that there is no place for standardized tests or, conversely, that all audiences want classroom-based assessment. The problem in the preceding examples was threefold: (a) The standardized tests didn't assess higher levels and meaningful application of literacy, (b) they didn't provide useful information to teachers and students, and (c) they were the *only* assessment used to meet the needs of administrators, teachers, parents, and students.

Some audiences—legislators, school boards, and administrators, for example—are not concerned about the performance of individual students or the achievement of specific learning goals; they need summary information on broad outcomes for large groups of students, and, generally, they need this information only once or twice a year. Standardized assessments such as writing samples or standardized reading tests usually provide the systematic and reliable information needed by these audiences outside the classroom. Sometimes this information provides a norm-referenced comparison of student performance, other times it provides a comparison with specific standards (criterion-referenced) (Taylor, 1994). Students and teachers, on the other hand, need information about individual performance, and they need to gather and think about that information almost daily so they can make good instructional decisions and set meaningful learning goals (Calfee & Hiebert, 1992). Their concern is with individual students' strengths and needs and with how to foster growth. They use ongoing collections of classroom-based assessment evidence to guide their decision making. Parents are usually interested in a combination of information, including standardized assessments and more specific and useful classroom-based assessment evidence (Flood & Lapp, 1989).

Although different audiences need different types of assessment, educators and policy makers caution against relying solely on any one indicator of student achievement. Instead, they call for a combination of different types of assessments (e.g., writing, performance assessments, projects, portfolios, interviews, videotapes) that might be used *together* to form a complete assessment system (Farr, 1992; Costa, 1989; Shepard, 1989; Wixson, Valencia, & Lipson, 1994). The National Council on Educational Standards and Testing recommended:

> No one test or assessment should be asked to serve all the assessment purposes. We need, at this point, a system made up of articulated components, glued together by their adherence to content standards, and serving explicit purposes for assessment. (NCEST, 1992, p. F-14)

Most remarkable, however, in all these new assessment efforts is the priority placed on classroom-based assessment—assessment carried out as a natural part of everyday classroom life, assessment like the portfolios I described earlier. Because classroom-based assessment grows out of classroom work, focuses on individual students, and feeds back directly to teachers and students, it is the most likely to improve teaching and learning. Teachers and schools are reemerging as the locus of assessment and decision making, and classroom-based assessment has become the linchpin in an effective assessment system. However, classroom-based assessment, by itself, will not be inherently better than past assessments simply because it is new or different. In fact, we know that most teachers have been inadequately prepared for classroom-based assessment (Hiebert & Calfee, 1989; Stiggins, 1991) and that there is a lingering mistrust of assessments that rely on teacher judgment. What *will* create effective classroom-based assessments is teachers who have a sound conceptual understanding of six basic principles of good assessment. Now we turn to these principles.

Principles for Sound Classroom Assessment

Now we describe six principles that will help you design a strong classroom assessment system:

- authenticity
- alignment
- continuous assessment
- multiple indicators
- collaboration
- reflection

These principles address some of the concerns of the past and set the stage for a new approach to assessment. We can think of no better way to put these principles into action than to implement portfolios in your classroom.

Authentic Texts, Tasks, and Contexts

During the past 15 years, literacy instruction has moved away from a focus on discrete skills and reading and writing of artificial texts to the application of skills and strategies and to reading and writing of more natural texts. Our assessments should reflect this authentic focus. Classroom literacy assessment must resemble "real" reading and writing activities that students might engage in as part of their daily lives in school and outside of school. This translates into three aspects of authenticity: authentic texts, authentic tasks, and authentic contexts in which students demonstrate their learning. All three aspects of authenticity are important.

Authentic texts. Authenticity is most obvious in the material students read; it is easy to recognize specially constructed texts that control vocabulary, sentence length, or concept load. If you read these artificial texts, it's also easy to see why students might find them uninteresting or confusing. Fortunately, since literature-based instruction and process-writing curricula have been implemented, classroom reading and writing materials now include a wider variety of real-world texts and purposes for writing. Students read trade books, full-length texts, magazines, informational articles, and books and use research material in school and out; these types of texts should be represented on assessments. In classes, students are writing for many different purposes and audiences; these should be represented in authentic assessments as well.

Authentic tasks. Authenticity of literacy tasks is a bit more elusive. An authentic task requires students to engage in an activity that is meaningful, realistic, and useful. Authentic assessments permit us and our students to evaluate the learning directly rather than indirectly. This is sometimes called *performance assessment* (Hiebert, Valencia, & Afflerbach, 1994; Taylor, 1994). The goal is for students to *demonstrate* the actual learning in meaningful contexts as much as possible. The real, authentic learning becomes transparent, readily seen and understood by students, teachers, and parents. When my sixth-grade students were asked to select the correct definitions from a list of five, they were not engaged in an authentic vocabulary task. A more authentic task might have asked students to read a selection which included several new vocabulary words and then asked them to discuss or to answer questions that relied on those words to understand important ideas in the selection. Vocabulary knowledge *is* important, but multiple choice tasks are not an authentic assessment of that knowledge.

Figure 1.1 is a poem designed to assess first graders' understanding of a particular decoding skill—short vowel sounds. It provides a good example of an authentic text used for an inauthentic purpose.

Although "Choosing" is an authentic poem, appropriate for most first graders, the task of circling all the short vowel sounds is an artificial task for reading this poem. Try to complete this task yourself. You will probably

Figure 1.1

> Read the poem.
> Then circle all the words that have short vowel sounds.
> The first line has been done for you.

Choosing
Eleanor Farjeon

Which will you have, a ball or a cake?
A cake is so nice, yes, that's what I'll take.

Which will you have, a cake or a cat?
A cat is so soft. I think I'll take that.

Which will you have, a cat or a rose?
A rose is so sweet, I'll have that, I suppose.

Which will you have, a rose or a book?
A book full of pictures? Oh, do let me look!

Which will you have, a book or a ball?
Oh, a ball! No, a book; No, a - -
There, have them all!

This assessment activity uses an authentic text, but circling short vowels makes it an inauthentic task, distracting students attention from the poem.

---

find yourself mouthing the words one by one, losing sight of the content of the poem, the humor, and even the rhyme. Certainly, this is not an authentic reading of the poem. Furthermore, after you have completed the circling task, you probably have little motivation to return to the poem just to enjoy it! Not only is this an odd task, one that students never actually do in life, but also completing it sends two unfortunate messages. The first is that the reason for learning short vowel sounds is to circle them in words, not because they help us *read* words that make up interesting poems and stories. The second message is that the purpose of reading interesting texts (poems) is to do odd things with them (i.e., circle isolated words) rather than to enjoy their meaning, the sound and sense of language.

Similarly, it would be inauthentic to ask students who have read *Charlotte's Web* to list in correct sequence the events in the book or in a chapter.

A more appropriate and authentic task for this text would be for students to trace the development of the friendship among the characters, a major theme of the book. Listing things in order, however, would be very appropriate for cooking or for providing directions for constructing a model or perhaps for reading a detective mystery. Writing a letter to the chamber of commerce to request information about a field trip the class is planning would be a functional and authentic use of letter writing; writing a letter to the main character in a favorite book is inauthentic, unlikely to get a response or to communicate with someone who is interested in what the writer has to share. The point is that literacy tasks, as well as texts, need to be authentic. They should fit with the purposes and unique characteristics of the texts children read and write.

Authentic contexts. The need to evaluate literacy learning in authentic contexts is apparent to anyone who has observed a child taking a standardized test. Not only are the texts and tasks often artificial, but also having students "perform" for 45 minutes to demonstrate ability is far removed from how students actually use and apply their learning. After completing a 40-minute writing sample about "an important day in your life," a third-grade boy asked his dad, "Will I always have to write everything in 40 minutes?" His dad's response was clear and thoughtful: "Not always, but there are times when you will have only a short time to write down what you need to." Writing about an important day in your life, without talking with a friend or spending a considerable amount of time deciding *which* day, is certainly not authentic. Perhaps writing a summary of the book you've just completed or a welcome note to a new student could be completed in a shorter time. Our assessment contexts should be as authentic as possible.

Alignment of Assessment, Curriculum, and Instruction

Classroom assessment must be aligned with curriculum and instruction. Simply stated, we should assess what we teach and teach what we assess. Furthermore, the learnings we ultimately decide to teach and assess should be those that we judge to be meaningful and valuable for our students (Wiggins, 1991; Wixson, Peters, & Potter, 1996). This requires careful thought and deliberation about what students should know and be able to do—often referred to as *content standards* or *learner outcomes*. Although this principle seems obvious, my early experiences with assessment demonstrate that alignment may not always be easy. Curriculum, instruction, and assessment may be misaligned in three different ways. We may (a) assess outcomes that have not been taught or practiced, (b) teach and stress particular outcomes that are not assessed, or (c) assess learning in a way that is different from how that learning is taught, practiced, and used in the classroom.

The first two misalignments can be thought of as opposite sides of the same coin. For example, several years ago a local school district decided to implement direct writing assessment instead of depending on multiple choice items as a measure of students' writing abilities. Students were given a choice of several topics and then spent three days planning, drafting, and revising their papers. Although district personnel were pleased about the move to a more authentic writing assessment, they were appalled when the results were released. Not only were scores low in all areas—organization, ideas, voice, sentence fluency, and conventions—but also there was little evidence that students had used the writing process to create their finished pieces. Discussions with classroom teachers revealed the problem: Few of the schools in the district had implemented process writing in their classrooms! Although the district now had an authentic writing assessment, it was not aligned with the curriculum and instructional strategies in most classrooms. Without this realization of misalignment, district personnel might have assumed that students hadn't learned to apply the writing process and needed "remediation" instead of considering the possibility that students hadn't been given adequate opportunities to learn and to practice process writing. Alternatively, the opposite might happen: Some important learning outcomes may be emphasized in classes but not assessed. For example, many local reading outcomes now include attention to literary interpretation, critical stance, and personal response (Langer, 1995), yet the majority of standardized reading assessments still include predominantly literal-level questions. Similarly, even with new forms of classroom-based assessment, such as portfolios, students may have learned particular outcomes that for some reason may not be included in the students' classroom portfolios (Valencia & Au, 1997). As a result of this type of mismatch, students and teachers may not know how well students can apply some of the important literacy outcomes they have learned.

The third type of mismatch occurs when there is a difference between the format of the assessment and authentic learning outcomes. A familiar example is to assess spelling by having students select the one correctly spelled word from a list of five instead of examining samples of students' writing. Not only is this type of assessment inauthentic, but also it is not aligned with the way spelling is taught and practiced in school and in life. Similarly, students' abilities to use and apply word recognition strategies are often assessed by having students identify words that contain similar sounds or circle words that have the sounds of, say, short /e/. However, authentic assessment of these word recognition abilities is best accomplished by observing how students apply their strategies while reading a real text.

Misalignments between curriculum, instruction, and assessment are not simply an inconvenience—they are a critical problem. When instruction and assessment are misaligned, students' true abilities are not assessed and our instructional decisions are likely to be inaccurate. Furthermore, when we realize that a misalignment exists, the tendency is to revise the curriculum, which may lead to our teaching isolated skills and to confusion about which outcomes are important; the test becomes the curriculum instead of the curriculum becoming the assessment. So not only does misalignment lead to misinterpretation of assessment results, but also it may negatively influence what is taught in schools.

Classroom-based assessments often have built-in alignment. If the assessment comes directly from what students are doing in the classroom, as compared with "drop-in" types of tasks, it is automatically aligned with the content and the format of instruction. However, this doesn't automatically mean that what is happening in the classroom is valuable or authentic. In the early days of portfolio experimentation, I reviewed a sample portfolio that contained a few student-generated stories and more than 30 fill-in-the-blank reading and writing worksheets. Not only were most of the worksheet formats artificial, but also the learnings that were emphasized were not important literacy outcomes; they focused on isolated skills such as matching words with the same sound, circling correct answers to comprehension questions, and writing words in alphabetical order.

In contrast, some teachers who are using classroom-based assessment keep track of student progress by creating a two-way chart. Important curricular outcomes are listed down one side, and next to each is a space for teachers and students to write progress notes for each outcome. In fact, one middle school teacher asks her students to complete the chart, listing the work they have completed, which demonstrates their accomplishments in each outcome. If the space is empty, the teacher examines both the student's performance and her own teaching. The exercise of thinking about, and constructing a framework for, aligning curriculum, instruction, and classroom assessment is a critical component of a strong assessment system.

Continuous, Ongoing Assessment

Good assessment is an ongoing process. It provides specific and immediate feedback to teachers and students so they can adjust teaching and learning, and it honors students' progress and growth over time. One of the frustrations with traditional standardized tests is that they fail to capture specific information about changes in learning over time. This is particularly true for students whose abilities are very far above or below their grade placements; standardized tests often don't include enough appropriate items for these students to demonstrate their abilities. Therefore, the results are not accurate indicators of what students can do. Furthermore, even when these tests are administered every year or twice per year, they don't provide specific or timely information about change. They simply provide scores. Javier, my sixth grader who had progressed from preprimer to second-grade reading level, couldn't answer more than 5 questions out of 40 on the sixth-grade reading test. His score didn't reveal any useful information about his achievement, and it provided *no* information about his growth since the beginning of the school year.

Without a doubt, teachers, parents, and students are concerned about students' progress over time. The most useful assessments for examining change and for making sound instructional decisions and setting goals are those that come from the classroom. Figure 1.2 shows three samples of writing collected from Jeffrey, a first-grade student, in September, October, and November. The growth over time for this emergent writer is dramatic. From September to October he has written a more complete accounting of his experience using a problem/resolution structure for his story. In addition, he has developed more conventional sound/symbol relationships in several of his words (i.e., in September *TE=tooth*, in October *TOF=tooth*) and has a better sense of word boundaries (i.e., in September *FOT=fell out*, in October each word stands alone). By systematically assessing Jeffrey's writing in September and October, Jeffrey and his teacher were able to set goals and focus instruction. As a result, the changes in the November paper are even more dramatic. In this piece, he describes two events and connects them in time for the reader. Not only has the story developed, but also Jeffrey now has a sense of sentences, and he uses end punctuation. Again, his sound/symbol spelling correspondence is progressing.

This is the kind of information needed to make good instructional decisions and judgments about learning. Honoring growth is integral to meaningful assessment. However, standards must be considered as well. Standards are specific benchmarks or indicators of learning that people agree are "worthy and tangible goals for everyone—even if, at this point in time, for whatever reason, some cannot (yet!) reach" them (Wiggins, 1991, p. 21). Standards anchor our expectations for students and assure that we have a clear vision of good performance. Wiggins (1993) points out the difference between making progress on a personal level and reaching an agreed-upon standard or goal. He says, "Teachers do students and parents a great disservice when they report results as growth and not progress (toward a standard or goal), because they invariably make it seem as if the student is closer to meeting a valid standard than the (growth) comment . . . really implies" (Wiggins, 1993, p. 286).

Imagine, for example, the conversation between Jeffrey's teacher and his parents if he were a fourth grader rather than a first grader. His individual growth still would be essential to discuss; however, so, too, would be his writing performance in terms of specific expectations for most fourth-grade students (e.g., story development, sentence structure, conventions, invented spelling). It is unfair—in fact, unethical—not to be honest and clear about student performance with reference to specific standards, especially when performance is far different than the expected standards or expectations set for students at a particular age or grade. This is not to say that growth is unimportant. It is. Instead, this is to say that both growth *and* clear, high standards are important for children. Unfortunately, students from nonmainstream backgrounds are often provided with lower-quality educational experiences and held to lower standards than are mainstream children (Au, 1993). A study conducted in 1975 highlighted the importance of having high standards for all students. The researchers found that although the teachers worked hard and had intentions of "being nice," they

Figure 1.2

MI TE FOT AND I LOVE IT

My tooth fell out and I love it.

9/90

MY TOF WOSS
LOSS OT WOSS
BEDEN ALOT BOT
I GOT SEM
WODR ON
MY TOF

My tooth was loose.
My tooth was loose. It was

bleeding a lot but I got some

water on my tooth.

10/90

Figure 1.2 *continued*

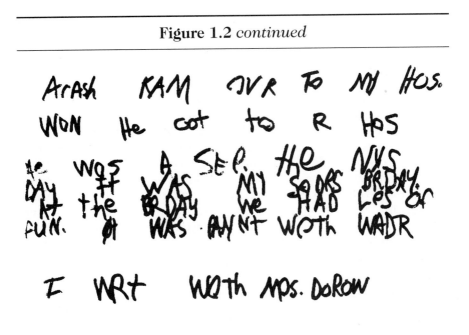

Arash came over to my house. When he got to our house, he was asleep. The next day it was my sister's birthday. At the birthday, we had lots of fun. I was painting with water. I wrote with Mrs. Dorow.

11/90

Samples of Jeffrey's writing over three months reveal his growth in several aspects of writing and reading.

---

had essentially stopped trying to teach African-American children in their classes. The researchers concluded:

> We have shown that oppression can arise out of warmth, friendliness, and concern. Paternalism and a lack of challenging standards are creating a distorted system of evaluation in the schools. (Massey, Scott, & Dornbusch, 1975, cited in Delpit, 1988)

Assessment must value both individual growth and clear, high standards for all.

Multiple Indicators of Performance

Student performance varies depending on the tasks and contexts. Some of the newer, more formal assessments use different types of tasks to tap students' performance under different conditions. For example, the New Standards Project has developed assessments in which students read and write different types of texts, use oral and written response modes, and work both independently and collaboratively (National Council on Education and the Economy, 1996). In Maryland, after students read several selections on a similar social studies or science topic, their written responses to comprehension questions are scored both for understanding of the content and for writing ability (Kapinus, Collier, & Kruglanski, 1994). And in Vermont, students are required to include evidence of writing for several different purposes in their statewide writing portfolio assessment (Koretz et al., 1994).

Classroom-based assessments provide more opportunities than these standard assessments to sample variability in student performance. Because they rely on a wide array of tasks that occur as a natural part of classroom life, students can demonstrate their learning under a variety of conditions. Look, for example, at the difference between Austen's reading comprehension performance when he wrote a response and when he dictated a response (see Figure 1.3). If we were to depend solely on Austen's written response, we might conclude that he was unable to read or understand the story. The dictated version of his summary shows just the opposite—his comprehension is quite good. He did, however, have difficulty understanding the assignment and organizing his thoughts in writing. Austen's teacher recognized the problem and tried another assessment strategy with him. Many students, like Austen, are placed at a disadvantage when classroom assessment relies on only one type of indicator (i.e., writing). This classroom sample not only exemplifies the importance of multiple modes of assessment, but also highlights how we can gain information about several important literacy outcomes—in this case, reading comprehension, personal response, and writing—from a well-crafted, authentic assessment task.

It is critical, then, to vary the type of assessment evidence we gather. We can think of the variety along several dimensions—type of evidence, level of support, type of text, and time spent (see Figure 1.4). Austen's reading comprehension performance is a good example of how the type of evidence influenced our understanding of his comprehension abilities. Unfortunately, other types of evidence such as oral presentation, discussions, conferences, and interviews are more time consuming and difficult to document. This is one reason why important learning outcomes such as oral language and dramatic interpretation of literature have not been given the attention that more easily documented learnings have received. Some teachers prefer informal anecdotal notes; others prefer prespecified observation checklists for documenting hard-to-gather evidence. Whatever your choice, it's important to vary the type of evidence to meet the needs of the students and the learnings you want to assess.

Students also perform differently depending on the amount of "scaffolding" or assistance they receive (Graves & Graves, 1994; Lidz, 1987). Whereas past assessments overrelied on individual, independent work, the risk for classroom-based assessments is that most tasks will be teacher-

---

Figure 1.3

Retelling

Name __Austen__

Date __Feb 4, 1992__

Selection ___How Spider Got A Thin Waist___

Number of pages __Six__

1. What do you think this reading will be about?   *misinterpreted question*
can't answer
~~How you retell a Story.~~ *after reading*

2. What do you already know about the topic?

eight legs
2 parts of body
lots eyes
diff shapes/colors

that I havft to read a Story and retell it

Retell the story as if you are telling a friend who hasn't read the selection.

Once upon a time there was a spider & sons, elder & younger. He was really lazy Then he was walking one day and then he remembered it was a feast day for the village. Then he walked upon 2 villages and he didn't know which to go to. So he went up and climbed up a tree & thought about it. Then he came up w. an idea

---

supported or collaborative. Knowing what students can do both with and without support is important. Similarly, the content and structure of different types of texts and the amount of time students spend on a task will influence their performance. Teachers could certainly add to the list of dimensions shown in Figure 1.4 or alter the descriptors for each (e.g., type of

---

Figure 1.3 *continued*

And he decided to go to one who
opened first. So asked elder son to take
one end of rope and take it to east village
& when that villages opened, pull rope hard.
He asked younger son to take end of rope
to east villages. and pull rope hard when
opens. Then awhile later the both elder
& younger son pulled at same time
Then ~~he it sque~~ he didn't know which
one to go to. The 2 sons dean't know why
father "not coming. So they pulled harder
end rope got so tight that it made
the spider's waist really skinny. up
                                                       until today.
1. How accurate was your prediction about the story?   he was skinny
        Forgot - went up tree twice to think
                    danced after each time.

2. What surprised you in the story?
        I thought when pulled rope. It
        wouldn't get stiff it would
        just set there

3. Who else do you think would enjoy reading this selection?
        Somebody who likes celebration
        like reading about surprises
        and parties.
        Or people who like insects.

---

*It would be easy to misinterpret Austen's reading comprehension from
his written responses. However, through his dictated responses, we
learn that his reading comprehension is quite strong.*

---

text—easy, average, difficult) to fit their individual classrooms. The point is
to ensure that we don't fall back into the trap of using a single approach or
format to assess the wide array of learnings and situations that occur in our
classrooms.

Figure 1.4 also shows a partial table of contents from a third-grade port-folio and the range of types of evidence included. By locating the pieces on dimensions, it is easy to see the approaches that have been overused and underused. For example, the majority of artifacts are written work—there are no records of oral presentations or observations and only one set of reading conference notes. Most of the final stories have received a good deal of teacher guidance, but few have been collaborations with other students, and few extended writing tasks have been completed independently. Most of the reading and writing have been with narrative texts. And there is a nice variety of brief activities and longer, more sustained projects. The point behind multiple measures is *not* to try to cover all the points on the con-tinua but, rather, to recognize that student performance will look different depending on the type of evidence, level of support, and amount of time spent on the task. By using multiple measures to assess student perfor-mance, we are more likely to get a complete and true picture of what stu-dents can do.

Collaboration among Student, Teacher, and Parent

Somehow, in the past, we came to believe that assessment ought to be secretive—the test content was "secure," the scores were entered on confidential student records, and the results were used by "others" to judge students and teachers rather than by the students and teachers them-selves. But these kinds of assessments are unlikely to produce the best re-sults or to encourage the best quality learning. Students and teachers cannot focus their efforts unless they have a clear, shared understanding

Figure 1.4

Dimensions of Multiple Indicators

Type of Evidence

written work	oral presentation	interview	observation

Support

independent	collaborative	some teacher support	carefully guided by teacher

Type of Text (Genre)

narrative	informational	poetry	persuasive	document/directions

Time

brief task	over several days	over an extended time

Figure 1.4 *continued*

Looking at Multiple Indicators
Table of Contents
(September–January)

A: Reading response journal
(*1,000 Cranes*)
B: Reading log (January–February)
C: Questions about reading log
D: Home reading record
E: "Sheila the Great"—character
profile and drawing
F: Personal writing goals for December
G: Buddy journal
H: "The Girl That Shrunk" (rough
draft and final)

I: "Training for a Meet" (final only)
J: "A Long Story" (planning, draft,
revision, and final)
K: Self-reflection on literature circle
discussion
L: Reading conference—teacher notes
M: Reading summary
N: "My Best Friend" (published story
with illustrations)

Dimensions of Multiple Indicators

Type of Evidence

A, B, C, D, E, G, H, I, K, M		L	
written work	oral presentation	interview	observation

Support

A, B, C, D, G, J	N	F	H, I, J
independent	collaborative	some teacher support	carefully guided by teacher

Type of Text (Genre)

A, F, H, I, J	I, M			
narrative	informational	poetry	persuasive	document/directions

Time

C, F, K, M,	B, D, E, I	G, H, J, L
brief task	over several days	over an extended time

---

*It is important to gather information about students by
using a variety of indicators. Their performance
will vary in different situations.*

of their goals and meaningful opportunities to evaluate their own progress toward those goals. They must work *together* to clarify the attributes of high quality work. Then, teachers must work deliberately to communicate, collaborate, and model those attributes clearly with the students.

Delpit (1988) discusses powerfully the importance of making standards explicit and clear, especially to students of color who may come to school not knowing the expectations. Although Delpit sees value in process approaches to teaching, she also demands that expectations and standards be clear to students. She writes:

> Teachers do students no service to suggest, even implicitly, that "product" is not important. In this country, students will be judged on their product regardless of the process they utilized to achieve it. And that product, based as it is on the specific codes of a particular culture, is more readily predicted when the directives of how to produce it are made explicit.
>
> If such explicitness is not provided to students, what it feels like to people who are old enough to judge is that there are secrets being kept, that time is being wasted, and the teacher is abdicating his or her duty to teach. (Delpit, 1988, p. 287)

We must move away from what Pearson calls "guess what's in the teacher's head" to a shared, clear, and specific vision of what we want to accomplish. When students and teachers realize that they are coassessors of teaching and learning, assessment loses its punitive connotation and becomes a shared responsibility that has value for all the participants. For example, poor performance on an assignment would not cause a student to become embarrassed or a teacher to become angry. It could, instead, motivate the student to ask for help or clarification, and it could encourage the teacher to think about how instruction might be improved. Collaborative assessment not only fosters a shared understanding of results, but it also fosters a partnership in the learning process.

Collaboration extends beyond teachers and students to a three-way collaboration among teachers, students, and parents (Daniels, 1996; Henderson & Berla, 1994). Although educators have always tried to involve parents, the task is made more difficult by once-a-year parent-teacher conferences and report cards that communicate learning in numbers and grades. But collaboration and communication can occur at any time during the year. Collaboration becomes easier when actual evidence of student work is shared and when the conversation is focused on *what* and *how well* the child is learning rather than on grades (Paratore, 1993; Salinger & Chittenden, 1994). Because students are discussing and collaborating with teachers in class, they can share the responsibility of collaborating with parents (Countryman & Schorieder, 1996), and likewise, teachers can benefit from parents' insights (Paratore, 1993, 1994). After reviewing and discussing classroom work with her son, one parent noted:

> I learned that Cole's reading comprehension has improved. Cole is becoming an avid reader which I think is great. I like his journal. He is getting better and better at including more detail in his writing. His penmanship is improving.

The teacher concurred with this mom's insights. Together, child, parent, and teacher were able to examine progress and set appropriate goals. It is this shared knowledge and vision that mark collaborative assessment.

Self-Reflection and Self-Evaluation

The most compelling change in assessment has come from the recognition that teachers and students should be active participants in the assessment process. Years of research indicate that students who are self-directed, who can assess their own strengths and needs, and who set appropriate goals are more likely to be high achievers (Biemiller & Meichenbaum, 1992; Pressley, Woloshyn, Lysynchuk, Martin, Wood, & Willoughby, 1990). The same is true for teachers. Those who are reflective practitioners, able to be thoughtful and critical of their own teaching, are more likely to be effective teachers (Ball, 1996). Traditional approaches to assessment might have been able to produce scores, but they certainly didn't produce teachers or students who learned about themselves from the assessment or who cared about the results. Whether they were standardized tests, teacher-made assessments, or exercises that were part of a textbook series, the strategy was for students to complete the assessment, for teachers or test companies to grade them, and for teachers to enter results in a grade book. There was little ownership for learning and little value placed on setting personal goals and evaluating progress toward them. These assessments were not "episodes of learning" (Wolf, 1989). Neither students nor teachers were able to use the assessment tasks or the results to gain insight into teaching or learning.

When reflection is part of the assessment process, students and teachers are reminded that assessment is *part* of learning, not something that they have to do for someone else. Reflection grows naturally out of classroom assessment because instruction and assessment are integrated. Both teachers and students learn that people improve by judging their own performance against exemplars and clearly defined standards. In turn, they become more expert at understanding what good work looks like, more likely to be self-directed, and more invested in their own learning and progress—all of which lead to success.

Sometimes this self-assessment of learning takes on a personal response, as seen in this eighth-grade student's comments about a piece she had written titled "The Stranger in the Motel":

> This is a true story and it happened to me and a close friend. It is a factual story and it felt very good for me to get it out on paper.

In other instances, self-assessment is more focused on specific criteria for good work. The following reflection, written by a sixth-grade student, shows clearly how the process of self-assessment can help students clarify what they have learned and give teachers insights about students' thinking:

> I have decided that "Katherine's Performance" is my worst piece because I accidentally got carried away and ended up writing 3 different plots which screwed up my story. . . . Next time, I'll take more time editing it.

There is little doubt that this student understands the importance of a clear, strong story line when writing narratives. She also recognizes that the problem might have been avoided if she had spent more time revising her work. From this reflection, both student and teacher have a clear focus for future instruction. Not surprisingly, the students' next attempt at narrative writing was stronger.

Self-assessment also changes the way teachers think about teaching and learning. Just as for students, some teachers find personal value in implementing classroom assessment. The process of integrating assessment with instruction and examining closely student learning seems to provide renewed enthusiasm and a sense of purpose for teachers. Marilyn, a first/second-grade teacher, reflected on her own growth by listing several changes in her teaching:

> . . . much less teacher directed learning, more student voice and choices, structure provided when and (for) whoever needs it . . . .

She reflected on her thoughts, concluding:

> All of the above changes feel good when they're happening—but I'm working harder than I ever have and am sometimes overwhelmed with the planning and organizing. I like what I'm doing and have more to do—so I didn't retire this year!

The hard work Marilyn describes includes more than the logistics of classroom assessments. It includes substantive thinking about what we want students to be able to do and about how to judge their progress. Just as reflection helps students clarify the attributes of good work, it also provides the same clarification for teachers. As a result, teaching becomes more focused and systematic.

Summary of Principles

These six principles of good classroom assessment—authenticity, alignment, continuous assessment, multiple indicators, collaboration, and reflection—provide a framework for designing sound classroom assessment. When they are put into practice, your classroom assessment system will have the following features:

- contains evidence that resembles authentic reading and writing
- uses direct evidence/demonstrations of what students can do
- assesses valued and meaningful learner outcomes
- is integrated with and grows out of high-quality literacy instruction
- provides evidence that is collected over time
- values and distinguishes between individual growth and performance against a standard
- is used by teachers for instructional decision making
- is understood by parents
- represents students' abilities across a variety of tasks and contexts

- requires students to reflect on their learning
- requires teachers to reflect on their teaching
- is a collaborative effort among teachers, students, and parents

This list presents a powerful approach to assessment, one that honors the needs of teachers and students and their power to make a difference in their own educational lives.

We can think of no better way to fulfill these requirements of sound classroom assessment than to use portfolios.

Defining Portfolios

A Philosophy of Portfolios

The term *portfolio* has many definitions. In Chapter 2, we will describe various portfolio models. However, just as a theory or philosophy of education and learning is important for effective instruction, so is a philosophy of portfolios essential to guide many of the daily decisions you will make about portfolios. No one could possibly prepare for, or anticipate, all of the portfolio decisions that surface during instruction. Having and understanding a portfolio philosophy protect against the risk of portfolios becoming just another container, another folder, or another requirement for you and your students. It offers coherence and integrity for what you do; it reflects your beliefs about teaching, learning, and assessment. Our philosophy grows out of the principles for sound classroom assessment just described.

Our definition of *portfolio* includes both a description of the physical container and a mind-set, or approach, to using portfolios (see Figure 1.5). The most obvious element of the portfolio definition is a description of the physical container itself. Three key concepts underlie the description: (a) "purposeful collection," (b) "range of student work and records," and (c) "of progress collected over time." A purposeful portfolio is not simply a collection of work generated in the classroom. It is focused and deliberate. The alignment principle helps determine the focus. By clarifying what you want students to know and to be able to do, you can focus your instruction and students' classroom work. As a result, there will be plenty of evidence generated in class that aligns with your curriculum. But you also want to be careful not to place too much in a portfolio. It can become so cumbersome and overwhelming that you and your students wouldn't be able to make sense of the information or to concentrate on the most important aspects of learning. Consequently, the portfolio wouldn't be used or useful. In Chapter 2, we describe further how you can become more focused in selecting work for the portfolio and strategies for helping you make decisions.

The second element of the definition, "a range of student work and records," emphasizes multiple indicators and authenticity. It is easy to fall into the habit of collecting only samples of student work, usually writ-

Figure 1.5

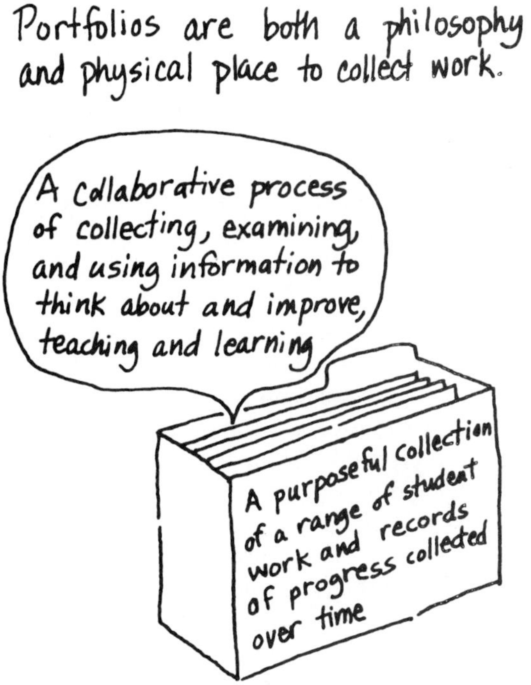

Portfolios are both a philosophy and physical place to collect work.

A collaborative process of collecting, examining, and using information to think about and improve, teaching and learning

A purposeful collection of a range of student work and records of progress collected over time

A portfolio is a physical container and it is a philosophy which encourages students, teachers, and parents to actively use portfolios to think about teaching and learning.

ten work. As we have seen, this is problematic for both teachers and students. Without multiple indicators we are likely to get a skewed picture of what students have learned and of how well they can apply their abilities to a variety of tasks. That is why we include "student work and records" as a reminder to include a wide range of strategies for documenting learning. Although not directly stated in this part of the definition, the assumption is that portfolio artifacts of all kinds—student work as well as teachers' notes and observations—must resemble authentic learning as much as possible.

The final part of this definition, "of progress collected over time," is based on the principle of continuous assessment. To keep the focus on student growth and change, portfolios must contain evidence that is dated and systematically collected over extended periods of time. If, for example, it is important to document growth in writing poetry, teachers will need to plan opportunities for students to write poetry throughout the year and then monitor portfolio contents to be sure they contain samples of poetry writing. Even if a poetry unit were a month long, students would need to revisit poetry throughout the year to enhance their understanding and to document their progress over time. Growth is impossible to determine if evidence is not collected over a sufficient period of time.

Most definitions of *portfolio* stop here, with a description of the physical container and what should be in it—*portfolio* as a noun. However, our experience has demonstrated that simply keeping a portfolio falls short of our expectations of how portfolios can help teachers and students. To make a difference, we believe that portfolios must be used and useful—they must entail action. Therefore, we add a second component to our definition—*portfolio* as a verb (see Figure 1.5).

Again, we can deconstruct this part of the definition into three elements: (a) "collaborative process," (b) "collecting, examining, and using information," and (c) "think about and improve teaching and learning." All three action-oriented elements grow out of the principles of reflection and collaboration. When portfolios are collaborative, they belong to the student, teacher, and parent. As a result, all have the right and responsibility to contribute artifacts, review the work, and use the information to evaluate progress and to set goals. This type of thoughtful decision making requires more than a shared responsibility—it requires time and knowledge needed for reflection. And this is where the principle of continuity comes into play again. Portfolios must be a process, an ongoing part of the classroom, rather than a fixed, one-time event, if thoughtful reflections are to reveal student growth and result in timely instructional actions. At the same time, the principle of continuous assessment reminds us of the importance of having a clear understanding of both standards and individual growth. By considering standards and growth side by side, we can set high expectations for students and support their progress toward those goals. As we will see in Chapter 2, this action-oriented stance is not a part of all portfolio models. However, because we believe that portfolios should be useful to both teachers and students and that they should encourage collaboration, we support a shared portfolio model. This active, shared thinking about teaching and learning is the heart of this book.

Conclusion

In this chapter we have provided six principles to guide your thinking about classroom-based assessment and to provide the rationale for using portfolios with your students. Our dual definition of *portfolio*—the physical container and the active engagement—embraces the principles of authenticity, alignment, continuous assessment, multiple indicators, collaboration, and reflection. As a summary, Table 1.1 presents a brief listing of the attributes of a shared portfolio. Unless a portfolio reflects the ongoing nature of teaching and learning in classrooms and unless it is used collaboratively among

Table 1.1
Portfolio: A summary

What it is:	What it is not:
a framework for clearly thought-out goals, tasks, and criteria	a place for "everything" or "anything"
an opportunity to use more varied, authentic, performance-based indicators of student abilities	a place to store indirect, outmoded literacy tasks
a continuous assessment process integrated with instruction	a once-a-year (or every grading period) assessment required by a person or agency outside the classroom
an open, shared, and accessible place to store student work and records of progress	a cumulative folder to record scores, grades, and confidential information inaccessible to children
an active process of thinking about, valuing, and evaluating learning and teaching	a place to collect samples of student work
a supplement to other criterion-referenced or standardized assessments	a way to avoid judging learning against standards

Attributes of a shared portfolio model.

students, teachers, and parents, it will be simply another container to hold work. If we lose the principles, we will lose the compelling parts of the portfolio. When portfolios are defined and characterized by these principles, they encourage us to expand the quality and quantity of information available for decision making and to engage students, teachers, and parents in the evaluation of progress. This is the ultimate purpose of assessment.

References

Au, K. H. (1993). *Literacy instruction in multicultural settings*. Fort Worth, TX: Harcourt Brace College Publishers.

Ball, D. L. (1996). Teacher learning and the mathematics reforms: What we think we know and what we need to learn. *Phi Delta Kappan, 77*(7), 500–508.

Biemiller, A., & Meichenbaum, D. (1992). The nature and nurture of the self-directed learner. *Educational Leadership, 50*(2), 75–80.

Brown, R. G. (1991). *Schools of thought: How the politics of literacy shape thinking in the classroom.* San Francisco, CA: Jossey-Bass.

Calfee, R. C., & Hiebert, E. H. (1992). Classroom assessment of reading. In R. Barr, M. L. Kamil, P. Mosenthal, & P. D. Pearson (Eds.), *Handbook of reading research* (2nd ed., pp. 281–309). New York: Longman.

Cole, N. S. (1988). A realist's appraisal of the prospects for unifying instruction and assessment. In C. V. Bunderson (Ed.), *Assessment in the service of learning* (pp. 103–117). Princeton, NJ: Educational Testing Service.

Costa, A. L. (1989). Re-assessing assessment. *Educational Leadership, 46*(7), 2.

Countryman, L. L., & Schorieder, M. (1996). When students lead parent-teacher conferences. *Educational Leadership, 53*(7), 64–68.

Daniels, H. (1996). The best practice project: Building parent partnerships in Chicago. *Educational Leadership, 53*(7), 38–43.

Delpit, L. (1988). The silenced dialogue: Power and pedagogy in educating other people's children. *Harvard Educational Review, 58*(3), 280–298.

Farr, R. (1992). Putting it all together: Solving the reading assessment puzzle. *The Reading Teacher, 46*(1), 26–37.

Flood, J., & Lapp, D. (1989). Reporting reading progress: A comparison portfolio for parents. *The Reading Teacher, 42*(7), 508–514.

Garcia, M. W., & Verville, K. (1994). Redesigning teaching and learning: The Arizona Student Assessment Program. In S. W. Valencia, E. H. Hiebert, & P. P. Afflerbach (Eds.), *Authentic reading assessment: Practices and possibilities.* Newark, DE: International Reading Association.

Graves, M. F., & Graves, B. B. (1994). *Scaffolding reading experiences: Designs for student success.* Norwood, MA: Christopher-Gordon.

Henderson, A. T., & Berla, N. (Eds.). (1994). *A new generation of evidence: The family is critical to student achievement.* (Report No.: ISBN 0934460418). Washington, DC: National Committee for Citizens in Education.

Hiebert, E. H., & Calfee, R. C. (1989). Advancing academic literacy through teachers' assessments. *Educational Leadership, 46*(7), 50–54.

Hiebert, E. H., Valencia, S. W., & Afflerbach, P. P. (1994). Understanding authentic reading assessment: Definitions and perspectives. In S. W. Valencia, E. H. Hiebert, & P. P. Afflerbach (Eds.), *Authentic reading assessment: Practices and possibilities* (pp. 6–21). Newark, DE: International Reading Association.

Kapinus, B. A., Collier, G. V., & Kruglanski, H. (1994). The Maryland School Performance Assessment Program: A new view of assessment. In S. W. Valencia, E. H. Hiebert, & P. P. Afflerbach (Eds.), *Authentic reading assessment: Practices and possibilities.* Newark, DE: International Reading Association.

Koretz, D., Stecher, B., Klein, S., & McCaffrey, D. (1994). The Vermont Portfolio Assessment Program: Findings and implications. *Educational Measurement: Issues and Practice, 13*(3), 5–16.

Langer, J. A. (1995). *Envisioning literature.* New York: Teachers College Press.

Lidz, C. (1987). *Dynamic assessment.* Hillsdale, NJ: Erlbaum.

Linn, R. L. (1994). Performance assessment: Policy promises and technical measurement standards. *Educational Researcher, 23*(9), 4-14.

Mitchell, R. (1992). *Testing for learning.* New York: Free Press.

National Council on Education and the Economy. (1996). *Performance standards: The New Standards Project.* Washington, DC: National Council on Education and the Economy.

National Council on Education Standards and Testing. (1992). *Raising standards for American education.* Washington: U. S. Government Printing Office.

Paratore, J. (1993, December). *Learning from home literacies: Inviting parents to contribute to literacy portfolios.* Paper presented at the annual meeting of the National Reading Conference, Charleston, SC.

Paratore, J. R. (1994, December). *Shifting boundaries in home/school responsibilities: Involving immigrant parents in the construction of literacy portfolios.* Paper presented at the annual meeting of the National Reading Conference, San Diego, CA.

Pressley, M. , Woloshyn, V., Lysynchuk, L.M., Martin, V., Wood, E., & Willoughby, T. (1990). A primer of research on cognitive strategy instruction: The important issues and how to address them. *Educational Psychology Review, 2*(1), 1–58.

Resnick, L. B., & Resnick, D. P. (1992). Assessing the thinking curriculum: New tools for educational reform. In B. R. Gifford & M. C. O'Connor (Eds.), *Future assessments: Changing views of aptitude, achievement, and instruction* (pp. 37–75). Boston, MA: Kluwer.

Rhodes, L. K., & Shanklin, N. (1993). *Windows into literacy: Assessing learners K–12.* Portsmouth, NH: Heinemann.

Salinger, T., & Chittenden, E. (1994). Analysis of an early literacy portfolio: Consequences for instruction. *Language Arts, 71*(6), 446–452.

Shavelson, R. J., Baxter, G. P., & Pine, J. (1992). Performance assessments: Political rhetoric and measurement reality. *Educational Researcher, 21*(4), 22–27.

Shepard, L. (1995). Using assessment to improve learning. *Educational Leadership, 52*(5), 38-43.

Shepard, L. A. (1989). Why we need better assessments. *Educational Leadership, 46*(7), 4–9.

Stiggins, R. (1991). Assessment literacy. *Phi Delta Kappan, 72*(7), 534–539.

Taylor, C. (1994). Assessment for measurement or standards: The peril and promise of large-scale assessment reform. *American Educational Research Journal, 31*(2), 231–262.

Valencia, S. W., & Au, K. H. (1997). Portfolios across educational contexts: Issues of evaluation, professional development, and system validity. *Educational Assessment, 4*(1), 1-35.

Valencia, S. W., & Calfee, R. C. (1991). The development and use of literacy portfolios for students, classes, and teachers. *Applied Measurement in Education, 4,* 333–345.

Valencia, S. W., & Pearson, P. D. (1987). Reading assessment: Time for a change. *The Reading Teacher, 40*(8), 726–732.

Valencia, S. W., Pearson, P. D., Peters, C. W., & Wixson, K. K. (1989). Theory and practice in statewide reading assessment: Closing the gap. *Educational Leadership, 46*(7), 57–63.

Weiss, B. (1994). California's new English-language arts assessment. In S. W. Valencia, E. H. Hiebert, & P. P. Afflerbach (Eds.), *Authentic reading assessment: Practices and possibilities.* Newark, DE: International Reading Association.

Wiggins, G. (1991). *Teaching to the (authentic) test: Assessment that measures and evokes quality student performance.* Paper presented at Performance Based Assessment: A Bridge to Change, Santa Clara, CA.

Wiggins, G. P. (1993). *Assessing student performance.* San Francisco: Jossey-Bass Publishers.

Wixson, K. K., Peters, C. W., & Potter, S. A. (1996). The case for integrated standards in English language arts. *Language Arts, 73,* 20–29.

Wixson, K. K., Valencia, S. W., & Lipson, M. Y. (1994). Issues in literacy assessment: Facing the realities of internal and external assessment. *Journal of Reading Behavior, 26*(3), 315–337.

Wolf, D. P. (1989). Portfolio assessment: Sampling student work. *Educational Leadership, 46*(7), 35–39.

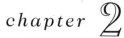

chapter 2

Designing a Portfolio System

SHEILA W. VALENCIA

> *This chapter provides a brief overview of several popular portfolio models, highlighting the different purposes, audiences, participants, and structures of each. After exploring the strengths and weaknesses of each model, we devote the major portion of this chapter to the composite portfolio, a model that we believe capitalizes on the strengths of others. We explore, in-depth, how student-selected work, teacher-selected work, and Common Tools work together in a composite portfolio to create a shared, action-oriented assessment tool.*

There are so many different ideas out there about portfolios—I just can't keep them straight. I know they are a good idea but I can't seem to get a handle on them.

T. R., intermediate teacher

Since 1990 hundreds of articles and books have been published about portfolios, yet readers often are confused by the different definitions, purposes, and models of portfolios presented in the professional literature. As a result, it is difficult for us to decide what should go into portfolios and how to implement them effectively in our classrooms. This confusion often leads to frustration and an unending search for "expert" answers to constantly emerging questions. Although the questions will never completely disappear (and they shouldn't), having a well-articulated portfolio model of your own will help you make good decisions. It will assure that your portfolios have a coherence that makes them useful to you and your students.

Portfolio Models

Portfolio models differ according to their purpose, audience, participants, and structure. Although there are few, if any, "pure" forms of the models presented next (see Table 2.1), thinking about the various aspects of these models will help you decide which model you want to adopt or adapt and will provide a framework for your decisions. As we noted in Chapter 1, there are

Table 2.1
Portfolio Models

	Showcase	Documentation	Evaluation	Process	Composite
Purpose	highlight best/ most mean- ingful work student ownership student self- reflection	document growth document performance/ achievement inform instruction	evaluate achievement report to others some student self- reflection	document process of creating product student self- reflection student ownership inform instruction document growth	document growth evaluate performance/ achievement student self-reflection student ownership inform instruction
Audience	student teacher parent	teacher parent	administrator	student teacher parent	student teacher parent administrator
Primary Participants	student	teacher	teacher student	student	teacher student
Structure	loose	moderate	tight	varied	moderate

Different portfolio models serve different purposes and audiences and they have different requirements and structures.

many different purposes for assessment. This is true even for portfolios—they can be designed to answer different questions and to serve different purposes. Just because information is collected in the classroom does not mean that all portfolios will serve the same purposes, nor does it mean that they will provide information to the same audiences. The degree of participation of teachers and students and the structure of the portfolio are related to the different purposes and audiences. In general, however, most portfolio models share a commitment to student and teacher participation in the assessment process.

Although there are important distinctions among the models, all of them rely on information collected in the classroom, and all are constructed to fit, as much as possible, into natural classroom events. Ultimately, they support the belief that assessment should be integrated with instruction so that it can be most useful to teachers and students. In the next section, we will present a brief overview of the advantages and disadvantages of four widely used portfolio models—showcase, documentation, evaluation, and process. Then we present for your consideration a fifth model—the composite model, which we believe combines the strongest features of the other four and is consistent with the principles of sound classroom assessment and a shared, action-oriented portfolio presented in Chapter 1.

Showcase Portfolio

A showcase portfolio is one in which students have total responsibility for selecting their best or favorite work (e.g., Hansen, 1994; Tierney, Carter, & Desai, 1991; Paulson, Paulson, & Meyer, 1991). It may include personal artifacts from home or school as well as samples of classroom work; students make those decisions. As a result, the work in each student's portfolio is different from every other student's portfolio in the class.

Simmons (1990) studied student choices for writing portfolios. He found that students selected pieces for very different reasons. Consider the reasons provided by three high school students from the same class (see Figure 2.1). The first student selected work that was difficult for him, and he recaps, in his reflection, important things that he learned. The second student presents a very different perspective on selection. He selected work that was easy for him. He was proud of the acknowledgment that his work received from his teacher—it received a good grade and was read aloud in class. The third student selected work that elicited a personal response for her—there is no reference to difficulty, grades, or others' opinions but instead an affective response to the honesty and emotional impact of the piece. Although younger and less experienced students may not be as articulate about the reasons for their selections, their rationale is equally varied (see Figure 2.2). Elizabeth, a first grader, has been working on writing a complete free-choice plan. She is proud that this one "has all of the elements." Andrew selects a piece that is funny, and Rosie likes that her mom affirms that she has created a "really cooll peice." Overall, these examples from elementary and high school students reveal the wide range of reasons

Figure 2.1

PORTFOLIO ENTRY

Why did you make this selection for your portfolio:

(include reasons, specific references to certain parts, the work you went
through, what you learned, how the writing affected you, etc.)

I made this selection because the hardest thing for
me to write is an analysis paper. I used the right format
for writing a paper; Intro, 3 body paragraphs, and the conclusion.
I worked hard organizing my ideas and developing a good
thesis and supporting material. I also learned that making an
outline makes it easier to organize and write a paper.

Evaluation

"Things fall apart" is my favorite peice of writing.
I like it because it was easy to write and I
did not have to struggle with it. Also, it recieved
a good grade and was read outloud in class.

Evaluation

I like this writing the best because
it is very honest, I wrote what I felt. Also,
I like alot of the words I chose, the images
are very vivid and I like that. I know they
are vivid because when I read it over it ticks
me in the stomach again and again.

*Students may use different criteria for selecting work for their
portfolios. These high school students from the same class demonstrate
widely differing reasons for their selections.*

that students use in choosing portfolio work when they are given free reign
in a showcase model. The examples also demonstrate vividly the insights
that students can develop about their own work through the process of selecting portfolio pieces. At the same time, the process enables teachers to
know their students in new and different ways.

Because the teacher has little control over what is selected for the portfolio and because students select work for a variety of reasons, the portfolio
may not provide evidence that the teacher wants or needs to make decisions about instruction or student progress on targeted outcomes; the focus
of the portfolio artifacts may not parallel the teacher's instructional focus.

Figure 2.2

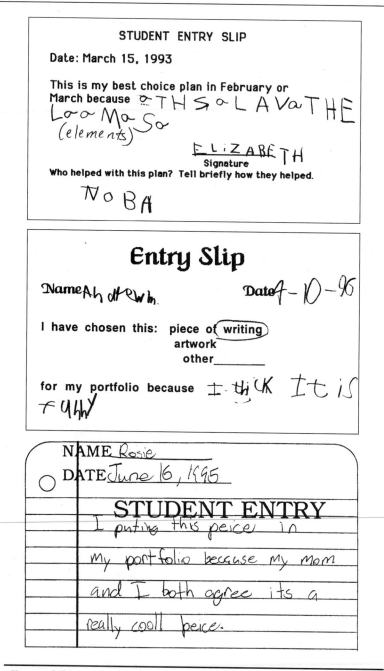

STUDENT ENTRY SLIP

Date: March 15, 1993

This is my best choice plan in February or
March because ᵃTHSᵃLAVᵃTHE
LᵒᵃMᵃSᵃ
(elements)

E LiZABE TH
Signature

Who helped with this plan? Tell briefly how they helped.

NO BA

Entry Slip

Name Ah drew h.   Date 7 - 10 - 96

I have chosen this: piece of (writing)
                      artwork
                      other_____

for my portfolio because I think It is
fully

NAME Rosie
DATE June 16, 1995

STUDENT ENTRY

I puting this peice in
my portfolio because my mom
and I both agree its a
really cooll peice.

---

*Young children also display a wide range of reasons for placing work
in their portfolios.*

The primary audience, therefore, in a showcase portfolio, is the student, and the primary purpose is to engage that student in ownership and thoughtful reflection about her work. If, for example, the teacher wants to use the portfolio to examine how well a student is applying reading strategies or experimenting with new forms of poetry, that work must be in the portfolio. If the student has not selected those types of pieces, the teacher will need to look elsewhere for evidence. This can present problems for teachers who want to use showcase portfolios to assess student progress and communicate with parents. Similarly, these portfolios may not provide enough systematic collection of evidence to show growth over time. Student self-selection, self-evaluation, and self-reflection take priority over standardization. The showcase portfolio does, however, provide teachers with interesting insights about individual students' reflections and their approaches to learning.

Evaluation Portfolio

An evaluation portfolio presents a sharp contrast to the showcase portfolio. The primary purpose of this type of portfolio is to use evidence collected in the classroom to systematically evaluate student learning and to report to others. These portfolios are scored or rated in terms of specific goals or learner outcomes (Au, Scheu, Kawakami, & Herman, 1990; Koretz, Stecher, Klein, & McCaffrey, 1994; Salinger & Chittenden, 1994). The impetus for evaluation portfolios usually comes from a state or district desire to report information about large numbers of students, sometimes in an effort to replace or supplement standardized tests with classroom-based assessment. The audience is primarily people outside the classroom who are interested in how well students are learning. As a result, it is important that evaluation portfolios can be scored reliably.

Scoring authentic student work is always complicated and even more so when each portfolio contains different evidence (i.e., showcase portfolios). Therefore, evaluation portfolios try to simplify the task by providing guidelines for what should be included as well as specific evaluation rubrics for scoring. Figure 2.3 shows the specifications for several different types of evaluation portfolios. The South Brunswick Early Literacy Portfolio (Chittenden & Spicer, 1993; Salinger & Chittenden, 1994) includes evidence of students' reading and writing, all of which is collected and stored by the teacher. Because this is an early literacy portfolio, many of the artifacts are teacher observations, notes, and interviews, and there is little student involvement in the portfolio. The artifacts are collected on a regular schedule from kindergarten through the end of second grade, providing valuable information for the teachers and enabling them to examine student growth over time. In contrast, the Vermont and Kentucky state portfolios permit students to choose some of the pieces from their classroom folders for their evaluation portfolios, and then students are required to write reflections on that work. However, specific guidelines must be followed and only required

Figure 2.3

South Brunswick Early Literacy Portfolio

self-portraits
interview with the child
interview with the parent
Concepts About Print test
word awareness writing activity
sight word list
reading sample (running record)
writing sample
class records
story retelling
optional forms

Vermont Fourth-Grade Writing Portfolio

Table of Contents
A single best piece, which is selected by the student, can come from
    any class, and need not address an academic subject
A letter explaining the composition and selection of the best piece
A poem, short story, or personal narration
A personal response to a book, event, current issue, mathematical
    problem, or scientific phenomenon
A prose piece from any subject area other than English or language arts

pieces are evaluated (Koretz, Stecher, & Deibert, 1992; Kentucky Department of Education, 1992–1993). These types of evaluation portfolios are collected only once a year and only at designated grade levels, similar to the schedule of many standardized testing programs. However, because students and teachers must choose the work from "somewhere," these evaluation portfolios often support more inclusive and ongoing classroom portfolios as well as more attention to student reflection throughout the year (Mosenthal & Jimerson, 1995).

Most evaluation portfolio projects are committed to involving some teachers in the scoring process. Many policy makers and educators realize that portfolio assessment can improve teaching and learning only when there is a direct link to what teachers do in the classroom. As teachers work together to review student work and evaluate it against a set of criteria, they

Figure 2.3 *continued*

Kentucky Fourth-Grade Writing Portfolio

Table of contents: title of each portfolio entry, study area for which the
  piece was written, page number in the portfolio
Personal narrative
Poem, play/script, or piece of fiction
One piece of writing, the purpose of which is to:

       1. present/support a position, idea, or opinion

           or

       2. tell about a problem and its solution

           or

       3. inform

One piece of writing from a study area other than English/language
  arts (any of the other portfolio entries may also come from other
  subjects)
A "best piece"
A letter to the reviewer discussing the "best piece" and reflecting
  upon growth as a writer

---

*Evaluation portfolios provide guidelines about portfolio contents so they
have some degree of uniformity and can be evaluated systematically.*

---

define what is important for students to learn, explore effective instructional strategies, and clarify expectations for student performance.

Documentation Portfolio

Documentation portfolios have their origin in early childhood education. Similar to the South Brunswick Early Literacy Portfolio described earlier, documentation portfolios include systematic, ongoing records and samples of student progress. Their purpose is to document student learning over time using a combination of teacher observations, anecdotal records, interviews, and student work (Chittenden & Courtney, 1989; Grace & Shores, 1991). Evidence is usually placed into the portfolio by teachers, although, in some cases, students select pieces as well. However, unlike the South Brunswick portfolio, documentation portfolios are rarely evaluated against predetermined criteria or a rubric. Instead, the work is used to describe student progress and is examined against individual teachers' expectations and against the child's own progress over time. Many teachers have been

Figure 2.4

Sample Artifacts in a Primary-Grade
Documentation Portfolio*

Art Activities (Fine Motor Development)
  drawings
  photos of block constructions
  samples of writing

Movement (Gross Motor Development)
  anecdotal notes
  observation checklists
  videotapes

Language and Literacy
  tape recordings of emergent reading
  oral story retellings (dictated or tape recorded)
  language experience stories
  journal/writing samples
  book log
  running records
  notes from book conferences
  writing samples

Personal and Social Development
  anecdotal notes
  checklists
  videotapes
  child's "choice time" plans
  notes from parent-teacher conferences

*Adapted from: Grace, C., & Shores, E. F. (1991). *The portfolio and its use: Developmentally appropriate assessment of young children*. Little Rock: Southern Association on Children Under Six.

> *Evidence in a documentation portfolio provides a rich record of a student's unique progress over time.*

---

keeping these types of documentation portfolios for years as part of their own record-keeping systems and as a tool for communicating with parents.

Figure 2.4 shows an example of the kinds of artifacts that might be found in a documentation portfolio. Although some pieces are directly aligned with the curriculum, other pieces are selected to capture important and unique aspects of the particular child. In other words, documentation "falls somewhere between the highly standardized formats of tests and the idiosyncratic quality of teachers' own record keeping practices" (Chittenden & Courtney, 1989, p. 117). The teacher and the parents are the primary audience for this picture of the child, using the information to gain a more complete understanding of the child's growth, to set goals, and to plan for instruction and home support.

Process Portfolio

Process portfolios chronicle the development of a larger project or body of work as well as the development of the learner. The PROPEL portfolios (Wolf, 1989) are a good example of this emphasis on process. Wolf describes the contents of PROPEL portfolios in terms of "biographies of works, a range of works, and reflections." The concept of process is embodied in

---

Figure 2.5

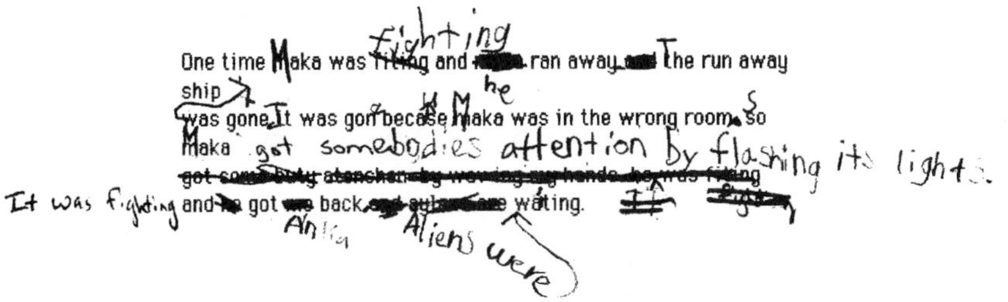

**One time Maka was fighting
and ran away. The run away ship
was gone. It was gone because
Maka was in the wrong room. So
Maka got somebody's attention
by flashing its lights it was
fighting and got Anka back and
aliens were waiting.**

Ben's rough draft with revisions and edits, and his final published book provide evidence of his process—a "biography" of this piece.

both the biographies and the reflections. A biography of a work includes the foundational work that eventually leads to a final project. For example, a biography of a student's published story might include planning notes and webs, rough drafts, teacher and peer feedback, editing checklist and notes, sketches and book layouts, and handwritten and typed final versions. Each of these pieces provides important insights about how the learner engages in the writing process and uses various writing skills and strategies. Figure 2.5 shows a small section of Ben's revising and editing of his story, "Space Stories." He worked on a plan, drafted on the computer, revised and edited by himself and then with the teacher, and published a final version, complete with illustrations and a dedication. By studying these pieces carefully, we can learn a great deal about Ben's writing process and skills as well as the kind of help his teacher provided throughout the process. These biographies honor the development of ideas, abilities, and the processes "behind the scenes" of polished work. Many of the work folders and project folders that teachers have students keep contain process work. However, these folders can become unwieldy. As a result, the work folder may be sent home at the end of each project, or selected pieces may be chosen by the teacher or student for entry in an ongoing portfolio. As noted in the showcase portfolio, the choices made at this step will influence whether the final portfolios are useful for looking at growth over time or if they are useful for looking at targeted learner outcomes.

A second aspect of the process portfolio is captured in student reflections. As students engage in reviewing and discussing their work, they begin to understand their own development and to assume more responsibility for evaluating their own work. Time must be allocated for students to step back from their work so that they can gain some perspective on it and on their growth over time. The emphasis in this portfolio model is similar to that in the showcase portfolio; students should be engaged in thinking about their work. The process portfolio, however, puts more emphasis on thinking about the process of creating work and the learning that accompanies its production. Using work in the process portfolio to discuss learning is more important than selecting the actual pieces, as is true in the showcase model.

Although there are often internal criteria for reviewing work, the process portfolio is rarely subjected to the kind of scoring typical of evaluation portfolios. The audience is more focused inside the classroom than outside. And, unlike some other portfolio models in which best or final work is most likely to appear (e.g., showcase, evaluation), process portfolios place greater importance on the process of learning and doing.

Composite Portfolio

The composite portfolio grew out of our review of various portfolio models and our desire to implement a model consistent with the principles of sound classroom assessment and the portfolio definition described in Chapter 1. Recall our dual definition of a portfolio:

- a purposeful collection of a range of student work and records of progress collected over time
- a collaborative process of collecting, examining, and using information to think about and improve teaching and learning

We found aspects of each type of portfolio that were useful. We were committed to the student involvement and ownership found in showcase portfolios; the consistency and comparability across portfolios and the focus on important outcomes found in evaluation portfolios; the rich descriptions of students found in documentation portfolios; and the student reflection and emphasis on process found in process portfolios. We tried to find a balance. As a result, we created a composite portfolio that has three components:

1. student-selected work: work selected by the student, often accompanied by a reflection (entry slip)
2. teacher-selected work: work selected by the teacher that helps describe a particular student more fully
3. Common Tools: specific assessment tasks or strategies designed to assess specific learner outcomes and used by all participating teachers on a regular schedule

Together, these three components create a portfolio and a portfolio culture that can be used to build student ownership and self-reflection, document growth over time, evaluate performance on important learning outcomes, inform classroom instruction, and report to others. We wanted to be sure that portfolios are useful to teachers and students in the classroom and, at the same time, that they can provide systematic, trustworthy information to parents and administrators outside the classroom. Next we describe each component in detail.

Student-selected work. Student-selected work is selected by the student and is often accompanied by an entry slip on which he/she reflects on why that particular work was selected for inclusion in the portfolio. Student selections are essential if students are going to share ownership of the portfolio with the teacher and if students are going to use the portfolio to become more reflective about their own learning. The entry slips provide a structure for the student selections, and they remind both teachers and students that the purpose of student-selected work is to engage students in becoming thoughtful respondents and judges of their own work. Unless we dedicate special attention to the *thinking*, student self-selection has the potential to become routine and superficial. The process of helping students reflect on their work will be discussed in more detail next and in Chapter 6. It is critical to note, however, that self-reflection and self-evaluation cannot simply be assigned to students; the process of selecting and completing entry slips requires the same time, modeling, practice, and discussion as any important learning. The goal is to help students learn to reflect on and evaluate their own work, not simply to select work or complete entry slips.

Figure 2.6

Name_____
Date_____

This piece is my favorite or the most meaningful to me because

_____
_____
_____

_____
Signature

Name_____
Date_____

I picked this piece as an example of my best work because

_____
_____
_____

_____
Signature

Name_____
Date_____

I selected this piece for my portfolio because

_____
_____
_____

Who helped you with this piece?

How did they help?

_____
Signature

Name_____
Date_____

Oh, Never, Never Again!

I have decided that this is my worst piece because

Some things that I learned from this lousy piece were

_____
Signature

L. Tipps, Bellevue Schools, 1992

Name_____
Date_____

Why did you make this selection for your portfolio (include reasons, specific references to certain parts, the work you went through, what you learned, how you feel about it, how it affected you, others' responses, etc.)?

_____
Signature

Using a variety of student entry slips helps students think about their work in new ways.

As we saw in Figures 2.2 and 2.3, students choose work for many different reasons when given free choice. However, our experience suggests that individual students tend to "fall into a rut" of superficial reflection (e.g., I worked hard) or select work for similar reasons (e.g., It's a good story) unless we conscientiously help them broaden their thinking. Using a variety of entry slips is one way to assure that teachers and students attend to many different dimensions of self-assessment. Figure 2.6 presents a few samples of entry slips that we have used successfully. Most common are student self-selections based on "favorite," "best," or "special" work; however, students can learn a great deal from work that is "unsatisfying" (Howard, 1990), difficult, or representative of accomplishing a personal goal. Similarly, questions such as "Who helped?" convey that collaboration is desirable. Providing students with different options for reflection reinforces the idea that there are different ways to review and think about our work. By using a combination of free choice and guided choice, student self-selections stay fresh, and teachers can guide students to examine work in ways that are aligned with instruction.

Teacher-selected work. Teacher-selected work allows teachers to target specific evidence for the portfolios. Sometimes that evidence is representative of a particular instructional emphasis or learning goal for all the students. For example, many fourth-grade teachers in Bellevue do a month-long unit on Washington State. The students conduct research, gather and organize information, use the writing process to write informational reports, and present the information in an interesting way to their peers. Because this project covers so many important learnings and because students spend a significant amount of time on it, many teachers include the reports in students' portfolios. Regardless of whether or not the report is a student's best work or whether he chooses it as a student-selected piece, the report is placed into the portfolio.

A second type of teacher-selected work is evidence selected especially for a particular student. For example, a teacher might include a copy of a specific reading journal page because it shows a student's new insights into the author's craft or demonstrates a student's first attempts at writing a poem. Or a teacher might include an audiotape of a new ESL student telling about her homeland in her native language and in English. Each of these teacher-selected pieces is placed into the portfolio because the teacher wants to document specific and unique accomplishments or needs of an individual student.

Many teachers have decided to attach teacher entry slips to their portfolio selections. Teacher entry slips are similar to student entry slips. The teacher may provide rationale, background, or specific reasons why she thinks it is important to include this work in the portfolio. We have found teacher entry slips to be helpful in communicating with parents and others outside the classroom as they examine the portfolios. Teacher entry slips provide the context for a particular artifact, making interpretation of student performance more meaningful. Teacher entry slips also help teachers focus their instruction and look more closely at student work. We discuss these teacher benefits in more detail in Chapter 8.

Figure 2.7

Teacher Selection

February, 1996

Student Biographies:

These are rough drafts of student biographies that the class wrote about each other. We discussed questions to use for interviewing a classmate of their choice. Interviews were conducted, notes taken of the answers, and then rough drafts were written.

Attached is the rough draft with student revisions and adult editing. There is also a Xerox of the final copy.

I included this
piece because it is
Lindsey's first
piece on the computer.
Typed in one sitting
(mrs. s.s. edited below)

Figure 2.7 shows three types of teacher entry slips that we have found useful. The first is a group entry slip, which might accompany an artifact such as a research report or class newspaper that might be included in most students' portfolios. It explains the purpose of the activity, the teacher's goal, and/or the type of support that students received. Some teachers duplicate the slip and have students attach it when they place the work into their portfolios. Other entry slips are created for a special selection, such as a student's first attempt at writing a story. These allow the teacher to note important information for a particular student. Finally, there is an entry slip that mixes both general and unique information, leaving the option for the teacher to include additional information as needed. Although none of these teacher entry slips is essential for a composite

---

Figure 2.7 *continued*

TEACHER ENTRY SLIP

Date:

I selected this piece of work to place in *Elizabeth* 's
portfolio because it represents participation in a group writing
activity to produce a class newspaper. Students with teachers
brainstormed article topics. Students then chose the article they
were interested in writing for the paper. Students submit their
pieces and work with the teacher for final editing, revising and
proofing the final copy.

PROMPT: Choose a topic you would like to research and write about
for the class newspaper.

ADDITIONAL COMMENTS: *This is one of the best
pieces Elizabeth has done to date. She is
excited about doing another piece for the
next paper about the zoo, Still gives her
an opportunity to write about animals which
is her passion, but moved her off the
house topic she* **Barb Baker/Marla English**
Continually replays. Signature

Who helped with this work? Briefly tell how each one helped.

*Mrs. English helped with editing
and revision. Elizabeth did editing
and revision on final proofing
copy.*

---

*Different types of teacher entry slips help parents and others outside
the classroom understand students work and teachers'
instructional support.*

---

portfolio, many teachers find them useful for communicating and evaluating student performance. They help distinguish the kind and amount of support that students received to produce a particular artifact.

Common Tools. Common Tools are specific, agreed-upon assessment tasks and techniques designed to assess specific student learning outcomes. They are intended to add consistency and focus to the portfolio, and, as such, they help teachers with instructional decisions and student evaluation. In addition to having clearly defined procedures and structures, Common Tools are used on a predictable schedule, for example, three times a year, so they provide documentation of student progress over time. In our view, Common Tools should be developed by teachers, drawing from their own classroom strategies and assessment needs.

Two problems motivated our development of the Common Tools concept. First, it became obvious that, very often, portfolios didn't contain the evidence that teachers needed to be able to assess student progress on important learning outcomes. If, for example, we want to know how well students use reading strategies, portfolios need to contain evidence of their reading strategies; if writing process is important, evidence about that needs to be collected as well. Sometimes evidence is missing simply because it is difficult to collect. For example, evidence of student writing is easily and commonly placed into portfolios, but evidence of reading strategies or self-evaluation is more difficult to document with typical samples of student work. At other times, evidence may be missing because the teacher has not focused instruction on that particular learning. One intermediate teacher cautioned her teammates, "Stop looking for evidence [in my portfolios] of critical response in reading. I just haven't taught it." As this teacher acknowledged, the process of looking for specific evidence can provide a good strategy for checking on our own instructional emphases. In both cases the portfolio is missing important information, and therefore it is not as useful as it could be for informing instruction, reporting to parents, and completing report cards. Similarly, if evidence is not collected consistently and systematically, teachers and students have difficulty examining growth over time. Common Tools are an effort to address the problem of missing evidence and to focus our own teaching.

The second reason for Common Tools grew out of teachers' desire to have some uniformity across portfolios within their class and across classes in their district. By definition, portfolios are complex; they contain a variety of artifacts, and the artifacts themselves are complex, providing evidence of many different aspects of reading and writing. It becomes difficult to make sense of all this information when every portfolio is different, especially if you want to use the portfolio information to communicate and report to others. Common Tools provide an anchor and a common thread of evidence across portfolios. In addition, we discovered that designing and evaluating Common Tools forced us to discuss and anchor our expectations for student performance.

Common Tools can be designed by individual teachers for use in their own classrooms, or they can be collaboratively designed by a group of teachers in a school or district. The objective is *not* to create a new or unusual task but rather to rethink and refine existing classroom practices so they can provide useful assessment information about specific learning outcomes. Of course, sometimes new assessment activities are developed in the process, but the aim is always to do a better job with instruction and assessment. Table 2.2 provides a sample list of Common Tools for specific

Table 2.2
Thinking About Outcomes and Instructional/Assessment Tasks

Outcome	Possible Common Tools (3 times)	Other Possible Indicators
construct meaning from text	written or oral summaries of selected & other texts, reading journal	response journals, book projects, informal reading inventories, observations, conference notes
interact with others about text	teacher observation checklist	literature discussion reflections, observation, book talks and recommendations
develop reading ownership	book logs kept for a 2 week "sweep," thinking about your reading reflection	journal entries, library records, teacher observation
use appropriate reading strategies	running records, informal reading inventories, conference notes	audiotapes, self-reflection questions, teacher observation
communicate effectively in writing	samples of writing	district writing sample, writing in other subject areas, reading responses
develop writing ownership	writing folders, journal entries, portfolio visit questionnaires	amount of writing, entry slips, self-reflection pieces on writing projects, teacher observation
engage in the writing process	evidence of process with one piece	editing worksheets, observation/conference notes, peer conference worksheets
engage in self reflection/evaluation	entry slips, portfolio visit questionnaires	self-evaluation built into projects, discussions, teacher observation, portfolio selection preferences

Common Tools are designed by teachers to systematically assess specific learning outcomes.

learning outcomes of Bellevue Public Schools and a list of other possible portfolio evidence that might provide information about each outcome. Five important points undergird this chart:

1. Common Tools are aligned with *your* specific learner outcomes; Bellevue's Common Tools won't necessarily work for you.
2. Common Tools grow out of good classroom practice and are easily integrated with instruction.
3. Common Tools may integrate assessment of several different learnings.
4. Common Tools work best when they are designed by the teachers using them; then they are most likely to be understood and useful for instruction.
5. Common Tools are only tools—they are not sufficient alone and are best supplemented by other evidence of student learning.

The process of creating Common Tools is perhaps one of the best exercises that you and your colleagues can do to clarify what you want students to learn and how you will determine their progress. Next, we offer several examples to demonstrate our thinking as we designed, tried out, and refined several Common Tools. The first, a tool for reading ownership, required the redesign of a strategy that teachers were already using; the second tool led to the development of new strategies for assessing self-reflection; and the third tool caused us to tackle the problem of collecting reading evidence and clarifying dimensions for reading comprehension.

Example 1—Reading Ownership. Many teachers, school districts, and state curriculum guides include an outcome about students' reading ownership (e.g., demonstrating positive attitudes toward reading; developing lifelong reading habits and reading preferences; reading widely and frequently). Portfolios provide an excellent place to keep track of this evidence, and reading logs are a logical and natural tool to collect that information. We began by defining what we wanted students to be able to do to demonstrate that they were developing reading ownership. We defined several dimensions of reading ownership (Hiebert, 1991) and decided that students should:

- read a variety of genres
- read frequently on their own
- enjoy reading

Then we reviewed various reading logs that teachers were using with their students, identifying the logs' strengths and weaknesses. Some logs included the number of pages read, others were organized by genre, and still others had a place for the date when students started and finished reading a book. After trying these out, teachers were disappointed. Although we could determine what students were reading, the information was superficial, the students seemed uninspired, and the message we were sending about reading ownership was wrong. Keeping track of books read was not the point; the point was to encourage reading widely and frequently with appreciation of the text and insight about one's own reading dispositions.

We designed a Common Tool that integrates several learner outcomes and promotes the kinds of behaviors that we hope to instill in our students (see Figure 2.8). The tool has two parts: a reading log and a set of reflective questions. The reading log is a way for students to keep track of the kinds of material and genres they read (books, magazines, newspapers, fiction, poetry, etc.), the frequency of their *unassigned reading*, and their personal responses to their reading. Many teachers have adapted the format of the log to meet their own needs; however, the essential information is always included. It is kept for a two-week "sweep" during each grading period rather than continually throughout the year—yearlong book logs lose freshness and purpose, and they are unmanageable for most teachers. Three "sweeps" during the year provide timely information to help plan instruction, and ample evidence to look at student growth and performance.

The second part of the tool is "Thinking About Your Reading", a set of questions that students answer by thinking about and reflecting on their logs at the end of each two-week sweep. These questions help us evaluate students' self-reflection in reading and help students and teachers set goals. The questions give meaning to keeping the log and they actively engage students in self-evaluation. Teachers spend time discussing students' observations about the types of books/authors they prefer, when and where they like to read, their goals for reading, what makes various reading material interesting/difficult/easy for them, and so forth. Students complete the questions individually, with peers, or in conference with the teacher. As with the log, several teachers have adapted the questions or added new ones. For example:

- When you look over your reading log, what do you notice about yourself as a reader (what you like to read, how much you read, where you read, etc.)?
- Overall, how would you rate the books you have been reading? Are they easy, medium, or hard for you? Tell why.
- Think about yourself as a reader. How would you describe yourself as a reader?
- What would make you a better reader?
- What would make you want to read more?
- Which is your favorite genre/author? Why?
- Which book was the easiest/most difficult? What made it easy/difficult for you?

Again, whatever adaptations teachers make, the focus on engaging in self-evaluation, setting goals, and identifying personal habits and preferences is always preserved.

As we worked on creating a meaningful, authentic Common Tool for Reading Ownership, it became apparent that we were tapping several learner outcomes and specific dimensions of each:

Figure 2.8

Two-week Reading Sweep - Reading Log

Student's Name Jennifer   Sweep Dates 12/95

	Book	Date(s)	Type	Read by	Comments
1	the mystrey teacher		Short chapter Book	Jennifer	This book had a bad Plot.
2	Number the Stars		Chapter Book	Jennifer	I liked Annmarie and Ellen.
3	It can't happen Hear		Chapter Book	Jennifer	A game is taken too sereisly.
4	A christmis with out Elisibeth		long chapter Book	Tennifer	A girl runs away and her famiien she has
5	The carnival ghost		chapter Book	Jennifer	It was so freaky I night lay awake all
6	The Evel 2		Chapter Book	Jenniser	This book was hard to understand
7	Fhe Evel 3		Chapter Book	Jenniser	This book scared me.
8	How I got my shrunken head		chapter Book	Jenniser	This book had a good plot

Two-week Reading Sweep - Reading Log

Student's Name   Sweep Dates

	Book	Date(s)	Type	Read by	Comments
9 / 10	The dino. that followed me home		Chapter Book	Jen	very funny book.
10	Lilas music vidow		chapter Book	Jen	very suspensive
11	Some of my best freinds are mondes		Chapter Book	Jen	I cracked up
12	Get well soon mallorey		Chap B	Jen	a girl go mononucleosis
13	Alex your glowing		Chap B	Jen	a girl gets drenched with an chemicaljan
14	Bet you can't		Chap B	Jen	Good ending
15	Bad news Babysitting		Chap B	Jen	what a plot!
16	witch Hunt!		Chap B	Jen	I got freaked

NAME Jennifer   DATE 1, 2, 96

READING SURVEY
Thinking about your reading

1. What makes you a good reader? I can read 126 pages in half an hour, and I understand what I read.

2. How often did you read during the 2-week reading sweep?

(every day)   most days   not very much

Figure 2.8 *continued*

3. How many different kinds of books did you read? Example: Did you read true stories or imaginary stories? Did you read stories about horses, plants, space, etc.?

    many different kinds (4 or more)

    (a few different kinds (2 or 3))

    ~~usually the same kinds~~

4. What strategies do you use when you come to a word that you do not know? _I sound it out. If that does not work I read around it._

What strategy works best for you? Why? _Sounding it out works best, Because most long words like Metomorphesis can be split example_

    Metlo|morph|es|is

5. How do you ~~feel about yourself as a reader?~~ Explain your thoughts. _I think I am a good reader. I was reading Nancy Drew in first grade._

6. Does anyone at home listen to you read or read to you? Who? _Nobody reads to me. I read to myself._

7. ~~How do you feel about yourself as a reader?~~ _____

_____

_____

8. Why do you think it is important to be a good reader? _It can take you to worlds beond your dreams._

9. What is your favorite thing to read? Why? _Chapter books, Because they have longer words and are more interesting_

10. What would you like to read next? _How I Survived my summer camp By Bruce coville_

& then ask if all those fail I for help.

Reading Ownership
- read a variety of materials
- enjoy reading
- read frequently on own

Construct Meaning From Text
- understand the gist, concept, theme, or problem
- take a critical stance and critically judge text (including understanding others' perspectives)
- relate text to personal experience, information, or feelings

Self-Reflection and Self-Evaluation in Reading
- self-assess reading habits, preferences, and processes
- develop preferences and goals for personal reading
- set personal goals

By using the reading log and accompanying questions, teachers and students can gain information about each of these literacy outcomes. Rather than leaving it to chance, we can be assured that we are teaching and assessing these goals. This example demonstrates how we were able to create a Common Tool to collect information on several critical outcomes simply by rethinking and redesigning a common classroom activity—the reading log.

Example 2—Self-Reflection and Self-Evaluation. As discussed earlier, we did not want to leave self-reflection and self-evaluation to chance. However, because most teachers had not been doing much self-assessment as a part of instruction, we could not rely on strategies that were already in place. Therefore, we had to develop something new—something that would provide both a meaningful instructional activity and an authentic assessment opportunity. We thought about the dimensions of self-assessment. Students should be able to:

- see strengths and weaknesses in a single piece and in work over time
- focus reflection on meaning and purpose as well as on mechanics and surface features
- set realistic goals in reading and writing
- develop appreciation of their own work

After several months of experimenting with ways to teach, encourage, and assess self-assessment, we came up with the idea of student entry slips that are now an integral part of student self-selections. And, as we've noted, it quickly became apparent that we needed to do a better job of teaching, discussing, and practicing self-assessment; we also needed to introduce students to a variety of ways of thinking about their work. This led to the creation of different types of entry slips (see Figure 2.6). Because teachers were concerned that students' writing difficulties might interfere with completing entry slips, they also encouraged students to collaborate with peers or to dictate to the teacher. We didn't want the form of assessment to obscure assessment of students' self-reflection.

Unfortunately, entry slips don't address all the dimensions of self-assessment that we want to teach and assess. Although they help students focus on a single piece, they don't help students to think about their learning over time or to set personal goals. We had provided an opportunity for goal setting in the Common Tool for Reading Ownership; however, those questions didn't seem to capture the breadth of reflection and evaluation that we wanted students to experience. As a result, we created portfolio visits (see Figure 2.9). Again, we created a conceptual framework and a schedule for the visits, developed and tried out a few models, discussed the instructional strategies that would support student performance, and then encouraged teachers to adopt or adapt the tool to meet their needs. Some primary teachers decided to interview their children and to use happy faces on the tool; intermediate, middle, and high school teachers made other adaptations. In contrast with the Common Tool for Reading Ownership, these tools caused us to explore a part of instruction with which we were less experienced and less comfortable. That meant our students were inexperienced and uncomfortable as well. However, the portfolios provided a perfect vehicle for self-assessment through the use of entry slips and portfolio visits. Development of these Common Tools for Self-Reflection and Self-Evaluation pushed our thinking about instruction as much as our thinking about assessment.

Example 3—Construct Meaning From Text. Creating a Common Tool for Constructing Meaning From Text (reading comprehension) presented a few unique challenges. First, we had to define the dimensions of reading comprehension; second, we had to find a way to document reading in a portfolio; and third, we had to confront the complex issues of text difficulty, text type, and teacher support during reading.

After reading and studying about reading comprehension instruction, we determined that students who can construct meaning from text should be able to do the following as they read different types of texts:

- understand the gist, concept, theme, or problem
- interpret and draw inferences
- distinguish and recall important information and important concepts
- synthesize and compare across texts
- take a critical stance and critically judge text (including understanding others' perspectives)
- relate the text to personal experience, information, or feelings

We began experimenting with retellings but quickly found that they encouraged students to recall everything about a selection rather than to be thoughtful and discriminating about what they were reading. We decided to move to reading summaries instead; summarizing was a meaningful and authentic way for students to demonstrate their ability to construct meaning from text. Teachers experimented with having students write summaries using many different types of texts. We soon had several important insights:

Figure 2.9

Name _Rosie_ _____ Date _Dec 5, 1994_

Portfolio Visit

Look at your portfolio work. Think about the learning that has been happening
for you in class and at home. Then answer these questions. They will help you
think about your reading, writing and math work.

1. How much do you like to read?

⬤ very much   ◯ some   ◯ a little bit   ◯ not at all

Why? I like reading a lot because it takes me to differnt worlds. I expereice the life of the characters.

2. What kind of a reader are you?
I like to read realistic fiction storys. Mysterys are o.k. so are adventure storys but I like realistic fiction the best.

3. How have you changed as a reader since the beginning of the year?
I have changed my reading miterel I used to like mysterys and horse storys now I like realistic fiction.

4. What do you think you do well as a reader?
strategy I think I can find the meaning of words rather easaly.

5. What reading goals do you have for yourself?
One of my reading goals is to start reading more picture books

---

1. Students had difficulty with summarizing.
2. The type of text influenced the type and quality of summaries that
   students wrote and the type of summaries that teachers expected.
3. The difficulty of the text students summarized varied dramatically
   both within and across students, and it influenced student
   performance.

Figure 2.9 *continued*

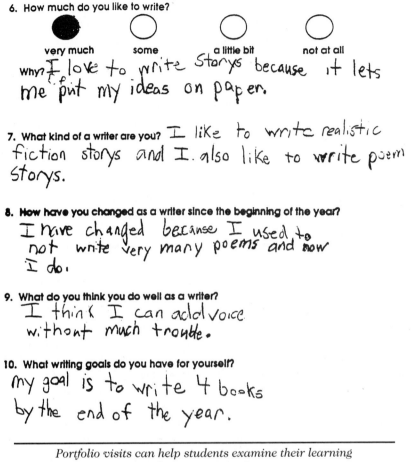

6. How much do you like to write?

very much　　**some**　　a little bit　　**not at all**

Why? I love to write storys because it lets me put my ideas on paper.

7. **What kind of a writer are you?** I like to write realistic fiction storys and I also like to write poem storys.

8. **How have you changed as a writer since the beginning of the year?** I have changed because I used to not write very many poems and now I do.

9. **What do you think you do well as a writer?** I think I can add voice without much trouble.

10. **What writing goals do you have for yourself?** my goal is to write 4 books by the end of the year.

Portfolio visits can help students examine their learning and progress over time.

---

4. Teachers who were not familiar with the text had difficulty judging students' summaries.

5. Summaries didn't capture all of the dimensions of constructing meaning that we wanted students to demonstrate.

These insights were not surprising given what we knew about the construction of meaning, but their influence on our Common Tool caused considerable concern. With all these factors at work, it was obviously very difficult to assess students' construction of meaning. As a result, we refined the Common Tool for Constructing Meaning From Text, adding more structure to the summary task and adding a second component to the tool.

First, we added structure by identifying a set of narrative and informational benchmark reading selections targeted for each developmental level. The purpose was to have a systematic and consistent way to estimate the reading difficulty of the texts and to include a variety of types of reading passages. Teachers needed a way to distinguish students' summaries of very easy selections from those summaries based on more representative grade-level texts. Because all the Common Tools were designed to tap growth over time, teachers agreed to choose at least two of these benchmark selections to use during the school year (recommended once in the fall and once in the spring). By using uniform passages, we are able to anchor a student's reading in terms of the text difficulty and text type. Additionally, because the content and genre of the reading selections were known, outside reviewers could evaluate student performance on the Common Tool for Constructing Meaning From Text.

Teachers were provided with a range of selections across several developmental levels. We agreed that teachers wouldn't need to use grade-level selections if, in their judgment, the grade-level selections were inappropriate for particular students. They were encouraged, however, to examine their expectations carefully and to try the grade-level selections to stretch their understanding of students' capabilities. They were also encouraged to use the summary tool with other classroom-based selections throughout the year.

Second, we made a commitment to learn more about *teaching* reading comprehension, including helping students understand the why, what, and how of summarizing. We realized that poor student performance on initial attempts at summarizing could indicate that summaries were inappropriate assessment tools or that students had not yet learned or developed the abilities that we wanted to assess. Therefore, by concentrating on instruction for a while, we could do a better job of judging if the problem was in the Common Tool itself. We focused on helping students to construct main ideas and themes, draw inferences, understand the author's point of view, take a critical stance, identify important information and concepts, synthesize information from different sources, form personal responses, and more. These were abilities that would help students with *all* reading tasks, not just summarizing and not just for our Common Tool. As a result of this concentrated effort on instruction, student performance on summaries improved dramatically.

Consistent with this emphasis on instruction, teachers were encouraged to use the anchor selections as part of instruction rather than as stand-alone assessment activities. This meant that teachers might want students to discuss, debate, respond, dramatize, or write about the selection. In addition, teachers were encouraged to use the anchors elections and the summarizing tasks as opportunities to teach and reinforce other reading and writing strategies. However, because we were concerned about distinguishing individual performance from teacher-supported performance, these activities were to take place *after* students had responded to the summary task on their own.

Third, we constructed several different formats for students to use in the summary task. When working with students at the early primary levels or with students who had difficulty expressing themselves in writing, teachers were encouraged to have students summarize orally. A story frame format was also developed to help primary students (The story began when, . . . Then, . . . Finally. . . .); at the intermediate and middle school levels, less structure was usually needed. In addition, because summarizing doesn't necessarily require personal response, we created follow-up questions that asked students to respond personally to what they read or to make connections with other texts.

Fourth, we developed a form for teachers to use to evaluate the summaries (see Figure 2.10). We found that the form helped us think about student performance in terms of specific aspects of constructing meaning and that it gave us a way to record the conditions under which the summary was constructed. For example, the form contains a place to note if the selection was above (difficult), at (average), or below (easy) grade level, or if the summary was written or retold orally to the teacher. Other information could be inserted as well. In addition to helping the teacher and student focus on these aspects of comprehension, the evaluation form enabled other teachers to interpret the summaries even if they hadn't read the material.

Finally, we decided to include a second component to the Common Tool for Constructing Meaning From Text—a reading journal—so that we could assess several of the dimensions that were not easily seen in a summary. The reading journal was defined as a "formal" place for students to respond to their reading. This journal could take on many forms: monthly letters to the teacher, reading response journals for books read as part of reading instruction, or responses to specific teacher-directed questions, to name a few. The purpose of adding this component is to encourage assessment using a wider range of texts and to prompt students to think about texts in ways other than summaries. By responding on a regular basis in reading journals, students learn to think about their reading, and teachers are given predictable opportunities to review students' reading comprehension as well as their reading ownership, self-reflection, and ability to respond in writing to what they are reading.

The process of creating and refining this Common Tool afforded us an opportunity to look more closely at construction of meaning than we had ever imagined necessary or possible. As with the other Common Tools, we found that we had integrated assessment of several learner outcomes:

Construct Meaning From Text
- understand the gist, concept, theme, or problem
- interpret and draw inferences
- distinguish and recall important information and important concepts

Figure 2.10

Student _Ben_   Teacher _Carnahan_
Date _2-6-96_   Name of text _Gloria_

Response mode: oral_____   written _✓_
Level of passage: easy_____   average _✓_   difficult____
Type of passage: narrative _✓_   informational____
Presentation mode: (K-1)listening_____   reading _✓_

Rate the summary (Circle)
     5-significantly above
     4-above
     3-at
     (2-below)
     1-significantly below

Check the appropriate description for each item.

1. Getting the gist, main idea, theme
     _ Includes theme, problem, main concept/idea, statement or synthesis of the critical content of the passage
     _✓_ Includes a weak or partial synthesis
     _ Unable to construct a synthesis of the passage

2. Includes significant information
     _ Includes significant information (e.g. plot, characters, resolution *or* **important** supporting details and concepts)
     _✓_ Omits some significant information or includes most details (**does not** discriminate)
     _ Includes little, if any, important information

3. Drawing inferences
     _ Includes conclusions, ideas that are not explicitly stated in the text
     _✓_ Suggests understanding of ideas that are not explicitly stated in the text
     _ Includes only information explicitly stated in the text
     _NA

4. Coherence and comprehensibility
     _Includes a richness, coherence, and comprehensibility that communicates the essence of the text
     _✓_ Includes some coherence but is not complete or does not flow
     _ Includes bits of information without much organization or flow

5. Constructs a personal response
     _ Includes a personal response to the major concepts, theme of the text
     _✓_ Includes a personal response to surface elements of the text or a simple statement of preference
     _ Unable to construct a personal response

6. Other observations

     Ben has not restated the main idea or theme. He has omitted important conclusion (inference) that J. liked G. because she did not laugh at him when he tried a cartwheel.

An evaluation form for reading summaries helps teachers foceus on specific attributes of a good summary and it provides documentation of the teacher's evaluation of student performance.

- synthesize and compare across texts
- take a critical stance and critically judge text (including understanding others' perspectives)
- relate text to personal experience, information, or feelings

Reading Ownership
- read a variety of materials
- enjoy reading
- read frequently on own

Self-Reflection and Self-Evaluation
- develop appreciation of own work

Writing
- write with clarity and organization
- communicate thoughts and ideas effectively

Developing the Common Tool for Constructing Meaning From Text was more challenging and rewarding than developing any of the other Common Tools. In addition to clarifying what students should be able to do, we had to consider the influence of text difficulty, genre, and mode of assessment. As a result, we came to a deeper understanding of what it means to construct meaning and instructional strategies that support students' learning.

Conclusion

This chapter presents several approaches to creating portfolios in your classroom. Each approach has its own unique strengths and weaknesses, and each can be adapted to meet your own needs. The most important point is that your decisions must be based on *some* model so that your portfolio is focused and useful to you and your students. You must understand the strengths and weaknesses of the model you create. Over time, your model and portfolio components may change as you become more comfortable with the portfolio process, as your students assume more and more ownership for their portfolios, and as parents become more accustomed to valuing portfolio evidence as a basis for evaluation. This flexibility and potential to "grow into" portfolios over time are truly two of the great strengths of a portfolio approach to assessment.

We strongly believe that portfolios should be a shared experience and that they must be useful to all the participants—teachers, students, and parents. If shared experience is not emphasized, portfolios may become containers that do little to advance teaching and learning. If they cannot provide reliable assessment information for teachers and others, they won't be valued and used. Portfolios take too much time and effort, and they offer too much promise to relegate them to becoming just another folder. That is why we have settled on the composite portfolio. Taken together, we believe that student-selected work, teacher-selected work, and Common Tools provide the basis for a shared, action-oriented portfolio.

References

Au, K. H., Scheu, J. A., Kawakami, A. J., & Herman, P. A. (1990). Assessment and accountability in a whole literacy curriculum. *The Reading Teacher, 43*(8), 574–578.

Chittenden, E., & Courtney, R. (1989). Assessment of young children's reading: Documentation as an alternative to testing. In D. S. Strickland & L. M. Morrow (Eds.), *Emergent literacy: Young children learn to read and write* (pp. 107–120). Newark, DE: International Reading Association.

Chittenden, E., & Spicer, W. (1993). *The South Brunswick Literacy Portfolio Project.* Paper presented at the New Standards Project: English/Language Arts Portfolio Meeting, Minneapolis, MN.

Grace, C., & Shores, E. F. (1991). *The portfolio and its use: Developmentally appropriate assessment of young children.* Little Rock: Southern Association on Children Under Six.

Hansen, J. (1994). Literacy portfolios: Windows on potential. In S. W. Valencia, E. H. Hiebert, & P. P. Afflerbach (Eds.), *Authentic reading assessment: Practices and possibilities.* Newark, DE: International Reading Association.

Hiebert, E. H. (August,1991). *The process of specifying goals and assessments.* Paper presented at the New Standards Meeting, Snowmass, CO.

Howard, K. (1990). Making the writing portfolio real. *Quarterly of the National Writing Project and the Center for the Study of Writing, 12,* 4–7, 27.

Kentucky Department of Education. (1992–1993). *Portfolio assessment 1992–93, Kentucky 4th grade students.* Frankfort, KY: Kentucky Department of Education.

Koretz, D., Stecher, B., Klein, S., & McCaffrey, D. (1994). The Vermont Portfolio Assessment Program: Findings and implications. *Educational Measurement: Issues and Practice, 13*(3), 5–16.

Koretz, D., Stecher, B., & Deibert, E. (1992). *The Vermont Portfolio Assessment Program: Interim report on implementation and impact, 1991–1992 school year* (CSE Technical Report 350). National Center for Research on Evaluation, Standards, and Student Testing.

Mosenthal, J., & Jimerson, L. (December, 1995). *Meaning and use of portfolios in different contexts: Making sense of the mandate.* Paper presented at the annual meeting of the National Reading Conference, New Orleans, LA.

Paulson, F. L., Paulson, P. R., & Meyer, C. A. (1991). What makes a portfolio a portfolio? *Educational Leadership 49*(5), 60–63.

Salinger, T., & Chittenden, E. (1994). Analysis of an early literacy portfolio: Consequences for instruction (focus on research). *Language Arts, 71*(6), 446–452.

Simmons, J. (1990). Portfolios as large-scale assessment. *Language Arts, 67,* 262–268.

Tierney, R. J., Carter, M. A., & Desai, L. (1991). *Portfolio assessment in the reading-writing classroom.* Norwood, CA: Christopher-Gordon.

Wolf, D. P. (1989). Portfolio assessment: Sampling student work. *Educational Leadership, 46*(7), 35–39.

PART 2

Using Portfolios Inside the Classroom

chapter 3

Managing Portfolios
Moving From Collections to Portfolios

ROBIN CARNAHAN

---

*Having a good system for managing portfolios can make the differ-
ence between reaping the benefits and giving them up. This chapter
provides practical suggestions for getting portfolios started in your
classroom, including introducing, constructing and storing portfolios. In addition, we provide suggestions for managing on-going student and teacher selection of work and other portfolio activities so
that portfolios become easily integrated into daily classroom life.*

I don't know if I'll keep a portfolio next year. Why? Well, I don't know if my
teacher next year will know how to do it. But, . . . I know, I can teach her.
That will be cool. *M. H., intermediate student*

Teachers have been keeping collections of student work for many years. In
fact, these collections and classroom-based observations form the basis of
instructional decisions far more often than do test scores (Hiebert & Calfee,
1989; Johnston, 1988; Stiggins & Conklin, 1992); that's why teachers have
continued to keep them. For example, teachers keep samples of student
work to help them make a particular point during parent conferences or
school guidance team meetings. They help teachers substantiate their
judgments and communicate with others, especially when those judgments
differ from standardized test results. Other times, collections are used to
demonstrate growth, to see the changes in children over the course of a
school year. And, in some elementary classrooms, teachers have children
keep special collections of work on long-term projects so the work can be
used throughout the project. Alternatively, teachers sometimes use collections from various students to demonstrate what they are teaching. These

teacher portfolios (Bird, 1990; Valencia & Calfee, 1994; Wolf, 1996) may be displayed, with student permission, during open houses to help parents understand the classroom curriculum; other times they may be shared with administrators; other times they are simply kept for the teacher's own use, to recall what was covered and how well particular activities worked with students.

My own experiences with collections date back to when I taught learning-disabled fourth, fifth, and sixth graders. I became increasingly discouraged and frustrated by the inordinate dependence of district and federal programs on test scores—I knew that my students were learning, and I knew that they could do better than those dismaying scores indicated. My frustration was small compared to that of my students'. They were discouraged by the sheer experience of taking these tests, as well as by the results. Their self-esteem suffered; the progress they knew they had made seemed to fade under the shadow of the standardized test scores. I knew I had to do something different.

I started saving work and projects—my "collections." Some of the evidence helped convince our school team to mainstream several of my students. We videotaped plays, conducted research and produced the "news" on videotape, took pictures of work and projects, wrote our own books—almost anything that would show parents and staff that these kids were learning and were able to have some successes in heterogeneous settings. The collections worked well for some purposes but not for others. They helped me share with students and parents what each student had accomplished over a period of time, usually a reporting period, and then the work was sent home. Parents and students were delighted. I felt I was on the right track, but I knew that my approach needed refinement. I didn't always have the evidence I needed, I didn't hold on to work for more than a few months, I wasn't systematic about focusing on each child, nor was I systematic about what I collected. Most interesting, now in retrospect, these collections belonged to me—not to the students.

When I returned to a regular education classroom, I had many of the same kinds of concerns about communicating student progress to parents and other educators. I also worried about students' ownership and involvement in their own learning. I continued collecting work, but just keeping a collection was not enough. It was at this point in my career, after 18 years of teaching, that I joined a group of district leaders and teachers who were interested in looking at alternative ways to assess children. Portfolios were the focus. I was excited then to join this group, and now, after six years, it continues to be a growth experience for me. Although most of the teachers in our group have had experience with collections in some form or another, we have learned a great deal about moving from collections to portfolios.

In this chapter, I will offer some suggestions about how to get portfolios started in your classroom—how to move from collections to portfolios. Specifically, I will provide some ideas for launching portfolios and managing them throughout the year. In the first section, "Launching Portfolios,"

I will present ideas for introducing, constructing, and storing portfolios and collections and a few strategies for developing early student ownership. In the second section, "Managing Portfolios," I will describe strategies for developing a "portfolio habit," selecting portfolio work, organizing the contents, and dealing with portfolios at the end of the school year. Our years of experience indicate that logistical issues such as these were huge concerns when we began. As a group, it took us three years just to get a handle on these logistics, and many of us continue to rethink them. I mention this not to discourage you but rather to encourage you to persist. Logistics and management are not trivial matters; they are important to many teachers implementing portfolios (Calfee & Perfumo, 1993). A good understanding of the issues makes it possible for you and your students to actually benefit from portfolios instead of just keeping them, or worse, giving them up.

Launching Portfolios

Most teachers who decide to implement portfolios believe in them (Calfee & Perfumo, 1993). Regardless of size or shape of the portfolios, teachers envision benefits that cannot be realized by other forms of assessment. They see a "real child" emerge from the selected work, a complete picture of the child's strengths, weaknesses, interests, and dispositions (Hansen, 1994; Howard, 1990; Reif, 1990). Teachers who have worked with portfolios for awhile can give a fairly accurate description of an unknown child from examining or scoring her portfolio; this amazes the classroom teacher of the unknown child (Valencia & Au, 1997). At the same time, teachers are eager to help their students become as invested in the portfolios as they are, to engage them more directly in their own learning and assessment of their progress. So, the first task is to figure out how to create this same understanding, enthusiasm, and ownership for portfolios in our students.

Introducing Portfolios

There are a number of ways to introduce portfolios to students and parents but, first, you must be clear in your own mind about the purpose and audience for the portfolios. Establishing a shared composite portfolio such as the one described in Chapter 2 requires that students understand that portfolios document growth over time, help students and teachers understand learning, and are a collaborative effort.

The first time I introduced portfolios to my second/third grade students, the concept was new for all of us. I asked them, "What is a portfolio?" They didn't have any good answers. I gave them the same question for homework, hoping they would get a range of answers from siblings, parents, and caregivers. The next day, most students knew that portfolios hold important work or documents. We elaborated by discussing and listing how we might use portfolios. The children's ideas were posted on a chart so we could

---

Figure 3.1

Year 1

What is a portfolio?

- holds work
- keeps your work safe
- helps you see what work you've done
- you can show it to your parents

Year 3

What is a portfolio?

- like a folder
- kind of like a safe
- keep things in it
- keep treasures in it
- keep samples of work
- keep it, don't lose it
- put year's work in it
- look at it when you're older
- see how you've changed
- show your parents
- show other teachers
- think about your work

---

*Students' developing understanding of portfolios is
reflected in their definitions before using portfolios (Year 1) and after
two years experience with them (Year 3).*

---

revisit and revise as we learned more (see Figure 3.1). I explained that we were going to keep most of our work in a working collection folder and then we would select special pieces from the collection to put into our portfolios. I told them how this would help me see the progress they were making because we would have work from different times during the year. Looking at the portfolios would help me determine what I needed to teach. I explained that portfolios would help the students as well. They would have fun looking over their work, seeing how they had changed. And it would help them determine what they needed and wanted to learn. I explained a bit about how we would be using the portfolios throughout the year, placing work into them and visiting them during conferences with friends, parents, and teachers.

We talked about artists' portfolios and about how our portfolios would be different than those—we all would be sharing the job of selecting work for the portfolio. I explained the different ways I would be selecting work for their portfolios, and I suggested that the special teachers in our school might also choose work to put into students' portfolios. I explained how each student would be selecting work to put into his portfolio, and I encouraged students to bring work from home. We also talked about how parents might contribute special pieces from home.

This distinction between an artist portfolio and a shared portfolio model is important. Artists' portfolios are completely under their own control. Individual artists enter and remove pieces at will to meet different purposes, and they are usually interested in presenting their best work rather than progress or growth over time. Too many teachers use the artist metaphor without realizing it can sometimes cause confusion and distrust. We have seen the problem surface at the middle school level where students may not want teachers to select work for the portfolio or may resist entering work that has not received a good grade. A shared composite model has a different purpose—not only to show off best work, but also to look at change over time and to assess important learning outcomes. The participants are all the people who have a stake in the students' education—teachers, parents, and students themselves. It is critical to set up a model of shared ownership from the very beginning.

Two years later the question, "What is a portfolio?" brought different responses from my class (see Figure 3.1). These students had been keeping portfolios for a year or two before they came to my second/third grade class. The addition of "think about your work" is significant because it indicates that students now understood that they were not just collecting perfect work; they were also looking at this work in order to reflect, evaluate, and set learning goals. They also recognized the value of looking at growth over time (i.e., "look at it when you're older," "see how you've changed"). In addition, students were aware of the varied audiences who might be interested in their work—parents, other teachers, and themselves—demonstrating their understanding of a shared portfolio model.

These differences from year one to year three demonstrate how students' understanding of portfolios had changed through their experiences. Just as we activate, assess, and build prior knowledge before students read (Anderson, Hiebert, Scott, & Wilkinson, 1985), it is important to activate and assess students' knowledge about portfolios. How else can we judge the best way to introduce them to portfolios? Even when students have been using portfolios for years, there are likely to be some differences between your approach to portfolios and that of students' previous teachers. For example, some teachers may be using a showcase model; others may be using a process model; others, a composite model (see Chapter 2). Rather than waiting for differences, or confusion, to surface, it is a good idea to explore understandings about portfolios with students early on.

Other teachers launch portfolios differently. Ann and Sharon, two colleagues who teach early primary grade children, introduce portfolios by discussing baby books and how, when the children were just babies, their important events were collected and recorded in a baby book. The teachers explain that now the children will be keeping and recording their special school events in a portfolio. Just as a baby book records developmental progress, a portfolio documents progress in school. Children can relate to the fun of looking back, and they have a sense of how precious these baby books are to them and their family members. But because baby books are not familiar to all children, Ann and Sharon also use other, more common, analogies such as scrapbooks or photo albums. These sorts of analogies work well for describing growth and change, but they are not as useful for communicating shared ownership. After all, babies don't actually contribute to their baby books! As a result, teachers are also careful to discuss the shared ownership of portfolios so that children understand that they, and their teacher, will play an important role in selecting work.

Several middle school colleagues present portfolios to their students as a means of documenting progress and of being accountable. This seems to work quite well because students at this level are concerned about grades and because teachers are eager for them to assume more responsibility and pride in their work. Linda, a middle school colleague, introduces portfolios by comparing student responsibility to real-life responsibility. She talks with her students about how a portfolio can represent a student's abilities just as a job application represents an adult's qualifications for a job. Similarly, Linda points out, after people get a job, they must demonstrate that their work is of good quality. Supervisors may observe them or request that they submit reports or evidence of their accomplishments. If the work is not going well or doesn't meet the expectations of the supervisor, evidence would be used to look back at the work and identify potential problems. Linda helps her students understand that, just like workers, students need to know how to evaluate their strengths and weaknesses and how to set appropriate goals based on their past work. Linda always tries to use examples from real-life situations to explain the purpose of a portfolio and to motivate her middle school students. Recently, a new principal was hired at Linda's school. The principal was asked to present his portfolio to the district hiring team, and he has since shared his portfolio with her students. This real-life situation has impressed Linda's students.

If portfolios are implemented schoolwide or if a group of students successfully used portfolios the previous year, teachers can use these knowledgeable others to help introduce portfolios to their new students. For example, several teachers ask "old friends"—former students—to return to lead a discussion with new students about portfolios. Teachers report that former students demonstrate remarkable insight and a sense of responsibility during these activities. They discuss why and how portfolios are kept, and they use evidence from their portfolios to show new students what they learned the previous year. They talk about their favorite pieces and their changes from September to June. This establishes a shared understanding early in the year, setting the expectations for learning and for the process of self-evaluation and reflection. The emphasis is on student ownership of the portfolio and a shared, collaborative model.

Just as special attention must be devoted to introducing portfolios to students, so must special attention be devoted to introducing portfolios to parents. Parents must be on board early in the collecting process because far less student work will be coming home. Parents need to know when and how they can have access to portfolios and how they may contribute selected items. They need to be partners in the portfolio process (see Chapter 9 for more details).

Setting Up Collections

If students are going to be encouraged to review work and then choose particular pieces for their portfolios, they must have a place to store the "portfolio candidates." The process of self-reflection and self-evaluation we want to foster through student-selected pieces (see Chapter 6) sometimes requires distance from the work and comparisons with other work. It is not always possible or desirable for students or teachers to know immediately that they want to select a piece for the portfolio. Therefore, teachers and students need a working collection that is distinct from the portfolio. For many teachers, this collection is similar to the work folders or working collections they have always kept. As we have noted, there are important differences as well. Teachers need to be clear about what goes into the collection, what is sent home, and how often work is selected for the portfolio.

When I first set up a collection with my students, we collected everything. All completed work was filed in legal-size file folders and kept in two large cardboard boxes, easily accessible to the children. I soon realized that it was confusing for students and for me to have too much in the collections, but I had difficulty determining what to keep in the collection and what to send home. Now, after several years, my colleagues and I have developed various strategies for determining what and how much to keep in the collections. Several common themes run through all of our strategies: (a) keep work that demonstrates important learning outcomes for your class; (b) keep work that demonstrates important learning for a particular student; and (c) set up a regular and predictable schedule for selecting work from the collection. Most teachers try to send some work home each week while, at the same time, placing the most important pieces into the collection. We also make sure to remind parents, through newsletters and parent entry slips sent home, about the portfolios so that parents are not concerned about the amount of work coming home.

At the primary level, many teachers have decided to collect work for one or two weeks and then, at the end of that time, the children and they make portfolio selections (the selection process is discussed next). The remaining work in the collection is sent home in a packet. Several parents have reported that they like receiving a packet of work on a regular schedule—there is less chance of children losing individual papers. Although parents can adjust to this schedule, it is difficult for many kindergarten and first graders who are eager to take their work home. This is why it is important to send a few pieces home throughout the collection time and to keep parents up to date on school activities.

At the intermediate and middle school levels, teachers choose a schedule that fits with their curriculum and their students. Because projects are larger in scope and more complex, the collections often are kept for a month or so, and then selections are made. It is important to strike a balance between having too few pieces and too many. Too few pieces may not challenge students to think deeply and critically about their work; too many will overwhelm them, leading to superficial thinking.

A different approach to collections is to use existing working folders as the source for portfolio selections. For example, some teachers have students keep a writing folder, reading response journals, math folders, and the like. For these teachers and students, establishing another collection might be an extra, unnecessary step. So instead, teachers have students return to these folders for their portfolio selections. As we describe next, students may need some guidance concerning what and how to select pieces. The critical issue when using multiple folders is to make sure work is conveniently preserved and accessible for portfolio consideration at a later time.

Establishing Early Ownership

Some teachers introduce collections early in the year as places to store work, and later they introduce portfolios as places for specially selected work. Other teachers introduce the collection at the same time they introduce the concept of a portfolio. Regardless of the sequence, it is a good idea to have the students do something related to the portfolio or the collection immediately after the launch. This helps establish ownership. What you do depends on the sequence of introduction.

If collections are introduced first, students can become familiar with the process of dating and filing work in their collections. They can actually locate the collection and place some of their completed work into it. Then, after a couple of weeks, portfolios can be introduced, and students can be guided to select a piece from the collection for entry into the portfolio. If collections and portfolios are introduced at the same time, students first need an experience with the collection. After placing work into the collection you can move to the next step by circling a date on the calendar when the students will be visiting their collections to select work for their portfolios. These types of activities solidify the distinction between a collection and a portfolio for the students, and they demonstrate your commitment to students' involvement in the process.

Figure 3.2

Students file work in alphabetized collections.

Constructing and Storing Collections and Portfolios

Collections. When I first set up collections, I had the students keep collection folders in their desks. This didn't work for my second/third graders—their papers got wrinkled and lost, and I didn't have easy access to them. Now collections are kept in legal-sized hanging folders that are stored in portable file boxes (see Figure 3.2). I usually have five or six file folders/students per box so students can have easy access to them. The file boxes can be easily stacked, placed onto a table in alphabetical order, or stored under a large work table. We keep our writing workshop folders in these collections also, although some of my colleagues prefer to keep writing folders separate because the students use them daily.

Some teachers use larger collection folders (e.g., a large piece of tagboard folded over) so students can store larger projects and artwork. As mentioned, other teachers simply use existing folders for their collection. The collections don't need to be decorative or special, simply easily accessible, temporary holding places for work.

Portfolios. The portfolios also must be easily accessible, and they must be sturdy. They must be able to withstand the constant handling that comes when students and teachers actively use them as part of daily classroom life. My first portfolios were the envelope type—two large pieces of tagboard with cloth tape on three sides. They were decorated with prints and patterns, and students' names were carefully written, by me, on the outside. Although these portfolios looked uniform and attractive, I soon realized that they did not reflect the personality or development of my second and third graders. These were *my* portfolios, not the students'. Now, when I introduce portfolios to my students, we also discuss how they can personalize their folders. Megan's portfolio is a good example of how students make portfolios their own (see Figure 3.3). Megan has drawn a brightly colored picture of a girl reading under a tree surrounded by nature—flowers, trees, clouds, sun, and birds. She leaves little doubt that she loves to read and that nature is important to her. In fact, Megan loves all the sciences, but especially natural science; she played a major role in planting our garden at school. Even without her name on the portfolio (she also designed the script

---

Figure 3.3

Megan's personalized portfolio cover depicts her interests and personality.

---

for her name), those who know her would identify the portfolio as Megan's. The cover shouts her personality, her wit, and her interests.

An alternative approach is to wait several weeks before asking students to decorate their portfolios. Provide several opportunities for students to place work into the portfolios and to use them to reflect on their own interests and abilities. Talk about how the portfolios will be shared with parents during "back to school night." After the students have had some experiences with their portfolios, they will begin to develop a sense of ownership and will be eager to make them personally distinctive. Although decorating portfolios may seem like a small consideration, children do develop more ownership and pride in their portfolios when they have a hand in personalizing the cover.

Across our school district, portfolios vary in size and shape. Figure 3.4 below shows several different forms. Some portfolios are quite large, especially at the primary grades, where students' artwork and projects don't conform to standard 8 1/2 x 11 paper. Figure 3.5 shows Robin's large envelope-type portfolio and several of her published books and pieces of

Figure 3.4

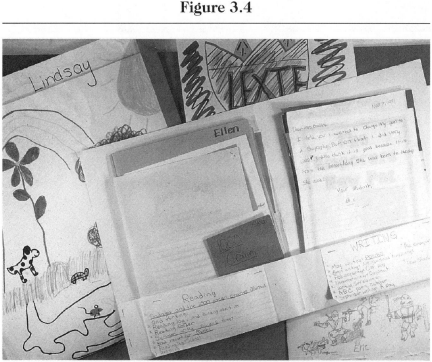

Portfolios come in all shapes and sizes: large envelopes, pockets, simple folders

Figure 3.5

Lindsay's first grade portfolio is large enough to hold her published stories and artwork.

artwork that are included in her portfolio. Other portfolios are simple file folders, and others are tagboard pocket folders.

In my first year of using portfolios, I used the large envelope style, hoping that the students would be able to include artifacts of various sizes and shapes. However, these envelopes were too big; I had to keep them flat, in a stack, and they were awkward and inaccessible. On the other hand, as Lindsey's portfolio demonstrates, other teachers use a large envelope style and have found handy ways to store them, such as filing them in a large, cut-off paper towel carton. It is clear to me now that portfolio holders must suit the personal and management styles of teachers and students.

Eventually I settled on a pocket portfolio with three sections that parallel our composite portfolio model: one section for teacher entries, one for student entries, and one for Common Tools (see Figure 3.6). The portfolio depicted has student work purposely spread out (they're not really this messy) to demonstrate that my portfolios always have more artifacts in the section designated for student selections (middle section) than in either of the other sections. This helps me stay focused on involving students in the portfolio. Although the number of papers may seem overwhelming, we have found that different teachers and students have different comfort levels concerning the amount of work in the portfolio. When students were interviewed about their favorite portfolio pieces, *none* of them had difficulty knowing exactly what piece they wanted to share and knowing exactly where to find it in their portfolio. The overwhelmed feeling seems to come from

Figure 3.6

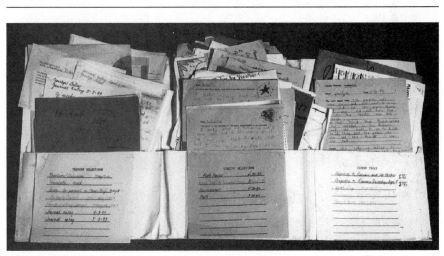

Robin's students use a three-pocket portfolio to hold teacher selections, student selections, and Common Tools.

those of us who are not familiar with the portfolio contents. Those who are, seem to know what is there. Nevertheless, you want enough pieces to cover the important learning outcomes and unique characteristics of each student but not so many that using the portfolio becomes a chore. In a survey conducted in several of our classrooms, most portfolios had between 25 and 45 pieces at the end of the school year.

Finding space to store portfolios can be challenging. The secret is to be sure they are accessible to students. Several of my colleagues have managed to set aside a corner for portfolios (or a portfolio center) where the portfolios are housed in some organized way (alphabetically, by group, by teams, by class seating arrangement), and all portfolio supplies are handy—student entry slips, parent entry slips, date stamp, and portfolio tape for strengthening seams. Other people use tubs that can be moved around the classroom as needed. When portfolios are visible and readily available, students will choose to use them more often, as Jocelyn and Nicole demonstrate in the photo below. They will be reminded to think about their portfolios, to show them to guests, and to share them with friends; they will come to

Figure 3.7

Jocelyn and Nicole retrieving their portfolios to share with each other

consider portfolios a natural part of the classroom rather than something separate. As a result, the process of reviewing and thinking about student work becomes a natural part of classroom learning for students and for teachers.

Managing Portfolios

Launching portfolios effectively is important, to be sure. However, management strategies usually determine whether portfolios succeed or fail. Make no mistake: Portfolio management is hard work. You must build a management system that is effective and efficient or else portfolios will get pushed aside when other things vie for precious classroom time. In this section I present four aspects of management: (a) establishing a portfolio habit; (b) guiding student and teacher selections; (c) organizing portfolio contents; and (d) handling portfolios at the end of the year.

Establishing a Portfolio Habit

One way to establish familiarity and ownership is to plan various opportunities for students to use their portfolios often—for example, at least every two weeks. This keeps the portfolios fresh and students' interest piqued. These opportunities need not be major portfolio evaluation activities but rather some other, less formal reasons for students to look over their work. For example, teachers often plan activities for children to do as soon as they arrive in the morning. One day, every couple of weeks, students could be asked to organize their portfolio work in sequential order or to find their favorite piece and share it with a friend or to search for a piece that will be especially interesting to a parent during conferences. Alternatively, students could be encouraged to share their portfolios during share time or to add a piece from home every month. These small activities make portfolios an integral part of the students' lives.

Another way to establish the portfolio habit is to establish a regular schedule for entering work in the portfolios and for visiting portfolios. Just as a predictable schedule for a writers' workshop allows students to prepare for writing before the workshop begins (Calkins, 1994), a predictable portfolio schedule encourages students to think about their work before the actual activity. Several of my colleagues have students write monthly reading letters so they can document students' reading interests. These letters are kept in a folder in the portfolio. On the first Monday of each month, students expect this portfolio activity. In fact, one teacher reported that she forgot to do letters and by Tuesday, her students had reminded her. In a similar manner, teachers and students can plan and mark the calendar with dates on which they select portfolio entries from their collections. Dates for quarterly portfolio visits also can be scheduled in the same way. Students look forward to these planned activities and soon develop an understanding of why they are keeping and using portfolios.

Guiding Teacher and Student Selections

Teacher selections. The majority of teacher selections my colleagues and I make are class decisions. That is, we suggest that all students in the class place many of the same projects into their portfolios. Because certain projects or activities cover many of the important learnings in the curriculum, they become important teacher selections for the portfolio. Teachers simply ask students to place these pieces immediately into their portfolios rather than storing the work in their collections. This saves time and space. If teachers decide to place a teacher entry slip on the work, it is easy to develop one generic slip, duplicate it, and have each child attach it before placing his or her piece into the portfolio. As we discuss in Chapter 2 and Chapter 8, the teacher entry slip helps others understand why the teacher selected the work and what type of support was provided. Because the rationale and background are the same for all students completing a class project, the same slip can be used for all children.

In contrast to teacher selections made for the entire class, sometimes a piece demonstrates a "breakthrough" for an individual child. When I notice this, I talk with the child about why I would like to choose that piece as a teacher entry and then simply ask the child to immediately place it into her portfolio. Again, placing the work immediately into the portfolio simplifies the selection process. Other times, I don't decide that a piece is important until I review the collection. In that case, I make my selection at the same time that students are reviewing their collections. Other teachers have a different strategy—they try to review a few student collections each week, tagging specific teacher selections for students to enter into the portfolio. Notice that all the strategies for teacher selections require the *student* to place the selection into the portfolio. No secrets here. Students and teachers work together, and, in the process, students gain one more hands-on experience with their portfolios!

Sometimes teachers see evidence of learning they would like to document, but it cannot be easily placed into a portfolio. For example, individual and group projects, oral reports, plays, artwork, and so forth are sometimes difficult to document. Therefore, I also use photographs, videotapes, audiotapes, and teacher narratives to supplement student work. Figure 3.8 is an example of how I used a photograph and teacher entry to document Michelle's oral report on hawks; rough drafts and notes were attached to the entry. Students spent several weeks researching, drafting, and preparing their oral reports. The activity included several important outcomes I had for my students—locating and reading several sources on their topic, synthesizing information according to specific categories, drafting pictures and captions that communicate important information, preparing a coherent oral report, and presenting the report using clear voice and interesting style. Without the

Figure 3.8a

Photo and teacher entry slip (on pg. 76) to document Michelle's oral report on hawks. The teacher entry slip is one that could be used for all the students participating in the project, but the addition of a few personalized comments elaborates Michelle's performance.

photograph and teacher entry, Michelle's portfolio would not have included documentation of her fine work and finished product.

Teachers vary in their use of entry slips for individually selected pieces. Some teachers don't use them very often, others create very brief handwritten comments while they are working with a student, and still others spend considerable time writing individualized comments. From a management perspective, I believe that a few class entry slips and a few individualized teacher entry slips are necessary but that they must not take an inordinate amount of teacher time. That's why so many teachers use the general class entry slip and then simply add an individual comment about a particular child when needed. My teacher entry slip for Michelle's project combines important background information that would apply for all

Figure 3.8b

Teacher entry for *Michelle*   Date 2-2-96

Research Project and Presentation

Students spent several weeks conducting research on an animal native to Washington State. They had to gather information from at least two sources, take notes, draft their report, conference with an adult or peer and revise. Their final task was to synethsize the information, organize it on an informative poster and present this information to the class in a 3-5 minute talk. They were expected to use a clear voice to communicate the most important information to their classmates and to be able to answer questions from the group.

Comments:

Michelle did a good job gathering research and summarizing for her presentation. Poster included photos and illustrations. She was unsure about where found in Washington.

Good, clear voice. Used notes effectively. Answered questions well. Peers enjoyed. RC

students in my class and some special information about Michelle's performance. An alternative to this combination entry slip is a brief personalized note on individually selected pieces, such as those seen in Figure 3.9. Some teachers have students leave teacher-selected pieces in a box

Figure 3.9

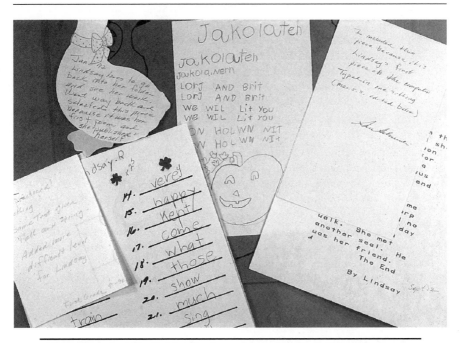

Three samples of individualized teacher entry slips. Although they are quite brief, they provide important insights about why the teacher selected the work to place in the portfolio.

so that the teachers can quickly jot down comments when they have a few moments (e.g., before school, while students are working). Others prefer to enter personal comments at the time they identify the selection. Chapter 8 presents additional ideas for deciding what to write.

Regardless of how teacher selections are made, it is important to be sure there are a sufficient number of teacher selections to cover important learnings and to demonstrate student growth over time. Sometimes the collections get away from us, and we find that we have neglected to select work. A good check is to be sure the portfolio includes at least one teacher entry each month or at least two teacher selections every grading period.

Student selections. Managing opportunities for students to select portfolio work is perhaps the most difficult task. In Chapter 6, we discuss how to help students become more reflective about their work. Here, I present some strategies for managing the task. Interestingly, the first hurdle we had to clear was our own fear that having students review their collections, conference, and place work into the portfolios was wasted time. In retrospect, this seems like a foolish fear—we now see this time as good quality teaching and learning time. However, in the beginning, we worried that it took too much time away from teaching. It is true that the first several months require extra teacher guidance, modeling, and practice, but with time, students are more efficient and more effective at making good portfolio selections.

We have found that students often are confused and overwhelmed by the process of self-selection. The selection field needs to be narrowed, at least initially. We have found that open-ended prompts such as "choose something for your portfolio" are rarely productive at the early stages of portfolio selection. By working directly with the entire class or with small groups of students you can structure the activity as much or as little as needed. For instance, a simple beginning task is to guide students to read through their journal entries to identify a piece with a specific attribute, for example, best, favorite, most interesting, least interesting, and so forth. At other times students can be guided simply to compare two to three different pieces. Eventually, students will become capable of reviewing several pieces and using a variety of entry slips like those in Chapter 2 and Chapter 6. At the beginning, however, limiting the number of pieces and the specific attributes helps students to become thoughtful and to make meaningful selections from the collection. As students gain more experience with the selection process, they enjoy free choices. Not only does it give them more choice, but also it helps teachers understand what individual students value.

Another strategy is to model or conduct a minilesson on how to think about work. For example, when discussing how to select a favorite piece, children can be guided to explore personal preferences and how those vary within and across students. Or when discussing how to select a best piece, criteria for good writing or good reading comprehension would need to be discussed. Figure 3.10 shows a bulletin board that could be used to help students understand various criteria for judging work. Alternatively, the bulletin board could be used to demonstrate the wide range of personal reasons why students choose pieces when given free choice. Bulletin boards of this sort might be used as part of a lesson or interactively so that students could continually post and share samples of their selections. Simply put, modeling the selection process makes student-selection go more smoothly.

Teachers can also help students by having them sort collections in different ways (i.e., chronologically, reading/writing, best work, favorite work, least favorite to most favorite books read, artifacts their parents would find interesting). The process of sorting puts students back in touch with the work; then teachers can provide more direction for making a particular type of selection.

Conceptually, it is most important to have students *talk* about their selections; it is less important to have them write about their reasons for selection. By having students work with partners or small groups, teachers can circulate to listen to students' thinking. As we discuss in Chapter 6, thinking is more important than completing the entry slip. As a result, not all student entries need to have entry slips. Nonetheless, it is useful at times

Figure 3.10

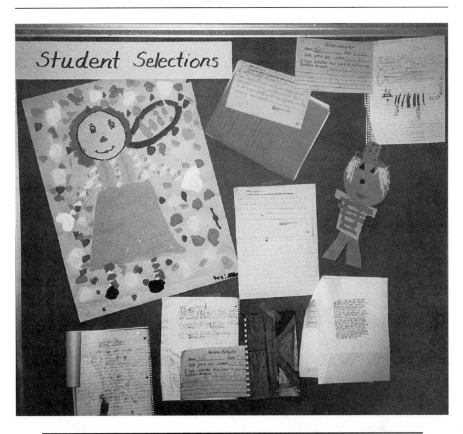

This constantly-changing bulletin board provides the impetus for class discussions about various criteria for making portfolio selections.

to have students document their reasons for selection. A first-grade colleague has developed an entry slip with a space for a picture and lines for writing. Students are given the choice of writing using invented spelling or drawing how they feel about a selection while the teacher circulates taking dictation from those who need help. In other primary classes, students dictate reasons to partners or older students. A simpler strategy with young students is just to have them sign and date a generic entry slip entitled "Student Choice" or to give them a sticker to affix to their choice. In my second/third grade class, students talk about their reasons with a partner and then write their own individual entry slips (see Figure 3.11). At the intermediate and middle school levels, students often spend 40 minutes or more discussing their work and writing entry slips. Obviously, this depth of reflection is not necessary or desirable all the time but, from time to time, it is useful. At all grade levels, it is a good idea to keep a supply of entry

Figure 3.11

After discussing their portfolio selections, two students work side by side writing entry slips.

slips easily accessible for students who are inspired to place work into the portfolio at unplanned times.

Parents may select as well. During the year students may take home the collection to share with parents. At that time students and parents may choose a piece or two to enter into the portfolio and return with an entry slip. I also send home blank entry slips for parents to have on hand for important things their children do at home. At conference time I remind parents that they can put a special piece into the portfolio, and I often provide time to look at the collection for this purpose. Parent entries are discussed in more detail in Chapter 9.

Organizing Portfolio Contents

Some teachers have added a table of contents to the portfolios. In addition to helping everyone know what is included in the portfolios, this portfolio activity requires a close examination of the work included. When my students construct the table of contents, I encourage them to take time to review each piece, and then we discuss changes they notice in their work. I have my students add a blank table of contents for each section of the portfolio at the beginning of each grading period. They update the table of contents each time they enter work in their portfolios. At the middle school level, some teachers construct for the portfolio a cover sheet that includes the most important learning outcomes for the semester. Students are required to go through their portfolios periodically and to list the pieces that demonstrate their abilities according to each learning outcome (see Figure 3.12).

Creating a table of contents, whether student-constructed or teacher-constructed, serves as a check on the work students are completing as well as on what teachers are teaching. For example, after asking her students to complete the cover sheet, Megan's teacher realized that she hadn't provided enough experiences for her students in writing ability and writing process during the fourth quarter. Megan had completed all her work yet had only a vocabulary worksheet as evidence of writing. Looking across the other students in the class, the teacher noticed that most of them had few pieces to consider as evidence. As a class, they discussed the problem and determined they would adjust instruction and portfolio selections accordingly during the last month of school. Had this problem appeared during an earlier quarter, there would have been more time to adjust.

A table of contents also provides a quick review before parent-teacher conferences to check for needed evidence that might have been completed but not entered into the portfolio. If more evidence is needed, the students or teacher can pull more work from the collection. In contrast, there are times when particular students have not completed work and there is little to place into the portfolio. All of my colleagues seem to have faced this kind of "empty portfolio syndrome" with at least one student at some time or another. Creating a table of contents is a good way for teachers and students to confront the problem before it goes too far.

Some teachers have developed other organizational tricks that help them organize portfolio contents. One strategy is to use different color codes for Common Tools and for teacher, student, and parent entry slips. Other teachers color code by grading period so they can easily extract pieces as they complete report cards. A different approach is to construct portfolios with different sections to correspond to a particular organizational scheme. My three-pocket portfolio (teacher entries, student entries, and Common Tools) is one organizational structure. Some teachers use two pockets—one for reading and one for writing. Others use four pockets, one for each grading period. The key is to be sure there is some sort of organizational scheme and that it meets your needs.

Portfolios at the End of the Year

Everyone who works with portfolios must decide what to do with them at the end of the school year. This is not always a personal or classroom decision. In some cases, it is a school or district decision. Interestingly, in most instances, portfolios are sent home, or in some cases, they "simply disappear" at the end of the year (Calfee & Perfumo, 1993). Our philosophy is simple: If there is no commitment or interest on the part of next year's teachers, the portfolios should be sent home. There is nothing worse than

Figure 3.12

REQUIRED ENTRIES TO THE PORTFOLIO

	1st Quarter Sept 1 - Nov 10	2nd Quarter Nov 10 - Jan 29	3rd Quarter Jan. 29 - Apr 9	4th Quarter Apr 9 - end
INTERACT WITH TEXT (Summarize important ideas and give personal response) * 1 Reading Summary	x. Owls Kiss	x. Rdg. Log	x. Flowers for algernon summary	x. Reading x. letter to Chelsea
CHOOSE TO READ FROM A VARIETY OF GENRE (Read a wide variety for pleasure) * 1-2 Week Sweep	x. 2-week sweep.	x. 2-week sweep	x Mexico Bibliography	x. Rdg Log
ENJOY READING (Choose to read wide variety and for pleasure) * 1 - List of Book Read	x. List of Books	x. List of books read	x. List of Books Read	x. Booklist
USE VARIETY OF STRATEGIES FOR READING & WRITING (Word attack, monitoring, planning, clarifying, etc.) * Comments on Entry Slips	x. G.S. Quiz	x. Letter Home	x. Summary Flowers for algernon	x. Book Report Jacket
WRITING ABILITY (Write with clarity, flow, and voice while meeting writing competency) * 1 Choice of writing you feel was successful	x. Owls Kiss	x. Storybook Final	x. Summary Rough Draft of mex. Report	x. vocab worksheet
WRITING PROCESS (Show complete process-planning, drafting, revising, publishing) * 1 Complete process paper	x. Nile Rough Draft	x. Nile Report	x. Mexico Report	
WRITING ENJOYMENT (Choose to write often; use it to communicate) * 1 Example of writing you enjoyed completing	1. Portfolio Evaluation	x. Storybook rough Draft	x. Jan's Chance	x. Storybook
SELF-REFLECTION/SELF-EVALUATION (Use realistic criteria and standards to evaluate work; more than mechanics) * 1 Portfolio Visit	x. Portfolio Visit	x Portfolio Visit	1. Portfolio Visit	x. Portfolio Visit

Table of contents for a middle school portfolio. Students sort through work in the collection and portfolio to find evidence that they have accomplished important learning outcomes.

dishonoring students' hard work and ownership in their portfolios by passing them along to people who will not value or use them. As the opening quote of this chapter demonstrates, students become very attached to their portfolios and to the process of keeping portfolios. In our opinion, sending portfolios home does not discount the good quality work and interaction that took place during the year. Portfolios can be as valuable within one year as across many years. On the other hand, if others are committed to portfolios, portfolios can become a powerful tool for students, teachers, and parents to use over time. Here the logistics can become complicated.

In one K–5 school with a schoolwide portfolio commitment, teachers have agreed to pass along a sample of work rather than the entire portfolio. Both the teachers and students select several pieces to send to next year's teacher, affirming the shared nature of the portfolio. Office staff attach labels indicating name, grade, teacher, and year to envelopes containing the selected pieces. The portfolio is sent home. The following year, teachers may go through the envelopes with their new students during the first few weeks of school. Depending on the grade, teachers and students may look back through envelopes from kindergarten up to the students' present year. Teachers use the portfolio artifacts as an opportunity to learn about their new students. They listen to students' comments, review work, and discuss entry slips with them. Sometimes the envelope is placed into the current year's portfolio. Sometimes it is filed separately but in a place where students can have easy access.

Exactly which pieces to pass on is best determined through a conversation among the participating teachers. Some schools hold cross-grade level meetings where teachers discuss what they would like passed on. Not only does this help with the portfolio "weeding" problem, but also it fosters a good discussion about articulated curriculum. Teachers have an authentic reason to discuss and coordinate what they teach at each grade. Alternatively, some schools and districts have compiled a list of required artifacts that are passed on. This type of schoolwide decision adds structure across the grades. In our district, many schools like to pass on the Common Tools and several other selected pieces. If a shared portfolio model has been implemented, it is critical to be sure students are also involved in selecting work to pass on.

In other schools, portfolios are forwarded in the fall after the new school year begins. The receiving teachers can review the entire portfolios from the previous year, and then, together with the students, they can select work they both want to save. Then the remaining work is sent home. The advantage of this process is twofold. First, current teachers have an opportunity to review complete portfolios and to select what seems to be most relevant to their needs. No one else has done the selecting for them. Second, many teachers enjoy using the portfolios for their beginning-of-year conferences with their new students. This helps students see the continuity of their learning and of their school experiences from grade to grade.

The transfer of portfolios from elementary school to middle school is a bit trickier. Although an increasing number of middle school teachers are requesting portfolios, individual schools or teachers make their own arrangements for passing portfolios. Our portfolios are sent to the language arts teachers because they have expressed interest in receiving them. In some cases, elementary teachers have arranged to send portfolios to English department chairpersons, who distribute the portfolios in the fall. In other cases, principals have become delivery agents of portfolios after students are enrolled in classes. Again, it is crucial to be sure the portfolios will be used and valued before they are collected and sent on. We know of several cases when portfolios have been lost in the transfer because middle school teachers were not using portfolios or were unaware that the portfolios were sent on. In addition, we haven't yet figured out how an elementary portfolio that might include math, science, and social studies would be passed along to the middle school where subjects are departmentalized. These are issues we will need to face as portfolios become more integrated into middle school instruction.

Whether portfolios are sent home or passed on, students need to have an opportunity to celebrate their progress and their portfolios at the end of the school year. Many teachers have students write letters to their new teachers at the end of the year (see Figures 3.13a & b). As with a portfolio

---

Figure 3.13a

June 18th 1996
Room 208
Eastgate Elementry

Dear 3rd graed teacher,
    I'm a good reader. I'm good at sounding out hard Words. In witing I have know probolems exsept for the spelling of cors. But other thahl that I could write all day. Math is not a thing I lilce alot in School but I don't haet it. I'm a good helper + a good friend but probdy the thing I'm best at helping people with is probdy math or Science. Next year I would like to learn about games food + Holfday in other contreys.

        Sinterely
           Hannah

Figure 3.13b

Dear,
Mrs. Carnahan,

Eastgate Elemetay
June 18th, 1996
Rm.203

I'm a ggood reader
& I like reading.
I don't like writing
but I'm good at
it. I don't like math
& I'm not that good
either.
I have lots of
friends & I like to
play. I like wacthing
T.V. & reading & Art.
Next year I want
to learn more about
Art & computers.

Sincerly, Matt

After reviewing and discussing their portfolio work for an entire year, second grade students wrote letters of introduction to their new third grade teachers.

visit, the students examine and reflect upon their work in preparation for writing the letter. Students can identify their strengths and needs, interests and expectations for the coming year, or other special information about themselves. Figures 3.13a and 3.13b are two examples of letters I received from second-grade students about to enter my third-grade class. I gain enormous insight about each of these students by reading their letters and reviewing the work selected by them and their teachers. I can examine the students' self-perceptions as readers and writers as compared with the actual work samples in their portfolios, and I can learn instantly about their preferences. For example, I know that Hannah recognizes her problem with spelling but that it doesn't interfere with her writing enjoyment or productivity; in contrast, I will need to find ways to interest Matt in writing, although he is fairly confident about his abilities. The processes of reviewing portfolios and drafting, revising, and sharing these letters are wonderful ways to celebrate the students' accomplishments at the end of the year; reading the letters together in the fall is a wonderful way to become acquainted with students at the beginning of the next.

Some teachers or schools have end-of-year portfolio events in which parents are invited to celebrate their children's portfolios (see Chapter 9). Others simply celebrate within the classroom. These culminating experiences are important to children, and they are another way to make the portfolio process important to them.

Conclusion

In this chapter, I have presented several strategies for launching and managing portfolios. Both teachers and students need to feel comfortable using portfolios, or else the portfolios will become what one student referred to as "dead folders"—places where old work is stored and never used again. The logistics of introducing portfolios and collections and of planning for their use takes time. Don't expect too much too fast. Think about how long it took most of us to become comfortable with other new ideas such as cooperative groups, literature-based reading, process writing, or writers' workshop. Think about how some of us are still working at them! Keeping and using portfolios require the same kind of organization and thoughtfulness as these other instructional strategies. Creating portfolios is more complicated than placing student work into folders. Those are collections, not portfolios. So, be prepared to give yourself and your students the time and support needed to develop a system that works for you.

As the management issues fall into place you and your students will really begin to see how useful and important portfolios can be. One of my students reminded me of this as she was cleaning out her desk in preparation for moving to a new school. Gillian gathered her papers and her portfolio, but then I noticed that she was sorting her portfolio. She told me that she had decided to take most of her portfolio work with her to her new school so that her teacher would know more about her. But, she explained, "I'm going to leave some work here so that everyone will remember me." Portfolios had become a part of this youngster's life, and they were about to become part of her new teacher's life as well. If her teacher doesn't know about portfolios, I'm sure Gillian will be able to teach her.

References

Anderson, R. C., Hiebert, E. H., Scott, J. A., & Wilkinson, I. E. (1985). *Becoming a nation of readers: The report of the Commission on Reading*. Washington, DC: National Institute of Education.

Bird, T. (1990). The schoolteacher's portfolio: An essay on possibilities. In J. Millman & L. Darling-Hammond (Eds.), *Handbook of teacher evaluation: Elementary and secondary personnel* (2nd ed., pp. 241–256).

Calfee, R. C., & Perfumo, P. (1993). Student portfolios: Opportunities for a revolution in assessment. *Journal of Reading, 36*(7), 532–537.

Calkins, L. M. (1994). The art of teaching writing. Portsmouth, NH: Heinemann.

Hansen, J. (1994). Literacy portfolios: Windows on potential. In S. W. Valencia, E. H. Hiebert, & P. P. Afflerbach (Eds.), *Authentic reading assessment: Practices and possibilities*. Newark, DE: International Reading Association.

Hiebert, E. H., & Calfee, R. C. (1989). Advancing academic literacy through teachers' assessments. *Educational Leadership, 46*(7), 50–54.

Howard, K. (1990). Making the writing portfolio real. *Quarterly of the National Writing Project and the Center for the Study of Writing, 12,* 4–7, 27.

Johnston, P. (1988). Teachers as evaluation experts. *The Reading Teacher,* 744–748.

Rief, L. (1990). Finding the value in evaluation: Self-evaluation in a middle school classroom. *Educational Leadership, 47*(6), 24–29.

Stiggins, R. J., & Conklin, N. F. (1992). *In teachers' hands: Investigating the practices of classroom assessment*. Albany: State University of New York Press.

Valencia, S. W., & Au, K. H. (1997). Portfolios across educational contexts: Issues of evaluation, professional development, and system validity. *Educational Assessment 4*(1), 1-35..

Valencia, S. W., & Calfee, R. C. (1994). The development and use of literacy portfolios for students, classes, and teachers. *Applied Measurement in Education, 4,* 333–345.

Wolf, K. (1996). Developing an effective teaching portfolio. *Educational Leadership, 53*(6), 34–37.

chapter 4

Collecting and Understanding Reading Performance

SUE BRADLEY

> *This chapter takes a close view of students' reading performance using portfolio artifacts. We describe several critical attributes of good reading and then discuss how evidence in the portfolios of three students can be used to understand their reading capabilities. Because reading performance is difficult to collect and interpret in portfolios, we close with some of the challenges to documenting reading.*

"As I think about portfolios and reading, I find myself working backward. "I think, I want to show that we are constructing meaning from text after reading four different books. . . . What can I have in the portfolios to show that the child successfully constructed meaning from the text or didn't?" So, it (the portfolio) is affecting my instruction quite a bit because even if I come up with what to put into the portfolio, I think about how I can set up the classroom to get that from students . . . you know it keeps going back and back."

S. B., intermediate teacher

When I was young, one phrase was guaranteed to create feelings of dread and foreboding in me. It was "a good educational experience." Whenever I heard my parents describe my upcoming chore in those terms, I knew that the chore would be one involving plenty of hard work, considerable extension of my skills, and probably tenuous immediate rewards.

Although my parents were not in charge of our portfolio committee, their admonition came through loud and clear as soon as committee members began work on the reading component of our assessment project. Unlike our work with writing, for which there was a rich legacy of evaluation material, we were entering relatively unmapped territory with reading. For my colleagues and me, our efforts with reading assessment definitely promised to fall into the dubious category of being "a good educational experience."

Five years of work demonstrated that that phrase was fitting for the task; our development of the reading portion of our literacy portfolio indeed proved to involve much hard work. Furthermore, we were continually called upon to extend our practices in reading instruction, frequently leaving meetings with action research questions to answer about teaching and assessment before our next meeting. And, if the rewards of a project are dependent on having all of the answers, we are certainly the unrewarded because the reading components of our portfolios are still evolving.

However, the comparison with any difficult individual childhood task ends at this point. We have instead found the process of defining, developing, and evaluating reading artifacts to be an incredible learning experience, with multiple opportunities for collaborative learning across many grade levels and at many points along the way. This chapter presents our insights in three areas: (a) our understanding of the components of good reading—the foundation for reading portfolio artifacts; (b) how to interpret and make sense of reading evidence in portfolios; and (c) our continuing questions and struggles with collecting indicators of reading performance.

What Is Good Reading?

At no place was collaboration more needed and more available than at the beginning of our work, that is, seeking an answer to the question, "What is good reading?" Before we could gather evidence of reading for the portfolios, we needed a shared understanding of good reading and what it might look like when we observed it in students and in their work.

As a group, we sought answers to these questions in many places. We searched for and shared professional articles and books that addressed the issues (e.g., Anderson, Hiebert, Scott, & Wilkinson, 1985; Paris, Lipson, & Wixson, 1983; Pearson & Gallagher, 1983; Dole, Duffy, Roehler, & Pearson, 1991). We balanced new ideas from the outside against what we knew as classroom teachers with many years of experience and varied developmental emphases. We also studied our district language arts outcomes to clarify our understanding of the theory, research, and practice underlying the goals of high quality reading instruction. Finally, we asked our students, "What do you do well as a reader?" "How do you know you are doing that well?" Their answers were reassuringly very similar to ours. All this extensive studying, rethinking, and questioning was essential before we could consider how reading might be manifested in our portfolios. We needed a deep understanding of reading processes and instructional practices if we were going to be able to make sense of and use portfolio artifacts. Next, I describe the attributes of good reading.

Good Readers Enjoy Reading

"I don't know what I am good at in reading because I'm just reading regularly. I just read all the time."—Katie

"Some kids when they read, they stop and goof off. When I start a book, I don't want to stop. It's exciting. One time I stayed up for four hours to finish a book

from the beginning word to the ending word. I looked at the clock , and it was twelve and then it was four when I stopped."—Will

"Good readers read good books 'cause some people think a book is good and others think it is yucky. Last summer my mom, my dad and my brother all read the same series of books but I couldn't get into them."—Ellen

Katie and Will are talking about the point at which the sheer enjoyment of reading makes it addictive, a disposition we would wish for all of our students. More realistically, teachers often talk about their desire to encourage "lifelong" reading habits or to have students experience the "joy" of reading or develop "ownership" of their reading. Ellen has developed a sense of ownership, knowing clearly that her preferences in books are different than those of the rest of her family. All three students know the enjoyment that reading can bring.

Motivation is one of the keys to learning to read. At the early stages, it allows students to sustain effort even when faced with the challenges of learning a new "code." At all stages and for all students, motivation provides a meaningful reason to practice, apply, and extend their reading strategies and skills. And we know from our own experiences that students with positive attitudes toward reading read more both in school and out. In the process, they gain knowledge, expand their interests, and develop automaticity and fluency, all of which lead to improved reading achievement (Anderson, Wilson, & Fielding, 1988; Anderson et al., 1985; Fielding, Wilson, & Anderson, 1986). Motivated, capable readers are better prepared to handle literacy tasks in school as well as those tasks that will be required of them later, as adults.

Naturally we wanted those advantages for all of our students. We conceptualized enjoyment to include behaviors such as: having positive attitudes toward reading, spending time in school and out reading, and developing reading preferences. In our portfolios, we wanted to be able to find evidence that students were catching the same reading fever as Katie and Will had caught. There were many possibilities. For example, home and school reading logs or a printout of a student's library checkout could provide evidence of how much children were reading. For information about attitudes toward reading, we could ask students reflective questions such as "How well do you like to read?" or "What kind of reader are you?" Anecdotal records could capture observations of students debating about their favorite authors or document engagement revealed in a spontaneous note to the teacher, "Sorry I didn't finish this story. I spent all my writer's workshop time reading."

So, instead of treating reading enjoyment as an altruistic and elusive goal, we found that we could, with a little concentrated effort, document student growth in enjoyment. Interestingly, however, we discovered that we hadn't gathered this kind of information in the past. Although we had always prioritized enjoyment, we had not tried to document it. We learned, however, that it provided enlightening and important information for us as we considered how to help children become engaged, motivated readers.

Good Readers Read a Variety of Texts for a Variety of Purposes

"I have been reading a book called Fun with French. *I am going to try to learn French."*—Kim

"I read my book report book. I finished it so that I could read Calvin and Hobbes *and all of his comics over and over again. I also read* Shipwrecked. . . . *When you read you can learn about other people's writing. You can figure our their plan for a book, like when you read a mystery."*—Will

"When I look at my reading log I notice that I like animals, poetry, adventure and science. I love science because it teaches you a lot. Like Greg's Microscope *teaches you good things to look at on a microscope and how to be careful with one."*—Jocelyn

If good reading involves enthusiasm and positive attitudes, it most definitely includes subsequent action. Many studies indicate that not only the amount of reading but also the breadth of students' reading is correlated with reading achievement (Anderson et al., 1988; Morrow & Weinstein, 1986; Taylor, Frye, & Maruyama, 1990). Furthermore, participation in a diverse, literate culture demands diverse reading (Guthrie, Schafer, Wang, & Afflerbach, 1993). So, it is not enough for students to read often; they must also expand their horizons, knowledge, and reading experiences by reading a variety of types of materials for a variety of purposes.

Kim, Will, and Jocelyn are moving beyond their decisions to simply engage in reading. They are beginning to develop awareness of the kinds of books they like and are experimenting with a wide variety of texts on their own and through assignments. As Will and Jocelyn are beginning to conceptualize, there are a host of purposes for doing that. For these third graders, reading is moving beyond an avocation to become a bank of resources that is useful for a wide range of purposes.

As we considered documenting variety and breadth of reading in our portfolios we began by thinking that reading records kept at school and at home during the year would be our best sources. Our interviews with students during reading conferences, their response journals for literature circles, and written answers to portfolio questions soon fell into place as additional sources of data. Now that these methods of documentation have become more routine in our classrooms, we have begun looking for data across curricula areas, asking ourselves, for example: What evidence is there of students' range of reading in social studies or science? Obviously, this question falls back on us as teachers and on the meaningful opportunities we provide for students to read across genres. In short, our students' days need to be filled with multiple reasons to read, and our portfolios need to reflect the same variety of purposeful reading.

Good Readers Construct Meaning From the Text by Interacting With the Text and With Others About the Text

"As I read, I visit other lands such as India and Russia, Persia and Arabia, to name a few. I have encounters with talking bears and wolves, meet enchanted people, and talk to trees."—Kate

"In literature circles we share answers from our logs."—Marc

"I am reading Tracken *so far his grandfather has cancer and it's by Gary Paulsen. It sounds kind of like* Hatchet *because they both have dying in them. I found out that* Hatchet *is by Gary Paulsen also!!!"*—Kim

Reading is the act of constructing meaning. It relies on the dynamic interaction among the reader, the text, and the social context in which reading takes place (Wixson & Peters, 1984; Wixson, Peters, Weber, & Roeber, 1987). Readers must interpret the symbols and pictures on the page in light of what they know about the written language, their background information about the topic, familiarity with the genre, and their understanding of the context of the reading situation. Meaning involves building relationships among people. Readers relate to the authors by reading, thinking about, and responding to their writing in light of the readers' own experiences, knowledge, and skills. Then, in many situations, readers interact with friends and family members, discussing and debating with others who have read the same or similar texts. In fact, emerging evidence suggests that reading instruction itself is not enough to increase the amount of reading unless the teacher also provides for interpersonal relationships that nurture sharing books (Guthrie et al., 1993).

It was not enough, however, for us to talk about "constructing meaning" as a generic, global ability. We had to define it more specifically so that we could clarify what we wanted students to learn and what our portfolio evidence might look like. From our readings and discussions, we determined that constructing meaning includes several dimensions: understanding the gist, concept, theme, or problem; interpreting and drawing inferences; distinguishing and recalling important information and important concepts; synthesizing, comparing across texts; taking a critical stance and critically judging text (including understanding others' perspectives); relating text to personal experience, information, or feelings; and interacting with others about texts. All this, we knew, was important for students to be able to do across a wide variety of types of texts. We concentrated on narrative and informational texts and the ways each of these various dimensions of constructing meaning is enacted as students read different types of text.

Kate's comment reflects the almost magical relationship between readers and authors, when the book can take readers beyond the confines of a room to practically limitless locations. Marc, too, has reacted to what an author has written, noted those reactions in his response log, and discussed his impressions in his literature circle with peers who have read the same book. Kim has started to make connections on her own among the books she is reading, and she is beginning to notice authors and their styles. These students are demonstrating some of the aspects of constructing meaning that we want to foster in our students.

In our portfolios, we needed evidence of how well students understood what they were reading and how well they could share and build upon those ideas with others both orally and in writing. Although we spent a substantial amount of time teaching and engaging students in constructing meaning, we found collecting evidence to be challenging. Most of our evidence, we discovered, was in the form of writing—literature circle response journals, comments about books on reading logs, book reports and reviews, letters about students' free time reading. Although these sources are usually rich with information, we realized that we also needed to include records of students' oral responses to reading. Often, these were the best indicators of students' abilities to build upon each others' thoughts. Portfolio artifacts such as teachers' reading conference notes, anecdotal records about discussions, and students' self-evaluations about literature circle experiences provided strategies for getting more and different reading evidence into the portfolios.

Good Readers Use Appropriate Strategies To Understand The Text

"Good readers read at a good pace and understand the words. They can tell you what the story is about. I used to stop between words and forget what the words were. Now I just go."—Lauren

"I develop a picture of what's going on [in the book] in my head. I know this works because the picture is good and clear."—Ben

"In literature circles I can keep up with what the teacher is reading. I'm good at sounding out stuff."—Sarita

"Good readers know the punctuation. Like if you didn't know what a question mark was, you wouldn't understand it."—Will

These students are talking about the complex decoding and metacognitive processes that good readers use. The reading process requires readers to flexibly use a variety of strategies—word identification strategies (e.g., phonics, context, word structure), self-monitoring strategies (e.g., checking for understanding, self-questioning), fix-up strategies (e.g., rereading, reading ahead), and study strategies (e.g., skimming, summarizing) as they read along. Being a strategic reader means more than possessing isolated skills and strategies. It means having a repertoire of strategies and knowing how, when, and why to put them into action to meet a particular purpose (Paris, Lipson, & Wixson, 1983). For example, good readers know that reading for enjoyment doesn't require the same detailed understanding or specific vocabulary knowledge as studying for a test. Similarly, good readers know when they are not understanding, and they stop to make adjustments. Poor readers often continue reading, unaware of the loss of comprehension (Baker & Brown, 1984; Paris & Myers, 1981).

Lauren, the fourth grader just quoted, knows that good reading involves fluency but always with a focus on understanding. Ben understands that reading involves organizing new information or developing images so that he forms a clear, coherent understanding of the text. And Sarita and Will recognize that they frequently need to work with their knowledge of word identification strategies and punctuation to make sense of the words. In short, all of these students are reflecting upon some of the strategies that readers use to construct meaning from text.

Early in our investigation of strategic reading we came to an important realization—we had sometimes wrongly concluded that our students were not employing reading strategies when the problem was actually in our assessments or our teaching. On one hand, we realized that when students are reading easily, without struggle, their strategies either are working at the automatic level or perhaps are not being called into action. Think, for example, of a fifth-grade youngster fluently reading *Charlotte's Web,* moving smoothly through the text, barely slowing down as the characters face an emotional crisis, and laughing as the story takes a funny turn. Although reading strategies may not be obvious, we might assume that they are working quite well to allow this student to read fluently with understanding. In other words, sometimes strategies "go underground" and are difficult to observe when students are reading easy texts. On the other hand, if the texts were more difficult, we might see some self-monitoring or word identification strategies called into action. We also realized that students were not accustomed to talking about metacognitive processes involved in using reading strategies. Sometimes they were not aware; sometimes they did not have the language to talk about what they did. Finally, we realized that for many of us, teaching reading strategies was a new focus. Students were not being taught to be strategic readers. We soon heard each other saying at meetings, "I guess there isn't any evidence in my portfolios because I haven't taught it!" None of these tasks (looking more closely for use of strategies, giving students language to talk about them, and providing strategy instruction) was impossible, but it meant that we had to extend our understanding of reading strategies before our students could extend theirs and generate portfolio evidence.

Good Readers Set Goals and Evaluate
Their Own Progress in Reading

"I started reading early because my sister was reading, but the first book I read I really didn't read. I memorized it. Then I read little books. Then I got into my sister's books and started reading her books. I don't know who's book shelf I'm going to read next."—Katie

"I'd like to read more challenging books. Gary Paulson is one of my favorite authors. I've been reading Dancing Carl, *and I want to read* Hatchet.*"*—Marc

"Last year I couldn't read a lot of words and now I can. I should practice because if there was a word that I couldn't read, I would skip it and the story might not make sense."—Jessi

Reading is the primary academic skill students need to succeed throughout school and throughout their lives. We can guide and monitor their progress, but ultimately we want students to be on their own, setting their own goals and evaluating their own progress (Costa, 1989; Perrone, 1991). In reading, self-reflection often takes the form of students planning what they want to read next and, sometimes, what they do well as readers. This combination of looking toward the future and stepping back to examine current performance builds the balance between the ambition, realistic expectations, and self-direction that are the hallmarks of a good reader.

Katie, Marc, and Jessi are beginning to do just that. They are observing themselves in relationship to their peers, against information that they have learned from the comments of others, and against their own expectations and progress over time. Katie recognizes the influence of her sister's role modeling. Marc has set a goal for himself on the basis of his familiarity with a popular author. And Jessi has recognized her progress in reading words so that she reads for meaning. All have a clear idea of where they have been as readers and where they are headed. How different their ambition and resolve are compared with those of others who have no idea of focus or appropriate challenge. These three students have established admirable standards for assessing their future reading success.

Using Portfolios to Understand Students' Reading Performance

The true test of the mettle of our many portfolio conversations came, of course, when we began to look at actual student work. We were not keeping portfolios just to collect evidence of students' work; we wanted to use that evidence to understand our students' reading strengths and weaknesses as well as our own instructional strengths and weaknesses. We wondered if we could actually use the reading artifacts in portfolios to gain a better understanding of students' reading abilities. Which aspects of good reading were easily seen, and which were less obvious or missing? How could we put together information from various pieces to form a detailed yet broad enough picture to shape our instructional decisions? The examples that follow are selected from the portfolios of two intermediate students and one primary student. Although space doesn't permit sharing the complete contents of the students' portfolios, these few samples provide some models and ideas for collecting and interpreting reading evidence.

An Intermediate Grade Example

Katie and David are two fifth graders in my multiaged classroom. Because both had kept portfolios since kindergarten, they were equally prepared to express their thoughts and reflections about their work. As a result, their work in reading has some striking similarities. More importantly, their portfolios capture evidence of their unique differences.

Reading enjoyment, habits, and preferences. Both David and Katie would bring smiles to a teacher's face. They both love to read. Evidence of their engagement, quantity of reading, and preferences is sprinkled throughout their portfolios.

Each month the students write to me about what they have been reading. Early in the process I might provide a few optional guiding questions to help them think about what they want to write about. For example, "Tell me about the book(s) you've been reading." "What is your favorite and why?" "Which character do you particularly enjoy? Why?" "When and where do you read?" "If you haven't been reading very much, why do you think you haven't?" I write a brief response to each student, establishing a meaningful audience for the communication. These reading letters not only give evidence of preferences, attitudes, and understanding, but also offer it in the child's own voice. You would think that students might tire of this activity, but they don't. In fact, they often remind me on the first day of the month that it's time for reading letters. I think the students especially enjoy taking a moment to think about their reading and knowing they will get a personal response from me! David's monthly letter to his reading teacher, my teammate, about what he had been reading reveals his eagerness to get home to read (see Figure 4.1). Katie's letters are informative as well. In one of her earlier letters, Katie put her own label on her penchant for reading, calling herself a "bookworm," and admitting she is proud of it. (see Figure 4.2.)

There are other indications of David's and Katie's enjoyment of reading. Both students consistently report that they enjoy reading "very much" on their portfolio visit forms. Their self-reports are confirmed by my classroom observations. Their reading logs, both from home and school, are amply filled out and have numerous comments beginning with phrases such as "I really liked . . ." or "My favorite chapter is . . ." (see Figures 4.3a & b, on pages 99–100 and 4.4a & 4.4b on pages 101–102). The comments reflect not only enjoyment but also the students' personal connections with the topic, content or, sometimes, genre of the books. Both students consistently spend time reading during this two-week sweep, and they write comments that demonstrate they are thinking and reacting to what they have read. An occasional expression of "I don't like . . ." indicates only that they have set standards for their enjoyment and indeed know if a book meets those standards.

It is especially exciting to see that both Katie's and David's love of reading does not diminish over the years. In fact, it increases. The accumulated evidence in their portfolios documents this. There are three years of monthly reading letters, several book logs from school and home, and numerous indicators of enjoyment embedded in other reading artifacts. Katie kept track of how many reading letters she had written over her three years as an intermediate student—31! In my reply to her last letter as a fifth grader, I wrote, "Dear Katie, Your last letter is just as great as all of yours have been. Your enthusiasm for reading books comes through loud and clear."

Missing from Katie's portfolio are anecdotal notes about all the times that I observed Katie reading in the midst of seemingly distracting

Figure 4.1

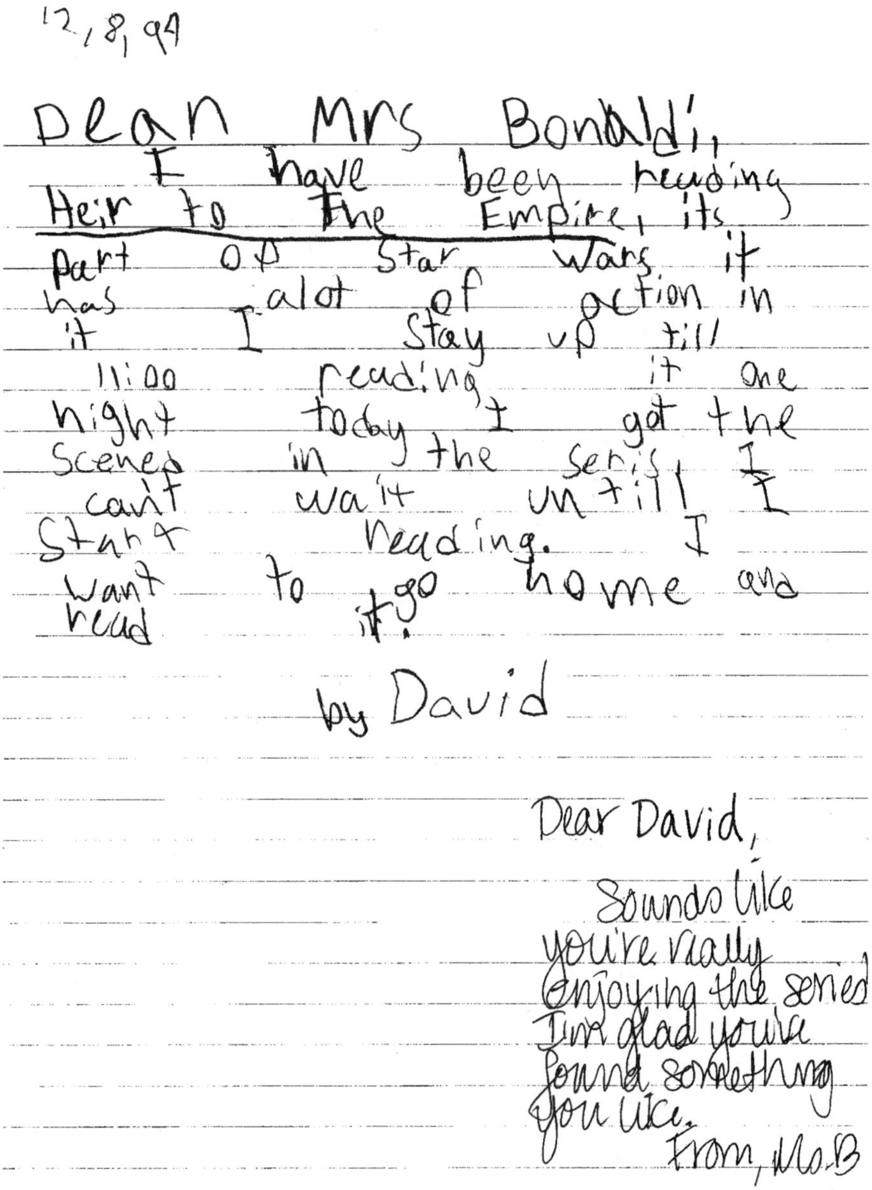

12,8,94

Dean Mrs Bonaldi,
I have been reading
Heir to the Empire, its
part of Star Wars it
has a lot of action in
it I stay up till
11:00 reading it one
night today I got the
scenes in the seris I
can't wait until I
start reading. I
want to go home and
read it.

by David

Dear David,
    Sounds like
you're really
enjoying the series
I'm glad you've
found something
you like.
        From, Mo.B

David's reading letter reveals his reading preferences and enjoyment.

Figure 4.2

May 24
1993

KATIE

Dear Mrs. Bradley

I have been reading Doll House Murders. I think it is a good book Because in the book a girl finds a doll house in her aunts Attic and all theese Strange things happen to the doll house. Molly recomended it to me and I think any one who likes mysterys will like the book. I like reading in my room and I also have almost Fineshd The Laura Engles wilder siries. I am a book worm and proud to be one, too.

From,

Katie

Dear Book Worm,
(Opps! Katie)
I'm glad I've gotten to know you & your love of reading. Sounds like you've got a good network for recommendations for books. Molly's advice is good. (You might want to try to write mysteries, too.) mrs B.

Katie is proud of her interest in reading and takes time to discuss books with her friends.

classroom hubbub. Likewise, missing from David's portfolio are teacher notes about the times David came in from an active football game at recess and was able to turn off his interaction with his peers in order to get into a book. Those "outsider's" notes would serve to strengthen even more the students' own "insider" comments.

Frequently even the most enthusiastic readers have narrowed their reading down to one or two genres, authors, or series and concentrated all their reading time with those books. This is why we balance our goal of having students develop preferences with a goal of encouraging them to read a

---

Figure 4.3a

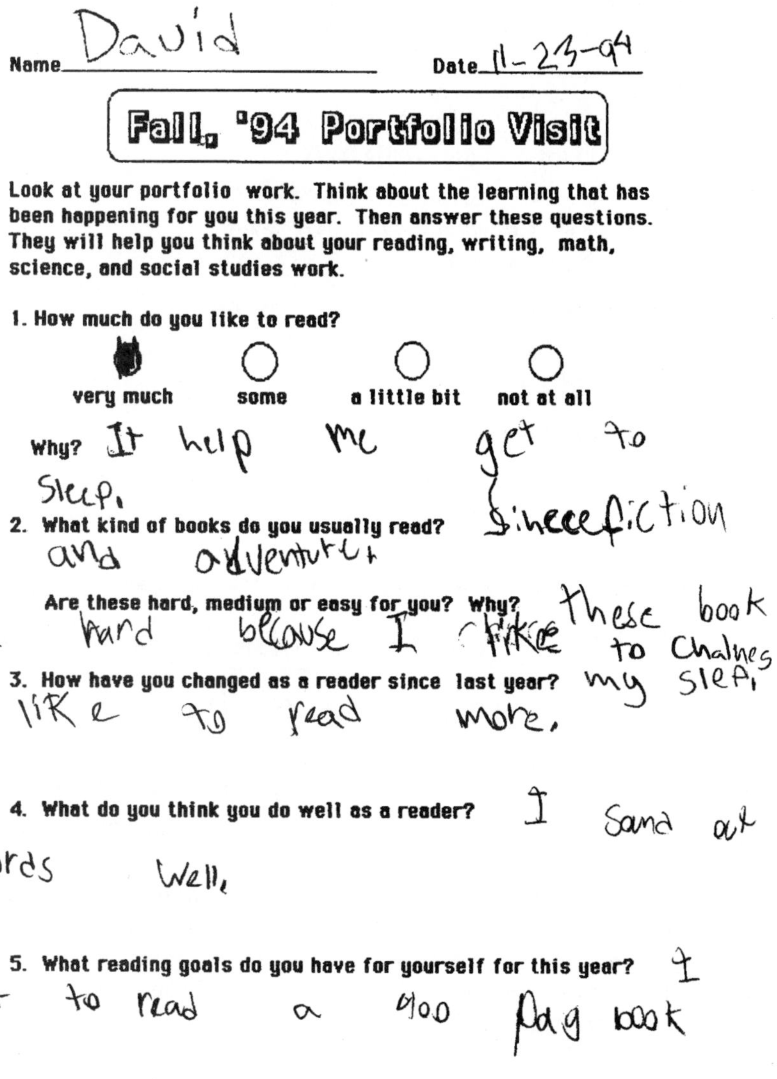

Name **David**   Date **11-23-94**

Fall, '94 Portfolio Visit

Look at your portfolio work. Think about the learning that has been happening for you this year. Then answer these questions. They will help you think about your reading, writing, math, science, and social studies work.

1. How much do you like to read?

● very much   ○ some   ○ a little bit   ○ not at all

Why? *It help me get to Sleep.*

2. What kind of books do you usually read? *Sinece fiction and adventure.*

Are these hard, medium or easy for you? Why? *Are hard because I like these book to chalnes my sleft.*

3. How have you changed as a reader since last year? *I like to read more.*

4. What do you think you do well as a reader? *I sand out words well.*

5. What reading goals do you have for yourself for this year? *I waht to read a 400 pag book*

Figure 4.3b

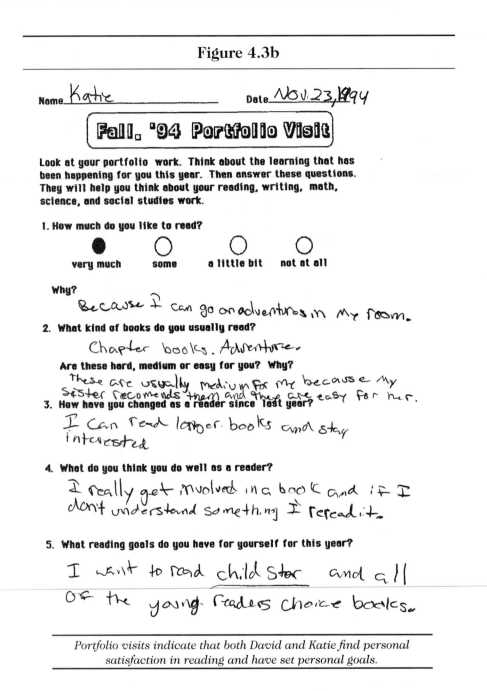

Name Katie   Date Nov. 23, 1994

Fall, '94 Portfolio Visit

Look at your portfolio work. Think about the learning that has
been happening for you this year. Then answer these questions.
They will help you think about your reading, writing, math,
science, and social studies work.

1. How much do you like to read?

● very much   ○ some   ○ a little bit   ○ not at all

Why?
Because I can go on adventures in my room.

2. What kind of books do you usually read?
Chapter books. Adventure.

Are these hard, medium or easy for you? Why?
These are usually medium for me because my
sister recomends them and they are easy for her.

3. How have you changed as a reader since last year?
I can read longer books and stay
interested

4. What do you think you do well as a reader?
I really get involved in a book and if I
don't understand something I reread it.

5. What reading goals do you have for yourself for this year?
I want to read child star and all
of the young readers choice books.

---

*Portfolio visits indicate that both David and Katie find personal
satisfaction in reading and have set personal goals.*

---

variety of texts for a variety of purposes. The balance can sometimes be
tricky to encourage, and it is complicated by the books that students choose
to read on their own. Some readers are tackling longer books and, as a result, do not demonstrate the same variety in their choices as students who
read many shorter books.

Figure 4.4a

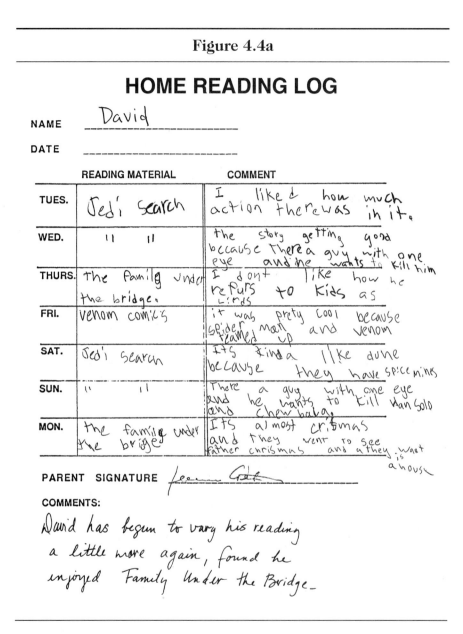

HOME READING LOG

NAME   David

DATE   _____

	READING MATERIAL	COMMENT
TUES.	Jedi Search	I liked how much action there was in it.
WED.	" "	the story getting good because there a guy with one eye and he wants to kill him
THURS.	The family Under the bridge.	I dont like how he refurs to kids as birds
FRI.	Venom comics	it was pretty cool because spiderman and venom teamed up
SAT.	Jedi searcn	Its kinda like dune because they have spice mines
SUN.	" "	There a guy with one eye and he wants to kill Han Solo and Chew baba.
MON.	the family under the bridge	Its almost crismas and they went to see father chrismas and a they want a house

PARENT SIGNATURE _____

COMMENTS:

David has begun to vary his reading
a little more again, found he
enjoyed Family Under the Bridge—

David and Katie both start out and remain readers with self-chosen preferences. As early as third grade, both of them stated in oral interviews and in written portfolio visits that they had a favorite genre, David's being science fiction and Katie's being adventure stories. David was familiar with popular authors such as Bruce Coville and Alfred Sloate, whereas Katie's definition of adventure tended to be realistic fiction that had enough action to keep her interest, such as *The Dollhouse Murders* or the *Little House on the Prairie* series.

Figure 4.4b

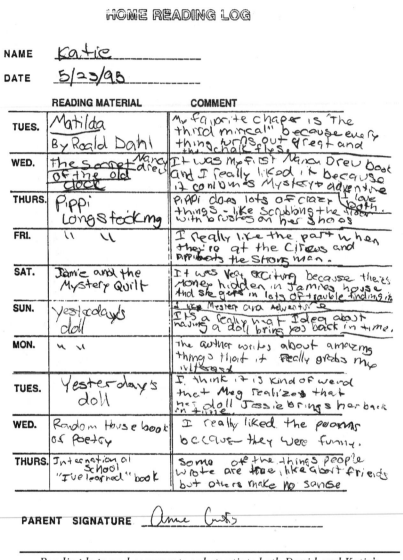

HOME READING LOG

NAME _Katie_

DATE _5/23/95_

	READING MATERIAL	COMMENT
TUES.	Matilda By Roald Dahl	My favorite chaper is "The third miracal" because every thing turns out great and the chalk flies.
WED.	the Secret of the old clock (Nancy Drew)	It was My first Nancy Drew book and I really liked it because it conbuns Mystery+ adventure
THURS.	Pippi Longstocking	Pippi does lots of crazy things - like scrubbing the floor with brushes on her shoes. I love both.
FRI.	" "	I really like the part when they're at the Circus and Pippi beats the Strong man.
SAT.	Jamie and the Mystery Quilt	It was very exciting because there's money hidden in Jamies house And she gets in lots of trouble finding it. I like Mystery and Adventure
SUN.	yesterdays doll	Its a really neat Idea about having a doll brings you back in time.
MON.	" "	The author writes about amazing things that it really grabs me with ease.
TUES.	Yesterday's doll	I think it is kind of weird that Meg realizes that her doll Jessie brings her back in time.
WED.	Random House book of Poetry	I really liked the poems because they were funny.
THURS.	International School "I've learned" book	Some of the things people wrote are true, like about friends but others make no sense

PARENT SIGNATURE _Anne Curtis_

Reading logs and comments substantiate both David and Katie's commitment and engagement with reading.

What is especially interesting to chronicle with the help of their portfolios is that although each of these students continues to have the same preferences in books three years later, both have grown in terms of what they are reading within that genre and have expanded to other genres. As a fifth grader, David recorded in his home reading log that he read five books of the *Star Wars* series, whereas Katie was choosing titles such as *Maniac Magee*, *Little Women*, and *The Voyages of Doctor Doolittle*.

For evidence of reading other materials and for other purposes, their school and home reading logs offer the richest evidence (see Figure 4.4). Katie recorded reading texts such as a middle school handbook, *International School, "I've Learned" Book*, to learn about her choice of schools, *Random House Book of Poetry* to enjoy the humor of some poems, a human sexuality book for a class assignment, and various picture books to entertain her younger brother. David, on the other hand, read historical fiction such as *The Family Under the Bridge* and *Weasel*, fantasy such as *Red Wall*, and books nominated for the Young Reader's Choice Award so that he could cast his ballot for the winner. In response to the last home reading log, David's mother wrote that she, too, has begun to notice his widening his interests beyond the time-consuming *Star Wars* series.

It is important to note that evidence about David's and Katie's reading enjoyment and reading breadth comes from reports of their recreational or free choice reading. Although I could speculate about their reading for other purposes such as the completion of social studies or science projects, at this point there is not much evidence in their portfolios to support that. As their classroom teacher, I have knowledge of those experiences but have not yet captured that in my portfolios.

It is tempting to stop now and say, "It's obvious that both of these students are good readers." But I need to go beyond enjoyment and variety to analyze documentation of other important aspects of reading, those that have traditionally not been documented, especially in portfolios. Specifically I want to know what kinds of reading strategies they employ, how well they construct meaning and interact with others about texts, and what goals they have for themselves as readers.

Reading strategies. Both David and Katie do some self-assessment about their reading strategies in response to questions in their portfolio visits (refer back to Figure 4.3). David wrote, "I sound out words well," and Katie said, "I really get involved in a book and if I don't understand something I reread it." Later in the year she wrote, "I read fast and can understand lots of words." What I discovered is that without my direct questioning about reading strategies, neither student automatically gave much evidence of his or her reading strategies. Because both were competent readers, chances were high that they effectively used several strategies but probably did so most of the time on a subconscious level. I gained insight into Katie's thinking in a one-on-one reading conference with her (see Figure 4.5). It was reassuring to me to know that Katie had developed a range of strategies she could apply when needed. Another technique I use for learning about strategies during a conference is to have students read a portion of their book that is difficult or confusing for them so I can observe strategies at work. We talk about the strategies the students use, and then I often use the opportunity to teach alternative strategies.

Figure 4.5

TEACHER SELECTION

These are notes from reading conferences that I have had with students. The books are their choices to read aloud to me. It may or may not be a book that they have read prior to the conference.

Katie

February 17, 1995

<u>Henry Ford</u> (the book for her biography book report) on p. 94

read fluently, little diificulty at all with vocabulary or phrasing of sentences, text was highly informational, about "surpluses, cash flow, profit sharing"

her opinion of the book? I think it is really neat. I learned about how they named the Oldsmobile and Mercedes Benz (named after Mr. Benz's daughter) thinks it is medium difficulty for her. Some words that I haven't heard of like (she scanned for a word) surplus.

goal update: I only have to read two more <u>The Ancient One</u> and I've started <u>Pickup Sticks.</u>

new goal: I want to finish all of the Little House books. I have half of one left.

What do you do when you read and don't understand? (we were interupted frequently)
1. Go back and reread.
2. Then I read the parts around what I don't understand to see if that has something to do with what I don't understand.
3. Look up a word that I don't understand in the dictionary.
   If there is more than one meaning try to figure out which meaning it is.
4. Ask someone if they understand it, like one of my friends because they might help me.
5. Like a computer manual, if I don't understand, I would go through bit by bit, step by step.
6. Game rules: I'd make up what I think it is and then keep going and see if that makes sense.

Notes from the teacher's reading conference with Katie provide documentation of Katie's reading fluency and use of reading strategies, aspects of reading that might otherwise be difficult to document in a portfolio.

I try to have formal individual conferences with most of my students three times a year (four to five times if they are experiencing difficulty), and recently I have begun to document what I learn. I have always had conferences but rarely kept records. My interest in assessing students' abilities to apply reading strategies has reaffirmed my need to document evidence. I have also seen how a focused conference can provide useful information about students' abilities to construct meaning and read fluently without having to rely on written work. I always share my written notes with the students and, of course, have them file the documentation in their portfolios. The students find the conferences enjoyable, and the addition of my notes interests them. They are able to see what I am looking for as part of good reading. In fact, during an interview with an outsider, Katie pointed to the conference notes as one of her favorite pieces in the portfolio, commenting, "I like these because this is what Mrs. Bradley and I talk about and I know what I do well and what I have to work on."

Because I didn't have direct responsibility for David's portfolio last year (my teammate did) there are no similar notes about reading strategies in his portfolio. Although my teammate could verbally tell me or David's parents what she had observed about David's use of strategies, there is very little evidence in his portfolio. Even though a portfolio may seem quite rich and thorough, it is obvious there is still a great deal of information about a student stored in the teacher's head. My teammate would read David's portfolio with more insight than I would because she is his reading teacher and I now see him only during our shared class activities. As a teacher once removed from his reading instruction, I am left to wonder about his reading strategies, just as his parents might. This points out the importance of documenting observations if the information is to be useful to others.

Construct meaning and interact with others about text. David's and Katie's portfolios provide compelling evidence of their different abilities to construct meaning and interact with others about text. For example, reading Katie's portfolio, I found many examples of how Katie was motivated to read in order to share her reactions with other people. In a self-reflection about her effort in literature circles, Katie wrote, "I really wanted to explain all about it." In response to another literature circle experience she explained, "I always talk about literature circles at home." David, on the other hand, seems to read primarily for his own personal satisfaction. He writes about choosing to read when he doesn't have anything else to do. His measures of successful reading tended to be the number of pages read or the number of days that it took him to read something.

Katie's written responses to texts are refined and to the point. Her written answers to questions about novels are consistently on target. By the spring of fifth grade she was demonstrating the depth of her thinking, even in her recreational reading. In a monthly reading letter, she spontaneously wrote an excellent summary of *December Stillness*, including the important story elements, a personal response, and her interpretation of the theme (see Figure 4.6). From the list of books and her comments, I can judge that Katie can independently read and construct a good understanding of at least fifth- to sixth-grade-level material. I also get confirming information about Katie's reading enjoyment, preferences, amount, and variety as well as her interaction with others about books, from her letters and from my conference notes.

It is never a good idea to rely on a single artifact or written piece to assess students' abilities to construct meaning from text; performance varies depending on the text and the kind of support that students receive. Therefore, I look for patterns across several portfolio entries. Katie's portfolio, for example, contains two reading summaries that are included as part of our Common Tools. Katie constructs well-organized, concise summaries of both these grade-level selections. In addition, Katie's portfolio contains a research report (note cards, rough drafts, final illustrated version) that she did on Washington State in which she used and synthesized information from several nonfiction sources. The process work and the final product both add information to support my analysis of Katie's abilities to construct meaning. Finally, several of her literature circle response logs confirm her ability to make personal connections (see Figure 4.7 on page 109). I sometimes provide questions for students' response journal entries so that I can be sure to prompt students to think of aspects of constructing meaning they may not automatically include in their responses. For example, I sometimes ask students to compare characters or books with others they have read to get information on intertextual connections, or I ask a specific question about a particular book to see if students are drawing inferences or understanding the subtleties of a complicated plot.

Examples of David's abilities to construct meaning are not consistently as strong as Katie's. After reading a grade-level passage that accompanies one of our Common Tools, David wrote a poorly organized summary, which included minor events and details along with important events (see Figure 4.8 on page 110). Nevertheless, David does demonstrate that he clearly understands the main problem and the overall theme of the story and that he is so engaged that he wants the story to continue. Others of David's responses similarly come close to the mark but are not as well developed as they could be. For example, when discussing the theme of *The Not-Just-Anybody Family*, a fifth-grade-level literature circle selection, David answered:

> I think the theme of the book was not to be greedy. Pap wouldn't have been in such a rush to get the money. He wouldn't of [sic] spilled them.
> The author wanted to say that old people can be your friend.
> I liked the book because they had a crazy family.

My teammate's notes to David point out that the evidence from the story doesn't substantiate David's first conclusion about greed as a theme but that his second thought about an intergenerational theme makes good sense. In addition, once again, David's lack of organization makes it difficult to understand his other comments about the story. So, although David can read and understand the important points and sometimes the theme of fifth-grade-level material, he needs to work on organization, distinguishing important from unimportant details and creating a focused summary.

Figure 4.6

5/3/95

Dear Mrs. Bradley,

During April I read, Pick-up Sticks, Stuart Little, and December Stillness.
I didn't really like Pick-up Sticks because nothing exciting really happened.
Stuart Little is one of my favorite books because it's about a mouse who gets into alot of trouble. Then he goes out looking for his best friend, Margalo, a bird. On his trip to find her he does some weird things.
My other favorite book is, December Stillness. Chelsea recomended it to me, and I'm glad she did.
It's about a Vietnam War Veteran who is homeless. He has all his belongings in two bags he carries with him. He spends all his time in the library reading about the Vietnam War. He doesn't want anyone to pity him, but one girl, Polly, tries to help him. He begins to trust her alright. She gives him some food that he eats, and some warm clothes. Then one night when Polly and her dad are driving, and they see that Mr. Weems, the vetran, got hit by a car and died. A few days later polly draws a picture of Mr. Weems to take to the Vietnam Memorial. She copys a poem.

continued

Figure 4.6 *continued*

onto his picture Called
"December Stillness". That was
a great book, even though it was
really sad. I saw how Vietnam
Can Kill peoples lives, with out really
Killing them.

From

Katie

Dear Katie,
Wow!! that's what I said when I finished
reading your letter. Your description and
summary of December Stillness was powerful.
That must be some book. Chelsey recommended
a great one for you. Where did she find it?
Did you see the Vietnam memorial when
you were in Washington D.C.? I would like
to see it some day, but as you said the war
killed even more than that memorial states.
I'm glad you were such a busy reader.
P.S. I agree with you about   Mrs B.
Pick up Sticks. That book
doesn't have a climax

*Katie's reading letter reveals more than her varied intersts and reading
ownership. It provides evidence of her understanding of the story plot
and theme as well as her personal responses.*

As a younger student, David had difficulty reading for important details, and although he had made progress in this area, it was something
that my teammate, David's mother, and I continued to work on right up
until the end of fifth grade. His mother told us that she would read with
him at night, having David start by himself and then orally summarize what

Figure 4.7

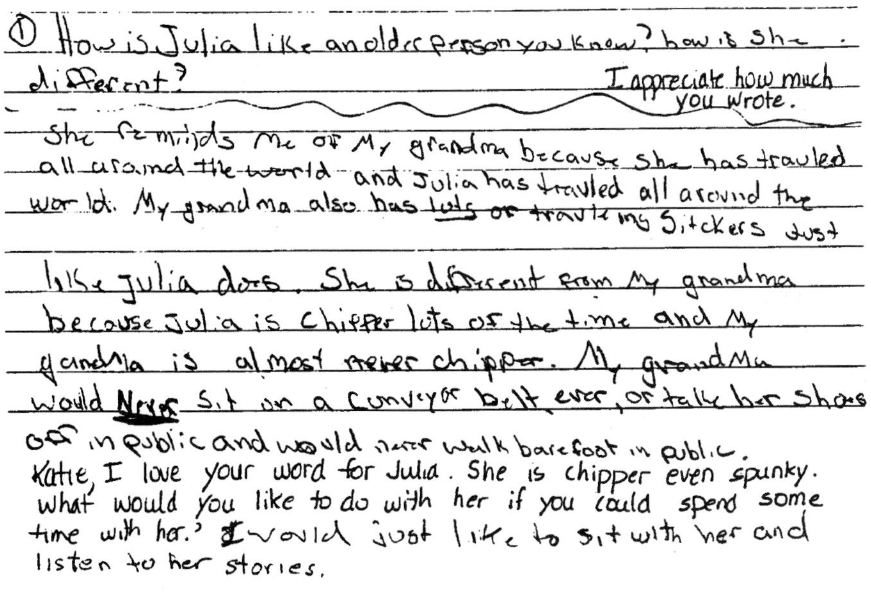

① How is Julia like an older person you know? how is she different?

I appreciate how much you wrote.

She reminds me of my grandma because she has trauled all around the world and Julia has trauled all around the world. My grandma also has lots of trauling Sitckers just like Julia dors. She is diffrent from my grandma because Julia is chipper lots of the time and my grandma is almost never chipper. My grandma would **Nver** sit on a Convyor belt ever, or take her shoes off in public and would never walk barefoot in public.

Katie, I love your word for Julia. She is chipper even spunky. what would you like to do with her if you could spend some time with her? I would just like to sit with her and listen to her stories.

Katie identifies important qualities of Julia, a character in her book, and she relates thoughtfully these qualities to her own grandmother.

---

he had read to her in order to bring her up to the point where they would start reading together. She felt, as we did, that this homework made him more attuned to important details. This is a prime example of a valuable anecdotal record that we could have encouraged David's mother to add to his portfolio to show the collaborative effort and focus we all had brought to helping David.

David's portfolio entries don't provide much evidence of his interaction with others about reading material. Unlike Katie, David doesn't spontaneously write about sharing in his reading letters or response journals. Nevertheless, it is important not to conclude that David doesn't participate and grow from his discussions with others. In fact, my observations suggest that David does talk about his reading with his friends and his family. The problem is not David. The problem is the documentation in his portfolio. It may be that the best way to document interaction with others is through a teacher observation checklist or anecdotal records. Alternatively, I could create an activity for students to complete in their literature circles that causes them to reflect on what they have learned from one another. Obviously, I need to consider both the documentation issues and the opportunities that I provide through my instruction for students to meaningfully interact with peers around books.

Figure 4.8

Name David
Date 10/20/94

SUMMARY OF READING, FALL 1994

Please write a summary of the story you just read. Remember to
include only the parts you think are important. A good summary is short,
but tells someone who has not read the story what it is about.

uncle   Title of the story: Making room for uncle Joe
Joe had down syndrome
So he needed some help
for taking car of him self,
One day Joe went out to
weed the graden but he was
Pulling out the flavers to.

one day uncle Joe went bowl-
ing with Danny, Danny saw
Some of his freinds uncle
Joe envited them to bowl danny

Danny was scared that
his friends were going
to make fun of
Joe but they dident uncle and
every body had a good time

Figure 4.8 *continued*

---

1. The theme or reason why the author wrote the story is *Jye*

PeoPle   by   whqt   Theme   like   not   what   they   do.

2. What are your thoughts about the story?   I liked it   bot   it   Should   be   a longer   Story

3. How hard or easy was this story for you to read?

hard---------------------------------easy

What made it easy or hard?   It   did'nt   have   any   hard   sPelling   on   any   thing

---

David's summary of a grade-level selection provides evidence of his strengths and weaknesses in constructing meaning from text.

Self-assessment and goal setting. Neither David's nor Katie's portfolio leaves any doubt these two students will continue as readers. Both give strong evidence of being able to set significant personal goals for themselves in reading. David frequently writes about wanting to read longer books. In November of fifth grade he stated in a portfolio visit, "I want to read a 400-page book," and indeed set out to read the longer books of the *Star Wars* series as his summer project. Challenge is a consistent goal for David throughout his reading self-reflections, and he can step back and notice that he enjoys reading more now than before (refer back to Figure 4.3). Other insights about David's self-assessment can be found in his reading log comments and monthly reading letters. He is acutely aware of those books that hold his interest (action, science fiction) as well as those books that are confusing, "I didn't finish the book because I didn't like it [and it] was very confusing." He makes comparisons across texts both among the *Star Wars* books and across others, often in terms of which ones have the most action. David's ability to reflect on his reading helps him make good choices. He enjoys challenge but knows when a book is out of reach for him. He sets appropriate goals.

Katie's challenges tend to come from her conversations with others about good books. She consistently sets goals to read books that her older sister reads, that friends recommend, or that have been nominated for awards. She even vows to read "all the comics at my grandmother's" when she visits over the summer. She knows that she loves to read ("I'm a bookworm") and yet continues to reflect on the importance of monitoring to be sure reading is making sense (refer back to Figure 4.3).

A Primary Grade Example

Educators and assessment experts point out that reading artifacts in portfolios are most often represented through student writing. They suggest that intermediate students may be more comfortable and more able to talk and write about their reading habits, strategies, and understandings because they have the fluency of language and the metacognition to do so. In the previous examples, Katie and David felt comfortable expressing themselves in writing, even as third graders. Their writing conventions and spelling were developed enough so that anyone reviewing their portfolios could form an impression of these students as readers. However, third graders are much more sophisticated than first graders. That raises the question of whether first-grade students' portfolios can adequately represent their reading abilities and progress.

As an intermediate teacher I reviewed the portfolio of one of my colleague's students. I wondered if I could form a clear impression of her student as a reader. Would I be able to use the evidence to determine the student's attitudes and experiences with reading? Could the portfolio help me understand how she went about the reading process, applied reading strategies, and constructed meaning from texts?

What follows is the result of my doing just that. I reviewed the portfolio of Becky, a first-grade student, to see what I could learn about her reading abilities and dispositions. This exercise proved to be not only a validation of portfolio assessment, but also an insightful process for me as a teacher whose students typically enter third grade as fairly developed readers. As I looked through my colleague's portfolio of an emerging reader, I gained a deeper appreciation of how my older students had started when they were five and six years old.

Becky had been with her teacher, Beth Marshall, as a kindergartener and as a first grader. Beth's conference notes from fall and spring (she simply adds to the fall notes to provide an ongoing progress report) of both years provide evidence of Becky's progress. When Becky was in kindergarten, Beth described her as an "emergent reader," a child who "enjoys and retells stories, uses pictures as clues to the story line, understands the conventions of print, and can point and match 1-1 as the teacher reads." By first grade, there is marked progress (see Figure 4.9). In the fall, Beth notes growth for Becky, now describing her as an "early" reader who enjoys reading. Beth uses classroom observations and interviews with Becky to substantiate her comments. In the spring, Becky's enthusiasm is still strong and is confirmed by her mother's note at the March portfolio conference stating that, "Becky has a healthy interest in books."

Also included in Becky's portfolio is a record of her reading abilities using a continuum that primary teachers in our district have developed (see Figure 4.10 on pages 116-117). Beth uses this continuum as a monitor of important learnings and as a vehicle for discussion with parents. Taken together, the continuum, samples of Becky's work, and conference notes provide important information on Becky's developing reading skills. Becky clearly enjoys reading and writing and is developing a variety of strategies for both reading and writing. Some tasks Becky can complete independently, and others still require teacher support. This is valuable information for the teacher and for Becky's parents. The continuum places Becky firmly on the way to success in second grade.

Clearly there were many aspects of reading that Becky's teacher observed. The nature of emergent literacy demands more teacher documentation than is typically needed at intermediate grades. Emerging abilities such as listening and talking about stories, concepts of print, book handling, and developing interests and motivation to read cannot be captured by students' written work. Without some type of teacher documentation (e.g., anecdotal notes, checklists, continua) these observations would simply be stored in Beth's memory, and thus neither colleagues nor parents would be privy to her insights. Nevertheless, although the teacher's notes are essential, they are not sufficient in our shared composite portfolio model. We rely, as much as possible, on both teacher documentation and actual evidence of student performance. As a result, I was able to use both Beth's records and student work to describe Becky as a reader.

Becky's portfolio work confirms that she is getting off to a good start as a reader. Becky's book log for independent reading provides evidence of what she is reading as well as how she is responding. It is unclear from her kindergarten book log whether Becky was beginning to read these books independently, looking at the pictures, or listening to them; however, she was making personal connections (see Figure 4.11 on page 118). By first grade, Becky is both reading and writing on her own and continuing her engagement with the characters (see Figure 4.12 on page 118). She is using sound-symbol correspondence in her invented spellings. Although this evidence suggests that Becky is developing positive attitudes toward reading, her responses to a Garfield Reading Attitude Survey included in her portfolio suggest that she may not choose to read during free time. Beth noted that for Becky, reading is a social act. Although Becky does read by herself, she prefers to read with friends. It will be important to encourage Becky's independent reading and to monitor her progress throughout the year.

Figure 4.9

Spring Conference
Ardmore Elementary
16616 N.E. 32nd Place
Bellevue, WA 98007

Becky
Ms. Marshall

Reading
       Students participate in Shared Reading, where we discuss reading strategies, vocabulary, phonics and punctuation. Students are read to, and read independently for an extended period of time each day.

Fall: Becky is an early reader. She enjoys listening to stories, chooses to read independently, shares ideas about books, participates in Shared Reading, is less reliant on illustrations as a clue to make meaning, uses phonics to confirm predictions, and expects to get meaning from text. Becky says, "I like reading. It is fun to do. I want to read chapter books."

Spring: Becky's reading skills have steadily progressed throughout the year. She is a fluent, confident reader who loves books and uses many strategies to decode grade level text. She is working on summarizing stories. She says, "Reading is fun because you get to read stuff you want to read. You can learn from books."

Writing
       Students have numerous opportunities to write during the day. For example, students create their own stories in Writer's Workshop, write letters at the writing table, and participate in teacher directed whole language activities. Writing is also integrated into the areas of mathematics, science, art and social studies.

Fall: Becky enjoys writing. She effectively uses invented spelling, writes sentences, is working on capitals and periods, is learning to leave spaces between words, and is confident about her ability to write. Becky is at the phonic stage of spelling development, and is working toward conventional spelling. She says, "I like writing. It is fun that you can do things like write things that are special to you."

Spring: Becky's writing skills have also progressed steadily throughout the year. She is currently working on handwriting, spelling high utility words, using punctuation, and creating a story with a beginning, middle and end. Becky says, "Oh, I love writing. I love that you can write your own stories and sometimes if you are at home you can have a lot of fun writing, if you don't have anything else to do."

The teacher's progress report provides documentation of Becky's reading and writing capabilities and dispositions that may be difficult to see in a first grader's portfolio work.

Additional evidence of Becky's choices of types and levels of books is documented by her weekly book bag selections (see Figure 4.13 on page 119). From these, we can see that Becky is staying fairly close to typical first-grade storybooks but that she is taking seriously the idea of challenge by trying, for example, *Aunt Harriet's Underground Railroad in the Sky* as her "challenger" book. She is setting appropriate goals and, in fact, does accomplish them. During conferences, Beth uses the book log entries and book bag selections to talk with Becky and her parents about Becky's enthusiasm for reading, choices of books, and her understanding of what she is reading. Beth supplements Becky's written responses with her own observations of Becky's ability to read and to construct meaning from first-grade texts.

Becky's portfolio also contains two modified running records (Clay, 1979) that provide information about her use of reading strategies. Comparing the record from spring of kindergarten with the one from fall of first grade, there is evidence of substantial growth in Becky's word identification skills. In kindergarten, Becky's miscues are proportionately quite numerous, although her attempts are close to the actual text. Beth wrote in her notes that Becky "knows basic sight words, sounds out with initial consonants, looks at the pictures, and tells stories about pictures." Becky's word identification skills are quite limited at this point, but she understands that reading should make sense and that pictures often help tell the story. The running record included for first grade documents much improvement (see Figure 4.14 on page 120). Reading from a first-grade text, Becky has a much lower ratio of miscues to correct word reading. Beth notes that Becky uses "pictures, sentence structure, and semantics-meaning" as observable strategies. She self-corrects, rereads, and uses initial consonants to handle the very few difficulties she has with this first-grade story. In response to Beth's prompt, Becky successfully retold the story, including an excellent summarization of the main points of the plot. This oral retelling was a good strategy for assessing Becky's understanding; her written responses were still quite limited at this time (refer to Figure 4.12). Becky commented to Beth that the passage was "just right" for her to read, and, in fact, she was correct in her self-assessment. This passage could be considered easy for her. The running record provides concrete evidence to support Beth's observations, continuum report, and Becky's other book entries.

Finally, two writing samples, one from the beginning of first grade and a section (four pages from a six-page story) from the end of first grade, provide striking evidence of Becky's growth in invented spelling, voice, and ability to communicate information (see Figures 4.15 and 4.16). Becky experiments with invented spelling using many of the sound-symbol correspondences she knows from reading (e.g., *bean* for *been*, *awaey* for *away*, *befor* for *before*), and she correctly spells many of her sight words (e.g., *the, to, for, going, have*). From these two pieces we also notice that Becky has not yet developed a sense of sentence structure or use of capitals and punctuation. These would be good areas for instruction through her reading

Figure 4.10

BELLEVUE LITERACY PORTFOLIO CONTINUUM/RUBRIC (Reading & Writing)
Primary (K-2)

Beginning of Kindergarten		Mid-Second Grade
I. Interacts with Text		
Listens to story	Listening to story:	Student reads grade level text:
Looks at text/pictures	Understands print carries meaning	Dictates - retelling
Pretends to read	Makes predictions (pattern books)	Constructs a personal response
	Listening to story!	- I liked the part where . . .
	Draws inferences	- that reminds me of . . .
	Compares and contrasts - alike and different using familiar story-line	- I did that, only . . .
	Recalls important **3/96** information	Child makes connection
	- begin/mid/end story	Understands sequence and cause and effect
	- verbal or picture type response	Understands that reading can be a tool to gather information
	Listening to story:	
	Understands plot/setting **3/96**	
	- what story is about	
	- where it takes place	
	Re-telling using pictures, verbal, or "3-part fold"	
	Reads independently	
II. Reads a Variety of Materials		
Random selection	Recognizes that there are books for different **3/96** purposes	Can choose appropriate **3/96** books at his/her own reading level
Handles books	Selects books based on purpose, interest and preference	Chooses different genres
Doesn't have a clear definition of reading		
III. Reading Enjoyment / Ownership		
Listens to picture books	Enjoys talking about books	Chooses to read for pleasure and information
	Voluntarily selects books which hold student's interest for a short time	Regularly shares reading **3/96** between home and school
	Enjoys listening to taped books	
	Enjoys listening to read- **3/96** alouds in different genres	

116

IV. Uses Appropriate Strategies

Pictures tell the story	Awareness that print carries the message; there is a beginning/ end of book; inventing the text	Uses directional movement: - knows where to start to read - knows which way to go— left to right and return - locates unknown words	Self-monitors by rereading, checking pictures, pausing, saying, "No, that's not right." Cross-checks by rereading, reading aloud, reading slowly, running finger under words *3/96* Searching: looks at picture/ text, skips word and comes back, searches environment	Uses self-extending strategies Learns to read by reading

I. Writing Development

emerging

Scribble/pretend to write with meaning Strings letters together with meaning Pictures carry meaning Left-to-right, top-to-bottom directionality	Pictures tell a complex story with some simple words Frequent use of a few known words (*name, Mom, love,* etc.) Labeling with first letter sound and some end sounds Beginning "lists"	Simple sentences Series of related sentences Spacing between words Some conventional spelling Many initial, medial and final consonants End punctuation and capitals inconsistent Pictures and text compliment each other	Story has a beginning, middle, end *3/96* Complete sentences *3/96* More importance placed on text than pictures *3/96* Detail in writing Experiments with different genres Experiments with punctuation (e.g., exclamation points, question marks) *3/96* Voice is evident *3/96* Blends, diagraphs, vowels *emerging 3/96* All syllables represented *3/96* Increasing use of conventional spelling *Sometimes* Legible and fluent printing *3/96* ☺	Sticks to topic Can write a long narrative over time Consistent use of end punctuation and capital letters *3/96* Varied sentence structure Appropriate details and information to develop topic Writes for self and other audiences "Bank" of fluent conventional spellings Uses specific action words and adjectives

II. Writing Process

Student draws a picture which may or may not tell a story	Student draws pictures accompanied by labels	Student develops story through a drawing Shares writing	Student draws a series of pictures which tell a story *usually writes first* Student writes the same theme which is repeated in subsequent stories *3/96* ☺	Planning, revising, editing *3/96* with teacher prompting

---

The continuum helps teachers note a student's developmental benchmarks, and it is useful for communicating progress and expectations to parents.

Figure 4.11

Date S-9-92

Title

Author Dirth of a Foal "Miller"

I would tell a friend to
read this book because it
shows how cats get born

Date 2-1-95

Title Dolphins!

Author Sharon Bokoske

I am like a dolphin
because I can swim really
good, and because I am
nice and smart.

Becky's dictated book log entries from kindergarten reveal her personal connections with the text.

Figure 4.12

Date 3-1-96

Title HENRY aND MUDG

Author CYNthia stevson

Date 6-19-96

Title Deling vath Dragigs

Author

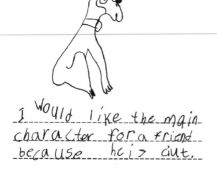

I would like the main
character for a friend
because he iz cut.

ifI was semring
I would tric to
Be friends wath All
of the Dragas

Becky's book log entries from first grade are written independently. She is reading on her own, continuing to enjoy the characters in her books, and experimenting with invented spelling.

Figure 4.13

Teacher Selection
Book Bags
9/95 & 3/96

Each week, students record the three books they have selected to put in their book bags. This list reflects the student's ability to self-select reading material, the student's book preference and the student's reading level.

Notes:

BOOK BAG

Name *Becky*

Date *3-11-96*

I know how to read

ing People House

I'm working on

the ghost Eye tree

My challenge book is

Aunt Harriet's
under ground Railroad
In the Sky

Becky's record of her "book bag" selections shows that she is choosing to read typical first grade books and that she is willing to challenge herself with more difficult books.

Figure 4.14

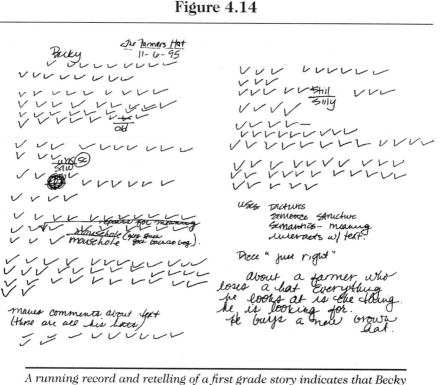

A running record and retelling of a first grade story indicates that Becky
is quite fluent at this level and that she understands what she reads.
The teacher's notes indicate that Becky is able to use a variety of
reading strategies.

and writing. Becky's experience with books comes through in her writing.
She tells many details about her upcoming trip to summer camp and
demonstrates a clear voice as she communicates with her reader. Becky
should be encouraged to continue reading and to make reading-writing connections. These areas will capitalize on her interests and strengths, and
they will be fun to explore with her.

Although the artifacts in first-grade portfolios are quite different from
those in intermediate grade portfolios, we can nevertheless learn about
students' reading enjoyment, variety of texts, self-assessment, and ability
to construct meaning and to use reading strategies. We have learned that it
is possible but not always easy to document reading. We still face many
challenges.

Figure 4.15

At the beginning of first grade, Becky uses invented spelling to label her picture.

Figure 4.16

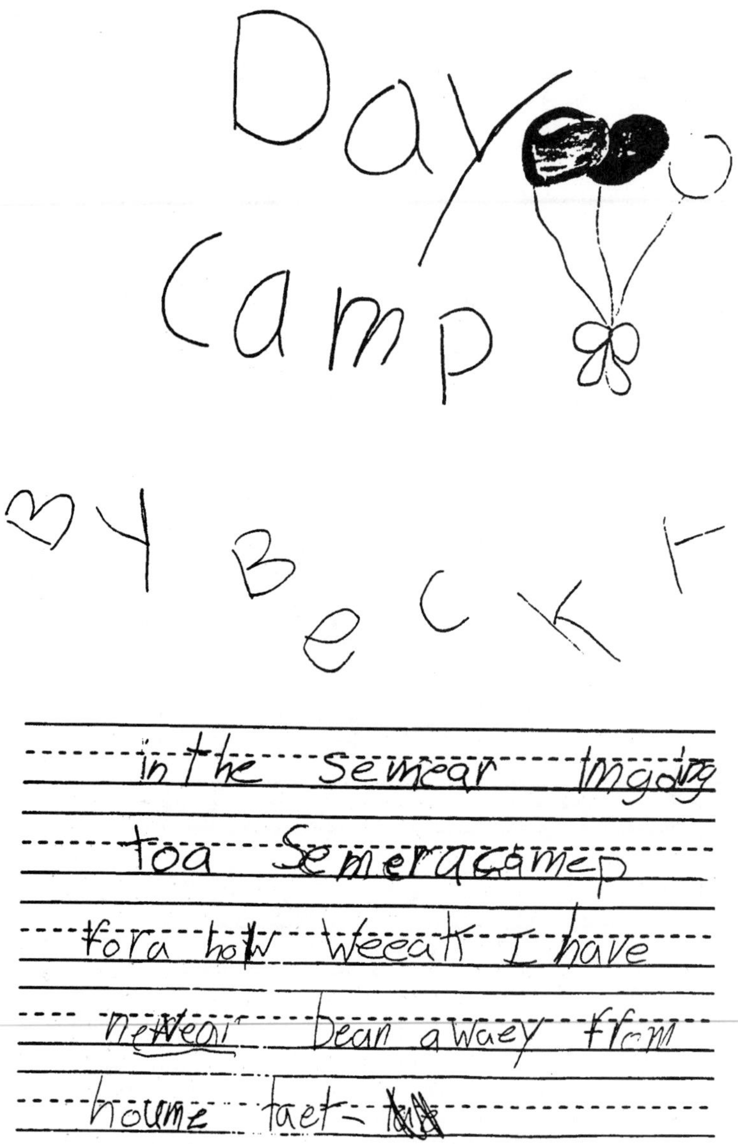

Day
camp
BY BeCKr

in the semear Imgoing
toa Semeracamep
fora how weeatt I have
neweai bean awaey from
houme taet—

"In the summer I'm going to a summer camp for a
whole week. I have never been away from home
that long before.

Figure 4.16 *continued*

i tis my frithast time
going to Sermer camp
I'm bring a flash Liegt
and my neow sleeping
bag my toeth Brash
lang befor I teln k im
going to have a
laet of fun their
and you no weat it
is goin ato be fun.

```
It's my firstest time going to summer camp.
I'm bringing a flashlight and my new sleeping
bag my toothbrush.  I think I'm going to have
a lot of fun there and you know what it is
going to be fun."
```

*At the end of first grade, Becky writes a long description of an
up coming trip to summer camp, providing good evidence of her
ability to communicate in writing and her developing conventions
(spelling, sentence structure, capitalization, and punctuation).*

Collecting Reading Evidence in Portfolios

Reading is a complex interactive mental process and, as we have seen, it is sometimes quite difficult to capture in a portfolio. Much of what readers do happens "behind the scenes," away from teachers' eyes and in the context of an informal, collaborative world of shared meaning making. Challenging as it may be, we continue to be committed to improving the reading components of our portfolios because of the benefits we have seen for our students, their parents, and our own teaching. Our challenges fall into four areas: (a) using good strategies of assessment for a range of developmental levels and a wide variety of situations; (b) evaluating individual students' progress and how it fits with grade-level expectations; (c) documenting the context of the reading situation and amount of support provided; and (d) finding time to document the "hard to see" in student work samples.

Strategies for Assessment

Our first challenge is to compile an ample menu of assessment techniques for assessing reading. There is no way that teachers can be limited to a few. Even after five years of work, we find that we cannot be sure when we will get the best and most needed information. We have discovered, however, that we *can* make some logical matches between assessment strategy, the aspect of reading we want to target, and the developmental level of the students. For example, an assessment strategy that might work for a beginning student, such as running records, might capture little about the strategies of a more advanced reader. Beginning readers and older struggling readers spend a considerable amount of time developing word identification strategies (context, phonics, sight words) and self-monitoring for meaning, both of which are easily observed using running records or informal reading inventories. However, although advanced readers still meet an occasional unknown word and certainly still need to monitor for understanding, they must apply their strategies to more complex, longer texts. Reading brief sections of text aloud will not provide the kind of information teachers need to evaluate students' abilities to monitor and fix up larger and more intricate units of meaning. It is one thing to read a paragraph from *The Giver,* another to be able to monitor, clarify, and resolve the problems that arise as you are reading the entire text. Similarly, if a student is a competent reader but has difficulty with writing, assessing text understanding may require additional individual conference notes, drawings accompanied by interviews, and observation checklists. Writing may underestimate how well the student understands. That is not to say that students should never write about what they have read, but rather that the written evidence is best supplemented with other evidence of understanding.

There are two main issues with respect to selecting good assessment strategies for reading. The first is that assessment strategies must fit the student, developmental level, and the task. Although we tried to stay open to many ways of collecting reading evidence, we found that our portfolio artifacts were still predominantly written work at the intermediate grades with more teacher notes at the early grades. Observation checklists were used by only a few teachers. In the same way, we found that even though several primary teachers tried to use audiotapes, they were seldom listened to, even by the teacher or the child. And we found that most reading artifacts represented narrative texts rather than the wide range of texts that we hoped our students were reading.

The second issue is that some aspects of reading are still difficult for us to document. We have discussed the difficulties collecting information about reading strategies, but we also continue to struggle documenting the social nature of reading. How can we capture the insights that come from collaborative discussions about texts and place them into portfolios? What are the other ways that students can demonstrate their interactions with others around reading? Our portfolios do not yet reflect this aspect of our curriculum.

We still need to experiment with new and better strategies for collecting and documenting student progress in all aspects of reading. Our menu of evaluation possibilities must be expanded to include both breadth of choices and depth of versatility. An added benefit, of course, is that by focusing on assessment of difficult aspects of reading, we are more likely to focus our instruction. This is why we need to continue to explore new assessment strategies.

Individual Progress and Grade Level

A second issue is how to address text difficulty in portfolio work. Unlike writing, reading has a strong tradition of evaluating student reading performance in terms of the grade level of the text. However, many of the characteristics of good readers are the same across developmental levels; it is the difficulty of the text that varies. Although we know that text difficulty is hard to define and that reading performance varies depending on the text, parents and teachers still ask the question, "Is this child reading material that is at or near her grade level?" At the same time, we ask, "Is this child making progress in reading, regardless of the level of material she is reading?" Both questions require attention.

Our experiences of using portfolios to communicate with parents, guide instructional decisions, and evaluate performance (see Chapters 9 and 10) suggest that we need a variety of standards by which to judge student success. On one hand, we are committed to teaching and assessing students where they are, moving them forward as best we can. If, for example, a fifth-grade student is still struggling with word identification and reading at a second- to third-grade level, we want to be sure his portfolio artifacts and classroom experiences capture those abilities. If he makes good progress, becoming more fluent and able to read more difficult books independently, we want the portfolio to show that growth as well. On the other hand, we feel it is essential to know that student is reading several years below grade level and to document, in some way, the level of his reading material. This is one reason why our portfolio committee decided to distribute a packet of reading selections representing a range of grade levels. The selections can be used by teachers to anchor their definitions of grade-level material, and they can be used with students as another indicator of reading performance. The selections are a helpful addition because it is often difficult for teachers to judge text difficulty, especially when students are self-selecting much of their reading material. That is not to say that a precise grade level can or should be indicated in the portfolio. Rather, we believe it is essential to honestly face the grade-level question and address it as we discuss portfolio artifacts with parents (see Chapter 9). And students are no less aware of text difficulty than are parents. We continue to struggle with how to address both reading growth and grade-level standards in our portfolios.

Amount of Teacher Support and Prompting Provided to Students

Just as grade-level issues are sometimes obscured in portfolio artifacts, so too is the amount of support that students receive. This is our third challenge. For example, many times portfolio artifacts represent strong retellings and story comprehension by first-grade students when the text is read aloud by the teacher. Listening comprehension is important at first-grade level, to be sure, but it is not the same as reading comprehension. Similarly, literature circles and reading response journals that are conducted with strong teacher support or shared reading don't represent the same student performance as do reading activities completed independently. These are tricky issues.

In another sense, we recognized that teacher support or prompting for a particular task might influence students' responses. The best example of this issue has been our experience with helping students write summaries of their reading. Our first attempts were called retellings, and by using prompts such as "Retell the story for someone who may not have read the story before," we indeed got exactly what we asked for—retellings and nothing more. As our discussions about summaries evolved we determined that although it might be developmentally appropriate to ask younger students for retellings, older students should be asked to summarize what they have read. We wondered what questions or prompts could best elicit a summary. If, for example, we expect students to mention the theme or big idea in their summaries, should we ask, "What is the author's message?" or "What is the theme?" or "What is the most important thing you took away from this story?" or should we leave it up to the students to remember that a theme needs to be included in a summary? Or, if we value students' personal connections to a reading, should we ask them questions that encourage connections, or should we wait to see if they will automatically make them? Summary writing is just one example of the issue of when and how much teacher prompting should be used. In reality, each of the activities and tasks we use in our classrooms and place into our portfolios raises questions about the teacher's role.

Although we haven't solved these issues, we have found that the best approach to dealing with level of support and teacher involvement is to vary the kinds of reading experiences that we provide for students in our classes, and thus to vary the nature of the artifacts collected for the portfolios. So, some reading artifacts would be created independently, some collaboratively, and others with teacher guidance or prompting. In addition, we have found it helpful to indicate on our teacher entry slips (see Chapter 8) or student entry slips (see Chapter 6) the level of support and prompting that students received for a particular activity. Even so, the variability in support for portfolio pieces continues to present challenges for documentation and interpretation of reading evidence.

Time

Although we were no strangers to time issues, we found the challenge became exacerbated as we tried to collect indicators of reading performance. Interviews, for example, can take precious one-on-one time in the classroom. Or summary writing—an excellent strategy for assessing how students interact with text—can be time consuming even after spending considerable time teaching students what is involved in a good summary. The time issue did, however, become less of a concern as we became more able to integrate our assessment methods into our regular reading instruction. This meant that our assessment measures were viewed as more valuable and engaging by the students and that we did not see them as something to add or superimpose onto a curriculum that was already in place. A good example of this is our home reading logs. The assignment of home reading for two weeks is usually viewed by the students—and definitely by the parents—as "good" homework, and we get valuable information about what students choose to read on their own as well as how they interact with what they have chosen to read.

We also observed that the more frequently any of these assessment techniques are used, the more adept even younger children can become in using the techniques efficiently; that saves time. Intermediate students, in particular, can become quite adroit at doing assessments with little supervision and can be very useful in modeling assessment techniques for younger students. In fact, it became apparent to us that teaching students how to "do the assessment" was in itself excellent teaching of reading. Rather than being an add-on, the reading assessments became a part of our typical instruction.

Conclusion

In this chapter, I have provided an overview of important attributes of good reading, and I have demonstrated how a variety of portfolio artifacts can be used to understand a student's reading abilities. We have learned that clearly and explicitly defining what you want to assess is more than half the challenge of the assessment task, especially in the area of reading. Documenting reading evidence in a portfolio requires both a clear understanding of the reading process and deliberate attention to collecting evidence. Although we still have several challenges to address, we are convinced that with careful attention, we *can* document students' reading capabilities and dispositions using portfolios. Documenting reading progress in a portfolio will probably always be more difficult than documenting writing. However, our work thus far suggests that the process of thinking about assessing reading has led us to better instruction and has led our students to improved reading performance. Difficult as it may be, we believe the effort will reap rewards.

References

Anderson, R. C., Hiebert, E. H., Scott, J. A., & Wilkinson, I. E. (1985). *Becoming a nation of readers: The report of the Commission on Reading*. Washington, DC: National Institute of Education.

Anderson, R. C., Wilson, P. T., & Fielding, L. G. (1988). Growth in reading and how children spend their time outside of school. *Reading Research Quarterly, 23*(3), 285–303.

Baker, L., & Brown, A. L. (1984). Metacognitive skills and reading. In P. D. Pearson, R. Barr, M.L. Kamil, & P. Mosenthal (Eds.), *Handbook of reading research* (pp. 353–394). New York: Longman.

Clay, M. M. (1979). *The early detection of reading difficulties* (3rd ed.). Auckland: Heinemann.

Costa, A. L. (1989). Re-assessing assessment. *Educational Leadership, 46*(7), 2.

Dole, J. A., Duffy, G. G., Roehler, L. R., & Pearson, P. D. (1991). Moving from the old to the new: Research on reading comprehension instruction. *Review of Educational Research, 61*(2), 239–264.

Fielding, L. G., Wilson, P. T., & Anderson, R. C. (1986). A new focus on free reading: The role of trade books in reading instruction. In T.E. Raphael (Ed.), *The contexts of school-based literacy* (pp. 149–160). New York: Random House.

Guthrie, J. T., Schafer, W., Wang, Y., & Afflerbach, P. (1993). *Influences of instruction on amount of reading* (Reading Research Report No. 3). Athens, Ga: National Reading Research Center.

Morrow, L. M., & Weinstein, C. S. (1986). Encouraging voluntary reading: The impact of a literature program on children's use of library centers. *Reading Research Quarterly, 21*(3), 330–346.

Paris, S. G., Lipson, M. Y., & Wixson, K. K. (1983). Becoming a strategic reader. *Contemporary Educational Psychology, 8*(3), 293–316.

Paris, S. G., & Myers, M. (1981). Comprehension monitoring in good and poor readers. *Journal of Reading Behavior, 13*(1), 5–22.

Pearson, P. D., & Gallagher, M. (1983). The instruction of reading comprehension. *Contemporary Educational Psychology, 8*(3), 317–344.

Perrone, V. (Ed.). (1991). *Expanding student assessment*. Alexandria: Association for Supervision and Curriculum Development.

Taylor, B. M., Frye, B. J., & Maruyama, G. M. (1990). Time spent reading and reading growth. *American Educational Research Journal, 27*(2), 351–362.

Wixson, K. K., & Peters, C. W. (1984). Reading redefined: A Michigan Reading Association position paper. *Michigan Reading Journal, 17*(1), 4–7.

Wixson, K. K., Peters, C. W., Weber, E.M., & Roeber, E.D. (1987). New directions in statewide reading assessment. *The Reading Teacher, 40*(8), 749–755.

chapter 5

Collecting and Understanding Writing Performance

Lynn Beebe

We examine students' writing abilities and artifacts in this chapter. We begin with a discussion of important writing outcomes, using examples from students' portfolios to demonstrate how these attributes can be seen and understood in student work. Then we discuss how a body of work in portfolios can help teachers, parents, and students understand writing capabilities. We close with challenges to collecting and interpreting writing evidence.

When I look at my writing I see that I need to includ more detals like where I went and how high the feris wheel was and what the people looked like.

K. S., grade three

Through my years of teaching I have always kept a file called "Children's Writing." This is where I put the stories that delighted me, poems written from the heart, notes with the first spontaneous written work of a child, and pages from a journal left behind by a student who moved away without notice, revealing thoughts I hadn't known. I thought of this collection as "neat stuff," too good to discard, but not specifically useful to my classroom practice.

I still have a folder of children's work, but it's now in a file on my desk, and it mostly serves to store unclaimed work that's too important to put into the trash. The pieces that I once saved for myself (and sometimes shared with parents or friends and colleagues) are now in the children's portfolios, with entry slips attached.

I have always realized the power contained in children's written work and have known that I could tell important things from the pieces I kept, but I didn't have a format for putting that telling together. There was no space on the report card for this knowledge and, besides, I didn't have the words to describe what I saw.

As portfolios became an integral part of my classroom and my practice, I realized they were much more than organized collections of student work. The writing that was put into these portfolios became more than the sum of the individual pieces. I found that as I further developed my own understanding and ability to assess children's writing, both my instruction and the students' work improved. Looking at the writing in the portfolios helps me be more explicit about what I teach and about the criteria I have for good writing; entering work into the portfolios makes my students more aware of the process of creating good writing and the abilities they have acquired in this process. Looking through the portfolios together helps the students, parents, and me to set appropriate writing goals.

Working closely with writing artifacts, the teachers in our portfolio group realized the power that using portfolios has to enhance our own understanding of writing curriculum, instructional strategies, and assessment. This chapter describes our rethinking about what students should know and be able to do in writing, how portfolio evidence helps us think about our teaching and our students' learning, and the challenges of collecting writing evidence.

Rethinking Writing

After the initial struggles with portfolio logistics (see Chapter 3), we began to dig deeper into thinking about writing. On one hand, many of us were comfortable with process writing and had collections of work we shared with parents at conferences. We delighted in the stories that children produced, and the children themselves appreciated each others' work at "Author's Chair" (Graves & Hansen, 1983) and other sharing sessions. Even many parents participated in our writing efforts, typing final copies, helping to publish collections of our students' work, and supporting students' writing interests at home and in school. And most of us felt that, in general, we could recognize good writing when we saw it. On the other hand, most of us were less comfortable with detailed analyses and discussions of children's work, and we were not sure that students were writing as well as they could. In terms of identifying more specifically what was good (or needing improvement), we could point out specific conventions, noting, for example, students' ability to use capitalization and punctuation, but rarely did we go further. We realized that we needed to specifically define the criteria of good writing and to develop a better understanding of children's written products, their writing processes, and their dispositions toward writing. What's more, most of us realized that we had never fully defined for students the attributes of good writing, such as the qualities of a good story or a persuasive piece. We often neglected to provide any sort of guidelines or feedback to our students beyond "add detail," "write about things you know and care about," and the usual "now edit for spelling and punctuation." We realized that there is more to good writing and good writing instruction.

We organized our thinking about good writing into four areas: qualities or traits of good writing (Spandel & Stiggins, 1990), use of the writing process (Graves, 1994), writing ownership (Au, Scheu, Kawakami, & Herman, 1990; Graves, 1994), and self-reflection and self-evaluation about the process and products of writing (Howard, 1990; Rief, 1990). Thinking carefully and specifically about each of these aspects of writing helped us create and assess important elements of a strong writing program. In the following, I describe in depth each of these important writing outcomes and provide examples of student work across a variety of developmental levels.

Qualities of Good Writing

Good writers communicate effectively through their writing. They produce pieces with clear, organized, focused, and interesting composition and content across a variety of genres and for a variety of purposes. We used analytic traits (Diederich, 1974), found in many state and district direct writing assessments, to define specific qualities of good writing—central purpose, voice, organization, word choice, sentence fluency, conventions (e.g., Kentucky Department of Education, 1992; Spandel & Stiggins, 1990; Vermont State Department of Education, 1994; Quellmalz & Burry, 1983). In general, these traits are applicable to many types of writing, such as stories, personal narratives, persuasive pieces, informational pieces, and poetry. Following, I provide a description and examples of each trait.

Central ideas and purpose. Good writers develop ideas and fulfill purposes. In fictional pieces, for example, writers express ideas that are significant and interesting, and they provide sufficient detail to enrich the central theme or story line. The ideas are well developed. With younger writers, the ideas may be in the form of pictures or letter strings. Later, as students begin to use words and simple sentences to express their ideas, the details may be found in the drawings that match or elaborate the written "text" or in a few sentences constructed around a topic. At more advanced levels, writers rely less on pictures. They can carry the central idea throughout the piece and shape the writing toward a desired outcome. In nonfiction writing, the author's writing stays with the topic. The main ideas create an informative and compelling content, and the generalizations are well supported with clear details that teach or persuade the reader. At all levels and with all genres, the writing is clear, focused, and interesting, written with purpose to communicate with others and/or the author herself.

Elizabeth's piece about Christmas and Erik's piece on World War III (see Figures 5.1a and 5.1b) demonstrate the mix of picture details with a few "words" or sentences. Elizabeth S., a beginning first grader, uses strings of letters that she reads back to her teacher (teacher's transcription is indicated in parentheses) to communicate her story about her favorite Christmas present. Erik, a more advanced student, still relies on the details of his drawings to add life to his writing; he also adds several sentences that describe the overall theme of his work. There is obviously much more to this story than he has chosen to depict through words.

Sam, a second grader, had teacher support in trying to keep her personal narrative focused on her main idea (see Figure 5.2 on page 135).

Figure 5.1a

10-27-92 ELiZABETH

SGAZ AS A PJRAVKS AZ JOZSRZMBKZAT
YMIFAVEVARTRMA ;M

This is a picture of my funnest
Christmas because it was my favorite
present. It was a rocking horse.

IJOZ KR CPAZ ATBKAZ IPADYCATT
HAMPTANRASMDA

(I chose this Christmas present because I
played with it the most on Christmas Day.)

This was last Christmas.

Elizabeth uses a combination of pictures and letter strings to communicate about Christmas activities. She read her writing back to the teacher, who wrote Elizabeth's thoughts below.

There were so many parts of the story she wanted to share that she found it hard to limit herself to one experience. Sam's first draft, written at the computer, contains several central ideas that paint a vivid picture of her experiences—her airplane experiences, explanation for the trip, airport pickup,

Figure 5.1b

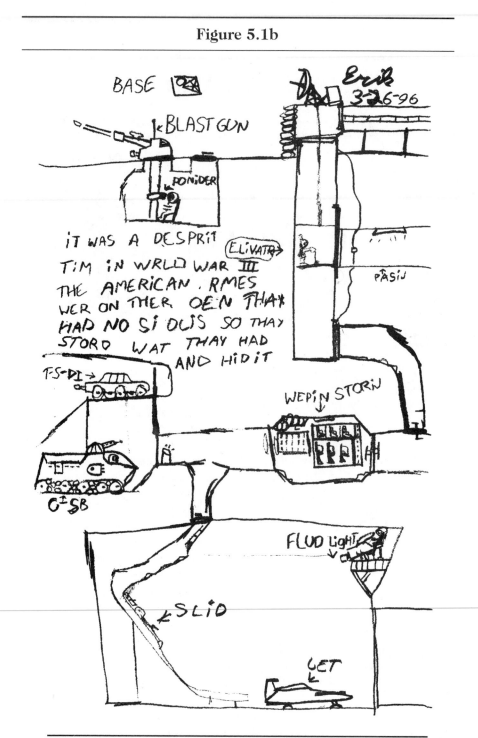

Erik uses detailed pictures and some sentences to tell his story. "It was a desperate time in World War III. The American armies were on their own. They had no silos so they stored what they had and hid it."

Figure 5.2

Entry Slip

Name Sam B   Date 3 - 20 - 95

I have chosen this Sacramento Story

for my portfolio because It was

Personal My narFirst Draft for a

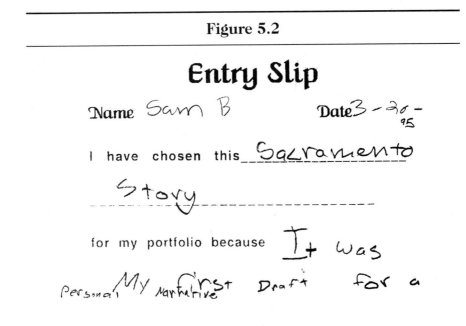

My Trip To Sacramento

There I was sitting next to my
screaming sister and sitting by the
window again. On the airplane my
ear hearting like a snake trying to
wiggle its way out. My sister
screaming for her mom on the other
row but she was a sleep. My dad
felt like saying bloody murder.
Well, we were on the air plane
because we were going to see our
reletives and celebrate christmas
because we are juish. When we got
off the plane our reletives picked
us up and they gave me and Lila my
sister a candy cane. So we got
home Ryan chased Lila around the
house. To my surprise the grounups
did not mind I guess they were to
busy chating. Well on christmas eve
I wrote Santa a letter and left him
a donut. The next morning I looked
at the fire place the donut was
gone and on the back of the note
there was a note from Santa.▯

Sam's first draft of a personal narrative about her trip to Sacramento.

playing at the relatives', and Christmas Eve episode. All of Sam's sentences stay on the central idea, "My Trip to Sacramento," and, for the most part, the story contains good detail to convey the mood and events. The story demonstrates some of the qualities of the "bed to bed" stories typical of second graders (Calkins, 1994), but it also demonstrates Sam's emerging abilities to add detail to some of the events. Next for Sam will be learning to focus on one or two important ideas and developing them more fully rather than briefly touching on everything that seems important.

Another student, Elisabeth, wrote a personal narrative about moving that demonstrates her ability to stick with a main idea throughout her story and her attention to supporting details (see Figure 5.3). Although I helped her edit this piece, the content and clear sense of focus came completely from Elisabeth. She develops three main ideas about moving in this segment of her longer piece: (a) statement about where she moved from, (b) her feelings about moving, and (c) a surprising positive aspect of moving. In addition, details such as "my medium-sized neighborhood," "sometimes I cried in my heart," and the explanation that "if we hadn't moved, there wouldn't have been room for James, my new brother" all give us a clearer picture of her feelings and the place she was to call home.

Voice. Voice is a quality we all recognize in good writing, and most of us can even identify individual students' work by what might be called their style or their voice. It is, however, much harder to describe voice to others or to instruct students in developing voice in their work. Voice is a sense that the writer is speaking directly to the reader in a way that is individualistic, expressive, engaging, and natural. Graves (1994) calls it "the imprint of ourselves on our writing" and reminds us that making a good choice of topic enables voice to emerge.

Even at the early stages of writing development, students demonstrate their voice in their own work, and they can recognize it in others' work as well. At more advanced levels, writers are consciously aware of creating voice in writing, eager to be heard and felt by their readers.

Elisabeth's voice comes across clearly in her piece about moving (see Figure 5.3). Her personal perspective rings through as she describes aspects of the move, leaving the reader with little doubt about the facts or the author's emotions. Elisabeth's voice is also evident in her poetry (see Figure 5.4 on pages 138-139). In her first poem, "Spring," she imparts a sense of delight and wonder in the world around her. Phrases such as "Morning comes, flowers bloom, roses sparkle in the sun" reflect her cheerfulness and love of life's small beauties. In a later poem, "Peasants," Elisabeth uses a more serious voice in describing peasant life, and she creates a rhythm to match the drudgery of the peasant existence.

Although voice seems easiest to hear, teach, and create in expressive writing (i.e., personal narratives, poetry) and fiction, it is also important to other genres such as descriptive, persuasive, and informational writing. Jeff and David, third graders in a multiage class, developed a strong and persuasive voice in their letter to Food Services (see Figure 5.5 on page 140).

Figure 5.3

When I Moved
By Elisabeth

When I moved, I left my friends and neighbors. I left my medium sized neighborhood in Bellevue.

When my parents told that we were going to move, I didn't want to go. I was very sad. I really did not want to move. I didn't want to leave my friends and neighbors. Sometimes I cried in my heart, when I thought about moving. But my Dad said, "We are going to move, because this house is too small."

Luckily we did move, because, although we didn't know it then, my mom was going to have a baby about a year later! If we hadn't moved, there wouldn't have been room for James, my new brother!

It was so boring looking for a house. I hated it! We had to drive all around around, sometimes in the relator's van and sometimes in

---

*A section of Elisabeth's final version includes clear focus and purpose.
It sticks to the topic.*

Reading the letter, you can almost picture these two youngsters discussing the problem and deciding how they will make their argument in a compelling way to Food Services. To their credit, the letter did its job—the director of Food Services responded! Difficult as it may be, it is important nonetheless to help writers develop voice in informational or report writing. In addition to knowing and understanding their content, students must develop their own sense of interest and importance in order to communicate the information effectively and with voice.

Organization. Organization includes the ability to use different text structures to communicate a clear sequence and coherence in the piece. The flow and structure should be appropriate to the purpose of the piece (e.g., stories with beginnings, middles, and ends; persuasive pieces with support for the stance; descriptive pieces that paint a vivid picture with the use of carefully selected details), and there should be coherence and transitions between ideas and paragraphs. Students' early attempts at organization may include a clear beginning but no ending, or a sense of story details without a plot, or experimentation with different forms of writing (letters, stories, poetry, journal writing, learning logs). These are important steps in learning about

---

Figure 5.4

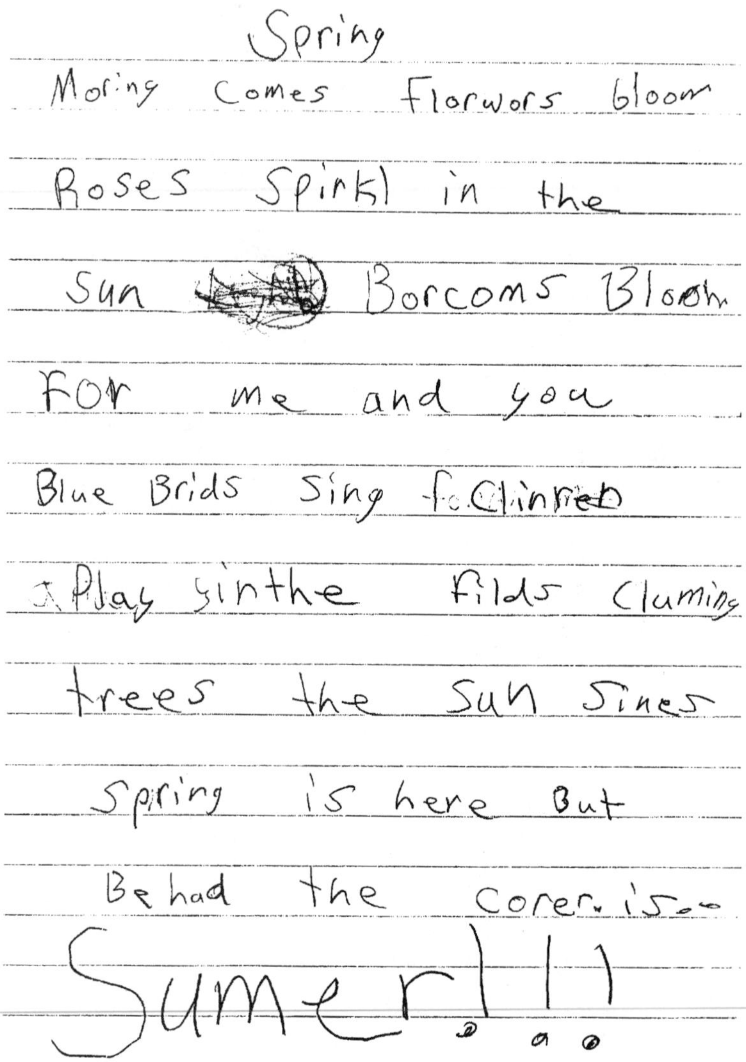

Spring

Moring Comes Florwors bloom

Roses Spinkl in the

Sun ~~Borcoms~~ Borcoms Bloom

For me and you

Blue Brids Sing foClinried

I Play sinthe filds Cluming

trees the Sun Sines

Spring is here But

Behad the corer. is...

Sumer!!!

Transcription of "Spring"

Morning comes, flowers bloom
Roses sparkle in the sun
Blossoms bloom for me and you
Blue birds sing
Children play in the fields climbing trees
The sun shines
Spring is here but behind the corner is
SUMMER!

Figure 5.4 *continued*

Peasants
A Poem by Elisabeth

Work
Work
Work all day
Play
Play
No play
Work in the fields
Plow
Plow
Shoo birds
Shoo
Go away
Stop eating
We're hungry too
Go
Go
Go away
Dinner has come
Porridge to eat
Sleep
Go to bed
Quick
Now quick
Morning comes
Work again

Elisabeth's poetry reflects her voice, whether the poem is light-hearted or quite serious.

Figure 5.5

Woodridge School
12619 S. E. 20th Place
Bellevue, WA 98005

10-1-93

Dear Food Services,

Some kids in this school district cannot buy lunch when you change the schedule, because they cannot eat certain foods. Example: I am a vegetarian. The schedule says cheese pizza. When I go to buy lunch, I see that !t is meat pizza. I cannot eat it. If it is possible, we would like you to serve what is on the schedule. When you do something like box lunch, we'd like to know exactly what is in it [especially for free lunch people because they have no other choice].

Sincerely,

Jeff +
David

communicating ideas in a clear, organized way. More developed writing will have a clearer organizational pattern that allows the writing to flow smoothly and easily. When writing nonfiction pieces, competent writers also organize their work around a central topic or question, providing a logical flow to the information, description, or argument that helps the reader understand the content and point of the piece. Often, difficulty with organization is related to the writer's struggle with her ideas, content, and purpose. When children's writing lacks organization, I often return to these fundamental aspects of writing before taking on issues of organization. At other times, organization requires a particular form (e.g., a business letter, an editorial, a cinquain) to communicate the ideas effectively.

Jeff and David's letter (see Figure 5.5) demonstrates organization on two levels. First, the boys needed a clear, logical organizational structure to make a convincing case for serving the food that is on the printed menu. Second, they needed to use the proper form for a letter so that it would be delivered and properly attended to by the people at Food Services. They were successful, with teacher support, at both.

Catherine, a beginning writer, has found a personally interesting and compelling topic for her writing—cats. Writing in complete sentences, she

---

Figure 5.5 *continued*

October 22, 1993

Woodridge School
12619 S.E. 20th Place
Bellevue, WA 98005

Dear Jeff and David:

Thank you for your letter of October 1, 1993, explaining your two
concerns regarding school lunch.

We do always try to serve what we have listed on the menu. When
the food listed is not the food served, it is almost always due to
the unavailability of the food to use from our supplier. In the
case of Cheese pizza, we had ordered it, however, it did not
arrive from the food purveyor. We, therefore, served our regular
pizza.

Your point is well taken regarding the box lunches. Both in
September and October I failed to list what was in the boxed
lunch on the menu. I will always list the foods from now on.

Thank you again for writing. It is always good to hear from our
customers!

Sincerely,

Anita Finch, M.S., R.D.
Nutrition Specialist

Bellevue Public Schools
District #405
P.O. Box 90010
Bellevue, WA. 98009-9010
12111 NE First /Bellevue, WA.

Jeff and David's edited letter exhibits their ability to use voice and
organization to make their case. They were rewarded with a response.

Figure 5.6

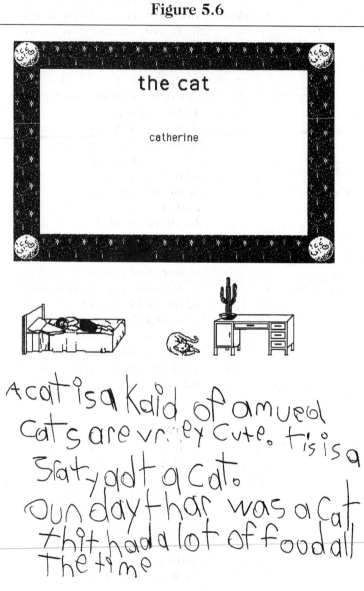

A cat is a kind of animal
Cats are very cute. This is a
story about a cat.
One day there was a cat
that had a lot of food
all the time.

Catherine enjoys writing about cats. She is beginning to try her hand at creating an organized story.

begins her stories easily but allows them to trail off at the end (see Figure 5.6). In "The Cat," she blends two ideas, fact and fiction, and seems a bit confused about whether she wants to write an informational piece about cats or tell a story with a problem and resolution. She knows the common "One day" beginning of many primary stories, but she hasn't yet developed her story structure. Blending the two genres is possible, but Catherine is not yet clear about her purpose; therefore her organization is confused, and she has not developed a satisfying closure to the piece.

Sara, a more advanced second-grade writer, has a clear beginning, a middle with climax, and an ending that ties up all the parts of her story, "Getting Even" (see Figure 5.7). She starts with a compelling story lead: "It was a regular first day of school and then Monica saw Jake and Jake saw Monica. They screamed. They were in the same class. When they were in first grade, they had hated each other." After giving her readers some background, Sara goes on to describe all the awful things Monica and Jake do to each other, leading up to the climax, where circumstances force them to spend the weekend together at Monica's house. Sara is able, at this point in her writing development, to write a story that has an interesting and well-developed plot. She takes her reader through several events that create a sense of heightened tension, creating the problem not by character choice (which would be inconsistent with the character development so far) but by an unexpected twist of fate. Finally, she carries the irony over to the conclusion, where the other characters in the piece (classmates and teacher) are shocked to learn of the twist. Sara demonstrates a strong sense of story structure and leads her readers through her creation in a compelling and logical way.

Word choice. This criterion refers to students' ability to communicate their intended message using precise, interesting words. Often this includes using lively verbs, strong imagery, and words that add interest and expression in a fresh, appealing way (Spandel & Stiggins, 1990). In addition, it involves avoiding clichés, slang, and wordiness (except when intentional and appropriate). But as Spandel and Stiggins (1990) remind us, word choice isn't "something that the writer reaches for out of need like an umbrella on a hook. The message comes first. Often the power in a successful piece comes less from esoteric or unusual words than from the writer's skill in using everyday words well" (p. 40).

At a beginning level, students are concerned with just getting words on paper to tell their stories. Very soon, however, they become interested in finding just "the right word" for a particular point, and they begin to experiment with new words for "tired words" (e.g., *exclaimed* or *shouted* for *said*; *colorful* or *shiny* for *pretty*). Older writers thoughtfully choose words and phrases to create particular feelings or tone in their writing. They vary their word choices to meet their purposes. In this way, word choice is often related to voice.

Figure 5.7

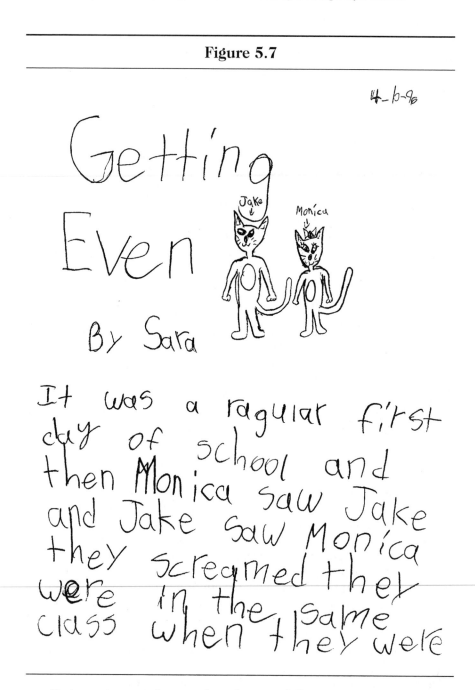

4-6-96

Getting Even

By Sara

It was a ragular first day of school and then Monica saw Jake and Jake saw Monica they screamed they were in the same class when they were

---

Katie, an intermediate student, has carefully selected words to create her characters and to set up the problem in her story, "The Groom's Dreadful Task" (see Figure 5.8). From just this beginning section of her five-page story, Katie's words leave little doubt that Peanut and Jimmy share a liking for one another ("Peanut was Jim's favorite horse, and Jimmy was Peanut's

Figure 5.7 *continued*

In first grade they hated eachother
Monica went to kick him but then the bell rang and Jake stuck his tung out at

her. Later in the after noon they had cemestry Partners and Jake and Monica were Partners Monica mixed them up wrong and Jake

favorite groom; Peanut nuzzled"), nor is there any doubt that King Richard is angry ("was in a rage," "'I must know what they are up to!!' yelled King Richard"). Katie's word choice also makes it clear that King Richard doesn't appreciate Jimmy ("worthless old groom") and that Saint Edward likes

Figure 5.7 *continued*

took a closer look
and kablue; it blew up
In Jakes face. Then at
recess Jake pushed Monica
down the slides and Monica
had togo to the nurses
office.

Then they got the worst
news Jakes parents were
busy so Jake was staying at
Monicas house for the
whole weekend That weekend
Jake arrived with his stuff
The guest Room was being
remodeld so Jak had

Jimmy and dislikes the job of giving him bad news. Katie's word choice
adds flavor and excitement to her piece, and as a result, the reader begins
to form a sense of the personalities of the three main characters in just a
few short paragraphs.

Figure 5.7 *continued*

---

to sleep in Monicas room! At
night, he layed out his sleeping
bag. They both thought it couldn't
be that bad. In the morning they
had breakfast then they went outs!
de to play they started a really
fun game and they were playing
together, over the weekend
they almost became

best friends. They stayed up almos
all night on saturday talking
about how much fun they had
over the weekend and how
wierd some of their classmate
were. On monday they walked in
talking there whole class was
pussled even their teacher.

Sentence fluency. Sentence fluency refers to sentence flow, rhythm, and variety. At early stages of writing, students are just beginning to understand the form of a sentence—that it has a subject and a predicate, that it contains a complete thought. They learn the difference between complete sentences, sentence fragments, and run-ons. But again, issues of form should

Figure 5.7 *continued*

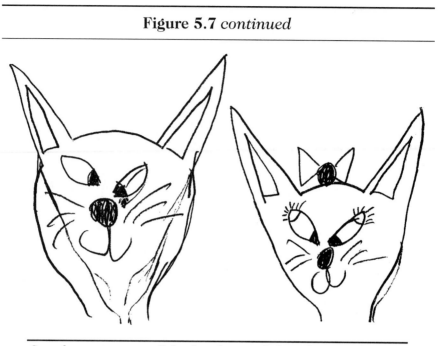

Sara demonstrates a well-developed sense of plot in her extended story about Jake and Monica.

always be secondary to issues of content and clarity of communication. Having students learn how to write complete sentences that are devoid of content and interesting ideas is not an admirable aim. Students should be able to use sentences effectively to get their ideas across. As they develop comfort with writing sentences, students begin to experiment with using a variety of sentence structures to communicate effectively.

Andrew, a beginning writer, is just feeling comfortable with writing journal entries (see Figure 5.9). Although he does not yet use sentences in his writing, Andrew is beginning to use writing to communicate ideas. I used evidence in his portfolio to help Andrew learn how to use sentences to make his ideas clearer and more important. In fact, even Andrew noticed his tendency to use *and* to connect his thoughts. He reflected on this to me: "I do have that problem. . . . I always use too many *and*s!" His later work shows an effort to reduce his use of *and* and to separate his ideas into more powerful sentences.

Katie's "Groom" story (see Figure 5.8) provides a good example of sentence flow and structure as well as evidence of how a variety of sentences can enrich the writing. Katie uses dialogue and compound, complex, and simple sentences to create interest and tension in her story.

Conventions. Conventions are the mechanical aspects of writing that make it easy for other audiences to read and understand an author's work. They

Figure 5.8

THE GROOM'S DREADFUL TASK
by Katie

1212 in Iralee, Ireland. January, 1st, the new year, King Richard's Castle...

"Naaaaayyyhh !" That was peanut coming up behind Jimmy. Peanut was Jimmy's favorite horse, and Jimmy was Peanut's favorite groom. Jimmy turned to greet Peanut. Peanut nuzzled as he was being groomed.
****

" I knew it !!" King Richard was in a rage. "I knew they would spy ". king Richards worst enemy's spy had just escaped. The spy had been in the royal weapon room, and had seem their latest weapon. Now it would not be a surprise weapon. "I must know what they are up to !!" yelled King Richard. He sent for Saint Edward to get a group of soldiors together to spy, as well as a worthless old groom named Jimmy.
****

"Jimmy ?" It was Saint Edward who came to get Jimmy and tell him the bad news. Saint Edward was one of Jimmmy's good friends and didn't want him to get killed by spying.

"I have some bad news Jimmy," continued Saint Edward, " You have to spy on Lord Jefferson for the King". Jimmy fainted from fear, because no spy ever returned alive from Lord Jefferson's castle.
******

Katie creates a compelling vision of the characters and the problem in the opening section of her story, "The Groom's Dreadful Task."

include grammar, capitalization, punctuation, usage, spelling, paragraphing, and legibility. These are the areas of writing that are easiest to see and teach and the areas that, in the past, consumed most of teachers' efforts. However, in most classrooms today, teachers emphasize that conventions are tools writers need to communicate with their readers. As such, conventions are best taught and learned in the context of children's writing and reading, where meaning is always the focus (Anderson, Hiebert, Scott, & Wilkinson, 1985; Graves, 1994).

On a continuum, usage begins with the correct use of pronouns and moves toward staying in the same person, using words like *there/their* correctly, and having subject-verb agreement. Spelling development proceeds through several stages as children become more conventional spellers. For example, Elizabeth is at the early stages of invented spelling, whereas Erik is at the transitional stage (see Figures 5.1a and 5.1b), and Katie is at the correct spelling stage (see Figure 5.8) (Gentry, 1982). Capitalization and punctuation begin with interest in sentence beginnings and endings; later, students learn to use more sophisticated aspects such as quotation marks, commas, colons, and possessives. And handwriting includes learning letter

---

Figure 5.9

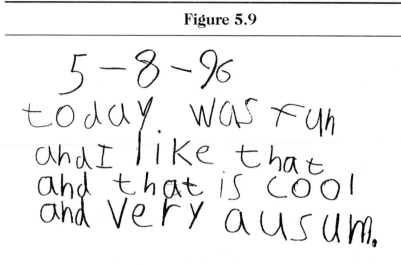

5 – 8 – 96
today. was fun
and I like that
and that is cool
and very ausum.

andrew m

---

*Andrew strings together ideas about a class trip. Although he knows
that sentences end with periods, he does not yet use sentences to
communicate his ideas. Transcription: "Today was fun and I like that
and that is cool and very awesome."*

---

forms and moves through organizing space on a paper (including formatting on a computer) toward clearly and legibly produced work. Graves (1994)
reminds us that handwriting should not be neglected because when children can control the mechanics of writing, they can concentrate on the information or story they are writing.

The six traits of good writing—central ideas/purpose, voice, organization,
word choice, sentence fluency, and conventions—described in this section
provide a useful framework for assessing writing in students' portfolios and
for thinking about our teaching. Having this common foundation and vocabulary for examining writing has moved us away from vague visions of
good writing to more specific understanding of what we want our students
to know and be able to do.

Writing Process

Assessing the products of writing is only one aspect of a total writing curriculum; students must also have experiences with the writing process.
Recognizing that documentation of the writing process in portfolios is cru-

cial, and sometimes difficult, we decided to include a Common Tool (see Chapter 2) for writing process: evidence of a piece (any genre) taken from first draft to final form. From this, we hoped to see the progression of the writer and the writing.

The writing process has been discussed by many researchers (e.g., Britton, 1970; Graves, 1994; Flower & Hayes, 1980), and many different labels have been given to the various recursive stages. We focused on planning, drafting, revision, and editing. Regardless of the labels, it is important to remember that these stages look different at various developmental levels and in various contexts. For example, planning a narrative might take the form of listening to a story, talking with a friend, or drawing rather than constructing elaborate webs or outlines that most teachers have seen in writing textbooks. Although planning, perhaps very good planning, may occur in these oral collaborations, concrete evidence may be difficult to find in the portfolio. In other contexts, such as writing a report, students might leave a better trail of their planning through their notes. Planning must fit the student and the task. Similarly, in the area of revision, many young writers manifest an understanding of revision in subtle ways. They may use their revision insights in future pieces rather than choose to make changes in an existing piece. In other words, they may not actually revise a first draft but may recognize changes they would make and simply apply these to future pieces. Looking across pieces, teachers might get a sense of this type of revision. Of course, as writers gain experience and skill, revisions such as making additions, insertions and deletions, reordering, focusing ideas, and making stylistic modifications become more common and more visible. And in the area of editing, students will reflect what they have learned; they cannot be expected to edit for skills they haven't learned, nor can they be expected to focus on all aspects of editing at the same time.

In addition to developmental and contextual variability inherent in the writing process, Graves (1994) points out that much of what most elementary students write is "simply flow," first-draft work. As a result, much of what is placed into portfolios will not provide documentation of the writing process, and it shouldn't. In our zeal to collect evidence of the writing process, we must not lose sight of the fact that the process must fit the purpose. Process for process sake is not the point.

The variability in students' use of the writing process becomes inescapably obvious when we review writing artifacts in portfolios. Maria, a beginning writer, used her drawings to help plan her story about seeing a fawn during the summer. Her picture had more detail than her writing. However, her hand was sure, and the words came easily after she drew as she wrote about how her mom let her take off her seat belt to better see the deer. The next day she wrote another piece about the fawn, this time without using pictures to plan. Her writing the previous day and her sharing with peers had served as her planning for the next piece. In contrast, Katie's planning was an integral part of her teacher's instruction on story writing (see Figure 5.10a, b, and c). As a result, Katie's portfolio contains

Figure 5.10a

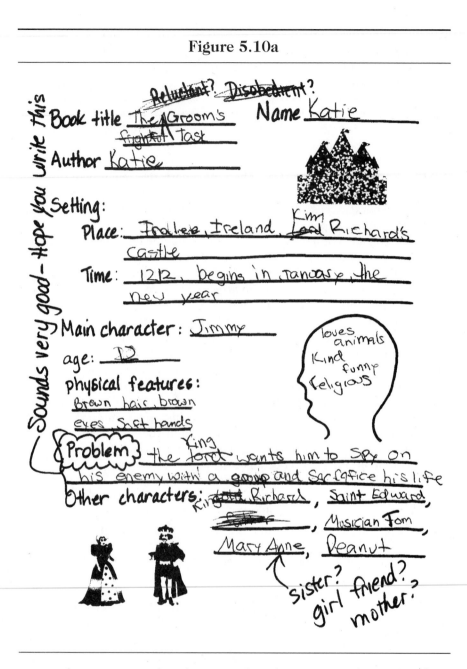

written documentation that she engaged in planning. It is also evident from reading Katie's rough drafts and final version of this story that she has used the plan flexibly, changing her ideas in later drafts and filling out the story with interesting character relationships and plot tension. Both Katie and Maria exhibit evidence of planning; one is just more easily seen in portfolio work than the other.

Figure 5.10b

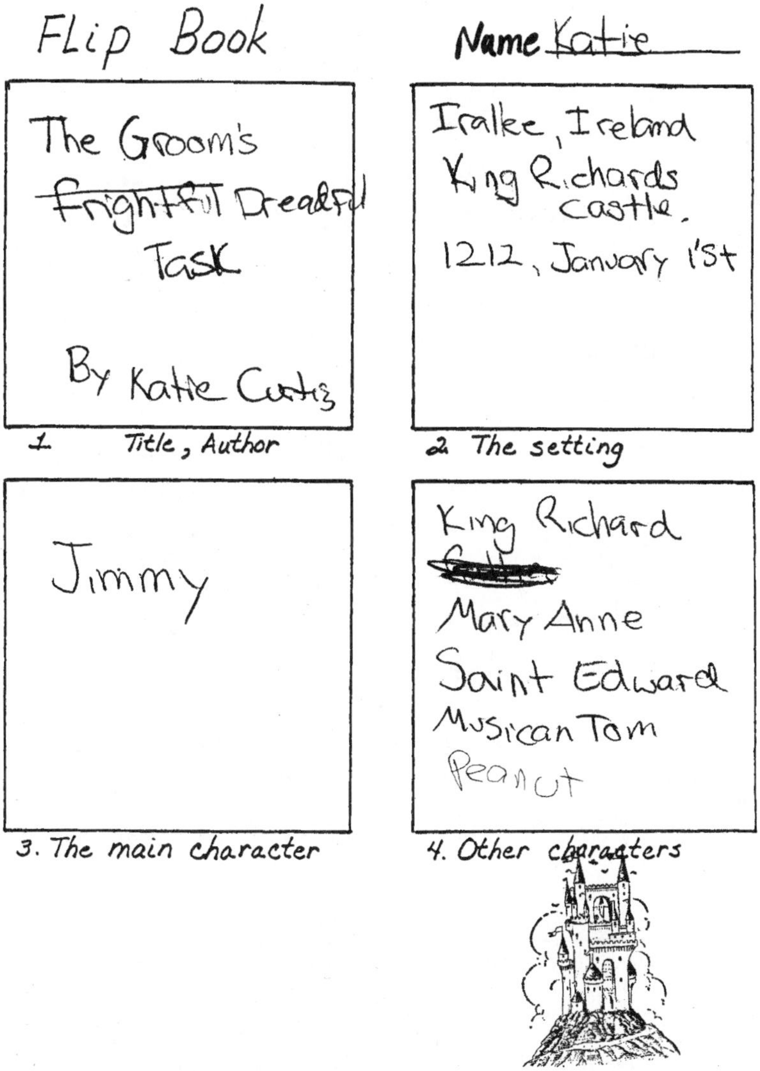

FLip Book   Name Katie

The Groom's ~~Frightful~~ Dreadful Task By Katie Curtis	Iralke, Ireland King Richards Castle. 1212, January 1st
1 *Title, Author*	2 *The setting*
Jimmy	King Richard ~~Castle~~ Mary Anne Saint Edward Musican Tom Peanut
3. *The main character*	4. *Other characters*

Catherine, a second-grade student, demonstrated her abilities to revise and edit as she went through three handwritten drafts over a period of two weeks while writing a narrative about her cat. In between each draft, she asked for help with spelling and for ways to make her story more compelling to her readers. Her drafts show that she took out some of the more mundane details, such as buying the cat, and added more about a time when the cat

Figure 5.10c

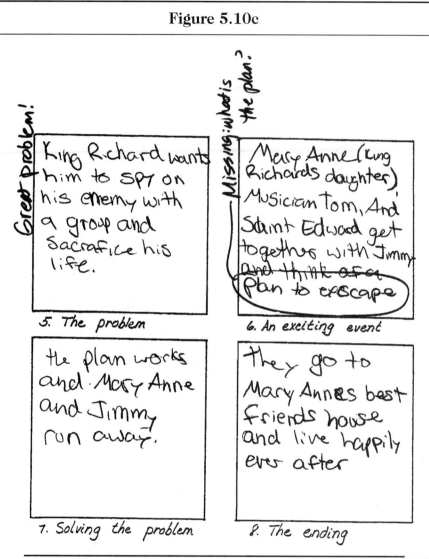

Great problem!

Missing: what is the plan?

King Richard wants him to spy on his enemy with a group and sacrafice his life.

5. The problem

Mary Anne (King Richards daughter) Musician Tom, And Saint Edward get together with Jimmy and think of a plan to escape

6. An exciting event

the plan works and Mary Anne and Jimmy run away.

7. Solving the problem

They go to Mary Annes best friends house and live happily ever after

8. The ending

Katie's plans for her "Groom" story outline provided a good starting place for her. Katie was able to develop these ideas more fully in her rough draft.

disappeared for several days. Lauren, adept with word processing, wrote two pages of "The Bear's Cry" and then asked for help with the dialogue and spelling. She continued this process for her lengthy story: writing, revising, and writing more.

In our portfolios, evidence of the writing process might be easily seen through artifacts such as rough drafts, pictures, planning webs, and student editing guides, but at other times evidence would need to be documented by teacher entry slips, anecdotal notes, or observation checklists. The teacher entry slip attached to Jeff and David's school lunch letter provides valuable information about the planning, revising, and editing the boys did in creating this letter, and it provides important information about the support they received from their teachers (see Figure 5.11). This teacher entry slip documents that Jeff and David were using the writing process in ways that enhanced their writing. Process is sometimes difficult to see in student work, yet it is important to document as part of the portfolio process.

Ownership of Writing

It is important to help children become competent writers, to be sure. It is also important to help children develop ownership and a sense of power about writing (Au, et al., 1990; Graves, 1994). *Ownership* refers to the characteristics of a lifelong writer:

- enjoys writing
- chooses to write voluntarily and frequently
- feels a sense of pride and confidence in writing
- appreciates writing as a valuable activity

What kinds of thoughts or feelings would reflect ownership of writing? What kinds of comments might reveal that students possess these important characteristics? The comments that follow, gathered from interviews, journal entries, portfolio visits, and entry slips, provide good examples of ownership at work.

Erik (grade two): "I have lots of ideas. I can't keep them all in! I have a good vocabulary for big words. I'm writing more now. My [amount of] writing is almost equal to my pictures."

Heather (grade one): "I am the best kind of writer! I can spell the words in the stories I make and I can help people spell. I think all my stories are good."

Kasshe (grade four): "I have a great mind and I can be creative in many ways when I write!"

Andrew's parents (grade-one student): "We are experiencing an explosion in Andrew's reading and writing skills and confidence."

Molly's teacher (grade-one student): "Molly's writing skills have steadily progressed throughout the year. She is working on spelling high utility words, using punctuation, and creating a story with a beginning, middle, and end. Molly says, 'I like to write because it gives you the feeling that you are making up stories about your life and you can have them when you grow up.'"

Katie (grade five):"When I showed my portfolio to my parents, they . . . thought it was kind of weird because I always write a lot of non-fiction stories and kids usually write fiction stories. But, I like to write non-fiction because I can just think of something that happened to me or somebody else and then I can just write about it. It's easier than just thinking up things."

Figure 5.11

TEACHER ENTRY SLIP

22102-10

Date _10-4-93_

I selected this piece of work to place in _____

portfolio because _it demonstrates the editing_
process; writing for a meaningful purpose;
and use of current understanding of business letter
Jeff practiced his name in cursive in the
signature block.

Additional comments:

    This is a personal and passionate situation
for Jeff, and I also await a response to their
letter.

> will add copy of   _Response received on 10-25 —_
response when it   _added to pace. MB_
arrives.   _Barbara J. Baker_
                                        Signature

Who helped with this work? Briefly tell how each one helped.

    Jeff did most of the word processing.
David did some.
    Both students proofread and edited, and
both Mrs. English + Mrs. Baker proofed and
helped them learn form and punctuation
of acceptable business letters.
    They shared the task of addressing the
envelope for the school mail system.

---

*In teacher entry slip for Jeff and David's school lunch letter. Their teach-
ers note the prior experience and instruction the boys have had on
related learnings, and they note the type of support the boys had
on this project.*

The preceding written documentation from students, parents, and teachers provides evidence that these children are developing ownership of writing. Ownership can also be observed—in the faces of children immersed in classroom writing, in children's willingness to share their work with others (in the "Author's Chair" or more privately), and in the ways students integrate writing into various aspects of their daily lives. Like the writing process, these incidental observations are sometimes difficult to document in a portfolio. Most often, my colleagues and I rely on students' responses to portfolio visit questions, entry slips from individual pieces, or teacher anecdotal notes. Rarely do any of us use observation checklists—they could be useful, we just don't tend to use them. On the other hand, some teachers create special activities that they hope will provide insight about student ownership. For example, some teachers have their students use writing logs to list the topics they have written about and to reflect on themselves as writers. From these logs and from a review of the amount of writing in the portfolio, teachers can get a sense of how much students are participating in and enjoying writing. There are many other types of teacher-created activities that can provide opportunities to learn about and document student writing ownership. Interestingly, after this outcome became a focal point for us, we began to see many more opportunities to observe and document ownership in the natural course of classroom activities than we thought were there.

Self-Reflection and Self-Evaluation

In the area of self-assessment, writers should be able to identify their overall strengths and weaknesses, as well as the strengths and weaknesses of an individual piece. They should be able to relate to ideas, themes, and personal experiences as well as to the surface-level conventions such as spelling and handwriting. In addition, writers must set realistic and important goals so they are engaged in their own learning. This is not easy for most students. As we discuss in chapter 6, becoming thoughtful about one's own work and setting appropriate, meaningful goals require knowledge, practice, and guidance. They are essential to becoming a self-directed writer (Graves & Sunstein, 1992; Howard, 1990; Rief, 1990).

Generally, we try to encourage students to engage in reflective discussions rather than always have them complete entry slips or portfolio visits; we want to privilege thinking and reflecting over recording. Because writing is so concrete, so visual, students tend to focus on length, spelling, and handwriting. They need to go further—to think about other aspects of their work as well. For example, sometimes children can respond in an affective or personal way, at other times they can take a more critical stance about the quality of their work (e.g., self-evaluation), and at still other times, they can think about their own writing process. All of these forms of reflection are important.

Self-reflection and self-evaluation enable writers to become self-directed and to develop plans for accomplishing their goals. At the same time, from students' self-assessments teachers can gain insights into the full range of their thinking about process, product, and affective response to writing.

For example, Jennie, a middle school student, wrote that, "As a writer I have improved my vocabulary and my sense of revising and editing." When asked about her goals, she commented, "I want to continue improving my editing skills by taking more time when I revise!" This student has a clear, worthwhile goal and one strategy—"taking more time"—for accomplishing it. Her teacher will want to monitor Jennie's progress to determine if she needs additional instruction on specific elements of editing or revising. Stephanie an intermediate student, spontaneously reflects on both her process and the quality of her work, "I think that I am a okay writer because I don't write a lot and I usually have to think a long time before I really write. I also never usually plan before I begin to write. What I do is I stay on one topic and have good endings." In contrast, Buddy focuses solely on the product: "I am a better story maker [this year than last] because I try to make stories creative and make them that other people could understand." And Christopher, a second grader, reports, "I want to be able to write longer stories and spell better and make my stories more interesting." Finally, Emily and Lauren, primary students, demonstrate personal responses to their writing. Emily, who has written several poems and stories about her young cousin's death, sees writing as a way "for me to remember my cousin." And Lauren, who is dealing with issues of friendship, says her stories about lost children and animals help her think about her feelings.

Each of these students provides a window into his or her thinking about writing. With this information, teachers can provide instruction and support to meet their needs.

Understanding and Interpreting Writing in Portfolios

We can gain much information about a student's writing abilities and skills by looking at single pieces of work, whether a teacher-directed, "on-demand" writing task or a student-generated piece. Even more information is available from a collection of writing gathered in a portfolio. Taken together, multiple samples of writing can provide a rich history of the writer—her abilities, interests, and insights—to document progress and to inform instructional plans. In this section, I discuss how writing evidence in portfolios can inform several different audiences. They can help:

- students learn about themselves
- parents learn about their children
- teachers learn about their practice
- teachers learn about students

Students Learn About Themselves

Because writing is so visible, looking through portfolio writing can provide students with a springboard for thinking about their writing. But, as we discuss in chapters 2 and 6, just looking will not automatically result in student self-understanding. Students must have meaningful reasons for review-ing their writing and guidance from the teacher. For many students, it is difficult to achieve the distance or separation from a single piece of writing that is needed for them to see their strengths and weaknesses. It is easier for all of us to examine work anew, from a different perspective, when we look retrospectively at our writing collected over time or let a piece "get cold." After this wait time, some students begin to see trends in their work, such as topics or voice: "I write mostly about animals, don't I?" or "My sto-ries are more exciting now!" Others focus more on mechanics and realize that their spelling or handwriting has changed over the year: "I can spell longer words now," and "I couldn't read some of my writing earlier in the year, but it's easy to read my new story." These insights contribute to stu-dents' sense of ownership and often lead to student-generated writing goals.

Portfolios can also help students problem solve about their writing. As I conferenced with Elisabeth and Sara, two second graders, about their story, they shared their general sense of frustration with it. It just wasn't working. We pulled samples of writing from their portfolios and discussed their writ-ing over the last few months. They had coauthored several stories, all fic-tional pieces, about friends who have some sort of adventure. As we looked closely at each successive story, discussing what was satisfying and unsatis-fying about each, patterns began to emerge. The girls recognized the source of their frustration; they wanted to be able to write stories like those they both liked to read. Those stories in books were exciting, but their stories seemed flat. As I asked them specific questions about the plot of their most recent story, and as we discussed some new ideas, their faces brightened, and they quickly began to add to their story. They realized that they hadn't said enough in their stories, that they had left out things they had discussed while sitting at the computer together. They found that they needed to more fully develop their ideas to satisfy their readers and themselves. By looking over the larger body of their work, the girls and I were able to identify the problem and to begin to work on its solution. Without that perspective over multiple pieces, the problem would have been more difficult to identify and the solution much further in the future.

In a similar way, students learn about themselves through the process of choosing work from their collections for entry into their portfolios. In asking students to choose their best work, or a piece they don't like, or a piece that demonstrates a specific skill, we help them explicitly define stan-dards, develop personal styles, and become their own "critical friends." The goal is to help students internalize the process of looking thoughtfully at their work so they no longer depend on the teacher to tell them how it's going. We have been mesmerized by videotapes of students in our colleagues' classrooms as they spend *hours* reviewing their collections, deciding which pieces they want to include in their portfolios. Whether the selection is guided by the teacher ("Today I want you to choose a piece that . . .") or is purely student-selected, the process of looking carefully at work helps students learn about themselves. The conversations we have observed re-veal that they are learning about themselves as writers.

Parents Learn About Their Children

Chapter 9 presents an in-depth analysis of helping parents use portfolio work to learn about their children, and chapter 7 presents information about student growth over time. What is most important to keep in mind is that parents are unlikely to have the same knowledge, experience, or expectations that teachers have when they look at students' writing. Often parents notice changes in spelling, handwriting, or length. These are obvious. But, we can also help parents focus on other goals we have for their children, such as experimenting with different genres, writing with organization and voice, and developing confidence and ownership in writing. We can also help parents to distinguish between pieces that are rough drafts, those that have been edited with adult help, and those that are self- or peer-edited. Sometimes parents are confused by the range of ability they see in the various portfolio pieces: "Well, he was a much better speller in October than now in February," or "Her early stories had nice endings. Now her stories are longer, but they don't seem to go anywhere." Teachers must help parents understand the different levels and types of support they provide as students try out new writing ideas and skills.

The real advantage of using the entire portfolio with parents is that they can see the patterns in their children's work (topics, skills, interests, voice) as well as the strengths and weaknesses of their writing. In looking through a portfolio, as opposed to focusing on one or two pieces of writing, parents can appreciate their children's writing development and, at the same time, gain a perspective on the work ahead. After a portfolio conference, one parent wrote, "I like . . . all the portfolio selections. Kendal's greatest confidence has always been in her drawing/artistic skills. I think I see now that she has more confidence in her written products and only uses the pictures for decoration. . . . Kendal's creativity and imagination in story-telling continue to amaze me."

Teachers Learn About Their Practice

Early in our portfolio work, we realized that not only were we collecting our students' work in portfolios, but also we were making our teaching practices visible. Because much of the work in portfolios is student writing (it is easier to document than reading; see Valencia & Au, 1997), our writing programs were the most open to review. Initially, this was an uncomfortable experience for most of us. We were forced to examine and expose our own writing instruction in much the same way that portfolios force students to examine and expose their own writing. As our confidence and interest grew, we found there was much to learn about our writing curricula, instructional strategies, and assessment practices.

Curriculum. I found that my students' portfolios could help me identify "holes" in my writing curriculum, both in terms of my class as a whole and in terms of individual students. For example, as I conducted a series of port-folio visits with students in the spring, I realized that only a few students were writing realistic fiction. We had been studying fairy tales and using fantasy stories as our read-alouds. As would be expected, these genres were finding their way into students' writing almost to the exclusion of other genres. I realized that I needed to vary my choice of literature or create specific opportunities for students to experience and experiment with other genres. The next read-aloud I chose was realistic fiction. After several days and many discussions about the book, several students began to write stories based in everyday reality. I used the opportunity to introduce other types of realistic fiction (e.g., historical fiction, mystery, humor), and, at the same time, I began to monitor my curricular decisions to be sure that my students were having meaningful opportunities to write in various genres.

During another series of portfolio reviews, I discovered that during writer's workshop one group of boys in my class was working exclusively in a cartoon format and exclusively with a single topic—aliens invading the Earth. After I brainstormed other genres and topics with them, some of the boys began a narrative story about "Bean Boy," inspired by our math work with beans! The format changed to story form, with illustrations added from time to time. Others in the group found it more difficult to move from the comfort of cartooning and needed more time and encouragement to vary their work. In these cases, I provided more individualized prompting and guidance to write and read using other forms. I tried to find the "hooks" to help these students expand their writing repertoires. The importance for me was clearly seeing that I needed to change and monitor my curriculum and students' self-selected topics for writing. The portfolio evidence provided the impetus for these changes.

Instruction. Teachers can also learn about the effectiveness of their writing instruction by looking at student portfolio work. One example that is easy to observe is in the area of conventions. For example, I thought I had successfully taught the use of apostrophes in several minilessons earlier in the year. I had noticed that many children were trying to use apostrophes in their writing early in the year, so I taught these lessons then, when students needed them. However, as I looked through portfolios prior to completing my spring reports, I realized that most of my students were continuing to add an apostrophe each time they added an *s* to a word—they hadn't made the distinction between possessives and plurals. Clearly, I had more work to do. Similarly, several intermediate and middle school teachers have discovered that although they have spent weeks working with their students on specific writing projects (e.g., biographies, reports, arguments), students often don't transfer these "project-oriented" abilities to other pieces of their writing. The teachers planned to provide more opportunities and more explicit instruction to help students transfer their skills.

Looking over a body of work reveals additional instructional follow-up that students may need. At the same time, it can also reveal successful student learning—writing assignments that produced interesting and complex work, goals that have been accomplished and demonstrated in several pieces, students' enjoyment in writing, and important changes and growth that have taken place over time.

Assessment. Teachers can also learn about their own criteria for good writing by looking through portfolios of students' writing. The comments we make and our suggestions for revisions reveal our priorities and the skills and strategies for which we hold students accountable. Noticing, for example, that most of our feedback is about spelling and grammar reveals a priority on conventions. Or noticing that, unconsciously, we challenge one student with our comments, whereas we ease off on another, causes us to rethink our expectations and standards for our class and for individual students. Reviewing portfolios provides an opportunity to review the intended and unintended messages we send to students through our assessment comments. It is a good check on our priorities.

Through portfolios, teachers can also identify assessment evidence that is missing. For example, recently I realized that, although my students write letters often (to thank parents for help or to express our appreciation to a special guest speaker), none of my students had letters in their portfolios. Because the letters were sent to the intended recipients, the students had no evidence of their letter-writing abilities in their portfolios. The skills of letter writing, both the mechanics and the ability to express thoughts clearly to an outside audience, were an important part of my curriculum, yet there was no documentation of these abilities. I have resolved that next year I will keep rough drafts of the letters and/or make copies of the final letters for the portfolios. Systematic review of the evidence helps teachers determine whether they are collecting the evidence that students, teachers, and parents need to assess important aspects of writing.

Teachers Learn About Their Students

The examples of students' writing in this chapter demonstrate how much teachers can learn about their students if they are clear and focused on important writing outcomes and if they look closely at student work. At the same time, this clear vision helps teachers become better observers of students in the classroom as they engage in writing. Looking across an entire portfolio of writing adds a complexity and richness to teachers' understanding that can't be found with individual pieces. Although individual pieces provide glimmers of what might be (both successful and unsuccessful), trends over time provide more reliable indicators of students' strengths, needs, interests, and dispositions. Sometimes the task of looking across multiple pieces seems overwhelming, leaving the teacher to conclude, "He's a great writer" or "She's improving"—general statements that are not particularly helpful for improving teaching and learning. It's important to bring the specificity and clarity of focus that we apply to single pieces to the larger body of portfolio work.

Figure 5.12

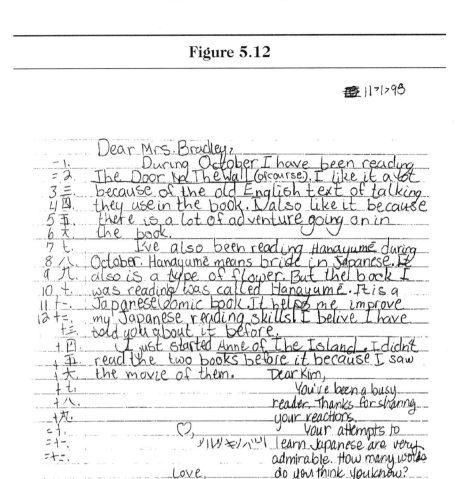

Kim's reading letter written in November demonstrates her writing ability, reading interests, and fascination with foreign language.

Figures 5.12 through 5.15 are selected writing samples from Kim's port-folio. Space doesn't permit us to include all the writing in this fourth grader's portfolio; however, through these excerpted samples and the teacher's comments, you can get a sense of how teachers can use portfolio evidence to understand trends in their students' learning. Kim's teacher, Sue, wrote the following after reviewing all the written work in Kim's port-folio. Sue had the added advantage of being Kim's third-grade teacher and having saved a few samples of Kim's work. Notice how Sue's references to

Figure 5.13

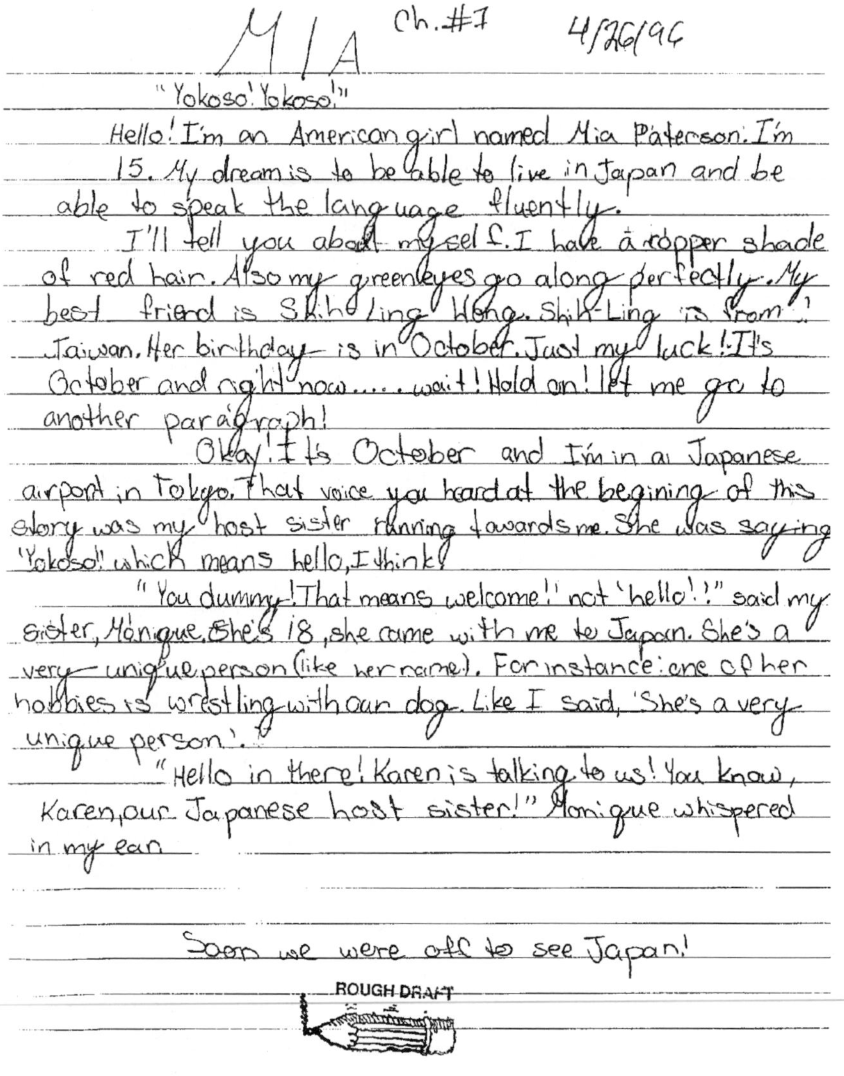

MIA   Ch.#1   4/26/96

"Yokoso! Yokoso!"

   Hello! I'm an American girl named Mia Paterson. I'm 15. My dream is to be able to live in Japan and be able to speak the language fluently.

   I'll tell you about myself. I have a copper shade of red hair. Also my green eyes go along perfectly. My best friend is Shih-Ling Hong. Shih-Ling is from Taiwan. Her birthday is in October. Just my luck! It's October and right now..... wait! Hold on! let me go to another paragraph!

   Okay! It's October and I'm in a Japanese airport in Tokyo. That voice you heard at the begining of this story was my host sister running towards me. She was saying "Yokoso!" which means hello, I think!

   "You dummy! That means welcome!" not 'hello!'!" said my sister, Monique. She's 18, she came with me to Japan. She's a very unique person (like her name). For instance: one of her hobbies is wrestling with our dog. Like I said, 'She's a very unique person'.

   "Hello in there! Karen is talking to us! You know, Karen, our Japanese host sister!" Monique whispered in my ear.

              Soon we were off to see Japan!
              ─── ROUGH DRAFT

A section of "Mia," a multichapter narrative story, written by Kim in April.

---

specific examples will help others understand and verify the points she wants to make.

Kim is committed to writing. She takes time to write, writes often, and is always eager to share at "Author's Chair." Her self-reports from her portfolio visits consistently indicate that she likes writing "very much" and has a strong sense of

---

Figure 5.14

ROUGH DRAFT   *4/5/96*   *Kim*

Trouble at Boggle School #3
The Mystery of the Pumkin Patch

Hi I'm Mrs. Googlebog. Here's the story of the day I went to the Pumkin Patch.

"Kid's! Hurry! We must get on the bus or we'll be late!"

Soon the weather turned bad and rainy and suddenly there was a loud CLAP! of thunder in the sky! All the children screamed in horror.

The bus jerked around the corner, stopped and shut off. The bus-driver turned around and showed his one-toothed-grin as he said "We're here.".The children rushed out of the bus whispering, as not to upset the bus driver.

As soon as we got inside of the barn, and were grabing towels out of backpacks to dry off, there was another loud CLAP! of thunder and a STRIKE of lightning. The lights went out and everyone was still, like they were waiting for something else to happen, but nothing did.The children were very obidient. They did what I said and stayed quiet.

When everyone was huddled together to make body-heat there was a dark figure slowly moving across the hard, wood floor. I counted quickly to make sure everyone was here. Everyone was, so that figure couldn't have been someone from the school.

I felt scared. Like I wouldn't ever see Andrew again.

Suddenly the lights came back on, and everyone was so relived(especially me!). I noticed that the figure wasn't there anymore. I wondered if anyone else saw it.

The End

Stay tuned for the next edition of "Trouble at Boggle School".

Draft of the first installment of a mystery story written by Kim in April.

---

ownership and confidence in her abilities. She says, "I like it [writing] because you can say anything you want in your writing." As a writer, "I get peoples [sic] attention and I get them to leave their body behind and put their mind into it." Kim's fascination with languages is apparent in her writing and, I suspect, this

Figure 5.15

MY SUMMER

Sep. 5, 95
Kimberly

    This summer I went to California to visit
my family. We went to Bass Lake (my cousins, my aunt and uncle)
for my cousin Katie's birthday. She turned 10. We
stayed in my Aunt Sue's house. It is right on the
lake. She has boats and seadoos. We go swimm-
ing every day. Then I came back to Washington and
had a Japanese exchaneged student come. Her
name is ゆかりまつせ Yukari Matsuse. She was 15
but she turned 16 in America. She was here
for 2 weeks. She left on August 12 (hatchigatsu
juuni nichi). Yukari and I cried a lot on that day. We
have been writing letters though. I just sent
a letter but I havent recieved a letter from
her.
    I also got a dog this summer. It's a 5 month
old female puppy. She is German-Sheapeard and
Beagle mix. I named her Shelby.

                    love,
                    Kimberly

                キ リ バ ー リ か ち き

Kim's beginning-of-year writing sample.

has contributed to her motivation to write and her facility with English [see Figures 5.12 and 5.13].

Last year, in third grade, Kim's stories were usually a type of realistic fiction-fantasy genre, a bit like *Matilda* by R. Dahl, in which things weren't like they appear to be and people/animals changed identities quickly. She was always eager to share these fanciful stories but her audience would be at a loss—the stories didn't have a middle and an end—just one more thing would happen.

Kim's writing has improved greatly this year. With the exception of "Midge and Mudge," a story she wrote in November, her other narratives have good story structure. She sets up interesting story problems and is able to carry them through to satisfying conclusions [see Figures 5.13 and 5.14]. She engages her audience through dialogue and asides in the text ("Let me go on to another paragraph," "As you might have guessed, I'm a teenage girl [14] who hates history!"). Her confidence as a writer comes through in her voice and her willingness to speak directly to her readers. For example, at the end of her "Biography of Amrita," she asks, "Don't you agree that my classmate sounds like a great person to be around?" Kim feels confident that she has persuaded her audience!

Kim is increasingly able to use her words as devices for creating images rather than just delineating actions. In addition, she has learned to vary her sentences and paragraphs and has grown in sophistication in sentence fluency and syntax [see Figures 5.12 and 5.15, written early in the year, compared with Figures 5.13 and 5.14, written later in the year]. Interestingly, Kim's final drafts are almost carbon copies of her rough drafts. She doesn't do much revision of ideas; she sticks with insertions and corrections of one or two words. This may be a reflection of the considerable thinking/planning she does before and during her writing as well as the fact that her spelling, grammar, punctuation (even dialogue) are often correct in her rough drafts.

Kim is self-directed in her writing and somewhat reflective about her work ("I am good at vocabulary," "I think stories through"). She has not yet developed a critical eye or the ability to examine the specific elements of her writing; this is consistent with her limited revision strategies. These would be good areas for further work. She sets realistic, challenging goals for herself. She is ready to be challenged to set some new goals related to exploring other genres since most of her current self-selected topics are personal narratives. With Kim's abilities and motivation, she's likely to continue to thrive as a writer."

Sue's description of Kim's writing addresses all of the areas that we've identified as important for good writing—qualities of good writing, use of the writing process, writing ownership, self-reflection—and Sue does so with attention to specific attributes of each. Looking across work provides teachers with an important and fresh view of students' writing abilities that is sometimes lost in individual pieces and the daily rush of classroom life.

Continuing Challenges

Although writing is perhaps the easiest of the literacy strands to document, we did not always find it easy to collect, document, or interpret student work. As we continued to look at and compare different portfolios, we began to have a better idea of the kinds of pieces that gave us the best and most helpful information and the areas in which we were still having difficulty. We realized that sometimes we did not have the evidence we needed to assess student performance or growth and at other times we were not sure how to interpret what we did have. These are ongoing problems for us.

Collecting and Generating Writing for the Portfolio

One of the challenges is having the right amount and variety of pieces in the portfolio to enable you and your students to use it for assessment and goal setting. This challenge arises from two sources: The first is simply a management issue—holding on to the work so that it can be placed into the portfolio; the second is a trickier curriculum issue—generating work that would be useful to have in a portfolio.

We all have experienced the management issue, regardless of how many years we've been teaching. Some children keep every piece of paper they have put a pencil to or printed out, whereas others lose everything they write (most of us discover this right before conferences!). Others keep only stories, whereas their neighbors keep only drawings. Some children date everything conscientiously, whereas others have difficulty recognizing their own unnamed, undated pieces. These management issues become a problem when we try to use portfolios with students, with parents, or for our own assessment purposes. Chapter 3 includes several suggestions for managing portfolios in general. In the area of writing, the primary management issues is deciding how to coordinate writing folders with portfolios and collection.

Some teachers ask students to store their writing folders in their desks; others keep them in a special writing folder bin; and still others integrate them into the collection or portfolio. If writing folders are not kept with the collections or portfolios, teachers must be sure to monitor, sort, and use the writing folders in the same ways we suggest using collections (see chapter 3). That means that students must be consistently guided to place their writing into their folders. When they review their collections for portfolio selections, they must also review their writing folders (this need not be done at the same time, but students must be reminded to review writing folders for portfolio entries). In addition, students may need to clear out writing folders on a regular basis rather than accumulate work for the entire year. When writing folders or collections become too full, choosing portfolio entries becomes difficult.

Teachers can simplify some of the choosing by requiring students to choose specific types of work. For example, we found that we didn't want to risk students not choosing a report they had worked on for more than a month or the *one* example of poetry writing they had completed this quarter. Therefore, many teachers have students place certain pieces of writing immediately into their portfolios as their teacher choices. At other times, students can be required to review their writing folders to select, for example, "your favorite poem" or a piece with "the most interesting lead," making sure that particular evidence would be kept.

The second problem—generating the work you would like to have in a portfolio—is not a management or collection problem. You can't collect what is not generated. Therefore, we also found that we needed to do a better job monitoring what our students were writing and what we were teaching. Although we realized early in our portfolio experience that it is important to include writing from across the curriculum and from many different genres, our portfolios still do not include a representative sample of the genres we hope to teach.

We have not yet solved this problem. For now, our best approach is to do a better job monitoring the types of writing experiences our students are having. Many of us are trying to build in more instruction and meaningful reasons for writing in different genres. We ask students to write in science, math, or social studies (e.g., keeping learning logs, writing responses to questions, formulating hypotheses for experiments, explaining a problem solution), and we value those as important writing artifacts. Even though most of that writing is first-draft writing, we understand it as an important indicator. When subject matter writing or journals are kept in spiral notebooks or bound learning logs, one option is to photocopy a few selected pages for the portfolio. Another option is to simply remove the pages from the notebook and place them into the portfolio with an entry slip. Both ways allow us to get everyday writing across the curriculum into the portfolio.

As noted earlier, most of us have committed more time to helping students work in a variety of genres—reading and writing fairy tales, mystery stories, letters, poetry, and the like. When we do special projects or units of study (i.e., research report, letters, poetry), we try to come back to that genre at other times during the year. We try not to "do the unit" and then "forget it" but rather to find other opportunities for children to use the abilities they have developed during the unit. In that way, students can transfer their skills, and we can document growth over time in a variety of types of writing. In sum, most of us tend to use a combination of student self-selected topics and teacher-generated projects and topics as part of our writing program. This gives us the opportunity to insert particular types of writing into the curriculum and to capitalize on students' personal interest.

Documenting the "Difficult to Document"

One advantage of portfolios is that they can provide alternative ways to look at important student learnings; a second advantage is that they are particularly good for documenting writing evidence. However, some aspects of writing continue to be difficult to document, even with a portfolio. Specifically, many of us struggle with evidence documenting writing ownership, self-reflection and self-evaluation, and, to some degree, writing process.

Other than a photo of a child engrossed in writing a story or reading her work aloud, our initial portfolios had no evidence to support writing ownership—enjoying writing, choosing to write voluntarily and frequently, feeling pride and confidence in writing, and having an understanding of writing as a valuable activity. We solved the problem somewhat by including questions about ownership on our regularly scheduled portfolio visits. For example:

"How much do you like to write?"

"What kind of writer are you?"

"What do you do well as a writer?"

"How have you changed as a writer since the beginning of the year?"

Students' responses to these questions provide us with insight into some of the aspects of writing ownership. We also are able to infer some of these characteristics as we read students' work and review the amount of writing they do. For some writers, the joy and reliance on writing come through in their journals ("I want to be a writer when I grow up"), and for some, writing has become an important and useful part of their lives. Nevertheless, we are aware that it is problematic to rely only on students' self-reports or sporadic comments in journals. We realize that we need to do a better job documenting our observations of students at work and of our individual conferences. One example of a brief checklist for writing ownership is the Kamehameha Elementary Education Program (KEEP) benchmarks (Asam, Au, Blake, Carroll, Jacobson, Kunitake, & Scheu, 1993), developed to help teachers focus and record observation. The checklist includes the following:

- enjoys writing
- shares own writing with others
- shows interest in others' writing
- shows confidence and pride in own writing
- writes in class for own purposes
- writes outside of class for own purposes

Although a checklist of this type is not as rich as having the actual artifacts, it at least reminds us to look for aspects of writing that might otherwise go unnoticed or undocumented. Anecdotal notes would provide more detailed information but are also more time-consuming to keep.

Our approach to documenting self-assessment and writing process has been similar, and it, too, remains problematic. On student entry slips and portfolio visits we have included questions about self-reflection and self-evaluation (e.g., "Why did you choose this piece? What does it show? What can we tell about you as a writer?" "What are your strengths as a writer? What do you want to do better?"). And some teachers have engaged students in using a checklist to think about their writing process. Again, these types of reports provide an important source of information, but they also provide only student self-reports. We need to continue to find other ways to document our observations of students' self-assessment and engagement in all the elements of the writing process.

Interpreting Writing Evidence

A challenge that affects the interpretation of all portfolio evidence, but most especially writing, is determining "whose work is it?" (Gearhart & Herman, 1995). Writing artifacts are often created with teacher or peer support, and often they are the result of collaboration among students. This is what we would expect in a strong writing program. However, interpreting individual student performance becomes difficult if we are unsure about the type and amount of support the student received. The problem is magnified even more when people outside the classroom—for example, parents or other teachers—look at the work. They don't have the intimate knowledge of the classroom context in which the writing was produced. This became apparent as we shared portfolios in our portfolio teacher group. We found that colleagues were frequently confused by what appeared to be inconsistencies in students' writing and were uncertain about how to evaluate student performance. Only after discussion with a particular student's teacher did we realize the full effect of having a portfolio filled with work supported by adults or peers, as well as work created independently. Obviously, what students can do with teacher assistance or with writing partners may be very different than what they can do alone. Both are important to know, and it is important to know the difference.

Although we haven't solved this problem, we have tried to address it in three ways. The first is to have questions on entry slips that ask, "Who helped you with this piece?" and "How did they help you?" Our motivation is twofold: (a) to document the kind of help students are getting with their writing and (b) to communicate clearly that we believe writing can be a collaborative process—that it is not cheating to have help. The second way that we have tried is to include more information on our teacher entry slips regarding the support students have received. The teacher entry slip attached to Jeff and David's letter (refer back to Figure 5.11) is a good example of how the teacher can indicate the kind of support students receive. The teacher can include information about any of the stages of the writing process, whether the writing is a first draft or has been revised, and the nature of the support provided for the student. The third way we have used is to monitor and provide opportunities for students to work both collaboratively and independently on writing projects. We recognize that not all writing in school and outside of school is collaborative and that we need to provide these opportunities for our students. As teachers, we need to be able to determine the needs of individual students so that we can both plan instruction and report accurately to parents and students themselves. In addition, we realize that when students take the writing assessment in our district or state, they are not permitted to work collaboratively. Although we believe that most writing is done in a collaborative, supportive environment, we realize that portfolio evidence should include a range of work that is both supported and independently created.

Conclusion

Although writing is perhaps one of the easiest curriculum areas to document in a portfolio, the thoughtfulness that goes into choosing pieces and the focus with which work is examined distinguish writing portfolios from the writing folders that most of us have kept in the past. When teachers and students think more deeply and more clearly about the qualities of good writing, writing process, writing ownership, and self-assessment about the products and processes of writing, the portfolio process becomes more than an activity—it becomes an integral part of teaching and learning about writing. Through the descriptions and examples of student work in this chapter, I have tried to demonstrate how teachers can use portfolio artifacts to understand their students' writing abilities in terms of specific writing outcomes.

I have moved a long way from my folder of "neat stuff" about kids to a place where I examine the intent behind my writing activities, instruction, and assessment. I still focus on the "neat stuff," the children's writing, but I now have the words to clarify for myself and others what I know about a student as a writer. My students have grown as well, developing a better understanding of good quality writing and a sense of themselves as writers.

Recently I overheard two students talking during a portfolio visit as one student shared his portfolio with the other. The student was organizing his entries and reflecting on his progress as a writer in preparation for a parent conference. The students sat, heads close together, looking at a piece written early in the year. The author commented on how sloppy his handwriting looked compared to now. His friend pointed out how good the drawings were. The author then started to reminisce about how that piece had been the beginning idea for the chapter story he was now working on. Both remembered that their classmates had loved the first chapter when it was read aloud in "Author's Chair" and how some had even started versions of their own. I never heard this kind of conversation about writing before portfolios became a part of my classroom and my teaching. As important as it is for me to understand and recognize good writing in my students, it is just as important that my students can do the same for themselves. Spending time with writing artifacts in our portfolios is a way to help us all think and learn about writing.

References

Anderson, R. C., Hiebert, E. H., Scott, J. A., & Wilkinson, I. A. G. (1985). *Becoming a nation of readers*. Washington, DC: National Institute of Education.

Asam, C., Au, K., Blake, K., Carroll, J., Jacobson, H., Kunitake, M., & Scheu, J. (1993). *The demonstration classroom project: Report of Year 1*. Honolulu: Kamehameha Schools Bishop Estate.

Au, K. H., Scheu, J. A., Kawakami, A. J., & Herman, P. A. (1990). Assessment and accountability in a whole literacy curriculum. *The Reading Teacher, 43*(8), 574–578.

Britton, J. (1970). *Language and learning*. Harmondsworth: Penguin.

Calkins, L. M. (1994). *The art of teaching writing*. Portsmouth, NH: Heinemann.

Diederich, P. B. (1974). *Measuring growth in English*. Urbana, IL: National Council of Teachers of English.

Flower, L. S., & Hayes, J. R. (1980). Identifying the organization of writing processes. In L. W. Gregg & E. R. Steinberg (Eds.), *Cognitive processes in writing* (pp. 3–30). Hillsdale, NJ: Erlbaum.

Gearhart, M., & Herman, J. L. (1995). *Portfolio assessment: Whose work is it? Issues in the use of classroom assignments for accountability.* Los Angeles: Center for the Study of Evaluation, National Center for Research on Evaluation, Standards, and Student Testing.

Gentry, J. R. (1982). Developmental spelling: Assessment. *Diagnostique, 8*(1), 52–61.

Graves, D. H. (1994). *A fresh look at writing.* Portsmouth, NH: Heinemann.

Graves, D. H., & Hansen, J. (1983). The author's chair. *Language Arts, 60*(2), 176–183.

Graves, D. H., & Sunstein, B. S. (Eds.). (1992). *Portfolio portraits.* Portsmouth, NH: Heinemann.

Howard, K. (1990). Making the writing portfolio real. *Quarterly of the National Writing Project and the Center for the Study of Writing, 12*(2), 4–7, 27.

Kentucky Department of Education. (1992). *Kentucky 4th grade students! What you need to know about your writing and mathematics portfolios.* Frankfort, KY: Author.

Quellmalz, E., & Burry, J. (1983). Analytic scales for assessing students' expository and narrative writing skills (CSE Resource Paper No. 5). Los Angeles: University of California, Center for the Study of Evaluation.

Rief, L. (1990). Finding the value in evaluation: Self-evaluation in a middle school classroom. *Educational Leadership, 47*(6), 24–29.

Spandel, V., & Stiggins, R. J. (1990). *Creating writers.* New York: Longman.

Valencia, S. W., & Au, K. H. (1997). Portfolios across educational contexts: Issues of evaluation, professional development, and system validity. *Educational Assessment 4*(1), 1–35.

Vermont State Department of Education. (1994). *Vermont writing assessment: Analytic assessment guide.* Montpelier, VT: Author.

chapter 6

Engaging Students in Self-Reflection and Self-Evaluation

SHEILA W. VALENCIA AND
SUE BRADLEY

In this chapter we describe two aspects of self-assessment—self-reflection and self-evaluation—both of which are important for helping students become self-directed learners. We present strategies for engaging students in self-assessment through everyday classroom activities. Then we offer specific suggestions for using portfolios to enhance self-assessment. Our philosophy is that self-assessment is an integral part of teaching and learning and that it must be part of classroom life as well as a part of the portfolio process.

While the mind develops, learns, and experiences, it can relate to previous work: compare and draw conclusions. A portfolio contains frozen expressions which we can analyze.

S.T., middle school student

No other aspect of new assessments has captured the attention of educators like student self-reflection and self-evaluation. When students' interests are at the heart of assessment, "first and foremost" assessment must encourage them to reflect on their learning, evaluate their progress, and set meaningful goals (Costa, 1989; International Reading Association & National Council of Teachers of English, 1994; Johnston, 1987). This is not important just for school, it is important for life. Our society depends on citizens who are reflective and thoughtful. How else can we deal with the choices and complex decisions demanded of living in a democratic society? Self-reflection and self-evaluation are essential elements of education, not add-ons.

We all yearn for students like S.T., the student quoted above, who are insightful and committed to their own learning. Unfortunately, they are not yet the norm. Instead, many students are passive learners (Johnston & Winograd, 1985), causing teachers to search for ways to "hook them," to engage them, to make them more responsible—to make them more like S.T. Ironically, we have kept students out of exactly where they need to be—involved in their own assessment. We have viewed learning as the students' job, assessment as the teacher's job. Yet, unless students are part of the assessment process, they will fail to take ownership, interest, and pride in their learning, and we will have failed to "hook them." More important, we will have failed to learn from them and to value them.

The relationship between learning and self-assessment is multifaceted. First, students who are involved in their own self-assessment do not become dependent upon others to determine what is important and how well they are doing (Farr & Tone, 1994; Rief, 1990; Short & Kauffman, 1992). They see learning as within their control (Hansen, 1992; Weiner, 1979). They gain a sense of voice, power, and responsibility. And they gain a sense of themselves as learners who have preferences and choices. Second, with this added sense of responsibility and ownership, students stay focused on their work. As a result, they are more likely to set and actually accomplish appropriate goals. Put another way, the more students know where they are and where they want to go, the more likely they are to get there (Rief, 1990; Stiggins, 1997; Valencia, 1990; Wolf, 1989). So, students who understand their own processes as readers and writers get better at both. Third, students who are clear about their own goals are more likely to help teachers focus instruction. Students and teachers can work together, rather than at cross-purposes, because they have a shared understanding of what they want to accomplish. Teachers gain insights into students' personal visions and priorities for learning and can adjust instruction to capitalize on them.

Our challenge is to find meaningful ways to engage students in self-reflection and self-evaluation. We must find ways to help students go beyond "feel good" kinds of self-assessment to more thoughtful, useful thinking about themselves and their work. In this chapter, we focus on how to do just that. We begin with a clarification of terms and then suggest two general ways to engage students in worthwhile self-assessment: (a) by integrating self-assessment into ongoing classroom life and (b) by using portfolio activities as occasions for self-assessment.

Self-Reflection and Self-Evaluation: Clarifying Terms, Purposes, and Contexts

Clarifying Terms

The terms *self-reflection, self-evaluation,* and *self-assessment* are used interchangeably in many settings and in much of the literature. However, for the purposes of this chapter, we draw a distinction that will help clarify what we want students to learn and how we can best support their learning. The distinctions we make are simple but important.

Self-reflection requires students to step back from their work or their learning to respond or react to it—similar to the way that we think of personal response or reader response (cf. Beach & Hynds, 1991). These thoughts and responses are not constrained in any way; they are simply carefully considered. Reflection may include:

- personal connections—*"I like this because its about how we made bread with our study buddies."* (grade one); *"It's about my grandma and I miss her."* (grade six)
- effort—*"I worked the hardest on it."* (grade two)
- surface features—*"It's long."* (grade four); *"I like the pictures."* (grade three)

In contrast, *self-evaluation* is the term we use to signify that students are evaluating their work against shared standards for quality. For example:

- standards for product and understanding—*"This story is confusing in the middle."* (grade four); *"I did a good job making my reader interested."* (grade four) *"I gave really good responses in my reading journal, like telling about the story so others would know."* (grade four)
- standards for process and strategies—*"This book is too hard for me— I don't know a lot of the words."* (grade two); *"I never revise my writing."* (grade six)
- standards for dispositions—*"My goal is to read books that aren't series books—I should spread out my interests."* (grade five)
- standards for surface features—*"It is my best cursive."* (grade three); *"My spelling and grammar were perfect."* (grade six)

Each of these comments reveals a student who has an understanding of some of the qualities of good reading and writing and of the reading and writing processes—these comments reflect the skills, strategies, purposes, and dispositions of reading and writing we described in chapters 4 and 5.

Finally, we use the term *self-assessment* to include both self-reflection and self-evaluation—any stance students take as they step back and use evidence or knowledge about themselves to think about or "sit with" (Wiggins, 1993) their learning or progress. In other words, we use *self-assessment* as the umbrella term, the broad concept, under which *self-reflection* and *self-evaluation* reside (see Figure 6.1).

Clarifying Purposes

You may wonder: Why bother with these distinctions between self-reflection and self-evaluation? A brief history of our early experiences with self-assessment will help. The first couple of years of our portfolio project, we asked students to attach entry slips to their portfolio selections telling why they chose a particular piece. We prompted with phrases such as, "Choose your favorite" or "Choose your best" and tell why. After two years, we analyzed student responses. Three trends became apparent (see Table 6.1). First, most of our students, at all grades, did not provide specific reasons for their choices. They selected pieces because they "liked them" or because they were "my best" or because they were "good"; students' rationales were gen-

Figure 6.1

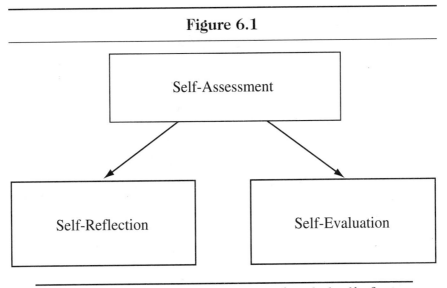

Self-assessment is the broad term we use to refer to both self-reflection and self-evaluation. We use self-reflection to refer to personal response and self-evaluation to refer to judging quality against criteria.
Both are important.

eral, often superficial. Second, few students referred to any standards (other than handwriting and spelling) for good quality work or demonstrated insight into their own reading and writing processes. Students did not seem to have criteria by which to judge their work. Third, there were no differences between the types of reasons that students provided when choosing a favorite or a best piece. Although we thought our prompts would help students distinguish high-quality work (best) from personally satisfying work (favorite), there was no difference. It was not that students equated best with favorite work, it was that they didn't seem to be able to think deeply about either concept. Even when interviewed, students rarely were able to provide additional insight into their learning.

We were humbled and shocked by these results. We thought that the process of keeping portfolios and asking students to reflect regularly on their work would result in students who were insightful and knowledgeable about their work. Instead, it produced flat, uninspired responses and students who did not like "reflecting" (e.g., "Do we have to do those entry slips this time?"). The kind of superficial, undifferentiated reflections we were getting were unlikely to produce students who took more responsibility for their own learning or who were likely to achieve their goals. Their responses simply were not thoughtful or useful enough to matter.

So, after much soul searching and studying, we drew two conclusions from our experiences. First, we determined that students could not be expected to engage in a kind of thinking they had not learned, practiced, or

Table 6.1
Student Self-Reflection and Self-Evaluation Comments
Year 2, Portfolio Project

% of students citing each reason

	Content (It's about)	Effort (Worked hard, long)	Surface (Spelling, handwriting)	Growth (I've changed)	General (Liked it, best favorite)
Primary	31	8	11	3	47
Intermediate	9	16	9	2	64
Middle School	9	25	16	19	31

Initially, students' self-assessments were global and fairly superficial.

come to value. We had to more actively teach and provide meaningful contexts for them to participate in self-assessment. Second, we realized that it is important for students to develop both personal responses to their work and the ability to evaluate themselves against commonly held standards. Thus, we came to distinguish *self-reflection* from *self-evaluation*. Focusing on one or the other is not enough. Students need to engage in self-reflection so they can take personal ownership for learning and can develop personal preferences and insights about themselves as learners. They need to engage in self-evaluation to clarify for themselves criteria for high-quality work; they must be able to realistically evaluate their work and to set appropriate goals. Although in practice self-reflection and self-evaluation often go hand-in-hand, we wanted to be sure that our students could and would engage in both.

Clarifying Contexts

We set our sights on figuring out how to help students develop both self-reflection and self-evaluation abilities and dispositions. We realized that one of the biggest mistakes we made when we began our portfolio work was relegating self-assessment exclusively to student entry slips and written or dictated portfolio visits (see chapter 2). Although thoughtful self-assessment can occur when students are selecting or reviewing portfolio work, it doesn't happen automatically. In addition, simply having students who can produce good "reflections" on demand, during portfolio time, seems to miss the point. We want students to develop a more pervasive, thoughtful stance toward their learning. Self-assessment should be a natural, self-initiated part of learning; it should be viewed as a disposition rather than as a specific task. As teachers, we must have strategies for engaging students in self-assessment, and we must take a more active role in teaching, modeling, and creating opportunities for students to reflect on their work in meaningful ways.

In the next sections we offer several strategies for integrating self-assessment into everyday classroom life *and* for using portfolios to foster self-assessment. The success of the latter, portfolio self-assessment, often depends on how well self-assessment has been integrated into other classroom activities.

Strategies for Engaging Students in Self-Assessment

At the center of all of the strategies we suggest is a focus on *discussion, instruction,* and *time* for thoughtful exploration (Camp, 1990; Howard, 1990; Rief, 1990; Wolf, 1989). Whether the conversations are between students, students and teachers, or students, teachers, and parents, the point is that, at least initially, there should be an interested audience on the other side. This forces students to take a fresh look at their work and their learning, and to bring their understandings to a conscious, verbal level. (See Pressley & Afflerbach, 1995.) Eventually, students internalize the processes and the purposes behind self-assessment and develop the "skill and will" (Paris, Lipson, & Wixson, 1983) to engage in it whenever they need to—the student himself or herself becomes the audience. But, as we have learned, this process takes discussion, instruction, and time.

Howard (1990) described in great detail the slow and careful process she used with her middle school students as they learned about self-assessment of their writing. She began by establishing a climate of reflection, encouraging students to share their work through discussion and to ask each other reflective questions such as, "What did you like about this piece?" and "What were you thinking about when you wrote this piece?" During this phase, the teacher modeled questions and supported students' thinking. From there, she guided students to written self-reflections and then to more evaluative stances such as, "one thing that is done well in your writing and one thing that needs to be improved." It was only at this point that she had students begin to select work for the portfolio and to answer specific questions about their writing. Finally, students compared pieces in their portfolios, analyzing pieces that were satisfying and unsatisfying to them. Howard's process is a good model of the discussion, scaffolded instruction, and time that it takes for students to develop self-understanding. What's more, it exemplifies the culture of shared self-inquiry that must be pervasive in the classroom if self-assessment is to become an effective part of the portfolio process.

So, whether students are engaged in self-assessment during normal classroom activities or focused on the work in their portfolios, they must have time to talk, to learn, and to think about their learning. Although, in the end, there may be fewer written reflections in students' portfolios, what is there will be more insightful and more useful to you and to your students. As you take time to listen while students are discussing their work, you will be rewarded with plenty of information to help you assess their self-knowledge and to plan your instruction.

Integrating Self-Reflection and Self-Evaluation Into Ongoing Instruction

There are many opportunities every day for students to think about their own learning and process of learning. Just by making self-assessment a natural part of classroom life, students will become accustomed to and learn the importance of self-assessment. We have found that it is easiest to engage students in self-reflection and self-evaluation when they have work in front of them or when the process of creating a project or participating in an activity is still fresh in their minds. It also seems easier, at first, for students to think in terms of a particular reading/writing task rather than to think globally about reading and writing. Next, we present suggestions for integrating self-assessment into your classroom.

Creating a Self-Assessment Environment

Creating a supportive environment for self-assessment requires a non-threatening, collaborative, inquiry-oriented classroom. Students must feel safe and interested enough to talk about what is going well and what is not. One strategy is to ask students to step back from nonacademic tasks to discuss their thoughts and responses. Artwork, classroom interactions, work preferences, and play activities all provide opportunities for students to experience self-assessment without fear of failure or uncertainty about expectations. For example, Christine, a third grader, reflected on a part of art in which she drew overlapping leaves. She reported to her teachers that she was proud of her work, saying, "I do great art, and I know how to combine two colors. One of my favorite things in this is to overlap. I tried to make it look real." In contrast, Lauren, a first grader, didn't seem to be engaged with her artwork or with the reflection task (see Figure 6.2). Although we might think she has done a remarkable job of creating and then drawing a replica of her puppet, Lauren doesn't seem to think so. Fortunately, as we look across her other early forays into self-assessment, we learn that she is discriminating and does, in fact, find other things about herself and her work that she enjoys. This was simply an activity she didn't enjoy.

Other teachers use interest inventories and school surveys to help students learn to be reflective; of course, at the same time, these also help teachers learn a great deal about their students. Lauren's "happy faces" and brief written responses reveal that she enjoys school but seems to want

Figure 6.2

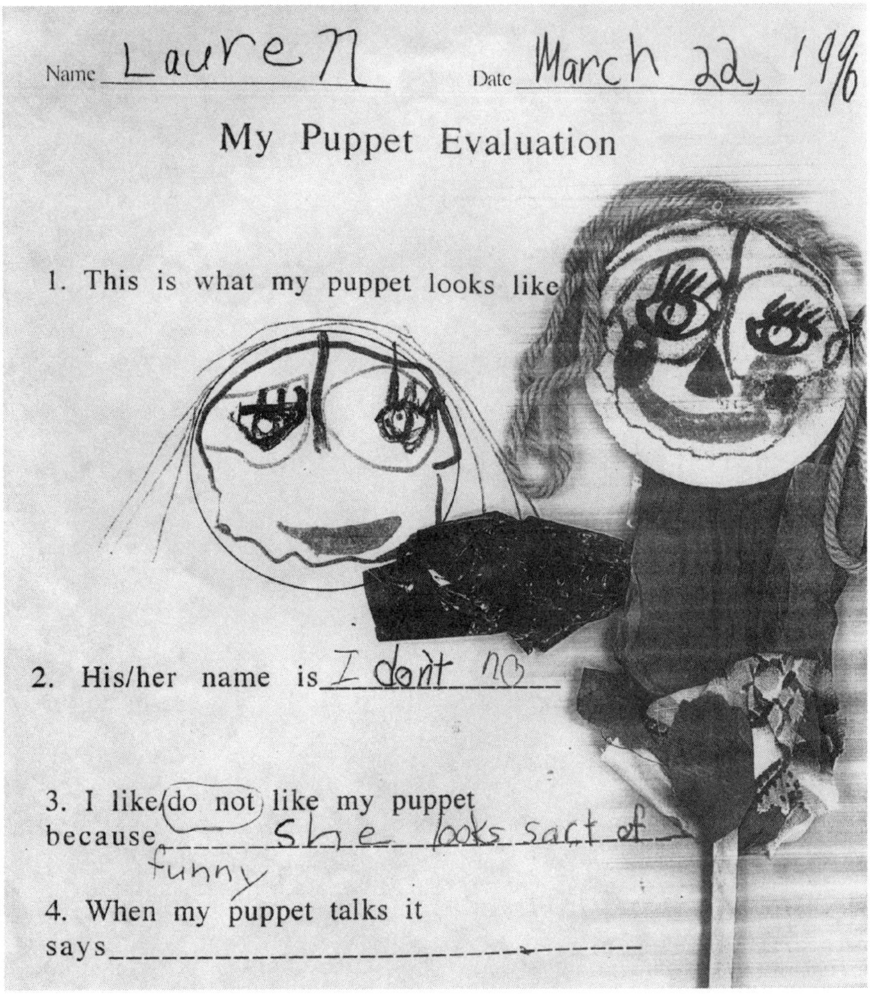

Name **Lauren**   Date **March 22, 1996**

My Puppet Evaluation

1. This is what my puppet looks like

2. His/her name is **I dont no**

3. I like (do not) like my puppet
because **She looks sact of funny**

4. When my puppet talks it
says_____

Lauren does a great job with her puppet, yet her reflection doesn't seem to indicate much engagement or pride in her work.

---

more friends (see Figure 6.3). Interestingly, she doesn't like to work alone but doesn't feel that she works well in a group. Lauren's teacher can use these self-reflections to help Lauren reach out to more children. These examples of self-reflections about art and school represent nonthreatening opportunities for students to develop self-inquiry skills and stances.

Figure 6.3

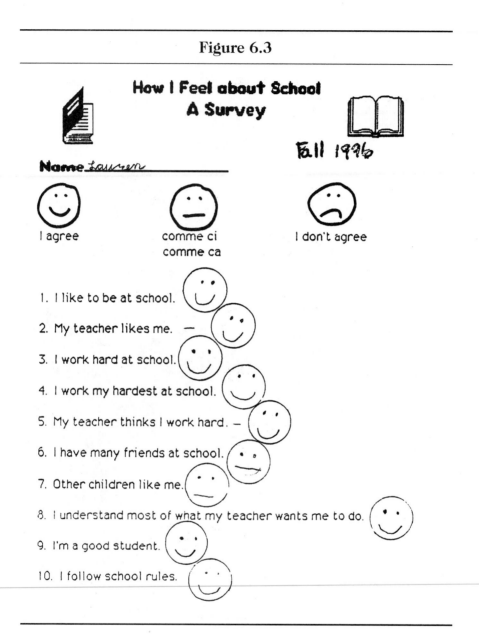

How I Feel about School
A Survey

Fall 1996

Name Lauren

😊 I agree   😐 comme ci comme ca   ☹ I don't agree

1. I like to be at school. 😊

2. My teacher likes me. — 😊

3. I work hard at school. 😊

4. I work my hardest at school. 😊

5. My teacher thinks I work hard. — 😊

6. I have many friends at school. 😐

7. Other children like me. 😐

8. I understand most of what my teacher wants me to do. 😊

9. I'm a good student. 😊

10. I follow school rules. 😊

Teachers can also introduce the concept of criteria to help students learn about self-evaluation in nonacademic tasks. For example, students could be asked to think about and discuss questions such as:

- How well are our learning centers working?
- Am I working well with my new table mates?
- How would I evaluate our lunchroom or playground behavior?
- What are some good ways to use my time if I finish my project?

Figure 6.3 *continued*

11. I'm a good reader.

12. I'm smart.

13. My parents think I work hard at school.

14. I work well in a group.

15. I like to work by myself.

Here's a picture of me with my friends: Cathrean veronca Haly Emaly Ali Shera

C. I wish I could **have more reading time and go on more feld trips** .

Interest inventories are a good way to introduce students to reflective thinking.

- What criteria should we use to select our "student of the month"?

To answer these questions, teachers would help students determine the qualities or criteria of good performance for each task. This evaluative stance toward ourselves and our actions sets the stage for self-evaluation about specific literacy learnings.

As students become more comfortable with the process of thinking about their work and behavior, questions specific to reading and writing activities can be posed, modeled, and discussed with the students (see Table 6.2). Again, it is most useful to tie these questions to a particular task and to have work in front of students as they talk about their responses (Higgins, Harris, & Kuehn, 1994). The more concrete the evidence, the easier for students to delve into their thinking. Notice how the questions in

Table 6.2
Questions to Foster Self-Assessment as Part of Learning

What do I like about this piece of writing?
Discuss one thing that is done well. Discuss one thing that needs to be improved.
Which part of creating this piece was difficult/easy for me?

What are my feelings about the story/book I read?
How do I think others would respond?
Which parts were interesting/confusing for me? Why?
How does this book compare with others that I have read?
How well does my summary capture the most important elements of the story?

Which research questions was I able to answer from this source? Which ones are still unanswered?
What new questions do I have about my topic?
What did I learn about X? What is still confusing for me?

What are my favorite topics for reading and writing?
How did I do on that task/activity?
What did I like best about X?

Table 6.2 involve both self-reflection and self-evaluation of specific tasks. As we pointed out earlier, students need to learn about both. In one sense, reflecting about specific reading and writing activities and processes is more difficult than general, nonacademic self-inquiry because it involves understanding of reading and writing. More difficult still is developing a sense of standards for the evaluative questions so that students can think about their work in terms of the standards. However, with appropriate support, even very young children are quite capable of setting standards for themselves (Higgins, Harris, & Kuehn, 1994). As you make questions like those in Table 6.2 part of your class discussions and model various ways of thinking, students will become more comfortable and adept at self-assessment.

Building Self-Assessment Into Predictable Classroom Activities

Most teachers have a few activities that are a regular, predictable part of students' days, weeks, or months. These provide another opportunity to have students practice self-assessment—they are opportunities for students to stop and think about their learning.

Journals. Some teachers weave self-assessment into the natural process of keeping journals (either reading or writing journals) by asking students to look through their journals, reviewing their work with a new eye. Sometimes students evaluate their work by looking for a piece that exemplifies a particular criterion (i.e., an effective description, a compelling beginning, good organization). At other times, students may be asked to reflect simply by selecting a favorite piece.

Katie and Kim, third graders, were asked to choose favorite journal pieces and to think about why they were their favorites. While the girls gain insights into themselves, their teachers also learn more about them (see Figure 6.4). Because the prompt is fairly open (i.e., "favorite"), we have an opportunity to learn what each youngster values. Katie's explanation shows

---

Figure 6.4

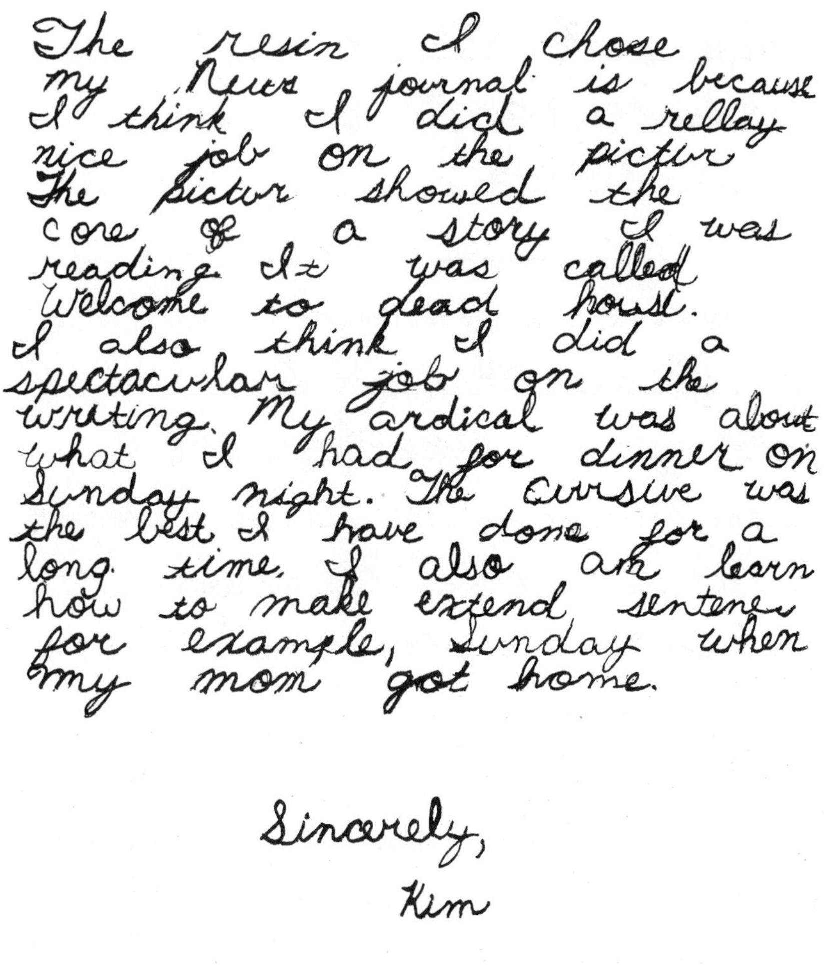

The resin I chose my News journal is because I think I did a relay nice job on the pictur The pictur showed the core of a story I was reading. It was called Welcome to dead houst. I also think I did a spectacular job on the writing. My ardical was about what I had for dinner on Sunday night. The cursive was the best I have done for a long time. I also am learn how to make extend sentene for example, Sunday when my mom got home.

Sincerely,
Kim

Figure 6.4 *continued*

Journal Response Reflection

NAME: *Katie*   Date: *5/8/92*

Choose your favorite journal response.

Why do you like it?

I like it Because it makes sense, it tells you whats happing in the Book and its long.

What does it show about you as a reader?

I show that I know whats happening in the Book, it shows I read complecated Books and it shows. I like horse stories.

Providing time for students to review their journal entries helps them reflect on and evaluate work that sometimes becomes routine.

---

that she is applying criteria to her choice. She believes that a reading journal entry should make sense, inform the reader about the plot, and be long. Katie also realizes that she is a strong reader ("I read complecated [sic] books") who has a personal interest in horses. Katie has developed some good criteria for this particular task—reading and writing must make sense;

her teacher learns that Katie might be encouraged to expand her criteria to include personal response or questioning the author, and she learns that Katie's self-evaluation of her reading abilities is consistent with the teacher's own analysis. Katie seems to have appropriate standards and an awareness of her own capabilities.

Kim chooses two pages from her journal as favorites. She comments on both surface features (the picture and cursive handwriting) and more substantive features of her reading and writing work. She is very proud of both. We learn that it is important to Kim that her picture captures the essence, perhaps the main idea, of the story she was reading ("The pictur [sic] showed the core of a story I was reading") and that she is learning how to write extended sentences. She even provides an example. This open invitation for reflection reveals Kim's broad range of personally satisfying aspects of her work.

Monthly reflections and letters. Other regularly scheduled activities such as monthly reflection letters or reading letters can help students build a habit of self-inquiry. Kristine's February Reflection (see Figure 6.5) is a good example of how Sue works with her students on self-assessment. Each month she creates the "lead-in" for the reflection by summarizing some of the things the students have been studying. The first part of every monthly reflection includes individual student goals and a plan for working on them (goals are discussed in more detail later). In addition, Sue works with the class to generate several questions that will help students think about what they have been learning and doing. This process, or minilesson, helps the students learn how and why to engage in self-questioning. The combination of teacher reflection, personal goal setting, and group-generated self-assessment questions creates a nice balance of modeling, personal choice, and instruction on self-inquiry.

Kristine's reflection includes two worthwhile goals. She has a good strategy for accomplishing one of them ("check my spelling with a Franklin speller") but not for the other ("I will make sure that I write longer stories"). This is an excellent example of how students often know what they want to do but don't know how to make it happen. Sue can help Kristine work on longer stories by helping her to identify her purpose for writing and to learn how to develop a narrative plot more fully. She can also help Kristine develop a repertoire of other strategies she can use to work on her writing goal. Other sections of Kristine's February Reflection are responses to questions generated by her classmates. She is encouraged to reflect on class activities, new reading genres (nonfiction), and the value of studying about inventors. Once again, a combination of self-reflection and self-assessment questions encourages students to think about their work in different ways.

Monthly reading letters like those we described in chapters 2 and 4 work very much like the preceding monthly reflection letters. However, they add an important element—a dialogue between teacher and student. As we noted, it is sometimes easy to lose sight of the importance of discussion in self-assessment, especially when students are engaged in written

---

Figure 6.5

𝔍ebruary

ℜeflections

𝒲hen you think of 𝔍ebruary, you think of 𝒱alentine's Day. 𝒲e did have a 𝒱alentine's party. 𝒲e also did a lot more in 𝔍ebruary. 𝒲e studied and wrote about 𝒜braham 𝔏incoln. 𝒲e continued our study of simple machines, and in math, we worked with patterns. 𝒲e finished our literature circles about the 𝒞ivil 𝒲ar. ℜight in the middle of 𝔍ebruary, we had a week off for mid-winter break.

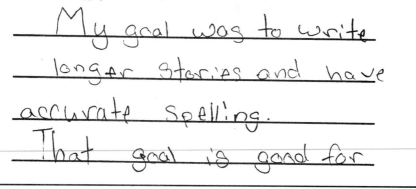

My goal was to write longer stories and have accurate spelling. That goal is good for

---

responses. The reading letters bring discussion, written dialogue, back into the picture. We have found them to be an excellent strategy to work on self-assessment in reading. They may be prompted with questions or completely open-ended, but they are always answered by the teacher.

Alyssa's letters demonstrate her insights into her reading, and they demonstrate the power of corresponding with a real audience (see Figure 6.6). Alyssa's December letter reveals her interest in story themes and her ability to relate to the characters. She wants Mrs. Bradley to relate

Figure 6.5 *continued*

me because I never write long
stories and I don't try to correct
my spelling. I will make sure
that I write longer stories and
I'll check my spelling with a Franklin
Speller

I liked the part of the
Valentine's Day party when
I played music for the class.
I think the party was o.k.
just the way it was.

If I could read any non-fiction
book, I would read about flowers
because I am interested in
flowers. I would never read
a book on Submerines because
I don't like them.

In inventing I learned that
inventors don't give up.
I would like to invent
a silly putty that would
do every thing that the
real silly putty would
do but a silly putty that
would not dry up.

*Monthly reflections are a predictable activity to help students set goals
and think about what they have learned and done in school. They are
also a good way to communicate with families.*

Figure 6.6

N Dec 18, 96   Alyssa

Dear Mrs. Bradley

I'v been reading
The Year of the Bear and Jackie Robinson.
I really enjoyed the book because...
.... It taught me a lesson that
said pay attition to anyone who
needs it. I also enjoyed doing it for
my book report. I'v also read alotof
Trixe Belden books! Diana Lynch
is my favorite character because she is
sentive and beautiful. Would you
like to Be

Trixe-Honey-Mart-
Brian-Jim-or Diana-Dan

Circle one

[signature]

Dear Alyssa,
Thanks for your
letter. I'm glad you
enjoyed In The Year....
I agree sensitivity to
others was one of the
lessons of that book. Were
there any other Themes?
I'm sorry I couldn't
chose a name. I don't
Know those characters well
enough to decide. Are you
still reading those books, too?

Mrs B.

Figure 6.6 *continued*

Feb 5 1997   Alyssa

Dear Mrs. Bradley
          I have been reading
more Trixe Belden the one I'm reading
now is called Trixe Belden and the Mystry
of the emralds. I will tell you about
each character in the book and then you
can pick one.
          Diana. She is the girl I picked
to be. Diana has black hair and violet
eyes, she is quiet but is very smart. Diana
likes Mart.

          Mart is Trixes brother. He has
blond hair and has a crew cut. He is a
smart alic to Trixe but really loves her. His
vocabulary is very wide he likes Diana

          Honeys really name is Madiline
but her hair color made her get
the name Honey. She is very sweet and
she helps solve mysteryses with Trixe.
Honey likes Brian.

          Brian is Trixes older brother. He
wants to be a doctor when he grows
up. Brian is as kind as they come. He
likes Honey.

---

to them as well. Remarkably, Alyssa takes on Mrs. Bradley's response by including a description of each character in her next reading letter so that Mrs. Bradley must "play." As you might expect, Alyssa and Mrs. Bradley continue to discuss book choices, characters, new genres, and other topics through their monthly letters.

Figure 6.6 *continued*

Dan is gruff on the outside but, is really very kind All his outfitts consist of A Black leather jacket, tight jeans, and cowboy boots

Jim is Honey's older adopted brother. He has a temper but he only gets it when someone is mean. He likes Trixe

Trixe is the really good mystery solver. She likes Jim and he likes her. Trixes best friend is Honey and they make a good team.

Circle One

Dear Alyssa,
Thanks for your letter. You explained each character well. There are so many.
    I think I like Honey but I'd have to read more to know for sure. Is Trixie your favorite? Does she appear as the main character in all the books?

Monthly reading letters can encourage collaborative reflection and discussion between students and teachers.

Student-teacher conferences. Our final example of a predictable activity that invites self-inquiry is the teacher-student conference. Many teachers use conferences to observe and assess students' reading strategies (see chapter 4), but such conferences also provide a perfect opportunity to build a collaborative model for self-inquiry. By engaging students in conversation about their reading goals, strategies, and preferences, teachers help students become thoughtful about their own processes, and they model that readers think and talk about such things.

Kathy's teacher takes notes on a classroom computer as she holds quarterly reading conferences with her fifth-grade students. Figure 6.7, an excerpt of her conference notes, shows how teachers can guide students' self-reflection and self-evaluation by joining them in conversation about their reading. Kathy's teacher begins the conference by checking in on Kathy's first-quarter goal "to read more mysteries because I really don't like them and maybe I will." Simply by referring back to Kathy's goal and asking how it worked out, her teacher is sending a message that we set goals for ourselves and then we evaluate our progress toward those goals. Goals are not set because they please the teacher but rather because they mean something to the student. The teacher goes on to talk with Kathy about her opinions of the book and her evaluation of the difficulty. By having Kathy read a section aloud, the teacher is able to judge whether Kathy's self-evaluation of difficulty is on target. It is. A few words are difficult for Kathy, but overall, judging from her oral reading and comprehension, the book seems just right for her. In the last part of the conference, the teacher and Kathy discuss new goals, and this is where we see a wonderful interaction about evaluating your own comprehension. The notes reveal that Kathy can discriminate between being bored by a book and truly not understanding, and she has well-developed strategies for coping with her confusion. Although the teacher took notes that were placed into Kathy's portfolio, the point of this example is that Kathy and her teacher took the opportunity of the regularly scheduled reading conference to engage in self-reflection and evaluation. Because Kathy was able to work collaboratively, alongside a knowledgeable other (Vygotsky, 1978), in this case her teacher, she was able to move into new areas of self-assessment that might otherwise not have been nurtured or attempted. And because self-assessment was grounded in Kathy's authentic reading experiences, she will be more likely to learn and apply her understandings in other situations.

Helping Students Develop Criteria for Self-Evaluation

Self-evaluation requires students to judge their work against a set of standards—individually constructed standards or shared standards. By definition, then, students must know the specific qualities of good work, and then they must be able to step back and judge their work or their activities against these standards. Teachers need to work with students to clarify expectations so that we all understand the performance standards (National Council on Education Standards and Testing, 1992). As we noted in chapter 1, being explicit about criteria for good work is not only fair, it is necessary (Delpit, 1995; Wiggins, 1993). Students cannot be expected to do high-quality work unless they are clear about what is expected. And working with students to develop standards is an important part of the process. In fact, one of our middle school colleagues coined the term *front-loading*

Figure 6.7

Kathy

January, 1995

Goal Update: Has read a mystery, Mystery on a Minus Tide (book report book). Also read a fantasy The Ancient One.

Today's Book: Stepping on the Cracks (books she was reading at her desk), on p.52, rereading the book ("one of my favorites"). Kathy spontaneously filled me in on where she was in the book with a succinct summary and interpretation of characters. Reports that she "loves" this book and would even read it again.

    read fluently and effortlessly, very rapidly

    added expression for dialogue as she went

Self-evaluation of the book difficulty: "basically easy though some words are hard."

    words decoded successfully:
        invincible = "gets in trouble, no, more like outgoing"
        undefeatable = "nobody can beat you" (I figured our the
defeat part)

New Goal: I think I will read Little Women again because I think I will understand it better this year than last. Basically I read it but didn't understand it. I haven't seen the movie.

Question: How do you know you don't understand something when you are reading it?

"You want to finish it but you are lost in the book. You just don't know what is going on, you get lost in the words. when I was in Little women and I didn't understand it, it dragged and seemed like would never end. It was different than Onion John. I'm just bored with that."

Question: What do you do when you don't understand?

1. Read it over again.
2. I don't go ask Mom, I try to figure it out myself. If it doesn't seem that important, I just keep going on. Q: Not important? If you're in the beginning, it's introduction, not the climax and usually that means it's not important.
3. Once when I was reading National Velvet, and I didn't understand, I watched the movie. I get something to back me up when I don't understand.
4. If there is a word that is the trouble, I write it down so that I look at it and think of what it means. Sometimes I look around that word to see if the other words help me figure it out.

The teacher's notes capture some of the collaborative self-assessment discussion that can occur during reading conferences. Kathy sets and accomplishes her goals, has developed opinions about books, and demonstrates good criteria to self-evaluate her understanding and use of fix-up strategies.

to describe what happens when she works with her students at the initial stages of a project to define the standards for good work. Another colleague suggests that sometimes students don't have a good sense of all the criteria of a good performance until they get a little way into a new project. Sometimes it takes a bit of experience with the topic and the assignment to build a vision of what would constitute good work. Conversely, it is unfair and not at all helpful for teachers to introduce criteria only after a project is completed. When students are involved in defining criteria and when they know, "up front," the criteria for high-quality work, they can use those criteria for self-evaluation throughout the learning cycle—before, during, and after activities and projects.

Next we present several approaches to developing and using criteria with students for self-evaluation on specific reading and writing activities. In general, they fall into three categories: (a) criteria generated by teachers, (b) criteria generated collaboratively between teachers and students, and (c) criteria generated by individual students. All three approaches rely on conversation and modeling.

Teacher-generated criteria. Figure 6.8 is an example of a teacher-generated form for students' self-reflection and self-evaluation about their literature circles. This represents a structured way to introduce students to self-assessment. Notice that several of the questions ask for self-reflection, opinions about the book, and who might enjoy it. The self-evaluation questions at the bottom are almost procedural, helping students focus on how often they did particular activities and requiring the students simply to rate themselves. The topics are important to the smooth functioning of a literature circle, yet they are fairly easy to evaluate. So, this section introduces thoughtfulness to important outcomes, but the task itself is structured to be easier for students. The statement, "I wrote thoughtful answers in my response log," provides a good opportunity to discuss with students just what "thoughtful answers" might be. And the task to set a goal for the next literature circle provides an opportunity to help students use their self-evaluation results to set new goals. In this case, the student decided to focus on the substantive content by improving his answers to questions.

Primary teachers have also used highly structured self-evaluations to model and discuss with children. For example, some teachers choose three or four areas on which to focus as students learn about and do research reports:

I can find my research books on my topic in the library.

I can write about my topic using my own words.

My report has interesting facts.

My pictures go with my report.

Teachers discuss these areas with the students before the students begin working on their reports and continue to refer to them throughout

---

Figure 6.8

LITERATURE CIRLCES–
SELF REFLECTION & SELF EVALUATION
TEACHER SELECTION   NOVEMBER, 1996

Students read books about slavery and the Underground Railroad:
        The Drinking Gourd by F. N. Monjo
        Wanted:Dead or Alive by Ann McGovern
        Harriet Tubman by Kate McMullan
        Two Tickets to Freedom by Florence Freedman

What did you like most about this book? *That it was of slaves running away. I liked their plan.*

Who might enjoy reading this book? *9 year olds*

Why might that person enjoy it? *because it tells about history*

Mark each of the following: 5 = always 4 = most of the time
3 = sometimes   2 = every once and awhile 1 = never

_5-_ I had my book and response log ready.

_4_ I wrote thoughtful answers in my response log.

_3_ I copied the questions and chapter numbers.

_4_ I kept up on the reading assignments and questions.

_5_ I listened well to others in our discussion group.

_5_ I took an active part in the discussions by asking
        questions and talking about the book.

What are your goals for the next time we have literature
circles? *To make good ansers on questions.*

---

*This fairly structured and simple form provides an easy way to help
students talk and think about self-reflection and self-evaluation.*

the week of work. When reports are completed, teachers again discuss these criteria, and students are then encouraged to respond in writing in a simple way. For example, they could choose from various "happy faces," or they could respond with number ratings.

A variety of teacher-generated criteria could be used for a wide range of projects and for students of all ages. As students become more comfortable with the process of self-evaluation, they can be guided to explore more substantive areas for evaluation and encouraged to provide more elaborate reasoning and evidence for their thinking. These structured activities are simply ways to get students used to thinking about criteria for good work and about how well they are meeting those criteria.

Student-teacher-generated criteria. By far, the best way to work with self-evaluation is to engage students in developing important criteria for specific projects. This teaches self-evaluative skills and helps students think like skilled readers and writers (Rowntree, 1987; Spandel, 1994). Lynn, a primary teacher, provides a good overview of how she works with her six-, seven-, and eight-year-olds to generate criteria. She begins the school year with discussions about criteria of a good school, classroom, teacher, and student. Dialogue and reflection are integral parts of the school day; students discuss current events, school problems, classroom difficulties. And they talk about their writing and reading with each other. Lynn models often; students have many opportunities to practice. This dialogue and discussion about general criteria lay the foundation for class discussions about explicit criteria for projects.

A good example of generating specific criteria comes from Lynn's experience with personal narratives. She began by introducing several personal narrative read-alouds. Each day, after listening, the students would talk about what made these stories satisfying or unsatisfying. Students also talked about interesting stories they had heard others tell about their lives or had told themselves to parents and friends. Then Lynn and the students worked on criteria for a good written personal narrative. She tells what happened:

> The children quickly and confidently raised their hands. The first child said, "There needs to be enough detail." "Yes," I thought, "they've heard me say this a hundred times." But the next child quickly added, "The story needs to make you feel like you were there!" "Great point," I thought as I wrote it on the board. A small, intense six-year-old was next. "The story must have soul," he said, and many of the group nodded knowingly. "Wait a minute," I thought, "What is going on here? How do these kids know all this? Why haven't I asked them before?" I asked them about "soul" in a story and, while the words were difficult to come by at times, they agreed that it had to do with engagement and the ability to pull the reader into the story in an honest way.
>
> At this point, all of my expectations about what the children knew about writing were gone. I was probably standing with my mouth hanging slightly open waiting for the next insight. They came quickly and with the same confidence as the first few. "Fun and exciting to read," "Interesting facts," "Feelings," "The

writer uses expression, just like you do when you read out loud, but it's in the writing." The children gave examples for each comment, and there was a current of understanding running through the group, with heads nodding and no disagreement, even from those students who could usually agree only if they had said it! "They really know this!" I realized.

Finally, as the group ran out of ideas, I tentatively mentioned spelling and punctuation. They calmly and somewhat condescendingly agreed with me, making it clear that, of course, these things were important, as I the teacher surely knew, but that they were not the heart of good writing. I divided the comments into two set of criteria, story and structure, and checked with the class to see if that division made sense to them. They understood the difference, it appeared. The structure criteria developed a life of their own and went on to be included with criteria for other writing projects since we found that they didn't change much from genre to genre.

The kids were eager to get started and filled with ideas for powerful personal narratives. I was more excited than the students; humbled, too, since I was sure that my own criteria would not have been as thoughtful or rigorous as theirs.

Lynn's experience of developing criteria with her students points out the importance of discussion, instruction, and time. She did a good job laying the foundation of a reflective classroom and took care to develop students' awareness of important criteria for a personal narrative in other parts of the school day. She honored the students' ideas and yet guided them to be clear, and monitored to be sure she was covering content that she wanted the students to learn. She gave the students time and support and then lots of practice using the criteria to evaluate their own writing and the writing of others. Along the way she provided lessons to students who needed more help—she used the criteria to guide her instruction.

This model could easily be adapted to develop criteria for other types of writing, projects, or reading activities. Figure 6.9 is an example of the criteria Lynn developed with her primary students; Figure 6.10 is an example of criteria developed with intermediate students for a state report; and 6.11 is an example of criteria developed for an oral presentation on famous inventors. Some teachers, especially intermediate and middle school teachers, assign points for each criteria, but even without points, the criteria help students focus on what is important. And because students have participated in criteria development at the early stages of the project, students' learning is enhanced, and students are more engaged in their work. At the same time, the criteria help teachers focus instruction.

Student-generated criteria. Eventually, we hope that students learn to generate their own criteria for self-evaluation; that takes support and time. Figure 6.12 is an example of a first attempt by fifth graders to develop four evaluative questions for a book report they did. The teacher worked with them on four general categories: clarity, interest, voice, and personal choice. Then, within each category, students created specific questions for their self-evaluation. Figure 6.12 shows a student's self-evaluation of her work and the teacher's evaluation of her work. It is interesting to see the

---

Figure 6.9

Rubric for a Personal Narrative

Name of Author: *Andrew*

Comments by: *Lynn Beebe*   *Fall 96*

Story *When I got sick on my trip to Montana*	Yes/No	Comments
1. Important details are included in the story.	*yes*	
2. There are interesting facts that make the story fun and exciting.	*yes*	*—being cold, using a sleeping bag*
3. The author makes you feel "like you are there" by including feelings and expression in the story.	*yes*	*I could imagine you getting sicker + sicker*
4. The author shows that he or she cares about the story. There is "soul" in the story.	*yes*	*seemed important to you*
5. The author shows that he or she knows enough about the idea or event to write a story.	*yes*	*lots of details – you remember this well*

---

justification provided by the student and by the teacher for their ratings. It's also enlightening to have students and teachers share their perspectives in writing and then in discussion. Generating personal criteria is a good task for students. It forces them to consider what is most important and to be responsible for attaining the criteria that they set. Nevertheless, students need support and guidance in developing their own criteria. To be sure, students need to develop personal criteria, but they also need to become aware of high standards and shared expectations for good work.

Figure 6.9 *continued*

Rubric, continued

Structure	Yes?	Evidence of this
1. Title	✓	
2. Correct spelling.	not yet	
3. Punctuation	Some	
4. Capital letters at the beginning of the sentences.	Some	Washington

These criteria for writing a personal narrative were developed by a multiage primary class. The teacher used the criteria in conference with Andrew and recorded their comments.

Figures 6.9, 6.10, 6.11, and 6.12 demonstrate criteria for different tasks, and they also demonstrate ways to gather different perspectives or feedback on student work. The personal narrative criteria have been completed by the teacher, attached to the work, and entered into the portfolio. Rather than have this second grader complete the form, Lynn used it as a way to discuss Andrew's writing with him. Because the criteria were developed by the class, Andrew was familiar with them and enjoyed talking about these aspects of his work with his teacher and with a peer. The second set of criteria, structure, was completed only for the teacher's record at this time. Lynn chose to stay focused on the story criteria during the evaluation of this piece to help Andrew concentrate on story content. In contrast, the state report criteria were completed by both the student and teacher. Notice that they don't always agree on the rating but that both can offer explanations. The process of completing the self-evaluation and talking it over with the teacher was extremely useful for Martha and for the teacher. Finally, the oral report criteria show Kyle's evaluative feedback from two of his classmates. What are not shown are Kyle's self-evaluation and the teacher's evaluation using the same criteria. So, Kyle received feedback from peers, his teacher, and himself. Interestingly, there is a big discrepancy

Figure 6.10

Martha   State   Report   Assessment

Content
1. Completeness - 5 points
    Includes information on geography, history, major points of
interest, special points for interested visitors; gives enough
information so the reader understands

④ You give good information about special places. You didn't include history of the state.

5. because I gave enough information for someone to know about the state and good places to visit

2. Interest - 5 points
    Captures reader's interest; uses vivid language; adds personal touch

4. becuse I didn't use alot of things like that

④ I agree. You did give a personal touch in places to visit but not in other places.

3. Writing - 5 points
    Written in own words; thoughts are organized; uses complete
sentences; organizes in paragraphs

5. I rote in my own words rote in sentences and organiced in paragraphs

⑤ Well organized

4. Process - 5 points
    Uses notes to write rough draft; revises with peer; edits for
spelling and punctuation

4. I didn't use notes but I did write in ruf draft. Jason helped me with my report

④ Yes, we will work on note taking for your next report.

Presentation
1. Readability - 5 points
    Neat handwriting or typing so others can read

5. because I typed it and I used some words that you might not read alot

⑤ Great headings in different fonts. Neatly done.

2. Visuals - Extra credit
    Pictures, maps or charts are included

0 because I do not use any pictures

⑥ No extra credit.

---

*Collaboratively developed criteria for an intermediate-grade research
project require the student and the teacher to evaluate performance.
Martha's self-evaluations are written directly below the criteria;
the teachers follow the circled scores.*

Figure 6.11

Your Name: **Jay**

Presenter's Name ~~_____~~ **Kyle**

Please fill out one slip for EACH presenter.

Points: You can give a maximum of three
points for each item on the list below.
    3 points = Great Job!
    2 points = Good job, a few mistakes.
    1 point: = Nice try, but could be
        better.

JOB	POINTS
GIVEN	
-spoke loudly and clearly.	2
-Used expression when talking.	3
-Looked at the audience when. talking	3
-Paid attention to partner and was following along.	3
-Information made sense (was in their own words and in order).	3
TOTAL POINTS GIVEN:	14

Please add one compliment for the
presenters.

you were very imformatived I liked your present-ation.

Your Name: **Mary**

Presenter's Name ~~_____~~ **Kyle**

Please fill out one slip for EACH presenter.

Points: You can give a maximum of three
points for each item on the list below.
    3 points = Great Job!
    2 points = Good job, a few mistakes.
    1 point: = Nice try, but could be
        better.

JOB	POINTS
GIVEN	
-spoke loudly and clearly.	2
-Used expression when talking.	1
-Looked at the audience when. talking	2
-Paid attention to partner and was following along.	3
-Information made sense (was in their own words and in order).	2
TOTAL POINTS GIVEN:	13

Please add one compliment for the
presenters.

I Like how he spoke very clearly and I like how he looked at the audience

---

*The criteria for oral presentation were developed collaboratively by
intermediate-grade students. Each student completed a self-
evaluation and received feedback from two peers and the teacher. Peer
evaluations are shown.*

between his two peer evaluators in "used expression when talking," which
may be confusing for Kyle. This points out a potential problem when peers
are providing feedback; teachers must be sure that students understand the
criteria, can distinguish personal opinion from shared criteria, and know
how to be considerate of each other. The request for "one compliment"
helps students learn to be helpful yet sensitive when providing feedback

Figure 6.12

How well did I
explain Custers life?

Very well. It sounded
like custer had a
short, interesting and
hard life. ⑤

⑤ What I especially enjoyed
was how smoothly your story
of his life flowed. You were
also considerate of the reader
& explained things (like his
nickname) that might not be
well-known.

Did it really sound
like I was Autie?

Yes

What made it sound that
way? I ~~wo~~ wrote like it
was really him telling
about his West Point
life. ⑤

⑤+ This section was exceptional!
You sounded like an extremely
enthusiastic plebe, and
I think that's what
Autie was.

Was my book report
interesting to read?

Yes

What made it interesting
or non-interesting?
It sounded like Custer
had accomplished alot
of interesting things
in his life ④
⑤ Yes. You told interesting
events and you added your
personal comments.

Did you understand
why I like having
a book about him?

Yes

What made you understand?
Give examples.
I said that Custer
was important back then.
④.5
⑤ Yes, you're right. You gave
several examples of evidence to
show why Custer is a worthy
topic for a biography.

---

*Students generated their own criteria for a book report and then
self-evaluated using the criteria. The teacher also provided feedback
and a score.*

to peers. This model of multiple sources of feedback is beneficial for students as they learn to establish and internalize their own standards for performance.

Goal Setting. Goal setting can be integrated into many of the activities we have presented (e.g., conferences, monthly letters, project criteria, discussion of projects). As Carroll and Christenson (1994) point out, simply setting goals is not enough. We must help students set appropriate goals (meaningful and reasonable), provide them with opportunities to work on their goals and receive needed instruction, and encourage them to thoughtfully evaluate their progress toward those goals. It appears that many students are being encouraged to set goals, but few of them seem to be assisted or given time to learn what they need to achieve their goals. This is especially true when students set personal goals and teachers are faced with 28 to 35 goals in one classroom! Furthermore, many student goals are stated but not revisited or self-evaluated. They are simply written, filed, and never looked at again.

Some colleagues have devised a monthly goal sheet on which the teacher states one or two goals for all of the students in the class and on which each student identifies one personal goal for the month. In this way, teachers can manage instruction toward a limited number of goals and be sure they are covering important curriculum. At the same time, by having students identify their personal goals at the beginning of the month, teachers can group students with shared goals to be sure they get needed instruction and practice. Another strategy, developed by Sue Bradley, is to reproduce four or five strips of paper with copies of each student's personal goal, and give the packet of those strips to the student. As he works on his goal, one strip is attached to the work so that student and teacher are reminded of the goal and can look for progress on that particular piece. This strategy reinforces the commitment on the part of student and teacher to work on the goal, and it reinforces the need to continue to work on a goal over time—there are four or five strips! Best of all, it's an easy way to keep track of goal work.

Using Portfolios to Engage Students in Self-Reflection and Self-Evaluation

The most common strategy for engaging students in self-reflection and self-evaluation is to use the portfolio or the collection as the vehicle for conversation. For many teachers, this has been one of the most appealing aspects of using portfolios. Some even argue that getting students to use their portfolios for "self-analysis, assessment, and evaluation is the prime reason for its existence" (Farr & Tone, 1994).

Portfolios contribute to self-assessment in two ways. On one hand, portfolios provide a reason for looking closely at individual pieces—a sort of microscopic view of work. As students review their collections to select work to place into their portfolios they must reflect on and evaluate candidate pieces. On the other hand, because portfolios provide ongoing documentation of student learning, they provide students with opportunities to self-assess the "big picture," a sort of "macroscopic," aerial view of themselves as readers and writers. As students are guided to review old and new work in their portfolios, they can develop insights into their strengths, weaknesses, and possible future goals. As we pointed out earlier, these portfolio experiences will be enriched by the ongoing self-assessment context that is a natural part of the classroom.

Selecting Work for the Portfolio: The Microscopic View

Student entry slips can be useful when placing work into the portfolio because they encourage thoughtfulness about work and because they become a record of students' reflections. They can be completed individually by students, or they can be the product of a conversation between students, students and teachers, or students and parents. They can be written or dictated. As we've noted, it is important to stress the conversation over completion of the entry slip and to vary the entry slips, or purposes for selection, over time. Various entry slips were introduced in chapter 2 and management strategies for selecting portfolio pieces were discussed in chapter 3. Here we focus on the different types of reflection and evaluation students can develop as they are guided to select work to enter into their portfolios. Figures 6.13–6.15 provide examples of how entry slips can help students think about different aspects of their work. The prompts on these slips could just as easily be used as conversational prompts. And we suggest that you engage students in these kinds of discussions more often than they complete entry slips.

"Free choice" entry slips ("Select a piece for your portfolio and tell why you selected it") open the possibility for students to select in any way, inviting both self-reflection and self-evaluation. As one teacher commented, "You need to accept whatever you get if you use an open question." The advantage is that because you haven't directed students' thinking, you gain insight into what students value. For example, we learn that Lauren, a first grader, selected a picture retelling of a story because she worked hard and had nice drawings; Lauren R., a third-grade student, chose a book jacket because she understood and liked the book; and fifth grader Amrita chose a story that she wrote because she made it sound scary and worked hard on it. We have not found any particular grade-level differences in students' preferences when they have free choice—responses seem to depend on the students and on the particular piece they select.

It is useful to vary entry slips—not just for variety but also to help students explore other aspects of reflection and evaluation. The samples in Figure 6.14 focus students' attention on what makes work personally meaningful or special. Pride, interest, personal connection, and high quality surface

Figure 6.13

Grade 1

Student Entry Slip

Name *Lauren*

Date *May 7 1996*

I selected this for my portfolio because

I weted herd on it and
I liked my drings.

Signed _____

Grade 3

Student Entry
Date *4/8/97*

I am choosing this piece to put into my portfolio

because *It showed that I under stood*
This book. And it shows that I liked
this book to. Waterworld was a-interesting
book because it pulled me in
right at the start

Grade 5

ENTRY SLIP

I have chosen this piece of work (reading or writing) to

enter into my folder because *I made it sound*
a little scary and because I put a
lot of hard work in to it.

Name: *Amrita*   Date: *11/22/96*

---

*Three open-ended entry slips show the wide range of responses that
students have to their work.*

Figure 6.14

Grade 1   Entry Slip for an Individual Piece of Work
Self-Reflection -- Primary 
Name *the princess* Date *4-20-42*

This piece is my favorite because *I add'd details that where interesting to me and they look like it's going to be a winner*

Grade 3

STUDENT ENTRY SLIP FOR *Name this continent* 
DATE *3-20-96 March 20, 1996*

This piece is my **favorite** or **most meaningful** to me because *My mom is from Korea and I am Korean. Korea is in Asia.*

Signature

Grade 6   ENTRY SLIP FOR AN INDIVUAL PIECE OF WORK – Self Reflection

Name *The Stranger in the motel* Date *4/3/92*

After thinking about your choice and why you chose it, complete the
following paragraph and attach this slip to that piece of work.

I have chosen this piece of work because it is my favorite or the most
meaningful to me. It is my favorite or most meaningful because *this is a true story and it happened to me and a close friend. It is a factual story and it felt very good for me to get it out on paper. I went through the whole writing process, which improved the story and put alot of thought into it.*

*Responses to "favorite" or "most meaningful" choices vary by student,
grade level, and piece selected.*

Figure 6.15

STUDENT ENTRY
Date 2-10-97

I am proud of this work because it ~~shows I know how to~~ I think that my writing is good and I made good discreptions. I also like my picture. I liked it when we painted the trees with stenol. I like my tree that is on the right. I like my discription "here and there, to and through, back and forth."

This is an example of entry slips that encourage self-evaluation of learning.

across these various entry slips, again providing insights into these individual students' personal responses and values about their work. Teachers can also focus students' self-assessment on particular aspects of learning: what they know how to do or need to work on, evaluation of a bad piece, writing process, development of strong leads, ability to persuade, and so forth. The entry slips shown in Figure 6.15 are directed toward students' self-evaluation and standards, and they provide information about students' criteria for good work. They also provide an excellent model for teaching students that there is a great deal to learn from taking a critical stance toward their work. An added benefit is that students learn that portfolios are not necessarily showcases or places to put only good work. The focus you select for entry slips will depend on your instructional emphasis and the needs of your students.

Two points are important to keep in mind as students select work for their portfolios. The first is that simply selecting work, or even completing

Figure 6.15 *continued*

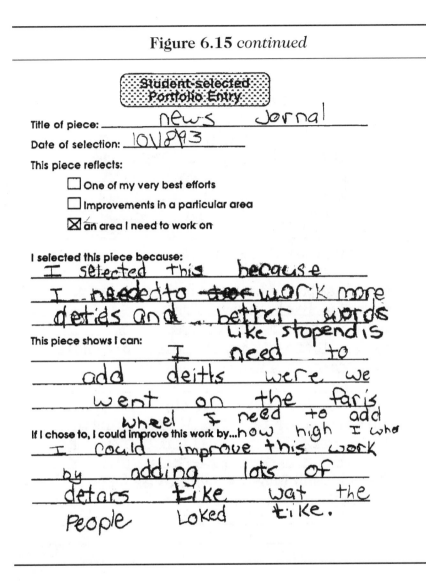

Student-selected
Portfolio Entry

Title of piece: _____ news   Jornal _____

Date of selection: 10\18\93 _____

This piece reflects:

☐ One of my very best efforts

☐ Improvements in a particular area

☒ an area I need to work on

I selected this piece because:

I selected this because
I needed to ㅡ work more
detieds and better words
Like stopend is

This piece shows I can: I need to
add deitls were we
went on the faris
wheel I need to add

If I chose to, I could improve this work by...how high I who
I Could improve this work
by adding lots of
detars like wat the
People Loked like.

an entry slip, doesn't assure that students are developing and learning about self-assessment. Teachers must guide and encourage discussions. The second is that students can expand their self-understanding if you guide them to look at their work in different ways, to take a variety of approaches or stances to self-assessment.

Portfolio Review: The Macroscopic View

Because portfolios contain concrete evidence of students' literacy accomplishments over time, they provide a good vehicle for discussions about long-range views of learning. In chapter 7 we discuss issues of growth and

---

Figure 6.15 *continued*

Oh, Never, Never Again!!!
(Aka For My Writing Portfolio)

I Have decided that the Candy Story
is my worst piece because It keeps on
jumping back and forth, and
it doesn't make sense at all.
The words are in the wrong
place and it's too long for
the kind of story it is.

Some things that I learned from this lousy
piece were that you don't use
candy bars to make long stories
I also learned that my grammer
wasn't correct.

. Thanks to this disasterous piece, I will
always remember to not use candy
bars in stories I will also remember
to out commas before a but
___. Wdors (oops!) Words I will never forget
how to spell:
1._____ 2._____
3._____ 4._____
_____5._____

These are examples of entry slips that encourage self-evaluation
of learning.

---

change, but here we focus on how to help students use that work to think
about, reflect on, and evaluate their learning. As we discussed in chapters 2 and 3, it is good to have a predictable schedule for students to visit
their portfolios, and it is best to focus initially on conversation rather than
on completing portfolio visit forms. In addition, giving students a task when
they are first sharing portfolios with peers helps them focus. For example,

one first-grade teacher asked her students to choose a partner for portfolio sharing. Their job was to take out all of the pieces, place them in chronological order on the floor, look them over, and then select one to share with their partners. They were to tell their partners how they had worked on the piece and what they liked about it. The partners were to ask one question. The teacher modeled and discussed with students how to go about the activity. She asked a few students to share various reasons for choosing a piece and asked others to suggest good questions for their partners. After this short modeling, the students were off on their own while the teacher circulated, providing help where needed and jotting down notes about students' insights. As we watched these little first graders with their huge portfolios', contents spread out like many Yellow Brick Roads, we were amazed at their engagement and the thoughtful way they selected one piece to share. After about 30 minutes, the teacher called the students together for a discussion about all of the different kinds of work the students had shared. As the students talked about their various reasons for choosing pieces, the teacher recorded their reasons on chart paper. These provided the basis for future portfolio discussions.

We observed a similar activity at a middle school. This time, students were asked to work with a partner to organize the contents of their portfolios. With a bit of discussion about alternative schemes for organization (sequential; preferences—like/dislike; topics; progress—worst to best; discipline—reading, writing, social studies), the students were off to work. The point of this activity was not so much to have students manage their portfolios as to get them closer to their work, to review and discuss learning with another person. In fact, as we observed these seventh-grade students sprawled on the floor deep in conversation with a peer, we noticed students reading each other's work, discussing strengths and weakness of each piece and comparing pieces across time. At the end of one class period the students were not finished with the task. They requested another class period to finish up!

There are many variations on this theme of having students use the contents of their portfolios to engage in discussion, each of which may have a slightly different purpose. For example, students might be asked to identify a piece or two that they are most proud of and to clarify what is meaningful to them; they could identify a piece that does not represent good work and analyze what was unsuccessful about it as a way to set new goals; or they could identify the projects that they most enjoyed as a way to gain insight into their interests and preferences. Notice that each purpose requires students to compare several pieces and to think deeply about their work, and it requires them to develop an understanding of criteria to fit these different purposes ("What makes me proud?" "What is personally meaningful to me?" "What is good work?" "What would I have to do to improve this work?" "What do I like to do?"). Our experience suggests that having a clear reason for portfolio review makes the activity more meaningful and more productive. Limiting the number of pieces that students review is also a good idea, especially when asking students more global questions such as how they have changed as readers and writers. For example, students could choose one piece of writing from the beginning, middle, and end of the year to analyze how they have changed. This is much more manageable than reviewing 10 to 15 pieces. And, it makes it more likely that teachers can help students clarify important areas of growth in writing.

The first few times teachers in our portfolio group asked students to conduct discussions like these, the teachers were concerned that it took so long. One teacher commented, "Yes, the kids were very engaged, more than I've seen in a long time. But I have so much to teach that I'm afraid to use my time this way." After several more months, one colleague offered a new insight: "I used to worry about how much time this took, but now I realize that this is not time away from teaching, it *is* teaching. I even spend *more* time now helping students get ready for the discussion so they know what they need to think about. My kids get more from this activity than some of the other activities I used to do with them. And the results of their efforts (or lack of it) are clear to them, not just the teacher."

In other chapters we have provided examples of portfolio visits and letters to next year's teacher. Figures 6.16–6.18 show several different forms that this long-range self-assessment might take. Figure 6.16 was written by a youngster at the end of second grade after she took a portfolio visit to review work for the entire year; Figure 6.17 shows a section of a midyear portfolio visit dictated by a third-grade child with learning difficulties; and Figure 6.18 was a fall portfolio visit of a fifth-grade youngster. Note how students can be guided to look specifically at the preferences, strengths, needs, and goals. It is best for students to complete forms like these *after* they have engaged in the kinds of discussion we described earlier. Self-assessment over time is difficult, especially if we want students to understand themselves in specific ways rather than simply understand that they are "better." They need time to study their work by examining concrete evidence of their learning. As a result, their self-assessment will be realistic, grounded, specific, and useful.

Conclusion

Self-reflection and self-evaluation are essential aspects of learning. Just like other important educational goals, self-assessment must be taught, practiced, and nurtured in meaningful contexts. In this chapter we have provided ideas for how to help students develop these dispositions as they work on everyday classroom activities and as they use their portfolios. We have stressed the importance of discussion, instruction, and time in helping students develop their self-assessment abilities. This is not to minimize the importance of written reflections and evaluations. Writing experts remind us that we write to learn, not just to record what we already know (Graves, 1994); in the same way, written reflections can help students learn about

---

Figure 6.16

What I lerned this year

by Lauren

1 **I lerned how to right much better then I did when school started I did not know how to right vary much but since the school year has encresed I have lerned how to right much batter then I did when the school year sarted.**

2 **At the begening of the school year I did not know how to reed vary much but thow the school year has gon past I have lerned a lot mere werds then I know when school stared like for instens here is tow werds that I lerned dering the school year**
1 **School**   2 **Beacuse**
now thes where hard to lern but I did lern themand I felt proud when I did lern beacuse and school and I also felt proud when I lerned ather woreds that I did not know beffer school started and I felt and stell fell now rilly happy and prowd that I did lern the words.

This end-of-year reflection by a second-grade student reveals her pride and general sense of growth.

---

themselves and their work. Our emphasis on discussion in this chapter is intended as a reminder not to use portfolios simply to have students complete self-assessment tasks, self-assessment "worksheets"—that would be a sad misinterpretation of the purpose of self-assessment and of portfolios. Portfolios can be valuable vehicles for exploring self-reflection and self-evaluation, as can many other classroom activities.

The self-assessment strategies in this chapter offer a range of support for students as they tackle new ways to think about their learning. In addition to advocating instruction and teacher modeling, we have tried to

Figure 6.17

```
┌─────────────────────┐
│  Portfolio  Visit   │
└─────────────────────┘
```

Look at your portfolio work. Think about the learning that has been happening for you in class and at home. Then answer these questions. They will help you think about your reading, writing and math work.

1. How much do you like to read?

   ● very much   ○ some   ○ a little bit   ○ not at all

Why? *~~Something~~ I like to read because ~~&~~ ~~then~~ I find stories interesting. The people are interesting too!*

2. What kind of a reader are you?

   I like adventure stories the best.

3. How much do you like to write?

   ● very much   ○ some   ○ a little bit   ○ not at all

Why? *I like to write because it ~~exercises~~ exercises my head.*

4. What kind of a writer are you? *I like to write adventure stories and poems.*

A third-grade student dictated his visit responses after spending time with his portfolio.

---

exemplify varying levels of structure and guidance that teachers can build into different self-assessment tasks, whether they are written or oral. For example, some tasks are highly structured, others are more open-ended; some require evaluation against standards, others require personal response; some require students to provide reasons, others ask for rankings or pictures. In addition, sometimes the learning task about which students are reflecting is difficult (complex research report, a piece taken through the writing process), and at other times it is less demanding (creating artwork, participating in literature circle, answering questions). Keep these

---

Figure 6.18

Fall Portfolio Visit

Reading

1. How good of a reader am I?

> I am a good reader because I can reread what I don't under-stand and then understand. I love to read! Especially mysterys!!!

2. What books have I read so far this school year? (at home and at school)

> I have read... Catherine called B The Midwifes apperantice, Nasty stinke Sneakers, dealing with dragons.

3. What can I do to be a better reader?

> What I could do to do be a better reader would be to get a book that is just right for me (my reading level).

---

factors in mind as you decide how to best help students learn the skill and the will of self-assessment.

Our goal is to weave student self-assessment into the fabric of everyday classroom activities and into portfolios. It gives students value and control over their learning. But it is not just students who benefit from their own self-assessment. If we are open to looking, we can also learn a great deal about ourselves, as teachers, from our students' self-reflections and evaluations. When the majority of our students talk about the importance of handwriting and spelling, we learn that we may be unintentionally sending the

---

Figure 6.18 *continued*

Writing

How good of a writer am I?

I have a great mind and I can be creative in many ways. I stay usually to one topic. I organize my writing so that it makes sense

How is the appearance of my written work?

My writing is very organize!

How are my editing skills?

I can identify miss spelled words when nobody else can!

What can I do to be a better writer?

I can plan before wirting and redd back/to see if I made any mastaiks. I can organize my ideas ly putti in my own words!

This fifth grader is able to identify her specific reading and writing strengths and needs.

---

message that these are most important in writing. Or when many students discuss how their work makes them feel, we learn that we are helping students develop meaningful connections and ownership of their work. If we are brave enough to engage in our own self-reflection and self-evaluation, students' insights can provide a rich data source for our own professional growth. This is the true definition of teachers and students learning together. And this is the only way for all of us to succeed.

References

Beach, R., & Hynds, S. (1991). Research on response to literature. In R. Barr, M. L. Kamil, P. Mosenthal, & P. D. Pearson (Eds.), *Handbook of reading research, Vol. II* (pp 453–489). New York: Longman.

Camp, R. (1990). Thinking together about portfolios. *The Quarterly, 12*(2), 8–14, 27.

Carroll, J. H., & Christenson, C. N.-K. (1995). Teaching and learning about student goal setting in a fifth-grade classroom. *Language Arts, 72,* 42–49.

Costa, A. L. (1989). Re-assessing assessment. *Educational Leadership, 46*(7), 2.

Delpit, L. (1995). Other people's children: Cultural conflict in the classroom. New York: The New Press.

Farr, R., & Tone, B. (1994). *Portfolio performance assessment.* Fort Worth, TX: Harcourt Brace College Publishers.

Graves, D. H. (1994). *A fresh look at writing.* Portsmouth, NH: Heinemann.

Hansen, J. (1992). Students' evaluations bring reading and writing together. *The Reading Teacher, 46*(2), 100–105.

Higgins, K. M., Harris, N. A., & Kuehn, L. L. (1994). Placing assessment into the hands of young children: A study of student-generated criteria and self-assessment. *Educational Assessment, 2*(4), 309–324.

Howard, K. (1990). Making the writing portfolio real. *Quarterly of the National Writing Project and the Center for the Study of Writing, 12*(2), 4–7, 27.

International Reading Association & National Council of Teachers of English. (1994). *Standards for the assessment of reading and writing.* Newark, DE: International Reading Association.

Johnston, P. H. (1987). Assessing the process and the process of assessment in the language arts. In J. Squire (Ed.), *The dynamics of language learning: Research in reading and English* (pp. 335–357). Urbana, IL: National Conference on Research in English/ERIC.

Johnston, P. H., & Winograd, P. N. (1985). Passive failure in reading. *Journal of Reading Behavior, 17*(4), 279–301.

National Council on Education Standards and Testing. (1992). *Raising standards for American education.* Washington, DC: Author.

Paris, S. G., Lipson, M. Y., & Wixson, K. K. (1983). Becoming a strategic reader. *Contemporary Educational Psychology, 8*(3), 293–316.

Pressley, M., & Afflerbach, P. (1995). *Verbal protocols of reading.* Hillsdale, NJ: Lawrence Erlbaum Associates.

Rief, L. (1990). Finding the value in evaluation: Self-evaluation in a middle school classroom. *Educational Leadership, 47*(6), 24–29.

Rowntree, D. (1987). *Assessing students: How shall we know them?* New York: Nichols.

Short, K., & Kauffman, G. (1992). Hearing students' voices: The role of reflection in learning. *The Whole Language Newsletter, 11*(3), 1–6.

Spandel, V. (1994). *Seeing with new eyes: A guidebook on teaching and assessing beginning writers.* Portland, OR: Northwest Regional Educational Laboratories.

Stiggins, R. J. (1997). *Student-centered classroom assessment* (2nd ed.). New York: Macmillan College Publishing.

Valencia, S.W. (1990). A portfolio approach to classroom reading assessment: The whys, whats, and hows. *The Reading Teacher, 43*(4), 338–340.

Vygotsky, L. (1978). *Mind in society: The development of higher psychological process.* Cambridge, MA: Harvard University Press.

Weiner, B. (1979). A theory of motivation for some classroom experiences. *Journal of Educational Psychology, 71*(1), 3–25.

Wiggins, G. P. (1993). *Assessing student performance.* San Francisco: Jossey-Bass.

Wolf, D. P. (1989). Portfolio assessment: Sampling student work. *Educational Leadership, 46*(7), 35–39.

chapter 7

Examining Growth Over Time

NANCY PLACE AND MARLA ENGLISH

This chapter takes a longitudinal view of learning—growth over time. Using portfolio artifacts collected over one, two, or three years, we look closely at several students and their progress over time. We examine the ebbs and flows of typical students' progress in reading and writing, special considerations of growth for students with special needs, and changes in literacy dispositions and self-assessment over time. We close with a discussion of special considerations for using portfolios to document student growth.

I've come so far this year. I'm come from Beverly Cleary to Edgar Allan Poe.

L. S., middle school special education student

Few assessments value individual students and their progress over time. Instead, most traditional assessments capture student performance at one moment in time, in an artificially constrained context, over a narrow range of literacy tasks. Although these snapshots taken with traditional assessments provide some useful information, they do not provide the full motion picture of a child's development. As teachers, we pride ourselves on bringing students along, taking them where they are, and helping them move to new levels of understanding and proficiency. This is the concept of growth we want for all of our students, and this is the unique type of information portfolios can provide.

Portfolios offer an opportunity for teachers, parents, and students to see directly changes in a student's learning and thinking over time (Simmons & Resnick, 1993; Valencia, 1990; Wolf, LeMahieu, & Eresh, 1992). Tangible evidence and accumulated "history" in portfolios draw attention to growth. So, in one sense, portfolios help us document what is uniquely changing or growing for a particular student. In another sense, portfolios help us *use* growth to set goals and to plan for instruction. By carefully studying a student's portfolio work, we gain an understanding not only of her capabilities but also of her unique learning trajectory. That is, we can understand the student's rate of learning, the level of support she needs to perform particular tasks, and her special interests and dispositions. As a result, expectations and instruction are better matched with the student's particular learning needs.

There are several ways to think about student growth. One way is to see growth (or the lack of it) in terms of a student's abilities to read and write more sophisticated or more complex texts. For example, Larry, the student quoted at the beginning of this chapter, reflects that he is able to read more challenging material at the end of the year than at the beginning. His teacher concurs that Larry now reads with greater fluency and comprehension and that Larry is able to use strategies to monitor and to adjust his reading. Larry's portfolio contains evidence documenting this growing sophistication, not just in terms of his reading and understanding of *Henry* and *The Raven* but in terms of other reading material throughout the year.

A second way to think about growth is in terms of students' progress against their own unique needs rather than against norms or grade-level expectations. This is critical for children with special needs, such as students in special education and limited English proficient students, who comprise a substantial percentage of school-age children. Surveys suggest that more than 10 percent of all school-age children receive special education services (U.S. Department of Education, 1993) and that more than 5 percent of all students are classified as limited English proficient (National Research Council, 1997). These are children for whom progress may not be visible using traditional measures. Often, their growth is judged against criteria specified in an individualized educational program (IEP) or individual measures of English proficiency—standards that require students to demonstrate progress but not necessarily to meet grade-level expectations.

A third way to think about growth considers aspects of reading and writing other than achievement—students' interests, dispositions, self-reflection, and self-evaluation. We know that amount and breadth of reading and writing are related to achievement (Allen, Michalove, Shockley, & West, 1991; Anderson, Wilson, & Fielding, 1988; Hillocks, 1984; Morrow & Weinstein, 1986) and that people who are capable readers and writers are more likely to be active participants in society and the workplace (Guthrie, Schafer, Wang, & Afflerbach, 1993). And we know that students' ability to engage in self-assessment will enhance their understanding about work quality, processes, and sense of self (Lipson & Wixson, 1997). Naturally, we want students to grow in these areas as well.

In this chapter, we take a longitudinal view of several students, using their portfolios to highlight these three aspects of growth in reading and writing. In the first section, we focus on changes in reading and writing abilities. Max, a beginning reader and writer, provides a good example of a student who is learning to deal with increasingly complex texts and who, in the process, is both advancing and regressing. In the second section, we meet Jason, a special education student, who demonstrates his growth in small but important ways, and Saori, a limited English proficient (LEP) student from Japan who is making a fast transition to English. For these children, portfolios show growth that would not otherwise be recognized. In the third section, we highlight growth in literacy habits, dispositions, self-reflection, and self-evaluation using artifacts from a variety of primary and intermediate students. Finally, we conclude with several special considerations for using portfolios to showcase student growth.

Growth in Reading and Writing Abilities

It would be convenient if students' abilities grew continuously, like a 45-degree angle on a graph, a steadily progressing journey up a mountain to its summit; performance would improve from November to January to June. However, learning is not that neat, and student performance is not that steady. The climb is not straight up a mountain but more likely up and down a series of peaks and valleys with many resting places along the way. This variability is to be expected from an interactive model of reading in which different factors come together to influence student reading and writing performance (Lipson & Wixson, 1997). *Student* factors (e.g., background knowledge, motivation, reading and writing strategies), *text and task* factors (e.g., topic, difficulty, structure, or type of text), and *context* factors (e.g., amount and type of teacher assistance or peer collaboration) all influence student performance and engagement.

These realizations about variability in student performance over time hold two important implications for examining students' growth from portfolios. First, growth will not be steady, but rather a series of painfully slow and surprisingly fast moments of progress. Students will even appear to regress as they take new risks and try out new strategies, texts, and tasks. Second, this variability will require us to look across many pieces over time. We will need to look for patterns of growth rather than rely on single pieces at specific points in time.

Max: A Developing Reader and Writer

Max's portfolio has followed him from first to third grade, providing us with a good example of the ups and downs of reading and writing growth. As a first grader, Max spent most of his time writing about *Jurassic Park* and its terrifying dinosaurs. Because Max wrote stories on the same theme throughout the year, his growth in writing was particularly visible. In the beginning of the year, Max primarily used pictures to tell his story. The text was usually a single sentence, dictated or written, which described the picture. However, sometimes Max would treat the picture and story as two unrelated pieces. Figure 7.1 is a good example of how Max relied on *Jurassic Park* pictures even when the story prompt and his dictated story were about something else.

A short time later, in December, Max used pictures and written text to tell a more developed *Jurassic Park* story (see Figure 7.2). Although the story line appears a bit vague, it is clear that Max has relied on the *Jurassic*

Figure 7.1

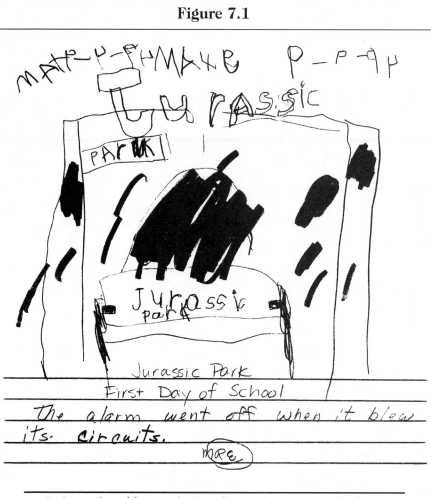

MAT-P-PHMAKE P-P-9H
JURASSIC
PARK
Jurassic
Park
Jurassic Park
First Day of School
The alarm went off when it blew
its. circuits.
MORE

In September of first grade, Max draws about Jurassic Park but dictates a story about the assigned topic: the first day of school.

Park story line to sequence his events. He began this story by retelling part of the movie to his teacher, then he drew pictures, and then he did his writing. In contrast to his early piece, Max now has stories that match his pictures.

Toward the end of first grade, Max still writes about *Jurassic Park* in his piece, "Jurassic Jungle" (see Figure 7.3 on page 227). Although the story is still related to the *Jurassic Park* theme in its title and general topic (boys meet terrifying animals), now Max tells a story that has original content. This story is a narrative with a connected sequence of events and related characters (except for the monkeys!); it has a clear beginning, middle, and end. Rather than using sentences just to label his pictures, Max used a variety of sentences in this second piece. We can see Max's developing sense of story.

We can also learn a great deal about Max's developing use of process writing from his teachers' entry slips (see Figure 7.4 on page 230). The notes indicate that Max prewrote with pictures in December but that in May he went directly to writing after brainstorming. In fact, "Jurassic Jungle" was originally written as four paragraphs without any pictures; Max generated pictures after he completed word processing for publication. We also learn that Max wrote first drafts of both pieces independently. In December Mrs. English word processed the story for Max, and he did no additional editing, proofreading, or revising for content. However, in May Max stood by, making many revisions to the content of his story, as Mrs. English word processed "Jurassic Jungle" for publication. In Max's words, "I wanted to make it more exciting." In this piece Max was telling a story for others, not simply remembering for himself. In addition, Max chose the text breaks and later added illustrations, a reversal from his earlier process in which the picture always came first. For Max at the end of his first-grade year, the text had become more important than the pictures.

Figure 7.2

Figure 7.2 *continued*

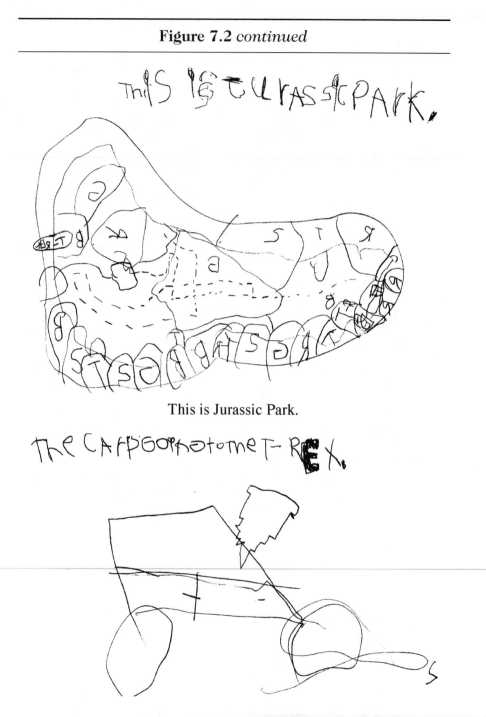

This is Jurassic Park.

The car is going to the T-Rex.

Figure 7.2 *continued*

The T-Rex is going to the car.

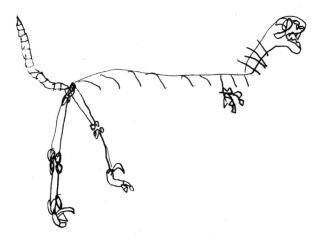

The power is (the) electric fence.

Figure 7.2 *continued*

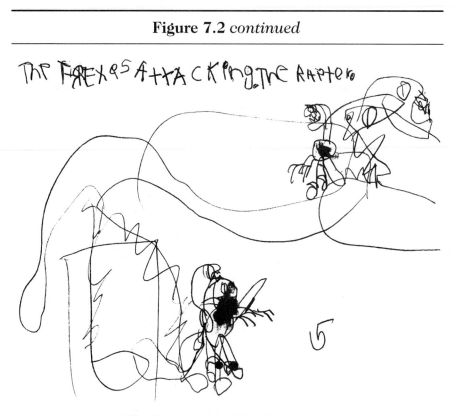

The T-rex is attacking the raptor.

Max's Jurassic Park story, written in December, follows many of the events in the movie. The full story reads: "This is Jurassic Park. The car is going to the T-rex. The T-rex is going to the car. The power is electric fence. The T-rex is attacking the raptor. [This is the T-rex. This is the boy. The Utah raptor is attacking Lex."]

Other aspects of Max's growth in writing are evident from a close review of these samples of his written work. Max's understanding of the conventions of writing (periods, capitals at the beginning of sentences, and capitals for proper nouns) has improved over time, and he has begun to edit for punctuation. On first glance, it may appear that Max's concepts of print and invented spelling have regressed. His writing is easier to decipher, and word boundaries are a bit more common in the December story. However, as Max takes on new content and writes more, as he does in May, he is trying out his skills in more complex material, making some of his skills more difficult to apply. At the same time, he has gained more confidence in his ability to use invented spelling to tell his story. A careful analysis of Max's

Figure 7.3

Jurassic Jungle

Cover

by Max

May 1995

This book is dedicated to Me.

Excerpt from page 1

One day two boys were going to the Jungle.

When they got in the jungle they found a tree house but they did not know that some monkeys were close by.

Excerpt from page 2

Figure 7.3 *continued*

They went to a pond and they saw a tiger on the other side. He chased them back to the tree house. The two boys climbed up the ladder with the tiger following them.

Excerpt from page 3

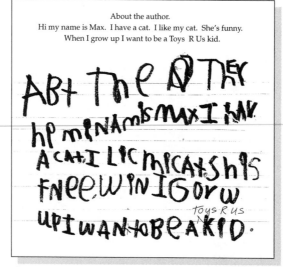

About the author.
Hi my name is Max. I have a cat. I like my cat. She's funny. When I grow up I want to be a Toys R Us kid.

Max's "Jurassic Jungle" story, written in May, demonstrates his creation of an original story inspired by Jurassic Park.

first-grade writing reveals that he is spelling many words correctly (*day, and, the jungle, in, tiger, tree, climbed, they, end*) and using his invented spelling effectively (*laeder = ladder, win = when, thm = them*).

Max's second-grade portfolio has very few writing examples. Two teacher entry slips indicate that Max has not been completing his writing. Mrs. English notes that Max has moved away from movie scenarios to his own stories but that he is having difficulty with endings; he seems to be reconceptualizing the concept of "what is a story?" On a classroom writing self-evaluation, Max has checked the line that reads, "I don't finish my stories" and lists as his goal to "finish stories." The pieces that are in the portfolio reflect different topics (one piece on rivers and wars, another piece done on the computer about animals), indicating some risk-taking on Max's part, but these pieces don't have a focus or purpose. They are disjointed, isolated bits of information. The last writing piece in the portfolio for second grade is a cohesive piece written on the *Jurassic Park* theme again, with the familiar introduction and a beginning, middle, and end.

In attempting new ground, writing stories that reflected his own imagination and not that of a movie scenario, Max was stalled as he tried to assemble the elements in a new way. At the end of second grade, he returned to his tried-and-true topic to complete a story. Then, at the beginning of his third-grade year, Max began writing his own complete stories on other topics. The pattern for Max was to explore writing in new genres, struggle, pull back, and then reengage with the challenge. As children come to new understandings, they often regress until they can reformulate the elements into something new. Portfolios can help teachers recognize the new thinking that students are doing even when they appear to regress. It is a natural process, but one that often obscures evidence of growth.

Max's portfolio also shows his growth in reading. As you might predict, his favorite books, recorded on his book log, were about dinosaurs, jungles, and *Jurassic Park*. His developing knowledge about these topics and his ability to make reading/writing connections are reflected as he used "official" dinosaur names in his stories and borrowed elements of plot and character from the movie. Running records (Clay, 1979; see also chapter 4) from November of his first-grade year show that Max was reading at primer level. At this time Mrs. English noted that he was an "impulsive reader" who depended on the pictures and the repeating structure of the language to get the meaning from the text. Later in the year (February) Max was able to read first-grade text, but Mrs. English noted that because he wanted to read quickly he still relied heavily on pictures, his background knowledge and on cues from the language structure to get meaning from the text. Although Max was able to read slightly more difficult text in February, Mrs. English noted that he still relied primarily on initial consonants combined with pictures and language structure to identify unknown words. He did not appear to use ending consonants, vowel patterns, or word families. Without such a careful analysis of Max's reading strategies, we might be misled by Max's ability to read more difficult text. He had, after all, progressed from primer

---

Figure 7.4

TEACHER   ENTRY   SLIP
Published Work

Date: __12-8-94__

I have selected this piece for __Maxwell__

portfolio because it demonstrates current best writing which was taken
through a publishing process to a final copy.
Additional comments:

_____Marla English/Barb Renfrow-Baker_____
Signature

Who helped with this work? Briefly tell how each one helped.

1.   PREWRITE ACTIVITY: pictures/mind map/class brainstorm/other?
      independently/with support *max has written almost
      exclusively about Jurassic Park.*

2.   WRITING: Wrote independently/with support-- *Mrs. English has done*
      --on a self-selected topic *Some structured writing on*
      --on a directed topic--prompt: *3 other J.P. stories using*
                                      key words. This story inde-
                                      pendently.

3.   EDITING: Did first editing for spelling/punctuation
      independently/with support. *N/A*

4.   SPELL CHECK: Used hand-held spell checker--yes/no

5.   WORD PROCESSING: Did word processing independently/with support
      or adult or class helper did all word processing *Mrs. Baker did all.*

6.   PROOFREAD word-processed copy for spelling/punctuation
      independently/with support. *N/A*

7.   EDITED FOR CONTENT on word-processed copy independently/
      with support *N/A*

8.   PRESENTED TO CLASS independently/with support

---

level to first-grade text. With a careful analysis, however, his teachers could
acknowledge this growth and still recognize his need to develop and apply
sound/symbol strategies.

Max's second-grade portfolio contains summaries of grade-level reading
passages along with modified running records of those passages. Mrs.
English took dictation of Max's summaries, "scaffolding" the task for him
(Applebee & Langer, 1983; Graves & Graves, 1994) so that Max's writing
wouldn't interfere with assessment of his reading comprehension. In October Max gave a sketchy summary of a second-grade story that he read (see
Figure 7.5). He omitted important information, and he included only information stated explicitly in the text. The summary was not complete. His

Figure 7.4 *continued*

TEACHER ENTRY SLIP--WRITING PROCESS

Date:_5-1-95_____

I have selected this piece for _Max_____'s portfolio because it demonstrates current best writing which was taken through a publishing process to a final copy.

Circle one: **The student requested to publish this story.

**The teacher suggested publishing this story.

Additional comments:

Who helped with this work? Briefly tell how each one helped.

1. PREWRITE ACTIVITY: picture or series of pictures/mind map/class brainstorm/other?   --independently/with   support

2. WRITING: Wrote independently/with support--
   --on a self-selected topic
   --on a directed topic--prompt:

3. EDITING: Did first editing for spelling/punctuation
   --independently/with   support.

4. SPELL CHECK: Used hand-held spell checker--yes/no

5. WORD PROCESSING: Did word processing independently/with support
   or adult or class helper did all word processing

6. PROOFREAD/EDITED word-processed copy for spelling/punctuation
   --independently/with support.

7. REVISED FOR CONTENT on word-processed copy independently/
   with support   *a word processing*
   --changed or added individual words   *was being done. Only*
   --revised or added individual sentences *added and changed*
   --restructured or added paragraphs   *some content. little*
                                            words "To make it more
8. PRESENTED TO CLASS independently/with support *exciting."*

_____Marla English/Barb Renfrow-Baker_____
Signature

Teacher entry slips from Max's December and May Jurassic Park stories record observations about his writing process.

---

teacher noted at this time that he was able to sound through parts of words he did not know and that he "appealed" (asked for help) to the teacher to verify that the word he had identified was correct. Max also noted that "the story was a little bit hard. There were no pictures and some long words. The pictures help me read a little better." Max was becoming aware of his own reading strategies. At the end of February Max read and gave another

---

Figure 7.5

OUTCOME: INTERACTS WITH TEXT

Format: Story Summarizing

Student's name: Max
Date: ~~3/2~~ *10/29/95*
Story title: Summer

PROMPT: Write or tell a summary of the story you have just read or heard. Your summary should be just long enough to include the most important ideas and information in the story. A good summary tells someone who has not read the story what it is mainly about.

Teacher Prompt: This story is about: " The story is about Mr. Pig, Mrs. Cat, Mrs. Dog and Mr. Frog. They visited each others garden. They thought that some of the gardens were good. They thought the bone garden was a dirt garden."
Teacher Prompt: What do you think the author wanted people to learn from reading this story/ " That there are lots of different kinds of gardens."
Teacher Prompt: What did you like about the story? " That it had different kinds of animals."
Teacher Prompt: How was this story to read? " It was a little bit hard. There were no pictures and some long words. The pictures help me read a little better."
Teacher Prompt: Did you like the story? "Not really, I like to read about real things not pretend things."

Teacher Prompt:
Does this story remind you of anything in your own life?"
Max— "No I'm not into gardening."

In October of second grade, Max's dictated summary of a second-grade story is incomplete.

---

summary of a second-grade story (see Figure 7.6). This time, the summary was coherent and included significant details and some inferences. He still had some difficulty understanding the author's message. This time, Max's teacher noted that he read aloud with expression. He sounded through words he did not know, and he reread to confirm after he had self-corrected. He did not "appeal" to the teacher. He noted that, "I could read almost all

---

Figure 7.6

OUTCOME: INTERACTS WITH TEXT

Format: Story Summarizing

Student's name: Max
Date: 2/29/96
Story title: Chicken Pox

PROMPT: Write or tell a summary of the story you have just read or heard. Your summary should be just long enough to include the most important ideas and information in the story. A good summary tells someone who has not read the story what it is mainly about.

Teacher Prompt: This story is about: " At first everyone got the chicken pox but Emily. She was mad because the other kids got to do and special things because of the chicken pox. But she didn't. Then she got the chicken pox but she was so sick. They were all over her and she was so sick she didn't get to do any of the fun stuff. Leo comes to Emily and he tells her the only good thing about chicken pox is that you can only get them once.

Teacher Prompt: What do you think the author wanted people to learn from reading this story/ " That you can only get the chicken pox once."

Teacher Prompt: What did you like about the story? " That some kids got to have choice all say when there was just a few left in the class. I would love to do that and have all the K'nexs and play the computer all day long."

Teacher Prompt: How was this story to read? "It was pretty easy. I could read almost all the words. If I didn't know the word I sounded it out.

Teacher Prompt: How were the main characters in the story? " Emily, Zack and Leo."

Teacher Prompt: What was the setting of the story? " It was mostly at school."

In February Max's dictated summary of a second-grade story is cohesive and includes important information.

---

the words. If I didn't know the word I sounded it out." He recognized and used new reading strategies.

Running records and summaries of reading passages are two assessment tools that Max's teacher included in his portfolio to show his growth in reading. Through these tools we can see Max's growth from the beginning stage of reading (using picture clues and repeating language structures with primer-level text) to a later stage when phonics cues are integrated with meaning and language structure as he reads a second-grade-level story. Not only did Max use these strategies, but also he was aware of them and therefore more likely to use them flexibly. At the same time, Max's summaries show an increasing understanding of story structure. Book logs and book projects in Max's portfolio provide added evidence of the kinds of books that Max was choosing as well as his developing reading preferences.

Looking across two years of reading and writing evidence in Max's portfolio, we see striking parallels in his growth. For example, Max's difficulty providing reading summaries paralleled the period in which he was struggling with writing stories, and his ability to rely less on picture cues and more on phonics paralleled a growth spurt in invented spelling. We also see a child who was taking risks in his reading and writing and who was becoming more metacognitively aware of his own reading and writing process over time. Max's portfolio provides a vivid picture of Max's growth. By looking at evidence of reading and writing ability over time, teachers, students, and parents are encouraged to take a broader view of development and to appreciate the ebbs and flows in learning.

Documenting Progress With Special Students

Portfolios have tremendous potential for demonstrating the growth of special education or limited English proficient students. It is difficult for these students—whose growth may be slow when compared with that of other students or who speak a home language other than English—to show progress on conventional measures. For these students, portfolios provide a method of seeing changes over the long term that might be missed in daily classroom interactions. Portfolios can provide a way of seeing strengths that are not visible on standard tests. They are also a way for students to validate their own growth and the impact that effort can have on their learning. Growth and progress can be seen and celebrated by assessing students against themselves rather than assessing them against a norm.

Jason: Growth for a Child With Special Needs

Jason is a child who suffered brain damage at birth. His speech, reading, and writing were delayed in developing and continue to be delayed. He is mainstreamed for most of the day in a multiaged classroom for grades one, two, and three. Although he is unable to obtain a score on conventional tests of reading and writing, his portfolio allows his teachers to see areas of great strength and growth. The changes are most obvious in the increased complexity and coherence of Jason's drawing and oral language.

Jason's self-portraits provide a graphic illustration of his growth in drawing, development, and representational understanding (see Figure 7.7). Jason's self-portrait at the beginning of second grade shows a long extended

Figure 7.7

Beginning of 2nd grade   End of second grade

Jason's self-portraits from the beginning and end of second grade reveal his increased representational understanding and fine motor control.

triangle with a circle at the top, two flipper-like arms protruding about one-third down the triangle, and two rectangles (feet) at either side of the bottom. The emphasis on head, arms, and legs with few details is representative of young children's drawings. His self-portrait at the end of the year shows a happy figure with a square trunk, arms, and legs, and a head with eyes, smiling mouth, cheeks, and hair. The figure is wearing a hat with a visor and a T-shirt that reads "Mighty Ducks." The increased detail and more accurate representation of a person reveal a substantial growth in Jason's development (Lowenfeld & Brittain, 1975).

The increasing differentiation and detail in Jason's drawings mirror the increasing differentiation in his dictation. At the beginning of first grade, Jason dictated only single words to describe his drawings—"policeman," "candy." At the end of second grade he wrote, dictated, and illustrated the following story.

> One day the bees were buzzing around a bee hive. They were making honey in their hive. A man made a bee trap. He caught the bees in the trap. The bears come [*sic*] and ate the honey because bears like honey. A man put the honey that was on a honeycomb into a glass jar. Then he took the honey home and ate it.

In this story, Jason tells a connected narrative using a variety of sentence structures, as opposed to single words. Although the story loses direction a bit between men and bears, it does have a beginning, a middle, and an end. Jason stays with the topic of bees and provides lots of information related to them throughout the story.

Jason demonstrated background knowledge about bees in this writing. At the time that he wrote this, some of the students in Jason's class were making "bee traps." There were many conversations about bees and honey. Jason included what he was learning about bees in his story. The portfolio provided one way for his teachers to see what Jason was getting from listening to class discussions. If we were simply to examine his written version of this story (see Figure 7.8), Jason's progress in oral language and sense of story would not have been apparent. For Jason, as for other special education students, portfolios may not solve the problem of documenting growth unless teachers adjust their assessment techniques to fit the needs of the student. In this case, the teacher included many more dictated pieces, drawings, work supported by an adult, and anecdotal records than she typically included in other students' portfolios. Portfolios have great potential for special education students, allowing teachers to adapt assessment strategies to meet individual students' needs.

Jason's portfolio also provided a record of his own sense of efficacy as a learner. In a portfolio visit at the end of his third-grade year, Mrs. English asked him, "How have you changed as a reader since the beginning of the year?" Jason spontaneously selected two books to demonstrate to his teacher how he had changed. Referring to a predictable preprimer book with two to three words per page, he said, "I used to read an easy book like *The Big Hill.*" Then, referring to primer-level book with several sentences per page, he proudly proclaimed, "Now I read a long book, *Down on the Funny Farm.*" When asked what he does well as a reader, Jason said, "I can remember the whole word." His goal was to be able to "read all the words."

Figure 7.8

Figure 7.8 *continued*

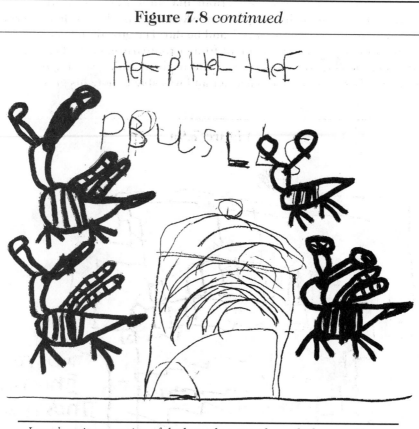

Jason's written version of the honeybee story bears little resemblance to his dictated story.

At this point, Jason realized that he was beginning to recognize words, and Mrs. English confirmed her observations that Jason was remembering words by sight rather than using sounds or context clues to identify words.

Jason also reported that he had changed as a writer since the beginning of the year. He indicated that he had learned the difference between words and letters when he said, "I used to just write lots of long letters. Now I can write words." Once again, he used evidence to make his point. From his portfolio, Jason pulled a second-grade sample that had random letters and an end-of-third-grade sample with a list of words he had copied from a book on lions that he had used for his research project (see Figures 7.9a and b). Although Jason couldn't write these words on his own and it was unlikely that he could read or remember them, he recognized them as words that carry meaning, and he was proud. In his portfolio was another drawing and sample of writing taken from February of third grade that demonstrate some words Jason could write on his own (Figure 7.10). Although the words don't match the picture, Jason's dictated entry slip reveals that he wanted to be able to write words and to use periods like all writers do. Again, he was proud of his accomplishments. When asked what he does well as a writer Jason stated, "I do great pictures," and he did. The growth in his fine motor control and organization is evident from a comparison of the beginning of second grade (Figure 7.9) with the end of third grade (see Figure 7.10). Jason clearly saw himself as a learner and was able to note his progress.

Figure 7.9a

Figure 7.9b

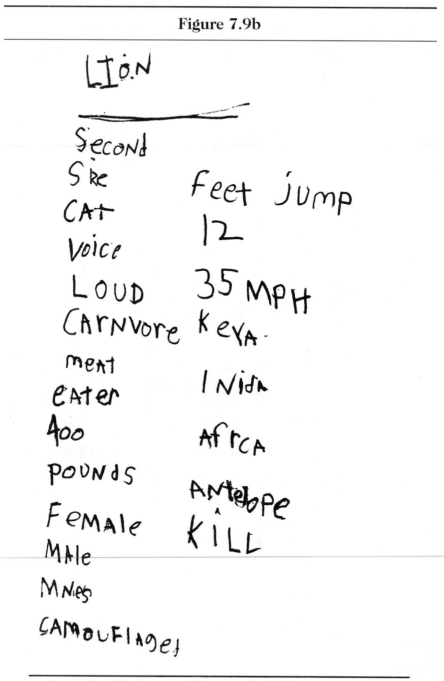

Jason selected two pieces of evidence from his portfolio—random letters from the beginning of second grade and self-selected words copied out of a book at the end of third grade—to demonstrate his writing progress.

Figure 7.10

Words written independently by Jason at the end of third grade don't seem to relate to the picture (the, go, to, on, he), but they do represent his understanding that writers use words to communicate.

Jason's Individualized Education Plans (IEPs) for his first-, second-, and third-grade years list the improvement of reading skills, written language skills, and math calculation skills as the academic goals. The focus in the IEPs over the three years is on developing letter recognition and sight vocabulary, reading easy books, and writing letters and sentences. The development of these areas can be easily tracked in Jason's portfolio, but it certainly would not be picked up on standard tests of literacy development. It is difficult not to compare the work of students like Jason with the work of more capable students, but to do so would diminish recognition of his progress. A portfolio can help us see the incremental steps, the small accomplishments not ordinarily valued, that add up to big steps for a student like Jason. Portfolios also keep us grounded in the reality of students as individual children with their own unique gifts and challenges.

Figure 7.11

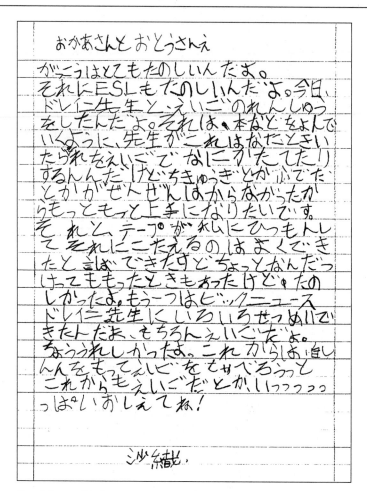

Dear Mom and Dad

School is fun. ESL is also fun. Today I practiced English with Mrs. Delaney. That is, like reading a book the teacher would ask "what is this" and I am supposed to answer that in English what they are but I didn't know how to say globe and pencil stand at all so I want to get better at it. Also, all in all I think that I did pretty well in answering the taped questions but there were times when I thought "what was it?" but it was fun. Also there is big news. I was able to explain some things to Mrs. Delaney. Of course it was in English. I was totally happy. From now on I want to speak English with more confidence. From now on keep teaching me looooots more English!

Saori

Saori's letter home the month (December) that she entered school was written in Japanese and placed in her portfolio. The translation was not done until several years later..

Saori: A Student With Limited English Proficiency

Students who do not speak English as their first language are at a disadvantage in many of our schools. Factors such as literacy in their first language, language spoken at home, support for first language in school, number of years in school, and instructional support all influence their particular strengths and needs and their rate of progress in learning to read and write in English. Progress for limited English proficient students is not easily seen on traditional tests. Furthermore, these students frequently work with other teachers (aides, ESL specialists, Title I teachers), which can limit communication between these teachers and the classroom teacher, and often results in fragmented instructional programs (Allington & McGill-Franzen, 1990; Anderson & Pellicer, 1990).

Saori spoke no English when she arrived in her third-grade classroom in December. An early portfolio entry is a letter home, written in Japanese, describing the first week of school (see Figure 7.11). Knowing that Saori was literate in her home language, her teacher, Mrs. Schmidt, included the letter as evidence of Saori's ability to use written language to communicate. Although Mrs. Schmidt didn't know for certain if the letter was clear and coherent, she did realize that Saori had lots to say and that she should be encouraged to maintain her home language. Interestingly, a translation of the letter done several years later reveals Saori's enthusiasm for school and for learning English, as well as her ability to communicate effectively in Japanese.

From that point on, Saori's rapid progress in learning to read and write English is evident in the portfolio. One of her first projects included in the portfolio is a state report written just after she arrived in class (see Figure 7.12). The report consists of labels and pictures of the state tree, state flower, state flag, and so forth. Classmates helped Saori with vocabulary and typed the words for her to paste under the matching pictures. Her dictated entry slip tells that she worked in a group and that she liked working with the other children. At this stage, Saori was still working on basic interpersonal communication skills (Cummins, 1981); she was listening in class and beginning to develop oral language in English. Mrs. Schmidt included these pieces in Saori's portfolio to demonstrate her ability to use oral language (English) through her dictation of word labels and entry slips. At this point, one month after entering school, Saori was still not reading or writing in English on her own, but her oral language was growing significantly.

A portfolio entry from March, contributed by Saori's ESL teacher, shows Saori beginning to write her own animal stories in English. Saori created a delightful tale of a rabbit and donkey who find a turnip and decide to search for a hungry animal who might like the food (see Figure 7.13). The story structure reflects Saori's familiarity with both Japanese and American stories and her emerging ability with English vocabulary and syntax. This is remarkable progress after just four months in the United States.

Saori was also making good progress in reading. Her reading log from February indicated that she was reading first-grade-level books, and her

Figure 7.12

State Bird
Willow Gold finch

State Bird

March reading letter to Mrs. Schmidt documented Saori's commitment to reading at home in English and Japanese (see Figure 7.14). It also demonstrated Saori's increasing competence in writing and English syntax. This growth in reading and writing was evident to Saori's parents as well. In a March parent portfolio visit, Saori's parents responded by writing:

> Saori had never written in English language before she entered E. school in December last year. We did not expect so much improvement in written and spoken English in 4 months. We are so pleased with all of Saori's work and the progress she has made.

At the same time, Saori's classroom teacher noted in March that "Saori is not ready to read and summarize in English." Although Saori was making good progress in reading, it was not surprising that she was not yet

Figure 7.12 *continued*

These are Saori's dictated labels for her state report, completed her first month in school, document her growing English speaking vocabulary.

Figure 7.13

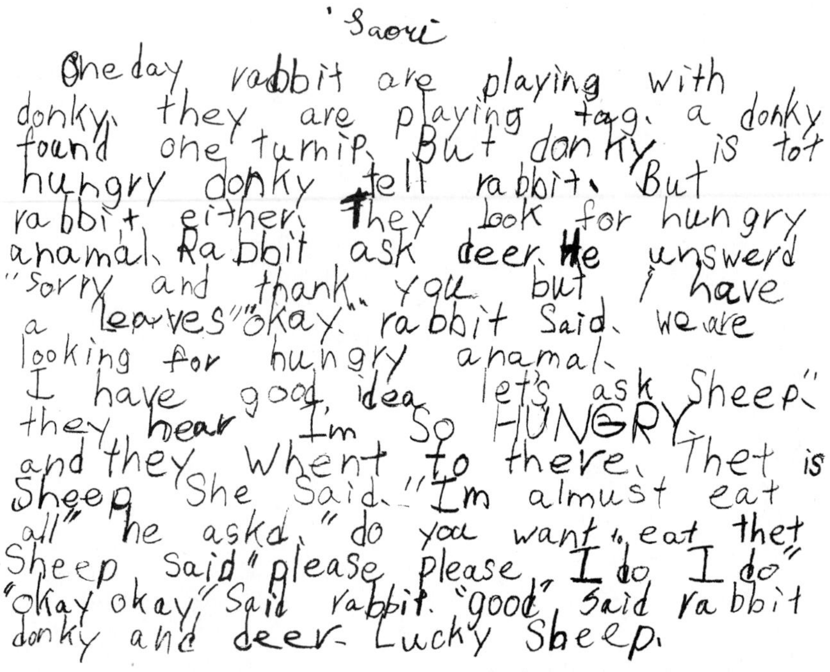

'Saori

One day rabbit are playing with donky, they are playing tag. a donky found one turnip. But donky is tot hungry donky tell rabbit. But rabbit either, They look for hungry anamal. Rabbit ask deer. He answerd "Sorry and thank you, but I have a leaves" "okay" rabbit said. we are looking for hungry anamal. I have good idea, let's ask Sheep." they hear I'm So HUNGRY, and they Whent to there, Thet is Sheep She said. "I'm almust eat all" he askd, "do you want eat thet Sheep said "please please, I do I do" "okay okay" said rabbit. "good" said rabbit donky and deer- Lucky Sheep.

Saori's story was written independently just four months after Saori had been in the classroom. It demonstrates remarkable progress in her knowledge of story structure, English syntax, and writing ability.

successful at the same reading tasks as were her third-grade classmates. Remarkably, at the end of May, her portfolio contained a written summary of a second-grade passage (see Figure 7.15). She was able to state the main idea of the story and several of the important events. Saori focused on details and was not yet able to draw inferences or construct a concise summary of the story. Nevertheless, no one who examined Saori's portfolio would determine that, just because she was not reading and writing as well as other third-grade students, she was at risk. In fact, Saori's progress was dramatic! Compare her end-of-year letter with the word labels from January (see Figure 7.16). The letter is further evidence of Saori's growing competence in writing and English syntax and her commitment to reading. At the same time, the letter alerted her teacher that Saori did not yet feel good about her reading and that she needed to be reminded of her excellent progress.

An interesting aspect of Saori's portfolio is that it was the product of collaboration between her classroom teacher and her ESL teacher. Both contributed pieces to the portfolio, providing a more complete picture of

Figure 7.14

3-5-96

Dear mrs Schmidt.

I like to read animal Stories.
I like all different kinds of animal
Stories.
I read about 50 minutes a day in English.
I read for about 25 minutes a day in Japanese
I would read more if I had more time
with my mom to help with English.
By June I'b like to be reading more
book in English.

Sincerely

Saori

Saori's reading letter reveals her commitment to reading in Japanese and English and her growing competence in writing.

Saori's growth. In parent conferences, both of these teachers were able to talk about the items in the portfolio, and they were better able to be, in the teachers' words, "in sync." These two teachers kept in contact with each other through the artifacts in Saori's portfolio and, as a result, Saori's program had a cohesion often lacking for ESL students. Saori was the real winner in the collaboration and careful documentation of her capabilities. In seven months she made remarkable progress that could be recognized and acknowledged by everyone.

Changes in Dispositions and Self-Assessment

As teachers, we have always known that it is important for students to enjoy reading and writing and to be engaged in their own learning. Terms such as "life-long reader," "literacy user," and "self-directed learner" have always been part of our vocabularies, yet we have rarely focused on documenting students' progress in these areas. Nonetheless, changes in students' literacy

Figure 7.15

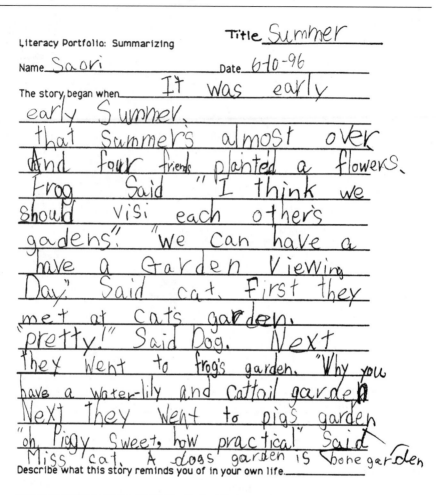

Literacy Portfolio: Summarizing   Title Summer

Name Saori   Date 6-10-96

The story began when   It was early early Summer. that summer's almost over And four friends planted a flowers. Frog Said "I think we Should visi each other's gadens." "We can have a have a Garden Viewing Day." Said cat. First they met at Cats garden. "pretty!" Said Dog. Next They went to frog's garden. "Why you have a water-lily and Cattail garden Next They went to pigs garden "oh Piggy Sweet, how practical" Said Miss cat. A dogs garden is bone garden

Describe what this story reminds you of in your own life.

Saori's summary of a second-grade reading selection reveals her ability to read and comprehend stories and her growing ability to communicate about her reading through writing.

dispositions and self-knowledge provide teachers and students with valuable insights. This is especially true for our struggling learners who rarely choose to read and write voluntarily, who view reading and writing as laborious, unpleasant activities, and who are passive learners (Johnston & Winograd, 1985). Ironically, it is precisely these learners who are most likely to benefit from concerted efforts to do more reading and writing and to develop self-awareness.

Figure 7.16

6-14-96

Dear Next Year's teacher,

I read 30 minutes. Because I want to de good reader. I like to read "The Boxcar children. Because I like the chacters and the Story I'm Japanese and I can't read very good and I'm reading easy books.
When I get Stuck I like to think for long time.
my favorite place to read is under my bed. Because it's Quiet and my cats are there

Sincerely,
Saori

Saori's end-of-year letter demonstrates dramatic growth in seven months.

Changing Dispositions

Max, the youngster described earlier, provides a good example of how students' writing interests may be slow to change over time. Max used the *Jurassic Park* theme consistently throughout his first-grade writing. His teacher was able to note this trend by reviewing Max's portfolio, yet she decided not to intervene but rather to use these interests to further Max's writing development. By second grade, Max's teacher was ready to encourage Max to branch out but, as we noted earlier, this proved frustrating for Max. By third grade, however, Max was beginning to successfully explore other topics and genres. Nevertheless, even in his piece about a visit to the zoo (see Figure 7.17), he returned to his fascination—*Jurassic Park*. After three years, Max made the break with the *Jurassic Park* story line but not with his interest in it. Fortunately, Max had moved beyond a single topic and genre, yet the transition took a long time and consistent monitoring by his teacher.

Figure 7.17

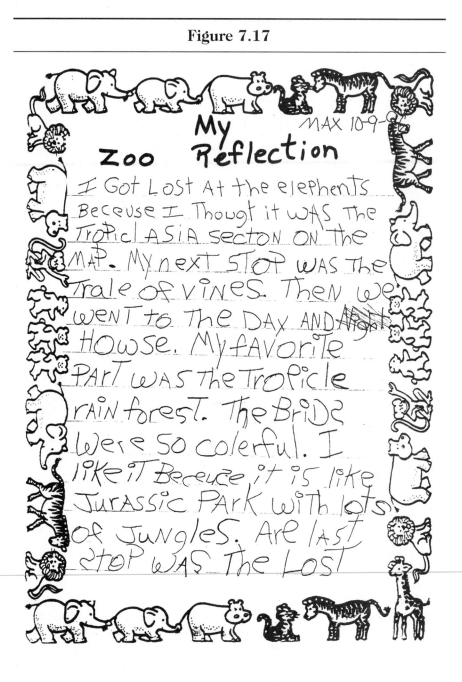

MAX 10-9-

Zoo My Reflection

I Got Lost At the elephents Beceuse I Thougt it WAS The TroPicl ASiA secton ON the MAP. My next STOP WAS The Trale of vines. Then we wenT to the DAy AND Night Howse. My fAvoriTe PART WAS The TroPicle rAin foresT. The BriDe were so colerful. I like iT Beceuze it is like Jurassic PArK with lots of Jungles. Are last stoP WAS The Lost

Amrita, an intermediate student, displayed a similar preoccupation with a single "topic" in her reading. During the first four months of third grade she was completely engrossed in the *Ramona* series; during the next couple of months she read books by Roald Dahl. At this point in the school

Figure 7.17 *continued*

AnD FOUND. We hAD
to FIND PAt's BACKPAC,
NOBODY hAD FOND it.
I relly liKED WATChing
The FAlKiNS eAT,
Ther rIP The FOOD like
RAPTORS.

At the beginning of third grade, Max finally breaks with the Jurassic Park theme but not with his interest in it. Max presents most of his thoughts in time sequence, adding his opinions and descriptions to enrich the text. Jurassic Park is still important, but it does not dominate content or structure.

year, with encouragement from her teacher, Amrita decided to set a goal of reading fantasy books. She even asked her teacher for title and author suggestions. However, notes from her reading conference several months later reveal that she didn't reach her goal—that she had instead drifted to *Babysitter Club* books. As she reviewed her book logs, Amrita noted that, "I love to read. . . . I read if I have nothing to do. . . . I read every day." She also noted that she prefers series books, "especially mysteries," providing her teacher with a useful clue to encourage Amrita to try mysteries that are not part of a series. Although Amrita's interests had not changed much over time, she was clearly the kind of voracious reader whom we hope to cultivate over time.

Max and Amrita exemplify students whose preferences and interests have served them well. Students like these remind us to balance both depth and breadth as we look for growth and change in students' interests. For Max and Amrita, staying with a topic enabled them to develop a depth and familiarity that "hooked" them to do lots of reading and writing. Although by one measure, these students did not grow and change substantially in their reading dispositions, other evidence suggests that they were flourishing as readers and writers.

Other students may cast a wider net, demonstrating more variety and change. Austen, a struggling intermediate reader, began third grade with little inclination to read and few interests (see Figure 7.18a). Although he reported that he "read" four books in school, he didn't offer any titles or authors. The teacher noted that Austen was simply looking through the pictures during quiet reading. By December Austen found *one* book that had captured his interest (see Figure 7.18b). Even when Mrs. Bradley gently probed about his repeated reading of this book, he replied by reminding her that this was one book that he could read. Finally in May there was a breakthrough in both Austen's book choices and his interest in reading (see Figure 7.18c). Once again, the choice of books was largely based on his ability to read and understand ("andesand") them. Now, however, he was beginning to identify topics that he enjoyed. Changes in Austen's reading interests and habits were very much driven by his sense of reading competence, thrusting him into a wide variety of easy reading books.

There is a delicate balance between encouraging students to try new topics and genres and supporting their interests and passions, between patiently waiting for new interests to take hold and gently prodding students to explore new ground, and between building students' reading competence and fostering motivation and interests. Although we want to encourage students to grow in their reading interests and habits and must continue to nudge students into new avenues, we must remember to "keep our eyes on the prize"—to keep students reading and writing.

Changes in Self-Reflection and Self-Evaluation

Changes in students' self-knowledge are the product of many factors (see chapter 6), so, as we might expect, defining just what is growth or change

Figure 7.18a

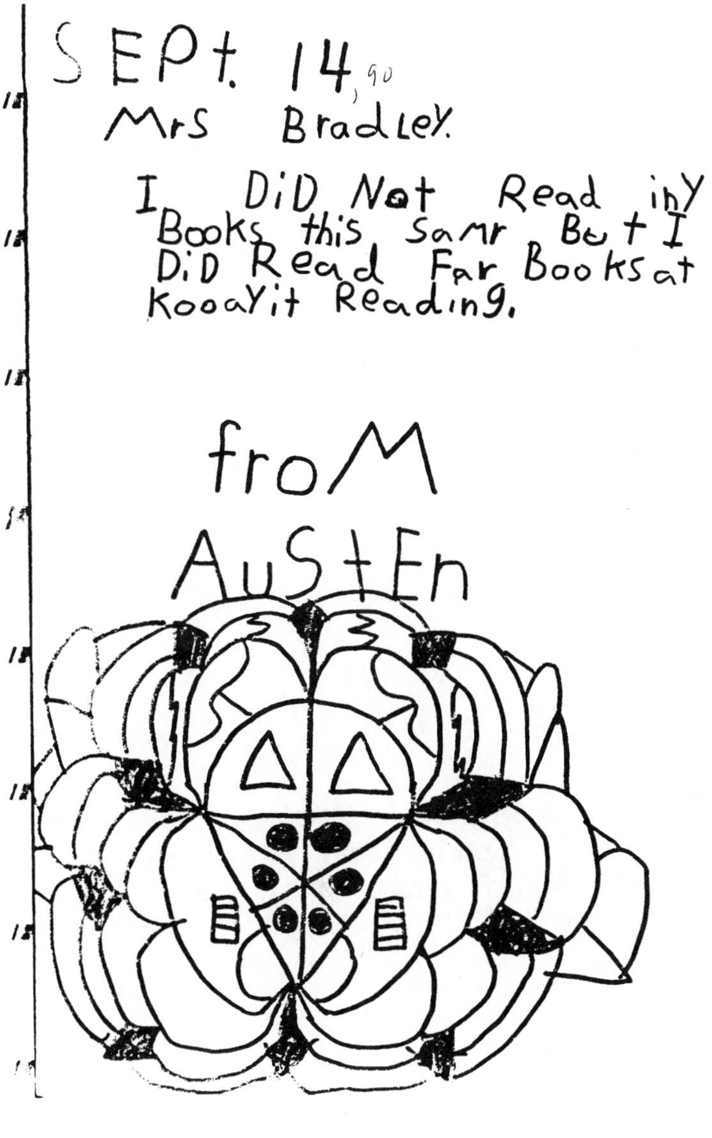

SEPt. 14, 90

MrS BradLeY.

I DiD Not Read iny
Books this Samr Bot I
DiD Read Far Books at
KooaYit Reading.

froM

AuStEn

September, 1990

Mrs. Bradley,

I did not read any books this summer but I did read four books
at quiet reading.

Figure 7.18b

Dec 6, 1990

Dear MrS. Bradley

I Sneaker Snatcher
at reading time it is
aBout two Boys traying
to Fiynd there Shakers.
it is Fun Becase It is
PeFikt for Me By the reading
I am oh 14.

from austen

Dec. 6, 1990

Dear Austen,
    Isn't this the book you read for your
mystery report? You've been reading it
many times. What makes it so good? it is
PeFRt For Me to read Mrs B.

December, 1990

Dear Mrs. Bradley,

    I [read] Sneaker Snatcher at reading time. It is about two boys
trying to find their sneakers. It is fun because it is perfect for me
by the reading. I am on 14.

Figure 7.18c

May 24, 1991

Dear Mrs. Bradley

I will name all the Books
I rade this week.
the life of a hamster, Dinamit,
Bean's on the roof, arms and arms
Birthday wishes, Camp out,
Dog for a day, the Buck stops
here, and then I will tell
you wich ones I liked.
Beans on the roof, Camp out,
arms a armer, Birthday wishes,
I liked Beans on the roof
Because I cood read it
and I cood ande sand it.
I liked Camp out Because it
had Bears in it and I like
Bears, I liked arms and
armmer Because it had hights
and I like hights.
I liked Birthday wishes Because
it was my Birthday and it was
a Birth Day Book, my favrit
Book is Beans on the roof Becqus
I can read it.

from austen

I will name all the books I read this week. The life of a Hamster,
Dynamite, Beans on the Roof, Arms and Armor, Birthday Wishes,
Camp out, Dog for a Day, the Buck Stops Here. And then I will tell
you which ones I likes. Beans on the Roof, Camp Out, Arms and
Armor, Birthday Wishes. I like Beans on the roof because I could red
it and I could understand it. I liked Camp Out because it had bears in
it and I like bears. I liked Arms and Armor because it had knights
and I like nights. I liked Birthday Wishes because it was my birthday
and it was a birthday book. My favorite book is Bears on the Roof
because I can read it.

Austen's reading letters show impressive growth in written
communication, reading interests, and habits over a year.

over time is sometimes difficult. For example, when selecting "favorite" pieces for their portfolios, students produce a wide range of reasons across an entire year: specific content ("it was about my grandmother and she is special to me"), genre ("it was my first poem"), craft ("it is exciting and tense"), and conventions and production characteristics ("my longest story," "best handwriting," "coolest pictures"). There doesn't seem to be a steady progression or pattern to these sorts of student reflections; they seem to reflect both personal and task specific factors. However, as with interests and habits, when we see that students are stuck in a particular way of thinking about their work, we try to expand their repertoire.

Within this variability there are some markers of growth that we have seen in students' self-assessments. The first is the ability of students to add specificity to their reflections, and the second is related to their understanding of the qualities of good work. Elizabeth's entry slips for "best piece of writing" over three years exemplify her ability to add specificity as well as her growing understanding of the elements of writing.

Grade One

> 11/92 *"It's my favorite book that I wrote."*

> 6/93 *"It was one of my first horse or pony stories."*

Grade Two

> 9/93 *"It was my first book this year."*

> 2/94 *"It was a lot of detail and I have a date and it has my initials on it."*

> 4/94 *"It has the environment on it like for mine it is African Savannah, and the continent, and facts about the animal."* (The report form had places for each of these.)

Grade Three

> 10/94 *"It had the most detail in the story. And it showed the kind of animal stories that I like. And it is one of the most writing."*

> 1/95 *"It has more episodes. It is more exciting because it's about a horse who wins lots of races."*

> 6/95 *"It has good spelling, all the sentences have periods, and I enjoyed writing about my favorite animal."*

Elizabeth has gone from broad reasons for designating a piece as "best" to more specific, writer-based reasons. In first grade, she focuses on producing writing; in second grade, production and fulfilling task requirements are important, although she is noticing the role of details in her writing. In third grade, Elizabeth is looking more closely at the internal structure of the writing and presentation, reflecting her awareness of audience. Notice that Elizabeth's personal connection and enjoyment persist throughout the three years but that, by the end of third grade, these are only two of several factors that define what makes a good piece of writing for Elizabeth.

Although a bit more difficult to see in students' comments about reading, changes in specificity and understanding also can be documented over time. For example, Angela, Kim, and Stephanie reflect on themselves as readers and on the strategies that they use at the beginning of the year and at the middle of the year:

> Angela (grade two)
>
> 10/93 *"I can sound out words."*
>
> 3/94 *"I can figure out what a word means by everything around it."*

> Kim (grade four)
>
> 10/95 *"I read the rest of the sentence."*
>
> 3/96 *"I sound it out, try to figure it out by the sentence, or ask an adult."*

> Stephanie (grade five)
>
> 9/94 *"[I'm] a good reader who reads alot."*
>
> 3/95 *"I think that I am a very good reader because I read books appropriate for my reading level, and even over. I always go back and reread stuff that I don't understand and if I still don't understand I go ask for help. I also stick to a book for at least four chapters and then I go back and see if I like it or not."*

Change is evident for each of these students over six months, and change is evident developmentally from second to fifth grades. All of these students reveal increasing specificity and sophistication about the variety of strategies that readers can use. Not only have they acquired more knowledge, but also their self-assessments indicate an awareness that will allow them to transfer these abilities to other reading situations.

These types of changes in self-reflection and self-evaluation are inextricably linked to the emphasis and guidance that we provide for students to learn about themselves and about reading and writing. As discussed in chapter 6, growth in these areas doesn't happen automatically for many students. Just like other aspects of literacy development (reading strategies, comprehension, interests, habits, etc.), self-assessment needs guidance and attention. During the first several years that we kept portfolios, we noticed that our students' self-reflections didn't seem particularly reflective. What's more, they didn't improve over time. We were hoping for growth, but it was not occurring. We discovered that observing desired changes in students' self-knowledge takes time, discussion, and instruction.

Special Considerations

Our examples in this chapter were selected to demonstrate the value of looking at student growth over time and the various ways that growth can manifest itself in students' work. What might be less clear from this chapter is that documenting growth using portfolios requires a few special considerations. First, as we have suggested in other chapters, growth cannot be documented if there is not enough evidence collected. Portfolio entries collected once or twice a year will not adequately record progress, especially given the uneven pattern of growth. In the same way, teachers who focus on a few large units of literacy study, such as poetry or research skills, may also find documenting growth difficult if the skills, strategies, and understandings for those units are not revisited at other times during the year. And, when most of the portfolio selections are left to the students, teachers may be unable to document growth in specific areas. Documenting growth requires careful, systematic collection of evidence.

Second, different aspects of growth are not equally easy to see in student work. For example, growth in reading and writing is most visible and most dramatic at the primary grades when students are progressing from emergent and beginning stages to more conventional reading and writing. Anyone looking at a primary portfolio can easily see changes in invented spelling, handwriting, and difficulty of texts that students can read on their own. At the intermediate and middle school levels, the changes are not as evident. More complex genres and purposes for reading and writing enter the picture, and students' growing sophistication is a bit more difficult to see. The differences between fifth- and sixth-grade reading material and increasing depth of understanding are not as apparent as the differences between first- and second-grade material and basic comprehension. In the same way, intermediate writing projects such as research reports and stories with strong character development require such different skills, processes, and products that it would be difficult to compare the student performance across projects for evidence of growth. The point is that growth occurs in both subtle and dramatic ways, depending on the grade level and the task. Teachers may need to dig deeply to recognize it and to share it with students and parents.

A final consideration is one we introduced in chapter 1 and will revisit in chapters 9 and 10—that of balancing individual growth against a set of common outcomes and expectations. As we evaluate and honor growth, we must also keep in mind the expectations shared by the "outside world" and the importance of having high standards for all students. This stereoscopic view of the student against himself and the student in the larger context can create a dilemma for teachers who are committed to student progress and empowerment. Yet, to attend solely to one or the other is to short-change students and parents. Portfolios can provide a vehicle for recognizing students' strengths *and* they can make visible the areas in which students need help. As a result, portfolios can empower students and parents towards meeting common standards and they can inform instructional decisions to better meet individual student needs.

For us, it is crucial to begin with the student, not the standard. By focusing on student strengths and interests first, we can create a situation in which student growth and outside standards converge, rather than diverge; we can value how much the student has gained, rather than lament about how far she is from the target. At the same time, by situating student work against the backdrop of shared standards, we all, students, parents, and teachers, are forced to look more closely at the quality of the work and to think more deeply about our assumptions and expectations regarding student learning. This dual set of standards—individual growth and common expectations—can provide the grist for conversations that enhance teaching and learning.

Conclusion

Portfolios have the potential to showcase the wonderful and idiosyncratic growth of individual students. This is one of the most compelling reasons to keep portfolios; no other assessment strategy can document with such clarity the ebbs and flows of student progress. In this chapter we have demonstrated that growth can be valued in many aspects of literacy—reading and writing capabilities, interests, dispositions, and self-assessment. Most important, we have reaffirmed that growth is not unidimensional, that it does not advance on a predictable or even trajectory. The unique abilities of the child and the demands of the task combine to produce the amount and type of growth we see in student learning.

When we collect evidence to document change and take time to study and value it, we create the best environment for learning. Parents, teachers, and students themselves come to understand teaching and learning in a new way. As one intermediate student suggested:

> Portfolios help us see our progress over the year. They help us see how much we have grown and what we need to work on. It's nice to look back and see what you have accomplished.

We agree. And add that it is important for *everyone* to have a record of where we have been so that we can celebrate where we are now and make plans for where we want to go next. This is the contribution that portfolios can make.

References

Allen, J. B., Michalove, B., Shockley, B., & West, M. (1991). I'm really worried about Joseph: Reducing the risks of literacy learning. *The Reading Teacher, 44*(7), 458–467.

Allington, R. L., & McGill-Franzen, A. (1990). Comprehension and coherence: Neglected elements of literacy instruction in remedial and resource room services. *Journal of Reading, Writing, and Learning Disabilities International, 6*(2), 149–182.

Anderson, L. W., & Pellicer, L. O. (1990). Synthesis of research on compensatory and remedial education. *Educational Leadership, 48*(1), 10–16.

Anderson, R. C., Wilson, P. T., & Fielding, L. G. (1988). Growth in reading and how children spend their time outside of school. *Reading Research Quarterly, 23*(3), 285–303.

Applebee, A., & Langer, J. A. (1983). Instructional scaffolding: Reading and writing as natural language activities. *Language Arts, 60*(2), 168–175.

Clay, M. M. (1979). *The early detection of reading difficulties* (3rd ed.). Auckland: Heinemann.

Cummins, J. (1981). The role of primary language development in promoting educational success for language minority students. In California State Department of Education (Ed.), *Schooling and language minority students: A theoretical framework*. Los Angeles: California State Department of Education.

Graves, M., & Graves, B. (1994). *Scaffolding reading experiences*. Norwood, MA: Christopher-Gordon.

Guthrie, J. T., Schafer, W., Wang, Y., & Afflerbach, P. (1993). *Influences of instruction on amount of reading* (Reading Research Report No. 3). Athens, GA: National Reading Research Center.

Hillocks, G. (1984). What works in teaching composition. *American Journal of Education, 93*(1), 133–170.

Johnston, P., & Winograd, P. N. (1985). Passive failure in reading. *Journal of Reading Behavior, 17*(4), 279–301.

Lipson, M. Y., & Wixson, K. K. (1997). *Assessment and instruction of reading disability* (2nd ed.). New York: Longman.

Lowenfeld, V., & Brittain, W. L. (1975). *Creative and mental growth* (6th ed.). New York: Macmillan.

Morrow, L. M., & Weinstein, C. S. (1986). Encouraging voluntary reading: The impact of a literature program on children's use of library centers. *Reading Research Quarterly, 21*(3), 330–346.

National Research Council. (1997). *Improving schooling for language-minority children: A research agenda*. Washington, DC: National Academy Press.

Simmons, W., & Resnick, L. (1993). Assessment as the catalyst of school reform. *Educational Leadership, 50*(5), 11–15.

U.S. Department of Education, Office of Special Education and Rehabilitative Services. (1993). *Fifteenth annual report to Congress on the implementation of the Education for the Handicapped Act*. Washington, D.C.: U.S. Government Printing Office.

Valencia, S.W. (1990). A portfolio approach to classroom reading assessment: The whys, whats, and hows. *The Reading Teacher, 43*(4), 338–340.

Wolf, D. P., LeMahieu, P., & Eresh, J. (1992). Good measure: Assessment as a tool for educational reform. *Educational Leadership, 49*(8), 8–13.

chapter **8**

Engaging Teachers in Self-Reflection and Self-Evaluation

SHEILA W. VALENCIA

Chapter 8 is about reflective teaching—teachers' own processes of self-reflection and self-evaluation. We begin by defining reflective practice and conditions that foster it. Then we descibe several strategies for building reflective practice into the process of implementing classroom portfolios. Our focus in on using portfolios as an engaging and worthwhile experience for teachers to think about their own teaching and learning.

My teaching has changed since I started using portfolios:
    I am more focused,
    I see each child differently (as he/she is);
    I teach differently—I am more reflective;
    I model more;
    I understand more about reading and writing . . .

               D. R., intermediate teacher

Portfolios help my teacher know how well she is doing as a teacher and if her teaching tactics are working.

               C. H., middle school student

When portfolios are action-oriented, both teachers and students use them to think about instruction. This careful, reflective, critical stance toward one's own teaching, students, student performance, curriculum, and instructional strategies is what is referred to as *reflective practice* (Schön, 1983, 1987; Valli, 1997). Without reflective practice, effective teaching cannot occur, nor can the benefits of portfolios be fully realized. Portfolios can be the springboard for reflective teaching, and they can provide documentation that reflective practice is at work. Just as we want self-assessment to become a disposition students develop, rather than just a task they complete with their portfolios, we also want teachers' self-assessment to carry over from work with portfolios to reflective practice in all parts of their professional lives.

In some respects, a separate chapter on teacher self-reflection and self-evaluation in this book is redundant; every chapter centers on teachers' *thinking* about reading and writing and about teaching and learning. We advocate portfolios in action and, by definition, teachers' active participation and inquiry into the design, implementation, and interpretation of portfolios. Nevertheless, as with student self-reflection and self-evaluation, insight doesn't come overnight for teachers, nor is it a *fait accompli* just because portfolios are in place. We include this short chapter, therefore, to provide a few strategies that will foster and support teachers' thinking about their practice and about their students as they work with portfolios. We begin with an overview of reflective practice and the conditions that facilitate teachers' engagement in self-reflection and self-evaluation. Then we provide several ideas for creating those conditions around portfolios so that teachers' self-inquiry can be nurtured.

Reflective Practice

Understanding Reflective Practice

What is it? Why is it important? Gone are the days when *assessment* was narrowly defined as a test and when teachers were designated as simply test administrators (cf. Stiggins, 1997). Gone, too, are the days when curriculum and instruction were scripted and when teachers were simply conduits or deliverers of information (cf. Snyder, Bolin, & Zumwalt, 1992). Teaching and assessment are so complex that teachers cannot merely apply what they have learned or what they have always done in a uniform way. They must be able to respond to constantly changing classroom contexts, determine what and how to teach, evaluate themselves and their students, and make adjustments. In other words, they must engage in self-reflection and self-evaluation.

Teachers spend as much as one-third to one-half of their classroom time involved in assessment-related activities (Stiggins & Conklin, 1992), and they make decisions about what and how to teach approximately every two to three minutes (Shavelson & Stern, 1981). They must have the ability to step back and reexamine their actions and consider other alternatives. As Dewey noted, reflective thought in teaching is critical because it *"emancipates us from merely impulsive and merely routine activity . . . enables us to direct our activities with foresight and to plan according to ends-in-view, or purposes of which we are aware . . . to act in deliberate and intentional fashion . . . to know what we are about when we act. It converts action that is merely appetitive, blind, and impulsive into intelligent action"* (Dewey, cited in Valli, 1997, p. 69). Teachers, then, are the actual tools of evaluation, the assessment instruments, as well as the instructional methods and materials (International Reading Association & National Council of Teachers of English, 1994; Johnston, 1987, 1989). Effective assessment and instruction depend on teachers' ability to be reflective, knowledgeable, careful, and critical in their thinking.

Reflective practice is essential for teachers who put portfolios into action. Teachers must make decisions about which learnings they want to document, the evidence that will be placed into the portfolios, and how they will engage students; they must judge the quality of student understanding from portfolio artifacts and use that information to make instructional decisions.

What conditions promote reflective practice? Research on professional development and on reflective practice suggests several factors that contribute to reflective teaching. First, teachers must have a deep conceptual understanding of subject matter so they can knowledgeably examine their own practice (Darling-Hammond, 1996; International Reading Association & National Council of Teachers of English, 1994; Shulman, 1987). Without a sound knowledge-base of reading and writing, teachers cannot determine what is worth teaching and what student learning might look like. Portfolio teachers, in particular, must grapple with identifying complex learnings that are embedded in authentic learning artifacts found in portfolios (Valencia & Au, 1997). In addition, they must interpret patterns of students' reading and writing performance as they look across multiple indicators and work samples found in portfolios (Johnston, 1987; Lipson & Wixson, 1997).

Second, reflective practice is fostered when teachers use actual artifacts (i.e., student work, videotapes) or actual experiences to inquire into their practice (Darling-Hammond, Ancess, & Falk, 1995; Richert, 1991; Valencia & Au, 1997). Artifacts ground discussions in the realities of authentic classrooms, and the results of those discussions are immediately useful and meaningful to teachers. Instead of staying at the theoretical or abstract level, self-reflection and evaluation using artifacts get right to the heart of complex daily instruction and student learning. And, because classrooms, students, and instructional goals are variable, teachers must problem solve around what is worthwhile and meaningful practice in a particular context (Lieberman, 1995; Richardson, 1990). Simple answers rarely apply.

Third, teachers benefit from becoming part of a collaborative learning community where problems of teaching can be explored. Collegial networks build ownership, expertise, and leadership among teachers who often work in professionally isolated situations—one teacher, one class (Darling-Hammond & McLaughlin, 1995; Lieberman & McLaughlin, 1992). Furthermore, unlike most professional development activities, which are usually "one-shot" meetings or "here's what to do on Monday" workshops, these professional networks are intended to provide teachers with the time and supportive community to dig deeply into their own teaching. Multiple voices, competing perspectives, and self-inquiry are nurtured in such an environment (Clark, Moss, Goering, Herter, Leonard, Robbins, Russell, Templin, & Wascha, 1996; Johnston, 1989; Richert, 1991). In fact, Valli (1997) suggests that if reflective practice is not part of a collegial community, it can backfire, "producing detached, idiosyncratic teachers" who end up reifying their own practices instead of opening to other perspectives.

It is not difficult to understand why the conditions just described are important for teacher self-reflection and self-evaluation; it is a bit more difficult to imagine having them all in place in your school or school district. However, when portfolios are in action, not just kept, they are uniquely situated to foster this climate—they require subject-matter expertise, rely on actual classroom artifacts, and invite in-depth discussion with colleagues. We believe that portfolios provide a wonderful opportunity for teachers to learn about children, themselves, and their practice. Next we describe four strategies we have used to build reflective practice into our portfolio implementation process: establishing a shared portfolio concept, participating in a professional community, using portfolios for discussion, and annotating portfolio artifacts.

Using Portfolios for Reflective Practice

Establishing a Shared Conception of Portfolios

Teacher self-reflection and self-evaluation start here, with the conception of the portfolio. Some portfolio models are designed to be used across classrooms, grade levels, schools, or districts. In these instances, the model is usually designed by central office staff or by a small group of teachers working with an administrator, so there will be some level of uniformity and coherence across sites. Other portfolio models are designed by a few teachers working on their own. In either case, it is critical for early conversations to focus on conceptualizations of portfolios, not on logistics. Although cost and time usually prevent all teachers who will implement portfolios from participating in these early conversations, our experience suggests that all teachers must have an opportunity to explore the conceptualization and definition of portfolios, even if a model or framework already has been developed by others.

During this first step in portfolio development, teachers get a chance to examine their own beliefs and practices about teaching, learning, and assessment of reading and writing. You cannot discuss a portfolio model without discussing what you believe is important for students to know and to be able to do. You cannot conceptualize portfolio contents without thinking about which instructional strategies and classroom activities you believe will help students achieve those goals. And, you cannot talk about a schedule or method of using portfolios without talking about your visions of classroom assessment and students' engagement in their own learning. In other words, we believe that all teachers must have an opportunity to think deeply about and to help construct the portfolio model that they will use. In our view, mandating portfolios without engaging teachers in in-depth discussions does not enable teachers to unpack deeply held beliefs and practices about reading and writing and to consider alternatives (Valencia & Au, 1997). As a result, portfolios that are not developed around a shared understanding often result in superficial adherence to portfolio requirements but little reflective practice in classrooms. A few examples from our experience may help make the point.

Clarifying learning outcomes. When we first began discussing portfolios, the school district had already developed and disseminated student learning outcomes in reading and writing. These were written by a representative team of teachers the previous year and had been disseminated to all teachers in the district, a process common in many school districts. We began our portfolio discussions believing that our portfolio group of 30 teachers, many of whom had worked on the district outcomes, could start by identifying what these outcomes might look like in a portfolio. We set aside an afternoon. What a surprise! No sooner had we started than we realized that we needed to have long and specific talks about what is meant by outcomes such as "students use a variety of reading strategies" or "constructs meaning from text," or even "read a variety of texts for a variety of purposes." Although we all thought we understood what these outcomes meant, we clearly had different operational definitions and expectations for students. Teachers had not had an opportunity to think through these complex learner outcomes nor to build a shared understanding with their colleagues. This, we discovered, was essential for effective portfolio implementation.

Clarifying a portfolio model. At the same time, we discussed our purpose(s) for keeping portfolios—who were to be the primary and secondary audiences, and which model would best suit our needs? We approached this development phase as a group problem-solving process, rather than simply choosing to adopt an already developed portfolio model. We read and analyzed articles about other models in light of our own needs. Because we were developing a model that would apply across classrooms, we tried to guard against a structure that was too formalized or one that would be too idiosyncratic across classrooms. It had to be usable by many but uniform enough to allow us to look across classrooms. These conversations were critical to successful portfolio implementation. Instead of producing teacher resistance to the model or to "required pieces," the conversations led to debates about *which* model and *which* pieces teachers wanted to be consistent across classrooms. The conversations also brought to the surface teachers' understandings about their unique approaches to classroom assessment and issues of sharing information with outside audiences. As a result, teachers decided for themselves on a portfolio model that was both desirable and feasible.

Developing Common Tools. Another example of reflective practice in the conceptualization stage of portfolios came with the development of our Common Tools. As we discussed in chapter 2, because these tools were designed to help us evaluate student progress on district literacy outcomes, we were forced to ask ourselves questions such as, "How will I recognize these outcomes in my students? What instructional strategies and activities do I have in my classroom that enable students to learn and apply these skills and strategies? Which of the activities might be good candidates for a portfolio or for a Common Tool?" Because tools were constructed by teachers and tried out, they became a sort of action research project (Noffke & Zeichner, 1987). As a group, we identified the problem (needing to collect information about a particular outcome), designed strategies to collect that information, tried out our strategies, and brought "data" back to the group for discussion.

For example, as a group, we developed tools for oral and written retellings to assess students' construction of meaning. We tried them out and brought student work back to the group. As we listened to a tape of one child's reading and retelling of *Fluffy the Porcupine,* some teachers suggested that the child had only a superficial understanding of the book and didn't seem to understand the humor and irony of the title. Others suggested that a child at the second-grade level should not be expected to understand the humor. The child's teacher commented that this child probably did not know that porcupines have sharp quills. Finally, someone suggested that we needed to check or build background knowledge before we had this child do a retelling or before we could evaluate her ability to construct meaning. This led to a discussion about prior knowledge, instruction, expectations for student performance, and another round of try-outs.

This inquiry-oriented process around Common Tools continues today, seven years after our project began. The discussions were, and continue to be, fascinating; they drive us to problem solve, to delve into the research, and to examine our own practices. So, when Common Tools don't produce the desired results, we have to determine if the problem is in the tool, in our teaching, or in students' performance. Through development of these assessment tools, we confront issues of curriculum, instruction, and student performance.

Three important insights for reflective teaching emerge from the conceptualization stage of portfolio development. First, the process is not linear. Our process of clarifying understandings about reading and writing outcomes was not "complete" before we launched into experimenting with a portfolio model or with Common Tools. It was easier to revisit the outcomes after we collected samples of student work than it was to talk about outcomes in the abstract. So, although we had to begin there, we did not reach closure before we started to implement portfolios. In fact, the student learning outcomes still undergo some changes each year. This applies to Common Tools as well. There is a recursive process of developing, trying, redeveloping, reconceptualizing, and so on that must happen if portfolios are to be effective and if reflective practice is to be fostered. Our understandings grow as we gain knowledge and experience.

Second, we found that even if we wanted to "mandate" certain procedures in our portfolio group, it never worked! We had to agree on certain guidelines to give ourselves structure, but we also had to build in flexibility and encouragement to become reflective practitioners so that teachers could experiment with alternative approaches. Teachers made individual decisions about some issues such as how they were going to organize portfolios, what they would look like, how to handle grading issues, how to share them with parents, and how to coordinate them with other work folders and classroom procedures. The balance between shared structure and professional prerogative is important not only to developing a shared portfolio model but also to building common experiences and a common knowledge base from which to grow.

Third, when newcomers decided to implement portfolios, they still needed to go through these processes of conceptualization. Although by year four, members of the core literacy portfolio group had worked out many of the logistical and conceptual issues for themselves, newcomers needed a chance to go through the process and be supported in their investigations. In many cases, newcomers benefited from the experiences of the "old-timers" and had a faster learning curve than the original group. Nevertheless, there are fundamental issues around teaching and learning literacy that everyone must grapple with in order to understand portfolios.

Participating in Ongoing Professional Networks

Continuity and structure. Teachers need regularly scheduled time to meet and discuss portfolio issues. We were fortunate to meet almost every month for the first three years of implementation. Sometimes we met after school; at other times, during the school day. Although not all teachers can be as fortunate as we were, being part of a professional network is critical to teachers' developing self-knowledge. Other portfolio teachers have found ways to get this time by using team meetings or study groups to get together. One principal even promised her staff that she would not spend any time in faculty meetings sharing information that she could put into writing; as a result, she was able to give over one faculty meeting a month to portfolio discussions. The essential elements here are predictability and continuity so that portfolio "thinking" and thus, reflective practice, become a regular part of teachers' lives, not special events.

What come from these ongoing meetings are shared interests, language, knowledge, and sense of inquiry. The group becomes a place where understanding about student learning, reading and writing, and instructional practice takes public voice and has a chance to be shared and tested against other perspectives. The continuity of the group allows trust and shared knowledge to develop. However, simply having meetings or time to talk "doesn't cut it," according to one of our participants. The discussions need to have direction, focus, and an intellectual edge.

Our regularly scheduled meetings had a structure. They always began with a time for teachers to talk about "how is it going?" Then we moved to discussions or activities in which we examined portfolio artifacts (discussed later in this chapter). Sometimes the group leaders would share with other group members their unresolved debates or differences in their perspectives about teaching, learning, or portfolios. They would think aloud about their perspectives and invite others to join in. The effect was that everyone was engaged in taking a critical perspective of the problem. Often, these discussions led to requests for additional information, articles, and research on the topic. So the meetings had a predictable format with room for individual agendas and opinions, all centered on problem raising and problem solving related to our portfolio work.

During "how is it going?" teachers felt free to raise concerns, tell stories, and share new ideas. Although we usually set aside a short time for this segment, it often took up more time than we expected. In retrospect, it was important to building community and trust. Initially, much of that discussion was focused on procedural issues: how to make portfolios that wouldn't fall apart, how to help students choose work to put in, color coding different parts of the portfolio for ease of management, or what entry slips worked best with students at various grades. As "off track" as these concerns may seem with respect to reflective practice, they need attention. Without a feeling of control over the logistics, teachers cannot give full attention to teaching and learning. However, these concerns can often take up hours of precious time. One good strategy for dealing with these concerns is to deal directly with them while also addressing conceptual underpinnings that are more substantive. For example, instead of focusing solely on the sturdiness of portfolios, we can explore how teachers are encouraging students to have hands-on experiences with their portfolios, how students are using portfolios, how often students are setting up portfolio visits, and what teachers want to happen during those visits. Or, when discussing different types of entry slips, we can discuss the kinds of reflective thinking we want to teach and encourage in our students. Most procedural issues have a conceptual analogue, and this is how reflective practice can be strengthened. Eventually, the focus on logistics gives way to issues of instruction and student performance.

Group membership. The composition of these collegial groups is also important to consider. We began with a representative group of approximately 30 teachers from grades K through 12. The middle and high school members were language arts teachers. The mix of grade levels was an advantage during those early years when we were conceptualizing the portfolio and discussing reading and writing. In fact, it was a perfect setting to build subject-matter expertise because we could capitalize on elementary teachers' knowledge of learning to read and write and secondary teachers' knowledge of literary understanding and written communication. However, as the years went on, we found that issues at high school were quite different, and those teachers broke away from the larger group. Later we reformed an early childhood group and an intermediate/middle school group so we could deal more directly with specific instructional issues. Overall, we found advantages to both K–12 and narrower grade level configurations that should be considered as networks are formed.

The meetings were both the "carrot" and the "stick" that kept teachers involved and interested. Teachers could not come unprepared. Part of being in this group was a commitment to sharing ideas and problems and to trying out ideas and bringing the "data" back to the group. In other words, if the group decided that it would try new ways of collecting reading comprehension information, then members were expected to do it. Or, if several teachers were interested in new ways of using portfolios during parent-teacher conferences, they would experiment and report back to the group. Sometimes, these projects were agreed upon by the entire group, at other times individuals simply took new ideas back to try out. In addition, teachers were expected to bring student portfolios to our meetings for discussion (see "Using Portfolios for Reflective Discussion" below).

These requirements were essential for productive meetings, and they were sometimes stressful. Teachers had to commit to keeping portfolios and sharing their teaching publicly. A few teachers were concerned that their portfolios didn't "measure up." Although these teachers never publicly said so, there were occasions when they simply brought nothing to share. Participating in a supportive network and being part of an "intellectually stimulating group" can counteract this fear. One teacher said, *"Being in this group kept me going. There were times when I was too tired or overwhelmed and wanted to give up, but I knew I wanted to come to these meetings, and I had to bring portfolios with work in them to share. So, sometimes I would do something the week of the meeting just so that I had something to share. It worked. Now [at the end of the year] portfolios are much easier. I can't wait until next year to begin again."* This teacher provides good reminders about setting up professional learning communities: (a) they must be worthwhile for teachers, (b) they should require commitment and active participation, and (c) they take time to develop.

Using Portfolios for Reflective Discussion

Portfolios provide the perfect vehicle for using classroom artifacts and personal experiences for teacher reflection. Grounding conversation in concrete evidence brings the conversation to real students and everyday teaching. There is no better way to get to the essence of reflective practice. Over the years, we have used four strategies to look at student work: description, alignment, moderation, and evaluation. In general, they build on one another, with description being the most general and evaluation the most specific. Each of the strategies requires teachers to share student work with a group of colleagues, usually four to six in a group. Next we describe each one.

Description. The description process requires teachers to bring a portfolio or folder of a particular student to share with colleagues. It is a good way to begin talking about portfolios, teaching, and learning. The conversation is very general: Describe what you notice about this student from his or her portfolio. This conversation is a gentle way for teachers to open their students' portfolios to their colleagues. It's like inviting a colleague to visit your classroom. We have found that although the conversation is supposed to focus on a particular child, it often strays to the portfolio artifacts themselves and questions such as, "How do you get your third-grade students to write like this?" or "Would you send a copy of these criteria for a research project to me?" or "Tell me how you run your literature circles." It is impossible not to think about your own teaching as you wander through another teacher's portfolio. By focusing on a particular child and a particular portfolio, teachers are thrust into critical inquiry about their students and their own practice in very specific and meaningful ways.

Alignment. One of the most difficult aspects of examining students' portfolios is identifying various learning outcomes in complex student work; that is, looking at a particular artifact and deciding if it provides evidence of, for example, "reading ownership" or "uses the writing process" or "constructs meaning from text." Because so many classroom activities involve authentic literacy tasks that require students to use many skills and strategies, evidence for several outcomes is often found in a single piece. More to the point, looking closely at portfolio evidence and the alignment with literacy outcomes prompts teachers to ask, "Why am I asking students to do this activity? What do I want them to learn or practice from this assignment?" This kind of discussion about alignment is not just about portfolio evidence, it is also about curriculum and instruction.

We have used a variety of forms to help these alignment conversations take place. Table 8.1 is an example of a generic form that can guide the discussion. You may notice that it is very similar to Table 2.2 (chapter 2), in which outcomes are aligned with Common Tools. The difference here is that teachers go through actual portfolio contents to determine what students are doing and learning. The column marked "Learner Outcomes" should include specific literacy outcomes already in place in the school, district, or state; alternatively if no outcomes are in place, this is a time to identify several important learning goals identified by the group. Our experience suggests that it is best to focus on no more than three or four outcomes the first time that teachers have this discussion. The middle column is a place to indicate all the evidence in the portfolio that provides insight into the student's capabilities with respect to a particular outcome. The final column is a place for teachers to think collaboratively about other indicators or classroom artifacts that could be used as evidence for a particular outcome.

Table 8.1 shows a sample analysis from Jose's fourth-grade portfolio, which includes many indicators of effective writing, several indicators of

Table 8.1
Alignment of Portfolio Evidence With Learner Outcomes

Learner Outcomes	Evidence Found	Additional Evidence Possible
Communicate effectively in writing	Daily journal Reading response journal Research report on Hawaii Pen pal letters Story, "The Case of the Dognapper" Two book reports	Expand genres to include poetry, descriptive, and persuasive writing
Construct meaning from text	Reading response journal Two book reports Reading log with limited responses	Informal reading inventory Teacher conference notes Observation of literature circle discussions Summaries using Common Tools or benchmark tools
Uses a variety of reading strategies	No evidence	Informal reading inventory Teacher reading conference notes Self-report question/survey Observation

Teachers can use a simple form such as this to think about the alignment of important learning outcomes with portfolio contents, classroom activities, and instruction.

reading, and no indicators of reading strategies. By using this form to structure their discussion of Jose's portfolio, a group of teachers talked about outcomes, instruction, student performance, and evidence of learning. For example, they discussed: various kinds of writing that fourth graders should be doing; the difference between reading artifacts that are generated in a class discussion and those that are generated independently by the student; reading strategies of fourth-grade students (what they are, how we can see them); and how literacy activities can be used to teach and assess several outcomes at once. As a closure activity, teachers discussed which artifacts in their own students' portfolios seemed to be rich, worthwhile learning experiences for students, which activities they might want to revise, and which they might want to eliminate in the future. After an afternoon of this activity one teacher commented, "*I find myself working backward. OK, if I want to show that the student can really understand and interpret what he reads, . . . what can I have in the portfolios to show . . . the child successfully constructed meaning or didn't? So, this whole process is affecting my instruction quite a bit because even if I come up with that [evidence], I think about how I can set up the classroom to get more of that from students. You know, it keeps going back and back to instruction.*"

Moderation. The moderation process builds on description and alignment with the added edge of encouraging various perspectives about the students' learning. In this setting, the teacher contributes a portfolio to the small-group discussion but does not participate in the discussion until the other members have discussed their observations. The group addresses four questions:

1. What did you learn about this child? How would you describe him/her? What are his/her strengths in reading and writing?
2. What reading and writing goals would be appropriate for this child, and what instructional strategies might be useful for helping the child achieve those goals?
3. What other things would you like to see in this portfolio to help you understand this child's literacy abilities?
4. How did the group's description and recommendations confirm, conflict, or add to the initiating teacher's perceptions?

Staying quiet while the group discusses their student is incredibly difficult for most teachers, who are eager to supplement the portfolio information with personal anecdotes and insights. However, the process of staying quiet is good for several reasons. First, it requires teachers to listen to one another and takes the presenting teacher out of the "hot seat" and out of a defensive stance. Because the conversation takes place with the initiating teacher present, there is a renewed sense of respect for peers and an acknowledgment of individual teacher knowledge and perspective. Second, it highlights the complexity of understanding literacy learning and teaching. Different perspectives are encouraged, all in the spirit of understanding a particular child. Amazingly, most teachers report that they not only learn from one another, but also that they gain confidence in their own abilities as they listen to peers. They have the rare opportunity to judge whether their interpretations of student performance are consistent with those of their peers. Third, by asking whether the portfolio adequately represents a particular child, we are also asking if we are collecting the necessary information. This is really a discussion about what is worth teaching and documenting; teachers benefit from hearing what colleagues value and how they interpret shared goals for literacy instruction.

Evaluating portfolios. We will discuss evaluating portfolios in more detail in chapter 10. However, here we want to briefly mention evaluation as an additional way to use portfolios for reflective discussion. Although there are strong feelings on both sides of the evaluation and scoring debate, we found that the discussions teachers had around evaluation were critical to helping us clarify standards for student performance at different grade levels. Nowhere else—not in description, alignment, or moderation discussions—were teachers forced to "put their feet down" and address issues of expectations. We concur with an intermediate teacher who suggested that the process of scoring portfolios "forces you to focus on criteria." She noted, *"It's difficult and frustrating but it sure makes you face your expectations. . . . I work better with a group of peers than by myself. . . . I can talk about expectations with them."*

A risk of scoring is that the conversation may become overly focused on a number and on interrater agreement. The key is to keep the conversation focused on understanding student learning and clarifying standards (Clark, et al., 1996; Johnston, 1989; Moss, Beck, Ebbs, Matson, Muchmore, Steele, Taylor, & Herter, 1992). One way to keep the focus on substantive, in-depth conversation is to spend a substantial amount of time discussing sample portfolios—a sort of moderation with a standards element. Another is to have teachers score in teams so that conversation is encouraged. Another is to require scorers to list evidence that they rely on to determine a score. All maximize the role of reflective discussion as teachers are scoring.

It is a good idea to specify the types of portfolios teachers bring to these various types of discussion: description, moderation, alignment, and evaluation. The aim should not be to bring those of the brightest or best students or the prettiest portfolios. We want to focus on students who stretch teachers' thinking. Sometimes we ask teachers to bring several portfolios representing a range of student abilities—high-, middle-, and low-achieving students; at other times they are asked to bring portfolios of students about whom they have questions. Recently, after six years of portfolio work, one teacher brought a portfolio to share with her peers. She placed the portfolio onto the table, sat back, and said, "I need help with this child. I am not sure my expectations are reasonable, and before I talk with the parents, I want your feedback. He's a third grader. Here he is." This presentation marked a dramatic change from the way the group worked the first several years. What is most notable is this teacher's own sense of self-inquiry and her eagerness to turn to colleagues for help. What's more, the group members didn't simply offer opinions, they referred specifically to work in the portfolio to make their points. More important, they *asked* questions of one another rather than simply answered them. The discussion was about what is important for students to learn, what good reading and writing performance looks like, what the evidence reveals about this particular student, and what instruction or support would be most helpful for him. This is truly reflective practice in action.

Annotating Portfolio Artifacts

We introduced the concept of teacher entry slips in chapter 2 and have referred to entry slips in other chapters. Interestingly, the discussions around portfolio evidence during moderation and evaluation actually prompted teachers to *ask* for teacher annotations and entry slips. Earlier research with teachers' portfolios had shown that teachers typically did not spend time annotating student work with entry slips (Vavrus & Collins, 1991). Entry slips didn't seem useful to teachers, and they required too much time. As a result of that research, we hadn't built teacher entry slips into our model. However, because teachers could not guide their peers or answer questions about their students during moderation and evaluation of portfolios, there emerged a need for teacher entry slips. The need came from both the initiating teachers and the reviewers. Specifically, the initiating teachers wanted to be able to communicate to others why particular pieces had been included: What were the goals and expectations for students doing a particular task? The reviewers often wanted to know how much support students had received for a particular activity so that they could distinguish between supported performance and independent performance. At the same time, we began to use portfolios more frequently during conferences (see chapter 9), and it appeared that parents had similar questions when reviewing their children's portfolios. So there was a real need for teacher entry slips that came from the teachers in our group.

The most interesting aspect of teacher entry slips is how they encourage teachers to examine closely their instructional practices and expectations for students. As teachers struggle with how to communicate what they value and do in the classroom, they reexamine many of their practices and beliefs. Figures 8.1–8.4 are examples of the types of reflection teachers engage in when they create entry slips. For example, the entry slip in Figure 8.1 reflects the priorities of Marla and Barb, two primary teachers. Just by the areas they include on the entry slip (prewriting, writing, editing, spell checking, etc.), they communicate what they value and work on with their students. Producing this entry slip required thoughtful inquiry into their curricular and instructional goals. In addition, the added space for special comments about Elizabeth and the distinction between independent and supported work provide good background knowledge for everyone who reads Elizabeth's story. And, it is clear that the teachers value this unique information about Elizabeth.

Figure 8.1

TEACHER ENTRY SLIP--WRITING PROCESS

Date:___6.12.95_____

I have selected this piece for __Elizabeth__'s portfolio because it
demonstrates current best writing which was taken through a publishing process to a final copy.

Circle one: *The student requested to publish this story.
**The teacher suggested publishing this story.

Additional comments:

Elizabeth's main theme in life is horses — she's had lots of lessons, takes care of horses, and reads fiction & nonfiction about horses. Her knowledge is reflected in her stories.

Who helped with this work? Briefly tell how each one helped.

1.   PREWRITE ACTIVITY: picture or series of pictures/mind map/class
     brainstorm/other?   --independently/with support
     Elizabeth says she read a series of books called "The
2.   WRITING: Wrote independently/with support--   *Thoroughbreds," in*
     --on a self-selected topic   *which there were*
     --on a directed topic--prompt: *2 horses "worden"*
     & "pride."

3.   EDITING: Did first editing for spelling/punctuation
          --independently/with support.

4.   SPELL CHECK: Used hand-held spell checker--yes/no

5.   WORD PROCESSING: Did word processing independently/with support
          or adult or class helper did all word processing
          Mrs. Baker did all.

6.   PROOFREAD/EDITED word-processed copy for spelling/punctuation
          --independently/with support.

7.   REVISED FOR CONTENT on word-processed copy independently/
          with support
          --changed or added individual words
          --revised or added individual sentences
          --restructured or added paragraphs

8.   PRESENTED TO CLASS independently/with support

_____Marla English/Barb Renfrow-Baker_____
Signature

---

*An entry slip created by two primary grade teachers reflects their think-
ing about the writing process in general and about Elizabeth's unique
interests, reading-writing connections, and independence
in creating a story.*

Figure 8.2

Teacher Portfolio Entry

Student's Name: *Lauren*

Date: *Apr. 29, 1996*

This piece was selected for a portfolio entry as a sample of your child's use of regular and invented spelling when writing sentences dictated by the teacher. This work gives an indication of your child's ability to analyse the words he/she hears or says and to find some way of recording the sounds he/she hears as letters. It is also an indication of his/her understanding of the proper use of capital and lower case letters and punctuation. The following are the sentences dictated by the teacher:

1. I have a big dog at home. Today I am going to take him to school.
2. The bus in coming. It will stop here to let me get on.
3. The boy is riding his bike. He can go very fast on it.

Lauren   April 29 1996
I have a big dog at home.
Today i am going to take him to
school. The bus is comeing
It will stop hear to let me get on.
The boy is riteingg his bike
He can go vere fast on it

A first-grade teacher entry slip communicates the teacher's expectations for writing and provides information about an end-of-year class assessment activity.

Figure 8.3

Reading Response Journal

The reading response journal is a place for students to respond to, write about, draw about, etc. their independent reading. It is a way for students to think about what they are reading. It is also a way for me to review students' comprehension on a regular basis. We share these journals during reading conferences.

When I read this journal, I am looking for:

_____ The main idea or theme of the book

_____ Significant information about the book

_____ Important ideas which were inferred

_____ Personal response to the ideas or writing

_____ Ideas that are clearly communicated in writing

A generic teacher entry slip for a reading response journal focuses on important comprehension goals for third-grade students. The slip also helps parents understand why the teacher has students keep these journals.

Figures 8.2–8.4 are less personalized but are still important reflections of teachers' thinking. Figure 8.2 clearly communicates this first-grade teacher's expectations for students' spelling (invented and correct), capitalization, and punctuation at the end of first grade. She even provides the prompt sentences so that parents can decipher their first graders' writing, a sample of which is attached. Similarly, constructing the teacher entry slip in Figure 8.3 helped this third-grade teacher clarify for herself and for outside portfolio readers what she hoped students would include in their response journals. The entry slip enumerates some of her reading goals for her students, and it also helps the teacher refocus instruction. The entry slip is stapled into the front of her students' reading response journals so the teacher can check off different areas of emphasis for different students or at different points in the school year. Figure 8.4 also reveals a teacher's thinking, this time about the writing process, reading-writing relationships, and qualities of a good story for intermediate students. A teacher who was less insightful about her own goals would not have been able to create such a succinct entry.

Figure 8.4

Teacher Entry Slip

Underground Railroad Stories

After reading and listening to several books about the Underground Railroad, the students composed their own stories about a fugitive slave. They did prewriting brainstorming and rough drafts at school with classmates. After conferencing with a peer or an adult, they revised to be sure the story was strong. We worked on stories having authentic settings, interesting problems, action and a clear beginning, middle, and end.

With the help of volunteers in the classroom or the parents at home, the students typed a final copy that we printed in a class anthology.

> *An intermediate teacher entry slip provides important background about how students created Underground Railroad stories. The teacher's insights about reading-writing connections, the writing process, and criteria for good stories are evident.*

Figure 8.5 is a personalized teacher entry slip created by a high school teacher to help others understand what she sees and values in a specific piece of student writing, "The Train." The teacher leaves little doubt that she knows what she wants to see in this piece and that the student also knows (and, in fact, challenges the teacher). It is also clear that the teacher values the student and her ability to self-assess.

The process of creating teacher entry slips can invite reflective practice. On the other hand, it can also be quite superficial, carried out without much reflective thought (i.e., "The students did this research report as part of our unit on South America"; "Children write about what they are reading in their reading response journals"; "Tanya worked very hard on this project and did an excellent job"). We have found that having a genuine, interested audience on the other side—colleagues, parents, administrators, or students—is a good motivator for generating thoughtful teacher entry slips. The added benefit, of course, is that teachers can communicate to others what they value and expect from their students. Others come to understand the thoughtfulness behind good teaching at the same time that teachers gain new insights into their practice.

Figure 8.5

Portfolio Entry: *The Train*

This piece tells me: *That Sara is very concerned about grades and expects a very thorough reading. When I was confused in my reading & thought I saw an inconsistency, she brought the paper back to ask me to reread it. She was right & I corrected my grade. She is very proud of this story - especially the twist in the end. I see a deliberate focus on dropping hints & creating suspense.*

> *This personalized entry slip reflects a high school teacher's understanding of a particular student's writing and her appreciation of the student's individual concerns and perspective.*

Conclusion

Reflective practice can be enhanced as teachers conceptualize, implement, and use portfolios. The strategies in this chapter require teachers to take a step back from and a step forward into their work. Portfolios require both. Reflective practice is driven by broad questions of what is important for students to learn and what is effective instruction. It is also driven by careful, knowledgeable analyses of student work and of specific instructional practices. The power of working with colleagues enriches our own self-inquiry with new perspectives, insights, and knowledge that we probably would not come to alone.

These are the kinds of professional experiences one teacher described as having an "intellectual edge"; another described them as "the most exciting and stimulating experiences of my teaching career." They push teachers out of the comfort zone into the challenge zone, where inquiry is the coin of the realm. When portfolios contribute to this quality of teacher engagement and reflective practice, they will certainly contribute to both teacher and student learning.

References

Clark, C., Moss, P. A., Goering, S., Herter, R. J., Leonard, D., Robbins, S., Russell, M., Templin, M., & Wascha, K. (1996). Collaboration as dialogue: Teachers and researchers engaged in conversation and professional development. *American Educational Research Journal, 33*(1), 193–231.

Darling-Hammond, L. (1996). The quiet revolution: Rethinking teacher development. *Educational Leadership, 53*(6), 4–10.

Darling-Hammond, L., Ancess, J., & Falk, B. (1995). *Authentic assessment in action: Studies of schools and students at work.* New York: Teachers College Press.

Darling-Hammond, L., & McLaughlin, M. W. (1995). Policies that support professional development in an era of reform. *Phi Delta Kappan, 76*(8), 597–604.

International Reading Association & National Council of Teachers of English. (1994). *Standards for the assessment of reading and writing.* Newark, DE: International Reading Association.

Johnston, P. (1989). Constructive evaluation and the improvement of teaching and learning. *Teachers College Record, 90*(4), 509–528.

Johnston, P. (1987). Teachers as evaluation experts. *The Reading Teacher, 40*(8), 744–748.

Lieberman, A. (1995). Practices that support teacher development: Transforming conceptions of professional learning. *Phi Delta Kappan, 76*(8), 591–596.

Lieberman, A., & McLaughlin, M. W. (1992). Networks for education change: Powerful and problematic. *Phi Delta Kappan, 73*(9), 673–677.

Lipson, M. Y., & Wixson, K. K. (1997). *Assessment and instruction of reading and writing disability: An interactive approach* (2nd ed.). New York: Longman.

Moss, P. A., Beck, J. S., Ebbs, C., Matson, B., Muchmore, J., Steele, D., Taylor, C., & Herter, R. (1992). Portfolios, accountability, and an interpretive approach to validity. *Educational Measurement: Issues and Practice, 11*(3), 12–21.

Noffke, S., & Zeichner, K. (1987). *Action research and teacher thinking: The first phase of the action research project at the University of Wisconsin, Madison.* Paper presented to the American Educational Research Association, Washington, DC.

Richardson, V. (1990). Significant and worthwhile change in teaching practice. *Educational Researcher, 19*(7), 10–18.

Richert, A. E. (1991). Case methods and teacher education: Using cases to teach teacher reflection. In B. R. Tabachnick & K.M. Zeichner (Eds.), *Issues and practices in inquiry oriented teacher education* (pp. 130–150). London: Falmer.

Schön, D. A. (1983). *The reflective practitioner: How professionals think in action.* New York: Basic Books.

Schön, D. A. (1987). *Educating the reflective practitioner.* San Francisco: Jossey-Bass.

Shavelson, R. J., & Stern, P. (1981). Research on teachers' pedagogical thought, judgments, decisions and behavior. *Review of Educational Research, 41*(4), 455–498.

Shulman, L. C. (1987). Knowledge and teaching: Foundations of the new reform. *Harvard Educational Review, 57*(1), 1–22.

Snyder, J., Bolin, F., & Zumwalt, K. (1992). Curriculum implementation. In P. Jackson (Ed.), *Handbook of research on curriculum* (pp. 402–435). New York: Macmillan.

Stiggins, R. J. (1997). Student-centered classroom assessment (2nd ed.) New York: Macmillan College Publishing.

Stiggins, R. J., & Conklin, N. F. (1992). *In teachers' hands: Investigating the practices of classroom assessment.* Albany: State University of New York Press.

Valencia, S. W., & Au, K. H. (1997). Portfolios across educational contexts: Issues of evaluation, professional development, and system validity. *Educational Assessment, 4*(1), 1–35.

Valli, L. (1997). Listening to other voices: A description of teacher reflection in the United States. *Peabody Journal of Education, 72*(1), 67–88.

Vavrus, L. G., & Collins, A. (1991). Portfolio documentation and assessment center exercises: A marriage made for teacher assessment. *Journal of Teacher Education, 18*(3), 13–39.

PART 3

Using Portfolios to Communicate with Those Outside the Classroom

chapter **9**

Communicating: Teachers, Families, and Students Together*

PHYLLIS RICHARDSON

> *In Chapter 9 we discuss two aspects of communication: helping families understand and support classroom learning and portfolios, and using portfolios to establish clear communication about student progress. We are committed to open communication among all the stakeholders in learning—families, students, and teachers—and offer several examples of how teachers can use portfolios to foster shared understanding and responsibility.*

In case of fire, first save the children, then save the portfolios.

Parent of intermediate student

Four years ago I participated in a district portfolio group. That experience forever changed the way I view instruction and assessment. It also helped me develop more meaningful and reflective ways to communicate progress and learning to students and families. This chapter explains my journey and that of many of my colleagues as we discovered how portfolios can become the centerpiece for meaningful, productive communication among teachers, families, and students.

I remember conference time at my childhood elementary school. My mother was called for a meeting—I was not invited. I was always apprehensive on these conference days because previous parent conferences had taught me that I was not a good student, and my own experiences of being in the "buzzard" group for reading and math reaffirmed my belief. I learned all of this by the time I was in second grade. On conference days I knew that my mother would come home and explain her disappointment in me.

*I use the term families to refer to the wide range of home situations and support provided to students.

It was a scene that was replayed over each of my 12 years in public school. Perhaps if I had been given the opportunity to be an active member of my conferences, I would have known exactly what I needed to do to improve. Perhaps I would have been able to gauge if I had made any progress at all. But I never heard those comments. More important, maybe if my teacher had kept authentic pieces of my work over time and talked about them with me, I might have seen my own learning progress and begun to believe in myself as an able learner. Maybe my mother would have, too. Now, as a teacher, I know that I do not want to instill in my students the negative feelings I felt as a young learner. I want my students to understand their own strengths and needs and to appreciate and own their learning. I want families to share in that knowledge alongside their children and the teacher. So, as my colleagues and I have implemented portfolios in our classrooms, we have made a commitment to use portfolios to foster a more open, clear, and effective form of communication with students and families.

Teachers have always communicated with families. We know all too well that without family interest, our job is more difficult and students fail to thrive (Daniels, 1996; Henderson & Berla, 1994). Portfolios add two challenges to this communication.

The first challenge is to help families understand the purpose and logistics of portfolios in the classroom. At one level, this simply means explaining what a portfolio is and how it works (i.e., keeping work at school, passing work along). At a deeper level, families need to understand a new view of classroom assessment. This involves understanding the curriculum—what we want students to know and be able to do; assessment—the strategies that teachers use to determine how well students are progressing; and student engagement—the role of students in evaluating their own work and setting goals (DeFina, 1992; Paratore, 1993).

The second challenge for communication is to help families understand student progress by looking closely at student work and other artifacts in a portfolio. Student performance is no longer hidden behind grades; now there is evidence to show strengths and needs, to document growth over time, and to reveal what students are learning. Families need help understanding that evidence so they know what their children are learning and how well they are performing against clearly articulated standards (Flood & Lapp, 1989; Hedman, 1993; Salinger & Chittenden, 1994). At the same time, we want students to be owners of that very same knowledge. The challenge is to establish collaborative communication among students, families, and teachers so they can look at work together, understand it, set reasonable expectations, and make decisions about next steps (International Reading Association & National Council of Teachers of English, 1994).

With these challenges in mind, we have two goals for communicating with families:

- There must be continuous communication with families to help them understand and support the process of learning and the complex nature of portfolio assessment.

- Teachers must provide clear and honest communication about student performance so that families will know what children are learning, how they are progressing, and how well they are achieving.

The first goal addresses the philosophy and logistics of portfolios, which may be new for families. The second addresses how we, as professionals, meet our responsibility to provide clear feedback to families about what their children are able to do and what are reasonable goals and expectations for them. The second goal also addresses how we involve students and families in a shared responsibility for evaluation and engagement in learning.

Communicating With Families About the Process of Learning and the Nature of Portfolio Assessment

Good communication is built on knowledge and trust. Each year, I begin to build that knowledge and trust with families by helping them understand the curriculum, learning activities, and assessment opportunities their children will experience throughout the year. I use three strategies to communicate with families about learning and assessment in our classroom:

- introductory portfolio letter
- monthly class newsletters
- Back-to-School Night

Introductory Portfolio Letter

The introductory portfolio letter is often the first exposure many families have to the concept of portfolios, student engagement in assessment, student self-assessment, and family participation in assessment. In the letter, I explain the concept of portfolio assessment and how it helps students, and I review generally what students are learning and how they are progressing. It is also important for families to understand that work will not be coming home as regularly as in the past. It's a good idea to explain clearly what will happen. For example, I explain that the students will review their collections monthly, make selections for their portfolios, and then take home the unused portions of their collections. Both the philosophy and logistics must be clear to families.

Figure 9.1 is a sample introductory letter I have used with my second-third grade class. Although some families will be familiar with portfolios (their children have used them in first or second grade), I find it useful to let families know *my* approach to portfolios. In the letter, I explain the concept of portfolios and just a little bit about how they work in my classroom. I also try to establish collaboration with families by encouraging them to contribute artifacts to the portfolio, talk with their children about school, and stop by our classroom to review the portfolio.

Other teachers use different strategies to introduce portfolios to families. Some wait until Back-to-School Night to explain portfolios, especially

---

Figure 9.1

September

Dear Families,

Assessment is a very important part of education today. As I teach and as students learn, it is essential to assess student performance. It's this assessment that helps me plan and helps students focus their effort. Unfortunately many of us have different memories of assessment—a pop quiz, standardized test, or Friday spelling tests, for example. The purpose of assessment was to be able to write down a grade, not to help teachers or students improve learning.

In classrooms today, assessment does not only mean tests. It means more. It means a continuous process of looking at students' learning, understanding, and progress over time. Teachers use a variety of methods to assess students' learning, not just tests. Anecdotal records, observations, samples of students' work, journal writing and special projects are just a few of the ways I assess students. The variety helps me gain a more complete picture of what your child knows.

We keep these different assessments in a portfolio, which is a collection of purposefully chosen work that is accessible to the student, family, and teacher at all times. The work in the portfolio is selected from actual classroom activities and is used WITH the students to set goals and look at progress. The students keep a collection folder which is separate from the portfolio. About once a month they select work from these collections to be placed in their portfolios. I also select pieces to keep in the portfolios. After we select from the collection, the remaining pieces are sent home. This means that you will be not be seeing as much work come home daily as you might be used to; you will get a collection of work about once a month and, of course, you are always welcome to look at the portfolio at school.

I encourage you to add pieces to your child's portfolio as well. Your perspective and involvement is an important part of the process. The process for your selection is simple. I will send home blank family entry slips with my monthly newsletter. You can select a piece from the collection your child brings home each month or you can select something your child has done at home that you think is important or interesting. On the entry slip, just briefly explain why you have made the selection. It's a good idea to talk about this with your child. Then, have your child bring the entry slip and work to school to put in his or her portfolio.

Portfolios help all of us understand that assessment is a vital part of instruction and learning. They provide a good representation of what your child is doing in school and they help me work directly with your child to review his or her progress and to set goals. These are the reasons why I use portfolio assessment in my classroom. We'll talk more about them throughout the year. I hope you will share the process of reviewing and contributing to the portfolio conversation.

Phyllis Richardson

My beginning-of-year portfolio letter introduces families to portfolios and our classroom.

if the concept is new to families and children in the school. In other schools where portfolios are being implemented schoolwide, principals include information in the school newsletter. Regardless of the strategy, it is important for families to be informed and to feel comfortable with portfolios.

Monthly Class Newsletters

Because portfolio assessment requires work to be kept at school over extended periods of time, it is vital that families are kept up-to-date about what is happening at school. In my monthly class newsletters, I explain activities, discuss learning objectives, and offer examples of student work completed or in progress. I try to include a bit of information about our portfolios each month. For example, I discuss how students are selecting work or how I am trying to involve students in self-reflection and self-evaluation of their work. I also use the newsletters to encourage family participation in the portfolios by including several family entry slips and providing some ideas for making selections. Often, the newsletters are rather lengthy, but I am committed to sharing important facets of our classroom with families. The newsletters are like a lifeline connecting our classroom curriculum and assessment to my students' home life. Figure 9.2a is an excerpt of the newsletter I sent home in November 1995. My style is friendly and personal; other teachers prefer a more formal style but still try to cover similar information.

My focus on family involvement is maintained through these newsletters. Each month, I ask families to become actively engaged in their children's portfolios by reviewing the monthly collections and making their own selections from the pieces that come home or from work done at home. Like the children, families are asked to complete an entry slip explaining the reason for their selection (see Figure 9.2b). Then, the entry slip is attached to the selection and sent to school so the children can place it into their portfolios. On one hand, creating the opportunity for families to be hands-on participants in their children's portfolios helps them understand the hard work of assessment and the kind of self-reflection their children are doing in the classroom. The process of reviewing work helps educate families about what their children are learning. On the other hand, family selections provide the teacher with another valuable perspective on the children's knowledge and abilities. I learn about my students' home literacy habits, their interests, and what the family values. Family participation in portfolios creates the opportunity for important two-way conversation between home and school (Lazar & Weisberg, 1996; Paratore, 1993, 1994; Rhodes & Shanklin, 1993).

Figures 9.3 and 9.4 are examples of the kinds of insights that families can provide. Nathaniel's dad has carefully observed his first-grade son's process of learning and shares his insights on the entry slip (see Figure 9.3). It is apparent that Mr. Jones appreciates Nathaniel's creativity, diligence, and independence. As a teacher, I learn that Nathaniel is encouraged to write and use invented spelling at home. Both father and son are obviously very proud to contribute this work to Nathaniel's portfolio.

Figure 9.2a

November 20, 1995

Dear Families:

Can you believe it? Thanksgiving is this week! It doesn't seem like it could possibly be here already. We have two more days of school, I have a major project due this week for the master's class I'm taking this quarter and I have eight people coming for Thanksgiving dinner on Thursday! I'm not sure I will make it in one piece! However, things always seem to work out—at least I have "farmed out" the pies!

Okay, enough about my personal life. I bet you want to know what your children have been doing lately—lots of things!!! To begin, I'm sure you saw the purple packet of work that came home on Friday. I hope your children told you the packet was a result of our first portfolio pull. The work brought home was work your children didn't select to become part of their portfolios. Each child selected 1-3 pieces for the portfolio and attached an entry slip on which he or she explained why the piece was included. I chose a few pieces for the portfolio as well. This time, we talked about selecting pieces the children felt demonstrated something about which they were particularly proud. Next time, we might have a different emphasis. I encouraged the children to think carefully about their reasons for selecting work and not to simply write, "I chose this piece because I like it…" or "…because it's good." They did a wonderful job thinking and writing about why a particular piece was important to them. I believe self-reflection is a critical part of the learning process and hope to help steer the children to even more in-depth reflections as the year goes on. Attached you will also find an entry slip for you. If you see any piece you would like to place in your child's portfolio, please fill out the entry slip and send it back with the piece you select-ed. We will put it in the portfolio. You may select from the work that came home on Friday or you may select something that your child has done at home.

In the reading area, our literature circles have been a fantastic success. The groups have finished reading their books and are beginning to create a group response to present to the class on Wednesday. This response will be a celebration of the end of the first Literature Circle groups this year and will feature all of the group projects. Group book responses are designed to help the students reflect on the meaning they constructed from the story. Often they find themselves going back into the book to look for an important part they might want to act out. Other times they have discussions about a certain event or a particular character which deepens their understand-ing of the story and helps them plan their project. The students have loved this Literature Circle time. All of the stories, which center around the theme of "Friends and Family," had thoughtful problems and themes which kept students' interest high. Now, students are busy organizing their responses. Some are writing poems to act out while others are creating puppet shows. I can't wait to see their presentations.

In math, we have…(I often include information about other subjects and special projects.)

During Writers Workshop we began a study of fairy tales and legends. We are looking at the structure and lan-guage of these two genres and are noticing the rich descriptions and details which are often a part of this type of literature. Ask your children to tell you about the Baba Yaga fairy tale we read–they loved it! In the next couple of weeks, after we've looked and talked more about fairy tales and legends, the children will be encouraged to write their own. If your children have favorite fairy tales or legends at home they'd like to share, we'd love to hear them!

Our study of our city has begun. Last week we started by looking at slides of old Bellevue and the Eastside that we borrowed from the Marymoor Park Museum. The class had a good informal discussion about why the Eastside was developed and how the community grew. We studied what a community needs to develop and reviewed a pic-ture book about a boy growing up and watching his community develop outside his bedroom window. This week, students will write words for this book, using their knowledge of what happens as a community develops. I extend an invitation to anyone who has information, stories, pictures, etc. of old Bellevue to share them with us. If you know people who were living during the early part of Bellevue's history, let us know. We'd love to have them share stories and history with us.

I hope you have a fantastic Thanksgiving holiday. Enjoy yourselves and don't eat too much turkey or pumpkin pie…YUM!

As always,

Phyllis

Phyllis Richardson

My monthly newsletters are informal. I try to help families understand what their children are learning and doing in class.

Figure 9.2b

FAMILY-STUDENT
ENTRY

DATE _____

I am choosing to put this piece
in _____

portfolio because I think it
shows he/she knows how to

_____
_____
_____
_____
_____
_____
_____
_____
_____
_____

Signed _____
Family member

_____
Child

I also provide a a family entry slip with my newsletters.

Jennifer's dad also shows a broad appreciation of his daughter's abilities (see Figure 9.4). He comments on Jennifer's understanding of complex issues facing the world as well as personal ("local") problems. He comments on her thoughtfulness about a dilemma that many third-grade students ponder—"How do you 'cancel' overpopulation and dying?" He also appreciates Jennifer's ability to structure a piece of writing and her sense of poetry. These are valuable insights for me as Jennifer's teacher. I learn that Jennifer is supported at home in her writing and thinking about important issues, and I have a vehicle for conversation with Jennifer's family.

At the end of each year I ask for feedback from families about my letters. It is important to me that I meet families' needs. Following is a representative sample of what I ask and what many families say:

Do my newsletters help you understand about learning in our classroom?

- *"Yes! It is nice to see the overall picture of what's going on in the class. Usually, I only hear about a favorite project."*

Figure 9.3

FAMILY ENTRY SLIP

Date ___5/31/93___

I picked this piece of work because *it is a good example of how Nathaniel works on a theme from many aspects. First he memorized "My country Tis of Thee." Then he sang it over and over. And then he wrote it in a fancy style that fits the importance and grandure of the song.*

___Dave___
Signature

Who helped you with it? Tell how they helped.
This was done all by himself at home, during the month of April!

- "Yes. I appreciate knowing exactly what approach is being taken in each subject.
- "Yes, but . . . much of the information is after the learning concept has already been fully explored. I would rather receive advance notice of the upcoming concept—to be able to help with reinforcement at home."
- "Your newsletters are very informative. It is important to us to understand your teaching goals and approaches. The letters add a new dimension to our child's descriptions of her classroom activities, and they enable us to reinforce the concepts and skills she is learning. We enjoy hearing about new teaching methods!"

It's rewarding to see how much families appreciate knowing what their children are learning. Even the concerned parent who would prefer to get the newsletters *before* we begin work on a new concept reinforces the importance of families' need for information. In response to this feedback, I now include a section in the newsletters about "Upcoming Events." Sending these newsletters, including entry slips, and asking for feedback from families have a secondary benefit as well: They reinforce my commitment to a two-way conversation. I want families to know that communicating about their child is our shared responsibility.

Back-to-School Night

One of my goals for Back-to-School Night in October is to help families understand that student portfolios will provide a more complete and verifiable documentation of student learning and progress over time. I arrange the classroom and my presentation around the portfolios, even though they are still very minimal at this time of year.

Figure 9.3 *continued*

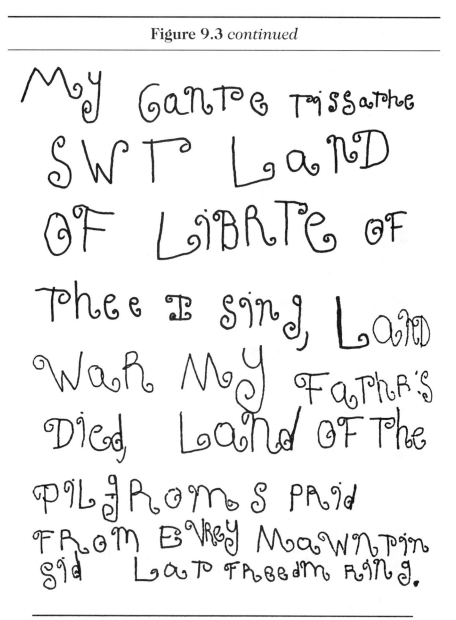

Nathaniel's dad notices and appreciates his son's approach to learning.

As families enter the room during this event, the first thing they see is student-illustrated portfolios. On every desk, students have left their own portfolios to announce to their families where they sit. The families sit at the desks. As the event begins, I share with families the importance of finding a more comprehensive way to assess students. No longer will one standardized test best judge what their children know. I explain that it is important to look at student work over time, to use a variety of assessment

Figure 9.4

FAMILY-STUDENT
ENTRY

DATE _____ 1/23 _____

I am choosing to put this piece
in *Jennifer* _____

portfolio because I think it
shows ~~he~~/(she) knows how to
write thematically.
~~It is~~ This poem shows
an awareness of global
(abstract) and concrete (local)
"problems" and is a good
exercise in structuring
her writing. It also presents
a fascinating dilemma: how do
you "cancel" overpopulation
and dying? Her parallelism
and use of "cancel" are strengths.

Signed _____

tools, and to encourage students and caregivers to become more involved
and responsible for student learning. Portfolios, I explain, are the assessment tool that can best accomplish these goals (Flood & Lapp, 1989;
Salinger & Chittenden, 1994; Valencia, 1990). I also explain the need for an
open and honest form of communication concerning their children's individual learning goals, which will be developed at the first three-way conference the following month (discussed later in this chapter). In addition, I

Figure 9.4 *continued*

If I Were In
Charge of the World.
If I were in charge of
the world I would get rid
of pollution,
If I were in charge of
the world I would cancel dying,
If I were in charge of the
world I would cancel over
population,
If I were in charge of the
world I would cancel bees,
If I were in charge of the
world I would cancel Poisonous things

---

discuss how I will structure the class to help students meet these goals and how we will use the portfolios to collaboratively assess students' progress. The families have time to browse through the first pieces we have entered into our portfolios. Usually, there are a couple of pieces of student writing, beginning-of-the-year math assessments, book logs, and a few pieces of art-work. These few pieces provide a way for families to get a first-hand experience of reviewing work with me close by.

Figure 9.4 *continued*

---

like   black   widows,

If   I   were   in   charge   of

the   world,   I   would   cancel   sickness,

If   I   were   in   charge   of   the

world   I   would   make   everybody

freinds,

If   I   were   in   charge   of   the

world   I   would   make   toys   and

candy   cost   nothing,

By   Jennifer.

---

*Jennifer's dad appreciates his daughter's engagement with the topic
and her ability to express herself in writing.*

Annette, a colleague who teaches an early primary class (multiaged, kindergarten, and first grade), also introduces the idea of portfolio assessment to her families at Back-to-School Night. Her explanations and examples are more specific and concrete because, unlike many of my second and third graders' families, her families have not received an introductory portfolio letter. More important, portfolios are a new concept for most of their young children and for many of them. Children's decorated portfolios are on their desks, along with actual collections of work the children have completed since the beginning of school. This is what the families see when they arrive. As Annette begins her meeting, she explains the reason why student work is not coming home daily or weekly. She explains the portfolio process to the families and has them review the work in the collections. She points out the need for students to keep these collections because some of the pieces will be selected for the portfolios. If the work were sent home, the students would not have collections from which to "pull" their self-selections.

Having families review the collections at Back-to-School Night provides a good opportunity to introduce the concept and process of family entries. We can help families learn to look at their children's work from a variety of perspectives—interesting, special, best, creative, evidence of change—just as we try to help the children reflect on various aspects of their work. Families can begin to appreciate the richness and value of using student work to assess progress. During Back-to-School Night, families might be encouraged to select one or two pieces from the collection for entry into the portfolios and to complete entry slips for their children to see the next day. The activity gives families a first-hand experience with the concept and logistics of portfolios and with possibilities for their involvement.

All of the preceding ideas (introductory letters, monthly newsletters, and Back-to-School Night) are examples of strategies to help families understand what happens in our classrooms and why and how portfolios are a central part of our work. At the same time these ideas help teachers understand families. Certainly, there are many other creative strategies to accomplish this first goal of communication. Whatever the strategy, we must be diligent in our efforts to introduce families to a new way of looking at student learning and assessment and to engage them as partners in the process. This kind of family involvement does more than help teachers and families communicate: It also increases the likelihood that students will learn and thrive in school (Daniels, 1996; Henderson & Berla, 1994).

Using Portfolios to Provide Clear and Honest Communication About Student Progress and Expectations for Learning

The second goal of communication is more complex than the first because it involves being able to articulate specific learning goals, helping families look closely at portfolio evidence to see students' progress toward those goals, and providing professional feedback on appropriate expectations and standards for student performance. Many families, like many of us, grew up at a time when students' learning appeared straightforward—each paper had either a letter grade, a number, or a plus or a minus inscribed in red across the top to indicate the quality of performance. Through the years, however, we have discovered that these numbers and symbols are not as objective or as clear as we thought—they are open to interpretation and often are assigned without clear understanding of what they represent (Stiggins, 1997). Examining genuine student work and portfolio artifacts can be more informative and meaningful than assigning grades if the process is linked to clear learning outcomes and standards for performance. However, families and guardians don't always understand what they are seeing or what are reasonable expectations for students (DeFina, 1992; Guyton & Feilstein, 1989). Three strategies can help families understand their children's learning and progress:

- three-way conferences
- linking portfolios to grading periods
- end-of-year portfolio celebrations

All of these strategies provide opportunities for teachers to help families understand the complex nature of their children's progress, and, at the same time, they provide a meaningful way for students to discuss what they know about themselves. As a result, students become "responsible experts" concerned about their own learning (Countryman & Schorieder, 1996; Darling-Hammond, Ancess, & Falk, 1995; Guyton & Feilstein, 1989; Hebert, 1992). Through discussion and examination of portfolios, we all join to become a collaborative team whose job is to understand students' progress, provide support for learning, and set appropriate goals.

Three-Way Conferences

Instead of the traditional parent-teacher conference, many of us use a three-way conference early in the school year (October or November) to review progress so far and to develop specific long-term learning goals. If students are going to be engaged in their own learning and assessment, they should be part of this conference. Some teachers invite the students to be present for the entire conference, others structure time for both three-way conferences and separate parent-teacher conversations.

In my classroom, each member involved in the conference must fulfill certain obligations before the day of the conference. Families complete a survey that they bring to the conference. It asks about their insights and goals for their children this year (see Figure 9.5). This family perspective adds a vital link that has often been left out of the information-gathering and goal-setting processes in school. Students also answer questions about themselves as learners on a student survey that is completed before the conference. Their responsibility is to identify their overall feelings about school and to describe three long-term goals they would like to work on during the coming year (see Figure 9.6). Some teachers work with their students to review portfolios as they complete their surveys. This reinforces *using* the portfolios to set meaningful goals. In addition to family and student surveys, I complete for each student an anecdotal record that documents my observations in the areas of reading, writing, math, and social/emotional development (see Figure 9.7). I often refer to the portfolio to help me think about and verify my insights about student progress thus far. The information from the family survey, student survey, and teacher anecdotal record is used at the conference to develop learning goals for the student. The point is that all participants must come prepared for the conference; each perspective is important because we share responsibility for goal setting and, ultimately, for student success.

On the day of the conference, the family, student, and teacher meet in a roundtable discussion to talk about progress so far and to develop a learning plan for the year. All members of the conference have their written documentation with suggestions for long-term goals. Because sound goal setting is based on understanding the child's current strengths and needs as well as personal goals, I begin by using portfolio evidence to talk about specific areas of improvement that I have noticed since the beginning of the year. Specificity is critical to this process. To be specific, I need to be clear about exactly what I value and look for in student learning (what I want to teach), what I see this particular child has learned, and what are reasonable expectations for this child who is now in my second-third grade class. Following are three examples of how I discuss "specifics" in writing and reading with families and children during the conference.

Looking at writing. I usually begin with writing because progress is so concrete for students and families to observe. Figure 9.8 (starting on page 300) presents two writing samples from Rosie's writing journal that were stored in her portfolio. The first sample was written early in the school year, the other two months later. During the fall conference I pointed out to Rosie's mother how Rosie's writing had improved. Specifically, I discussed the amount of detail in the November sample that was not present in the September sample. For instance, in November Rosie wrote, "On Sunday at 3:00 my dad my brother and I went to the airport to pick up my Grandma." In this opening sentence Rosie mentioned the time of day, who was present with her, and why they were with her. Later in the story, she included her feelings in a very natural way: "I'm glad she's here but its to [sic] bad about her clothes and its [sic] to bad about we did not get our present because they were in her bag." I also pointed out specific changes in the mechanics of Rosie's writing (e.g., spelling, capitalization). In addition, Rosie had begun to use the element of time to make transitions between her thoughts: "After we got her. . . ." During the conference, I made a special point of asking Rosie to add to my observations or to contribute her own. I wanted to be sure that we knew what Rosie thought was going well for her writing as well as what I thought was going well. By my using concrete examples and very specific feedback, Rosie's mother could see the growth in Rosie's writing over the first two months of school.

It is also important for families to gain an understanding of expectations and standards for good work. Therefore, during conferences I focus on areas of need as well as of growth. For example, Rosie's mom wanted to know if Rosie's work was in line with what I expected and what Rosie needed to work on. I pointed out that Rosie needed to clarify her use of homophones (e.g., *to, too,* and *two*) and that she was ready to learn more about paragraphing and complex story structures and plots. This was pointed out to Rosie and her mother in a kind and respectful way. It provided critical information about reasonable expectations for Rosie's writing and was essential later in the conference as we developed appropriate learning goals.

Figure 9.5

Student's Name _Kendal_   Date _11/1/95_

FALL GOAL SETTING CONFERENCE

The purpose of the Fall Goal Setting Conference is to share
information, evaluate progress and set goals for the coming year.
Please take a few minutes to fill out the following survey before
coming to the Fall Goal Setting Conference. This survey will help to
deepen my understanding of your child and will create a framework
by which we (student, parent, teacher) can begin to develop some
yearly goals as we look ahead to the remaining part of the school
year. It is important that you bring this survey with you and your
child to the conference.

1. What do you see as areas of strength for your child?

   Reading
   Written and oral Communication skills

2. What do you see as possible areas of growth for your child
   this year?

   Math skills and confidence
   Basic geography

3. List five attributes you see in your child.
   Kind, compassionate, imaginative,
   self-reliant, intelligent

4. Write a short paragraph describing your child in his/her home
   environment.

   Kendal is always very happy. She has a
   positive outlook on life and shares her happiness.
   She is very caring and looks out for her little
   brother. She would rather play in a world of
   her imagination than do anything else.

5. What academic or social goals would you like us (student, parent,
   teacher) to work toward this year?

   Confidence in math skills - This is a must.
   Become more of a self-motivated student.
   learn, challenge, expand her mind because
   She wants to.

---

*Kendal's parents complete this form before the fall conference. It helps
me understand their perspectives and expectations for Kendal.*

Figure 9.6

Name Kendal   Date 10-2-95

FALL GOAL SETTING CONFERENCE

The purpose of the Fall Goal Setting Conference is to share information, evaluate progress and set goals for the coming year. This student survey is where you get to tell your family and I how you are feeling about yourself and what new things you would like to learn this year. Please take your time answering each question honestly.

1. **List three things that you are really good at in the classroom.**
   1. I'm good at writing.
   2. I'm good at art.
   3. I'm good at math.

2. **List as many different ways you show kindness to your friends as you can.**
   I share snak.
   I help people with story ideas.
   I take people to the ofic if they are hurt.

3. **Who do you feel comfortable sitting by?**
   I feel comfortable sitting by, Stephane, Kalla and Aurby.

4. **I wish I had more time at school for...**
   I wish I had more time for W. Workshop.

Looking at reading strategies. Finding evidence of reading strategies in our portfolios and discussing them with families have been more difficult for me until recently (see chapter 4). I have always used reading journals, event posters, book jackets, and story maps in portfolios to talk about students' abilities to construct meaning from text, but documenting reading strategies has been more challenging. Not only are strategies difficult to observe and to document, but also families often are overly focused on one strategy—phonics. I have begun using running records, informal reading inventories, and anecdotal notes to document reading strategies that students use as they are reading. These tools provide concrete evidence to focus our

---

Figure 9.6 *continued*

---

5. At school I wish I didn't have to...

At school I wish I dident have to
do junnle stories.because it's hard to
rember what you did over the weekend.

6. At Choice Time I like to...

At choice time I like to make 3-D
houses of pattern bloxs.

7. What things about your school day do you share with your family?

I do not tell my famly aneything
because they hardly ask and I
somtimes forget.

8. What goals (things you want to get better at) would you like to work on this year?

1. I would like to make more friends.
2. I want to read 100 paged chapter books.
3. I would like to write beter cursiv.

Kendal also takes time to think about herself and her learning as she completes this form before the first conference.

---

discussion on sight word recognition, sound-symbol correspondence, context clues, and self-monitoring strategies.

Neal, a second-grade student, was experiencing some difficulty in reading. Early in the first grade he began participating in the Reading Recovery Program at our school. During the fall conference I shared sections of several running records with Neal and his family (see Figures 9.9 and 9.10). I noted that in October Neal was reading at level 14 independently (reading level: first grade) but that he was reading slowly and hesitantly. I also pointed out (and provided specific examples) that although most of his errors began with the same initial consonant as the word in the text, Neal had difficulty with middle vowel sounds and endings of the words (e.g., *dill* for *down; kich* for *kick*). In addition, many of his errors did not make sense in the sentence. He was not using context or sentence syntax to cross-check for meaning; he was not using self-monitoring strategies. I explained that I had used this information to plan my word identification instruction for Neal. I began to work on teaching Neal to use meaning (context) and sentence structure, in addition to improving his use of phonics. I also

Figure 9.7

ANECDOTAL RECORDS

Name _Kendal_

Date _10/95_

Reading

* Reads a variety—WEBLog   *ambitious, maternal*
* Branching out—biographies—Amelia Earhardt—some words are
  Challenging but she understands main ideas—
* Rereads + Self corrects

Writing

* Oreo story is wonderful—Everyone loves it
  * Suspense—Original
* Wonderful spelling—
* Descriptions "scarfing down a piece of cake" Valentines Day
* Punctuation is excellent—Journal Stories

Math

* Number patterns—excellent
* Add + Sub w/regrouping—wonderful — Beginning mult + double digit *just learning*
* Word problems—Yes!
* Wonderful at open ended problems—Milk+Cookies
* Reads + understands a graph.

Social

* A good person
* Works well in groups—
* A leader

Suggested Goals

* Extend... book projects, variety of genres
  Math projects—individualized
  Fiction stories with Clear Problem/solutions
  Geography.

I use an anecdotal record form to summarize notes for the conference.

---

worked on developing Neal's reading fluency and automatic word recognition by providing many opportunities for him to read easy books.

Next, I compared the October record with the November running record. There was some progress that I wanted to be sure everyone understood. First, this text was two levels higher than the October record and his accuracy rate was still high—97 percent, his former performance rate at the "easy" level. Neal's word identification and fluency had improved. He was able to use his knowledge of phonics, beyond initial sounds, to read unknown words such as *mistake* and *pretended*. In addition, Neal had begun

---

Figure 9.8

Sept 12, 94

On saturday I went to the mall whith my friend Megen and my mom. We went to a muffy bear convention. I had Megen and I had are Picturse taken. I had a great time,

Rosie, what is a Muffy Bear convention? I have never heard of it. Do you have the picture? I'd like to see it! Mrs. R.

---

to pay more attention to the meaning of the text as a whole instead of word-by-word meaning. This was evident from his increase in self-correcting while reading. I pointed out specific examples in which Neal misread a word (e.g., *over* for *very, teared* for *tore*) and then self-corrected so that the sentence or passage would make sense. This, I told his family, is a strategy good readers use. So, Neal had also expanded his repertoire of reading strategies.

After pointing out the specifics of Neal's record, I provided some suggestions to support his reading at home. For example, I suggested that Neal needed lots of opportunities to read easy books at home in a relaxed, supportive environment. This would build motivation, enjoyment, and reading fluency. In addition, I suggested that if Neal misread a word while reading with a family member, he should be encouraged to read to the end of the sentence and then asked if what he had just read made sense. If not, he should be encouraged to go back and reread, looking closely at the letters in the words and paying close attention to the meaning. I also suggested that Neal's family play word games with him. For example, Neal might enjoy playing Hang Man or rhyming games in which he could substitute different initial consonants in common word families (e.g., *l-ick, st-ick, k-ick*). These activities would help Neal become aware of common spelling patterns and would be useful to him as he encountered unknown words while reading.

Figure 9.8 *continued*

Grandma   Nov 21 99

On Sunday at 3:00 my dad my
(When)   *(who)*

brother and I went to the airport
                                          (where)

to pick up my Grandma. After we got
        (grandma)(grandmay)

her we went to baggage claim and

gess what only one of her lags

cane in. It was not the ome

with her clothes. Im glad she's here

but its to bad about her clothes.

And its to bad about we

did not get aue present becarse

they were in her bag.

Rosie,
You write very
interesting stories!
Your cursive is looking
wonderful! Very neat.
Mrs. B.

---

*Samples from Rosie's journal help her mother see specific elements of
Rosie's writing as we discuss Rosie's strengths and goals.*

Figures 9.9 and 9.10

RUNNING RECORD OF TEXT READING						
NAME: *Neal*			DATE: *10-20-94*	LEVEL: *14*		
ERROR RATE: 1:36	ACC.: *97* % *independent, but hesitant*	S.C. RATE: 1:		*1*	cues used	
Page	TITLE: *The Kick-a-lot Shoes*	WORDS: *368.*	E	SC	E	SC

```
2.   ✓ ✓ ✓ ✓ ✓
     ✓ ✓ ✓
     ✓ ✓ ✓
     ✓ ✓ ✓ ✓

     ✓ ✓ . dill      (ow sound)           1
           down
     ✓ ✓ ✓

3    ✓ ✓ ✓ kich ✓    (ck sound)           1
              kick
     ✓ ✓
     ✓ ✓ ✓ ✓ ✓ ✓ ✓
     like  ✓ ✓ ✓ ✓
     I'll                                  1
     ✓ ✓ ✓ ✓
     ✓ ✓ ✓ ✓ ✓ ✓
     ✓ - ✓ . ✓ ✓

4.   ✓ ✓ ✓ ✓ ✓ ✓
     ✓ ✓
     ✓ ✓ ✓ ✓
     ✓ ✓ ✓ ✓ ✓
    |✓  going  ✓| ✓ ✓-✓-✓ ✓               1
         got
     ✓ ✓ ✓

5    ✓ ✓ ✓ ✓ ✓(with help) ✓ ✓
                 after
     ✓ ✓ ✓ ✓

6.   ✓ ✓ ✓
     ✓ ✓ ✓ ✓
     ✓ ✓ ✓ ✓
     ✓ ✓ ✓ ✓ ✓ I                          1
                 crying
```

As Neal and his family left the fall conference, they had a better understanding of his actual level of reading and his ability to use reading strategies. They also had some ideas for supporting Neal's reading at home. In addition, we all decided that becoming more proficient at using a variety of reading strategies was a good goal for Neal. Everyone would work to help Neal become a successful reader.

Because my students stay with me for two years, Neal and his family had the advantage of seeing his reading growth and development over an

Figures 9.9 and 9.10 *continued*

RUNNING RECORD OF TEXT READING								
NAME: Neal			DATE: 11-29-94		LEVEL: 16		
ERROR RATE: 1: 37	ACC.: 97% (easy)		S.C. RATE: 1:				cues used	
Page	TITLE: My Sloppy Tiger goes to School		WORDS: 227	E	SC	E	SC

Although running records are difficult for parents to understand, they help me explain which reading strategies I am trying to emphasize with Neal.

extended period of time. In the spring of Neal's second year with me, I was able to show his family a current running record that indicated he was reading "at grade level" and using a variety of strategies (phonics, context, sentence structure, and self-monitoring) while reading. I supported this evidence with another indicator—results of an informal reading inventory—that also indicated Neal was "at grade level" both in his word identification abilities and his ability to comprehend third-grade-level material. The evidence in Neal's portfolio helped me demonstrate to Neal and his family Neal's progress in using reading strategies. Because two years earlier we had reviewed work, set goals, and focused our efforts, Neal had made good progress. We all had worked hard, and we were rewarded.

Looking at comprehension. A final example of how I discuss progress during conferences is in the area of constructing meaning from texts—reading comprehension. At the fall conference, I usually have two or three pieces of evidence that the student or I have included since the beginning of the year. These pieces might include a response journal, a reading summary, a research report, a book log with comments about the student's reading, or a mind map.

As I sat with Rosie's mom at the fall conference I pointed out specific entries in Rosie's reading response journals from *The BFG* and *Bridge to Terabithia,* both at third-grade level or above. She had read *The BFG* mostly on her own. Although the students met in literature circles to discuss the book with me, Rosie and her group read each chapter independently, without teacher support. Using my reading conference notes, I noted that Rosie was a fluent reader and writer and that her ability to identify with a character and to synthesize important information was quite developed. I also shared a couple of Rosie's journal entries from *The BFG* (see Figure 9.11a and b).

On her own, Rosie had chosen to write from the perspective of the main character, Sophie. This creative and insightful approach revealed Rosie's ability to understand the character's thinking and actions. Reading through other journal entries, we were able to see that Rosie had a good understanding of the problem, plot, and resolution of the story. She chose to write about events that were important to the story development, and her use of language revealed her strong vocabulary and understanding of the affective elements of the story (e.g., "I'm glad snozzcumbers are repulsive"). We also noticed that Rosie's entries stayed fairly close to the story line; she didn't draw many inferences, make connections to other texts, or write about her personal responses. Although I had observed Rosie's abilities in these areas, I told Rosie and her mom that I planned to focus more of my instruction and more of students' journal responses on these higher levels of comprehension. Rosie's journal entries provided an opportunity for me to talk about Rosie's progress and my instructional goals. As a result of this conversation, Rosie's family had a better understanding of the complex nature of reading and of Rosie's developing abilities.

In contrast, Neal's second grade journal contained responses to *Henry and Mudge,* a second-grade book (see Figure 9.12 on p. 310). Meeting with

Neal's family, I would point out that Neal read this book as part of a teacher-led small group of instruction. He would have had difficulty reading it on his own. Even though Neal's writing is fairly limited, I can demonstrate, through journal entries, that Neal is beginning to understand story characters. I provided prompts for this journal entry, and Neal responded in a personal but limited way. Without prompts, Neal's comments are often restatements of the information in the text. I would explain that Neal is working hard to read more challenging texts and that sometimes his comprehension remains quite literal. I plan to work with him, as with Rosie, to develop more inferential understanding and personal response.

The preceding examples of sharing information about student progress may seem one-sided, with the teacher doing all of the talking. In practice, they are not. However, I *do* feel it is important that teachers share their professional knowledge and that families understand and interpret what they are seeing. At the same time, I am equally committed to engaging all of the participants in a three-way collaborative conversation about specific strengths and needs. Therefore, as we peruse the portfolio together, I continually ask the family and the child to offer their comments, perspectives, and concerns. Conversation comes naturally because it is focused on the evidence in the portfolio. As the year goes on and as we all become more experienced and comfortable with three-way conversation, the child begins to take more of a lead (see the following discussion of the end-of-year).

Figure 9.11a

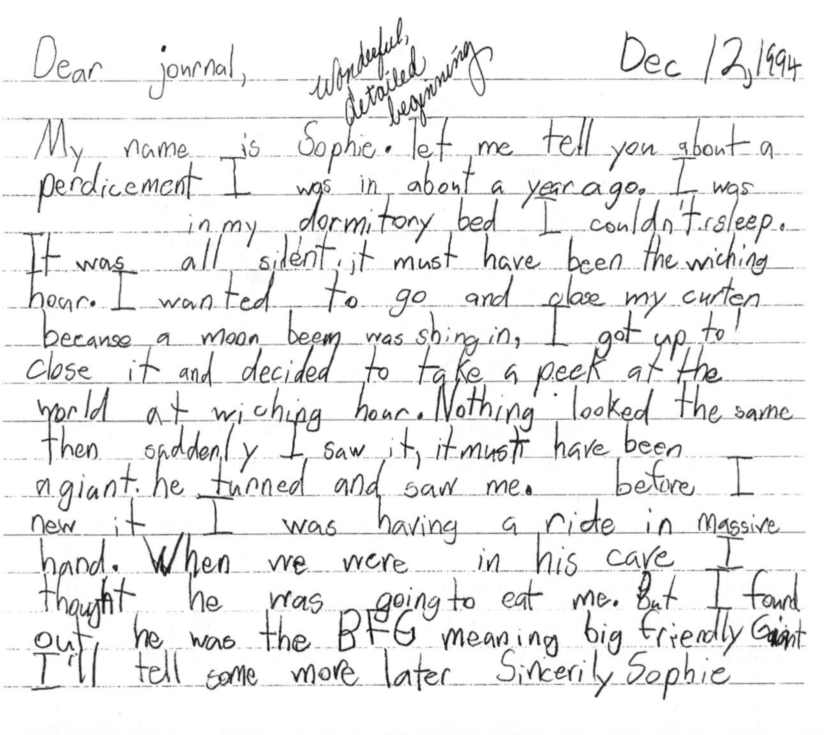

Dear journal, — wonderful, detailed beginning   Dec 12, 1994

My name is Sophie. let me tell you about a perdicement I was in about a year ago. I was in my dormitory bed I couldn't sleep. It was all silent, it must have been the wiching hour. I wanted to go and close my curten because a moon beem was shing in, I got up to close it and decided to take a peek at the world at wiching hour. Nothing looked the same then suddenly I saw it, it must have been a giant. he turned and saw me. before I new it I was having a ride in massive hand. When we were in his cave I thought he was going to eat me. But I found out he was the BFG meaning big friendly Giant I'll tell some more later Sincerily Sophie

Figure 9.11b.

Dear journal,   great idea!   Dec, 23, 1994

Let me tell you about one of the scaryest parts of my stay with the BFG. Well you see me and BFG were talking and all of the sudden one of the people eating giants barged in I was scared I had to think fast I saw the snozzcumber I decied to hide behind it the people eating giant ask the BFG what the snozzcumber was as he reached down to grab it so I jumped inside an end that had been chewed of how was I to know that the BFG would convince the giant to eat it before I knew it I was in his mouth and pretty soon I was out of his mouth I'm glad snozzcumbers are repulsive.

          Sincerily

            Sophie

Goal setting. The second part of the fall conference focuses on setting specific goals for the child. First, we review the goals that student, family, and teacher brought to the conference, looking for commonalities. We discuss how the goals match our detailed discussion of progress so far this year. We discuss how to prioritize, combine, or revise goals. In Rosie's case, for example, goal setting was simple. She wanted to "write at least one humorous story," and I felt that further work on writing in different genres would be a natural extension to her writing abilities. Her mom agreed. We set a goal of supporting Rosie's writing skills by facilitating more writing in different genres, including a focus on humor. The process of discussing worthwhile goals continues until the conference members have agreed on three to four long-term goals.

Setting goals is not always so easy. I can remember one particular child who had a speech delay that seemed to be affecting his written communication. Before the conference, the communication disorder specialist (CDS) and I worked together gathering evidence of the child's speech patterns to share with his family. We found some specific areas that needed work. At the conference I suggested that we include a speech goal that could be supported by the family at home as well as by the CDS and me at school. I also suggested formal speech testing. The child's family rejected the goal and the formal assessment; the family did not want the child to be singled out in any way. Even after further discussions and more explanations, the goal was not accepted by the family. Therefore, special services and home support were not provided as part of a long-term goal. However, as the classroom teacher, I continued to work within the classroom on oral communication skills with this child. I had learned important information about the family's attitude toward the problem and accepted that I would have to work on this goal myself, without home support.

Fall conferences are scheduled over several weeks. After having the opportunity to see and to discuss portfolio artifacts, families, students, and teachers have a better shared understanding of the students' accomplishments and areas of focus for continued work. All have discussed, asked questions, and voiced their concerns or agreement about the learning needs of the individual child. About a week after the conference I send home a written summary of our conference that includes the agreed-upon goals. This communicates my understanding about the decisions that were made during the conference and invites the family to make changes or clarify misunderstandings. With this narrative document, we then begin the year's work to support student learning.

Other models. Not all teachers communicate with families during the fall conference as I do. Sue, an intermediate teacher, gives her students a bit more responsibility for leading the fall conference. In addition to having older students, Sue has worked with most of her students for two to three years—she has a multiaged class. Therefore, most of the students and families have experienced these conferences before.

Sue works with her students for several days helping them prepare for the conferences. They review portfolio work and discuss how they have changed in reading and writing since the beginning of the year. They also identify favorite pieces to share with their families during the conferences. On conference day, the child and family are encouraged to spend approximately 15 minutes reviewing the portfolio before meeting with Sue. This gives them time to browse through the portfolio in a private, relaxed way. Some teachers even provide sample prompts for families who may be overwhelmed or reluctant to "intrude" on their child's work. For example:

"Show me your favorite (or best) work. What is special (good) about it?"

"Tell me how you worked on this piece."

"What piece do you think would surprise me most? Tell me about it."

These sample prompts help families understand that their job in this setting is not to judge the work, but rather to help their children think carefully about what they are learning. When Sue joins a family and the child, she begins by asking the child to talk about what he or she does well. Then Sue shares her insights, as the teacher, about what the child does well. Next, she asks the child to suggest personal goals and then adds her goals to the discussion. The family members are asked about their goals as well. After this three-way conference, Sue spends some time alone with the family members, making sure that their questions and concerns have been addressed. The specificity and focus that I include in my conferences (described earlier) are also part of Sue's conferences. The difference between her conferences and mine is that she provides more opportunity for the student to take the lead.

Another colleague, Lynn, actually makes home visits each fall with portfolios in hand. She feels that by visiting each child's family at home, she is creating a team effort and demonstrating her commitment to both the child and the family. On the day of the home visit, Lynn and the child go through the portfolio, making sure that they have all the entries they need and discussing how the child will share the work with his or her family. They make sure there are a few examples of writing, projects, and student selections with entry slips, as well as Lynn's beginning-of-the-year assessments (e.g., running records, sight words). Lynn drives the student home and, after a brief introduction and invitation for the student to share a favorite toy, picture, or other special part of his or her life, Lynn begins the portfolio visit with the student at her side. In the spring, the child will lead the visit, but in the fall, Lynn leads. Lynn explains the reasons for each entry and shares the process of collecting work. The family members' questions and comments are discussed and noted on a home visit record that is entered into the portfolio. Together, the student, family, and Lynn set goals for fall and winter and enter these into the portfolio.

Three-way conferences of all types have been so successful that many teachers and schools are trying to find a way to schedule two or three during the year. Regardless of how often they occur or how they are structured, an essential element of successful conferences is providing specific, honest, and supportive three-way conversation. As we noted in chapters 2, 5, and 7, confronting standards is part of good assessment. In addition to the frank conversations described earlier, some teachers have found it useful to use anonymous samples of other students' work (best if from a previous or different class) so that families and children can understand the continuum of student performance. Along the same lines, several teachers have begun using developmental continua when meeting with families. Annette attaches a writing continuum to the writing pieces in her K-1 students' portfolios (see chapter 4) to help families gain a perspective of their children's current level of accomplishment in comparison with developmental goals for learning. These types of strategies for dealing with standards are not intended to intimidate or to foster competition but rather to provide concrete examples of what students can do. When families and teachers develop a common understanding of students and of appropriate performance standards, they are better able to provide support and to have clear expectations and goals. As a result, students are more likely to learn.

Linking Portfolios to Grading Periods

Although most teachers schedule major portfolio events at the first conference period and the end of the school year, many teachers also find ways to use portfolios to communicate with families at other times. For example, some teachers invite families to participate in their classrooms on a regular basis. The children are encouraged to share their portfolios with families any time the families are in the building. Because the children are familiar with their portfolios and they are easily accessible, these informal visits don't require special teacher attention or time.

One of our colleagues at the middle school, Linda, ties family selections to each grading period. She has students take home their collections, and a family member then selects a piece and writes an entry slip to be placed into the portfolios. This strategy requires the family to look through all of the work in the collection for one grading period, giving the family a sense of what the child has been learning and producing. The family entry is then brought back to school, placed into the portfolio by the student, and used as part of their quarter self-reflection and self-evaluation activity.

Linda also plans a family-child portfolio visit each grading period. Because middle school teachers often have only 5 to 15 minutes to confer-ence with families, and because attendance at middle school parent-teacher conferences seems to be extraordinarily low, Linda also has developed a "take-home" portfolio event each grading period. She sends a letter home asking each family to make an appointment with the child to review the portfolio. The letter is returned, and Linda arranges with the students to take portfolios home on the appropriate day. In the portfolios, she includes a "letter of expectations" that provides very clear directions for families about reviewing the portfolio work with their children. The portfolio must be returned the following day in exchange for the report card. This assures that the portfolio is returned! The students prepare for their family confer-ences in class by examining their work and role-playing how to explain to their families what they have been learning. Although this strategy doesn't include the kind of direct teacher input found in most elementary school conferences, it is an effective way to keep families informed about what their children are doing, and to have students assume responsibility for dis-cussing their work and progress. As a result of this process, families are rarely surprised by the report card grades their children receive. Our mid-dle school teachers have documented fewer phone calls and questions from families and fewer complaints from students about report card grades as a result of these systematic ways of sharing portfolio work.

End-of-Year Portfolio Celebration

By the end of the year, the students have had many experiences reviewing their portfolios and reflecting on their growth as readers and writers (see chapter 6). They are proud of their accomplishments, thoughtful about what they have learned, and eager to share their progress with their fami-lies. So, each spring we hold a Spring Portfolio Celebration during which families, students, and teachers come together to honor the students' learn-ing. This conference is different than the fall conference. During the fall we are looking at early evidence of student work and setting goals for the year. The spring conference is truly a celebration and reevaluation of the work

Figure 9.12

I would like
to introduce
you to Henry
and mudge.
Henry is a boy
He wanst a
dog. He gets a
dog it gose to
one hundred and
eighty pounds
and there happy!

Figure 9.12 *continued*

If I was 11/6/95
mudge I woald
loes waeti
If I was aunt
sally I would
eats les and
hog the tv,.

Neal's literature journal helps me discuss the kinds of books that Neal is reading and his comprehension.

that has been completed and placed into the portfolio. The portfolio selections are used as evidence to support accomplishment of the fall goals. It is a student-led discussion, giving more responsibility during the conference to students and their families.

Logistically, it helps if an entire school commits to a portfolio celebration, but it can be successful even if a team or individual organizes the event. The first year we held Spring Portfolio Celebrations in my school, we invited eight families into the room while the other students carried on with their daily learning responsibilities. This was much too confusing. Now we schedule the celebration on an early release day and schedule families into one of four time slots approximately one to one and a half hours long. So, there are six to eight families and students in the classroom during any one time.

It is important to prepare families for this event. After they arrive, I provide an overview of the schedule. I assure them that they all will get equal time with me, and I post a list of their names and the times when I plan to meet with them. I also tell a story about an event that happened at my first portfolio celebration. On this particular day, one father proceeded to erase all of his son's answers on a math computation sheet of which his child was very proud. The father's purpose, I think, was to see if his son could actually do the work. The son appeared embarrassed but was nevertheless able to prove to his father that what was in his portfolio was truly his own work. He had worked the problems correctly and could, even on demand, replicate his abilities. I watched this father humiliate his son and then explained, once again, that this is a time of celebrating accomplishments. I have thought of this event many times over the years and wished that my message to this father had been stronger. I retell this story before families and children begin their celebration in order to communicate the standards and expectations that I have for the day. It is a time for thoughtful reflection and celebration of accomplishments. I also help families prepare for the celebration by providing some suggestions for moving the conversation along if their children become shy or confused (see Figure 9.13). I also ask them to take a moment to think about what they have learned and felt from the celebration experience and to share it with me in writing (see Figure 9.14). My objective is to guide families to engage with their children in a meaningful and positive way. I have learned, the hard way, that I must clearly prepare and follow up with families, just as I do with my students, if the celebration conference is to be successful.

It is also important to prepare the students for this event, especially because they will be leading the conference. We begin two weeks in advance with the third portfolio visit of the year (see chapters 2 and 6). Students work alone or with peers to compare past work with current work and to answer questions on their Portfolio Visit forms explaining how they have grown as learners. During the portfolio visit there is a lot of laughter and giggling as students share their past work with friends and comment about how "silly" some of their early work looks. I circulate, guiding students to think carefully about how they have grown as readers and writers. Enthusiasm eventually turns to more quiet reflection and sense of pride as students begin filling out the Spring Portfolio Celebration form that they will share with their families.

The Spring Portfolio Celebration form is a three-part carbon report with sections for student, family member, and teacher to comment about student progress and current issues. I help my young students organize their thoughts by giving them two to three questions to answer. For example, "How have you improved as a reader and writer?" or "How have you supported our classroom of friends?" They can add other information as well. I fill out my section after the students have completed theirs. Then the students bring the forms to the celebration conference. The families complete their section after meeting with their children and me. One of my colleagues, Sue, has her intermediate students and their families complete their sections of the forms together during the celebration conference as they look through the portfolios. Sue commented, "Students need to talk to

---

Figure 9.13

Today you're going to have the opportunity to look at your child's portfolio and celebrate what he/she has learned since the beginning of the year. The portfolio hold's work that your child and I have selected. Some has been done independently, some in groups; some work is in rough draft form and some is polished or published. This is a time to honor the progress your child has made, not to point out mistakes. If you have questions, we can discuss them when I meet with you and your child or we can schedule a separate time to talk.

Below are some ideas that might help you talk with your child about his/her work. They are designed to open conversation about <u>how</u> he/she is learning, <u>what</u> he/she is learning, and how he/she <u>feels</u> about the work. They are simply suggestions; feel free to enjoy your child and his/her accomplishments any way that works best for you.

- Tell me about your favorite pieces in your portfolio. What makes them favorite?

- Tell me how you have changed since the beginning of the year.
  Show me some examples from the beginning of the year and now.

- Tell me what you're really good at doing in school. Show me.

- Select a piece you are curious about. Ask your child to tell you how he/she created it.

Please take a moment to complete the attached evaluation form and return it to me before you leave. Thanks for being part of our celebration and part of your child's learning. Enjoy!

These ideas are helpful for some families as they celebrate the portfolio.

---

their families about their work and, in some cases, I felt like this was one of the rarer times that this actually occurred."

In addition to making a portfolio visit and filling out the conference form, my students role-play exactly what they will say to their families about the evidence in their portfolios. I explain that their job is to help their families understand the work in their portfolios, what they have learned, and how they have grown. I post the following as we discuss what they might say:

Reading:
- Tell your family about the book you are reading now.
- How is it different from the books you were reading in the fall (easier/harder, different type, more/less interesting)?
- Show your family something in your portfolio from your reading work.

Writing
- Tell your family about the piece of writing you are working on right now. Tell what it is about.
- Explain the process of writing in our room.

Figure 9.14

EVALUATION

Please take a minute to share your thoughts and feelings about today's portfolio visit.

I learned...	I liked...
Kendal is showing an increasing sense of personal pride in doing her very best. I am thrilled because I think this trait is essential to self esteem and accomplishment. Kendal's creativity and imagination in story-telling continue to amaze me.	All the portfolio selections. Kendal's greatest confidence has always been in her drawing/artistic skills - I think I see now that she has much more confidence in her written products and only uses the pictures for decoration.

Parent feedback helps me evaluate parents' responses to the celebration and revise my procedures to meet their needs.

- Show your family some of your writing from the beginning of the year. Explain how you have changed as a writer.

The students then choose a partner to role-play their portfolio presentations. Although they sometimes need focus, students never seem to be at a loss to discuss themselves!

Robbie, a second-grade student, provides a good example of how all of these pieces come together on Spring Portfolio Celebration Day. Robbie and I each had completed our sections of the celebration form before the conference (see Figure 9.15). Robbie had struggled to find ways to feel good about himself. Learning to read was a powerful tool that helped him feel successful. This was so important to Robbie that he chose to write about it in his section of the celebration form. I observed from afar as Robbie and his family immediately became engaged with his portfolio. I could see that he was doing a good job explaining his work and that everyone was excited and proud. As I joined Robbie and his family, I listened and added my own observations. For example, I commented about how Robbie had improved as a reader. Although he had written on his form that he reads well because "I can sound out most of the words," I also pointed out that he had learned

Figure 9.15

SPRING 1995 PORTFOLIO VISIT & CONFERENCE
Bellevue Public Schools--Newport Heights Elementary

Student ___Robbie___   Date ___March 30?___

Parent/Guardian(s) ___Joyce + Lane___

Teacher _____

Student comments: I think I do well at reading and writing because I can sound out most of the words in reading. In writing I try to do good stories and put lots of deatails in. School is okay to me. In the class I try to be quiet during SSR. This helps the class.

Parent/Guardian comments:
Robbie's learning to read has been a break-through in the "enjoying school" area. His ability to write has also assisted him with an improved self-image.
Thank you for complementing him in these areas — it has encouraged him to read + write more + more. We also encourage it at home.
I see an improved attitude about school in general. He's interested in many more things — not bored at all.
He sometimes gets discouraged & "quits." Your complements + encouragement have helped here too.

Teacher comments: Robbie has made some progress in learning to engage himself in learning. I have seen him gain confidence and he is beginning to feel good about himself especially in the area of writing. He still talks when others are talking, however this behavior has decreased since the fall.
Robbie's writing skills have really blossomed! His first story (The Robber that Robbed Banks) was very brief with little detail, problem development or supporting details. Now, in his most recent published story Robbie develops a problem, adds detail, uses specific language (hissed the witch, said the witch acting as Bra[in]s voice") and develops his ending! What wonderful progress!
Robbie has also become a budding poet and artist. He is very thoughtful with his words and other students have commented on how well they liked his pictures!

The three-part celebration form is completed by the child, family members, and the teacher.

---

many other strategies to help him unlock the author's message and make sense of a passage. I explained that he also had learned to use context clues to figure out unknown words and that he always made sure that he understood what he was reading. I then modeled with Robbie exactly what this meant so that when Robbie read at home with his family, family members could remind him to use these strategies.

Robbie's family and I also discussed my section of the celebration form. I explained to his family that my comments were directed at the goals we had developed at the beginning of the year. One of Robbie's goals was to practice writing stories that are organized sequentially and include a purpose along with supporting details. In my comments I compared an early story ("The Robbers That Robbed Banks") and a recent story in his portfolio. Robbie showed his family these two stories, and I specifically pointed out the areas of increased detail and sentence development. I also commented that Robbie had increased his use of specific language in his writing. This type of concrete evidence of growth helped his family understand Robbie's learning more fully.

After meeting with other families, I returned to Robbie's group to discuss his family's written comments on the celebration form. Robbie and I were very pleased that they, too, were able to see and honor his reading progress. Robbie is a child of few words, but his smile and dancing eyes were enough to show that he felt proud of his accomplishments and the recognition he had received.

As with the fall conferences, there are many ways to organize celebration conferences. The most important point is to plan some way to honor the children and their portfolios at the end of the school year. This is especially important if portfolios are not passed on to next year's teacher. In our school district, some buildings have a process for passing on portfolios and others don't. We don't believe that portfolios have any less value if they are not passed on. What is critical about portfolios is the shared communication that is established among students, families, and teachers during the year, when portfolios are used. But, at the same time, students become very attached and proud of their work, so it is important to celebrate their accomplishments in some way at the end of the year. The Spring Portfolio Celebration brings an exhilaration to the classroom that is difficult to explain. Rarely can you find families huddling with their children over school work and talking about wonders they have achieved. Every year I hear comments like, "I'm thrilled at all the learning that ———— has achieved this year. He feels a real sense of accomplishment" or "I learned so much about you. I didn't know that you. . . ." I look forward to Spring Portfolio Celebrations each year as a way to bring a sense of completion, accomplishment, and pride to all of our efforts.

Conclusion

Using portfolios to establish communication among teachers, families, and students is like any other new teaching strategy we try—it takes planning, time, adaptation, and perseverance. I'm still learning about portfolio assessment and about ways to communicate effectively using portfolios. The experiences that my colleagues and I have had suggest that it is important to start small, setting one or two goals for yourself the first year. For example, you might begin with an introductory portfolio letter and monthly or quarterly newsletters that include family entry slips. Alternatively, you might decide to use portfolios in your parent-teacher conferences without asking students to lead the discussion. Or, you might implement a couple of "take-home" portfolio events so that families and children have opportunities to spend relaxed time reviewing portfolio work. Whatever you choose, the key is to establish three-way communication, not just two-way communication between family and teacher, and to use the portfolio as part of the communication process. There is no right or wrong way to begin. We all need to follow our own styles and preferences for communicating.

I would be negligent if I didn't say that portfolios and continuous communication take more time. At first, it seems like an additional burden to our already busy days. But, as with any new learning, after the pieces are in place and after you have developed a routine, the time requirements decrease and the benefits increase. At the same time, I would be negligent if I didn't admit that this kind of communication reveals more about your teaching, your classroom, and your students than anything we have ever shared before. We put ourselves and our students on the line when we communicate so clearly and explicitly. Similarly, families put themselves on the line when they contribute to portfolios and engage in frank discussions of their expectations. As a result, we all need to be prepared to answer questions and to discuss curricular and instructional decisions that were not part of our past conversations. This is new and potentially frightening territory for all of us, yet it is territory that must be explored. Be patient with yourself, your students, and their families. The effort will result in a partnership in which we all are winners.

References

Countryman, L. L., & Schorieder, M. (1996). When students lead parent-teacher conferences. *Educational Leadership, 53*(7), 64–68.

Daniels, H. (1996). The best practice project: Building parent partnerships in Chicago. *Educational Leadership, 53*(7), 38–43.

Darling-Hammond, L., Ancess, J., & Falk, B. (1995). *Authentic assessment in action: Studies of schools and students at work.* New York: Teachers College Press.

DeFina, A. A. (1992). *Portfolio assessment: Getting started.* New York: Scholastic.

Flood, J., & Lapp, D. (1989). Reporting reading progress: A comparison portfolio for parents. *The Reading Teacher, 42*(7), 508–514.

Guyton, J. M., & Feilstein, L. L. (1989). Student-led parent conferences: A model for teaching responsibility. *Elementary School and Guidance Counseling, 23*(2), 169–172.

Hedman, R. (1993). Parents and teachers as co-investigators. In S. Lytle & M. Cochran-Smith (Eds.), *Inside outside: Teacher research and knowledge* (pp. 220–230). New York: Teachers College Press.

Hebert, E. A. (1992). Portfolios invite reflection—From students and staff. *Educational Leadership, 49*(8), 58–61.

Henderson, A. T., & Berla, N. (Eds.). (1994). *A new generation of evidence: The family is critical to student achievement* (Report No.: ISBN 0934460418). Washington, DC: National Committee for Citizens in Education.

International Reading Association & National Council of Teachers of English. (1994). *Standards for the assessment of reading and writing.* Newark, DE: International Reading Association.

Lazar, A. M., & Weisberg, R. (1996). Inviting parents' perspectives: Building home-school partnerships to support children who struggle with literacy. *The Reading Teacher, 50*(3), 228–237.

Paratore, J. (1993). *Learning from home literacies: Inviting parents to contribute to literacy portfolios.* Paper presented at the annual meeting of the National Reading Conference, Charleston, SC.

Paratore, J. R. (1994). *Shifting boundaries in home and school responsibilities: Involving immigrant parents in the construction of literacy portfolios.* Paper presented at the annual meeting of the National Reading Conference, San Diego, CA.

Rhodes, L. K., & Shanklin, N. (1993). *Windows into literacy: Assessing learners K–12.* Portsmouth, NH: Heinemann.

Salinger, T., & Chittenden, E. (1994). Analysis of an early literacy portfolio: Consequences for instruction. *Language Arts, 71*(6), 446–452.

Stiggins, R. J. (1997). *Student-centered classroom assessment* (2nd ed.). New York: Macmillan College Publishing.

Valencia, S. W. (1990). A portfolio approach to classroom reading assessment: The whys, whats, and hows. *The Reading Teacher, 43*(4), 338–340.

chapter 10

Grading Practices
and Portfolio Evaluation

SHEILA W. VALENCIA

Chapter 10 provides perspectives on grading practices and portfolio evaluation. These issues are controversial and decisions about them frequently are made at a school, district or state level rather than by teachers themselves. Nevertheless, we believe that grading practices can and must be improved, and that the process of evaluating portfolios can enhance teachers' learning. We begin with a brief background on grading followed by several suggestions for making portfolios and grading mutually supportive. Then we provide four different models or rubrics for evaluating portfolios which focus on discussion and deliberation of learning outcomes, standards, and instruction.

The portfolio process has been extremely helpful because it has given me a chance to meet with supportive peers and to check my expectations for kids' work against those of other teachers. It has definitely helped me make better instructional decisions.

J. B., intermediate teacher

"Judging is a teacher's professional responsibility" (Mitchell, 1992). To make good judgments, teachers must be clear about their expectations and standards for student performance. This is a daunting task, to be sure, yet we are engaged in setting standards and making judgments all of the time. We decide, for example, that Jason needs extra work organizing his stories or that Pam should be reading easier books to build fluency or that Latrice should be referred for special education assessment or that Wally should be encouraged to write about his personal experiences. These judgments go beyond analyzing students' strengths and weaknesses to determining what students should be able to do and how well they are performing against a standard. What makes rendering these kinds of judgments different than assigning grades or evaluating portfolios is that the standards often are not publicly communicated or deliberated.

Teachers have always struggled with grading and evaluation—public forms of judging student performance. Our long-standing reliance on standardized tests has not helped the situation (Hiebert & Calfee, 1992; Mitchell, 1992; Pearson & Valencia, 1987; Shepard, 1989). The public and teachers themselves have lost confidence in teachers' ability to make sound judgments. But the loss of confidence is easy to understand. After all, teachers have not had much training in assessment (Aschbacher, 1994; Stiggins, 1991); standardized tests have seduced the public into believing that a single score is objective and representative of real learning; and, when the bases for teacher judgments are made public, others frequently question them (Stiggins, 1997). But those of us who work with portfolios know that we must make judgments and that by keeping portfolios we take the process of making judgments out of a secretive, adversarial role into an open, collaborative one among teachers, students, parents, and administrators. If we don't use portfolios to help us grapple with evaluation and standards, we will be missing a valuable opportunity to change the nature of teaching and learning.

Every chapter in this book deals with standards in some form or another. It is impossible to understand student reading and writing performance, communicate clearly with students and parents, or make good instructional decisions without understanding standards and expectations for student performance. For assessment to influence teaching and learning, the information must be specific, immediate, and contextualized. It must take into account the student, the task, and the situation in which the student produces the learning. Therefore, the best, most useful type of feedback and judgment of student work is the kind of narrative interpretation that we have modeled in chapters 4, 5, 7, and 9. Even so, we must still come to terms with making judgments and feel comfortable and confident reporting them, whether we produce narrative reports, letter or number grades, or have face-to-face conferences.

In this chapter, we address two difficult but important issues facing portfolio teachers: assigning grades and evaluating portfolios. Teachers, schools, and school districts have widely varying perspectives and requirements with respect to these issues. With full acknowledgment of those differences, we offer several suggestions for grading and for evaluating portfolios that are more in line with our philosophy of portfolios as a collaborative process of collecting, examining, and using information to think about, and improve, teaching and learning.

Grades

In elementary school, students usually receive narrative report cards or letter grades. In middle school and high school, narrative reporting is rare; letter and number grades are more common. The appeal of grades is threefold: (a) they appear to be "objective"; (b) they are symbols with which most people are familiar; and (c) some people believe that grades may motivate students. Unfortunately, research indicates that this appeal is unfounded: Grades are not that "clean" or that "simple."

In general, teachers' grades reflect many different priorities and values. We all have experienced the shock of learning that work that received an *A* in one classroom, school, or district did not receive an *A* in another. So, too, what teachers choose to include on narrative report cards varies dramatically depending on their purpose, audience, and the individual teacher and child (Afflerbach & Johnston, 1993). More to the point, grades seem to be an idiosyncratic mix of achievement, effort, attitude, and aptitude (Stiggins, 1997). Certainly all of these attributes are important for success in school, but mixing them together for reporting and grading is problematic. For example, when aptitude or overall ability is figured in, high-ability students are shortchanged by holding them to higher standards, and low-ability students are shortchanged by holding them to lower standards. When effort and attitude are prioritized, the message to students is that working hard is enough, regardless of the results, or that personality traits make up for lower-quality work. Furthermore, both effort and attitude can be easily manipulated, leading students to teacher-pleasing behavior and superficial motivation rather than to intrinsic motivation and achievement. When achievement, effort, attitude, and ability are mixed into one grade, the message to students and the standards used to judge performance are ambiguous.

Stiggins (1997) cautions that we must pull apart these various influences on grading and focus on achievement. Reporting effort, attitude, and aptitude is fine, he maintains, but not mixing them into a grade that is intended to denote achievement. So, a general rule of thumb is to be clear about the learning outcomes you are targeting and to examine student achievement against standards for those targets. That should be the grade. When this message is clear to students, they understand their task and the criteria for good work. A middle school student commented:

> *I noticed that the pieces I worked hardest on and that I felt the best about didn't always get the highest grade.*

This student's effort and personal response were not driven by a grade; they were separated from standards for achievement. All were valued in his classroom, and he knew that.

Portfolios and Grading

For some educators, portfolios and grading are in direct conflict. These educators can't reconcile teacher control of grading with student ownership of portfolios. But for us, portfolios and grading can be complementary. In the next section, we offer suggestions for how they can be mutually supportive.

Portfolios provide evidence behind grades. Whether you use narrative report cards, letter grades, or numbers, portfolios provide a trail of evidence (Moss, Beck, Ebbs, Matson, Muchmore, Steele, Taylor, & Herter, 1992) that others can follow to see how you have made your grading decisions. Our experience is that there is less disagreement, conflict, or bad feelings around report cards when portfolio evidence is present. As we demonstrated in chapter 9, parents, students, and teachers can use specific portfolio evidence to develop a shared understanding of standards, achievement, and growth. When grades are given, the evidence provides an "explanation" of sorts to ground everyone's understanding of the standards for grades. This is particularly true at the middle school level, where grades seem to take on new importance and power. Our middle school teachers report fewer phone calls and follow-up meetings requested by parents after report card grades when parents have had a chance to review portfolios. In the same way, we have had parents report insights such as:

> *I always thought my son had difficulty truly understanding what he read, but now I can see that for myself. This work shows pretty limited comprehension. I can see why he got a B. What can we do at home to help?*

When portfolios are used alongside grades, the conversations are more collaborative and focused on shared problem solving than when grades are reported alone. Portfolios not only provide evidence behind grades, but also they help teachers stay focused on actual student performance (achievement) rather than confounding it with effort, ability, or attitude.

In addition to providing tangible evidence, portfolios help parents and students become knowledgeable "consumers" of grades. As a result, teacher judgment may be questioned. The parent quoted earlier whose concerns about his son's comprehension were verified by the portfolio and the report card grade also reported that his son had received As in reading for the past three years. He questioned why this was the first time evidence had been presented with the grade and why no other teacher had noted his son's difficulty. Essentially, he was questioning the judgments of previous teachers now that he had a sense of the standards and evidence used to grade his son. Similarly, another parent took a middle school teacher to task because, in her opinion, the portfolio evidence did not support the low grade the teacher had assigned. In this case two issues caused the problem: First, the parent needed guidance in reviewing work in the portfolio—she wasn't sure how to interpret the work, nor was she clear about the expectations or standards the teacher had made clear to the students. The parent, teacher, and student did not have a shared understanding of learning or standards. The second issue was that the portfolio represented only a partial indication of the student's performance. In addition to the work in the portfolio, the teacher's grade book included other evidence: scores on tests, grades on special projects, and a record of work that had not been completed. This is a good reminder that portfolios may not include all of the information needed for grading. At the same time, it is a good reminder that confusion can occur when effort (assignments completed) is included in a grade that is supposed to signify achievement. In our opinion, both of these parents exhibited the kind of active participation and involvement that we want to foster around grading. And, the portfolio provided the springboard for their knowledgeable involvement.

Stiggins's (1997) advice about making final decisions for report card grades is excellent, and it has particular meaning for teachers who use portfolios. He suggests:

Don't give up the details until you absolutely must. And when report card grading time arrives, share as much of the detail as you can with your students so they understand what is behind the single little symbol that appears on the report card. Then boil the richness of your detail away only grudgingly. (p. 444)

Good reporting and good grading—those that are useful for improving teaching and learning—can be greatly enhanced by the "detail" in using portfolio evidence to determine and explain grades.

Aligning report cards with portfolios and learner outcomes. Report cards, portfolios, and learner outcomes should be aligned (see Figure 10.1). Report cards should reflect the important learning outcomes for your students, as should portfolios. Therefore, report cards and portfolios should work together. In our experience, the grading-portfolio connection has been hampered by report cards that are not aligned with portfolios. In most cases, the portfolio reflects a new assessment system and new learning outcomes, whereas the content and form of the report card reflect an older model of curriculum and assessment—often skills based. In Bellevue, as in other districts, when report cards were redesigned to bring everything into alignment, grading and reporting became much simpler and clearer. The opposite is also true. Middle school teachers in Bellevue have been required to use a bubble-in report card with two pages of indicators of student performance. Only a few of these indicators are aligned with the student learning outcomes. The result is that keeping portfolios becomes distinct and separate from giving grades. Before elementary report cards were aligned, one teacher reported:

> *I used to do progress reports [report cards], and I'd keep portfolios. They seemed totally unconnected. I thought, "I will never survive." This just isn't the way it's supposed to work. It seemed that I was working harder and that it was not helping me. Then our school redesigned our report card. Now I actually use portfolios as I write up progress reports. Now this makes sense to me, and it makes sense to the kids. We keep what we value in the portfolios, and these are the things we are responsible for learning and reporting out.*

Grading individual assignments and portfolios. Teachers have a variety of approaches to grading individual student assignments. A full discussion of grading is beyond the scope of this chapter; however, in general, we agree with Au, Carroll, and Scheu (1997) that "grading should be used sparingly." Nevertheless, students still need to know and to be held to clearly articulated standards (Delpit, 1995; Stiggins, 1997; Wiggins, 1993), and they still need to get timely, specific feedback on their projects, with or without grades. The rubrics for individual projects and teachers' "front loading" of expectations during instruction, that we described in chapter 6, are good examples of making standards clear to students. And many of these strategies integrate scores or grading into the standards.

Although grading individual assignments is often an issue of personal teaching style or school policy, it can have an influence on portfolios. Generally, when most of the work students do receives a grade, student-selected

---

Figure 10.1

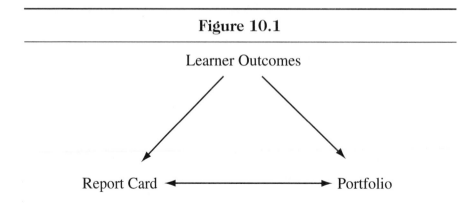

portfolio entries are very much influenced by the teacher's criteria. It is a bit more difficult to work with students on the range of self-reflection and self-assessment strategies that we described in chapter 6 after work is graded by the teacher. Furthermore, it may appear that student goal setting and criteria are just "window dressing," that the only one who truly holds the evaluation power is the teacher. In other words, we are more likely to get showcase portfolios—to show off or to please others—when students have only graded pieces from which to choose. Students tend to enter mostly "A" pieces. Certainly, there are some ways around this problem. For example, the "worst piece" entry slip in chapter 6 or careful teacher encouragement to choose work for other, more personal reasons can counteract some of the effects of the teacher's grades, but it will take great effort to overcome the teacher's influence. So, as you make decisions about how much and which classroom work to grade, consider the influence that it might have on the content and student ownership of portfolios.

Evaluating Portfolios

There are still many unanswered questions about the feasibility and desirability of scoring portfolios. Educators and psychometricians are uncertain about whether portfolios can be scored reliably or whether they are valid measures of student learning (Gearhart, Herman, Baker, & Whittaker, 1993; Koretz, Stecher, Klein, & McCaffrey, 1994; LeMahieu, Gitomer, & Eresh, 1995; Valencia & Au, 1997). Advocates argue that if classroom evidence, in general, and portfolios, in particular, are to be taken seriously and are to mediate the effects of standardized tests, there must be some way to report the findings to outside audiences (Valencia & Calfee, 1991; Wixson, Valencia, & Lipson, 1994). Those educators taking an alternative position argue that the essence of portfolio assessment—the richness of the information, the responsiveness to individual student needs, the student engagement, and the potential to influence teaching—may be lost if portfolios are scored

(Farr & Tone, 1994; Hansen, 1994). Regardless of their position, most educators agree that the process of portfolio evaluation is a valuable professional development experience (Koretz, et al., 1994; LeMahieu, et al., 1992; Valencia & Au, 1997). That is the position we take here: Evaluating or scoring portfolios is an essential component of portfolio implementation because it elevates teachers' thinking about outcomes and about criteria for student performance.

In the process of evaluating portfolios, teachers have to make judgments, not simply describe what they see. They need to understand the criteria for student performance and to decide how good is good enough. In the process, they learn that students cannot be evaluated for learning that has not been documented or that has not been taught. They confront gaps in portfolio evidence that, in turn, may reflect gaps in teaching and classroom assessment. They must examine their instruction and expectations for students beyond their individual classrooms and anchor those expectations against those of other teachers. They must deliberate their expectations with peers, seeking to understand and judge the performances of a wide range of students. No other aspect of portfolio implementation raises these issues as clearly as does scoring. So, our approach to scoring is that it must be seen as an integral part of effective, meaningful portfolio implementation. As such, scoring is not an end in itself but rather a means of helping teachers gain a deeper understanding of portfolios in relationship to learning outcomes and standards that cut across classrooms. The comments of a fourth-grade teacher who participated in several days of evaluating portfolios capture our stance:

> It [the process of scoring portfolios] forces you to focus on criteria. You wouldn't necessarily want to publish scores or do anything with them, but when we had to score the portfolio, the conversation was different. Scoring helps you focus on how you want to teach. The scores don't show you that, but our debates and conversations do.

Next we present samples of several rubrics used for scoring portfolios. Our purpose is to demonstrate various ways that scoring and evaluating can be conceptualized and used as a basis for discussion about student work, standards, teaching, and learning. Each rubric was designed to be used with the particular learning outcomes of each local school district. So, these rubrics cannot be imported to other districts or schools. Nevertheless, they represent interesting and different approaches to fostering discussions about standards and scoring.

Holistic evaluation of specific learner outcomes: The Bellevue Evaluation System. In Bellevue, we spent more than a year engaged in description, alignment, and moderation discussions (described in chapter 8) before we began to discuss scoring. The next year, we deliberated around an evaluation rubric that was aligned with the eight literacy learning outcomes for the district (e.g., constructing meaning from text, use appropriate reading strategies, communicate effectively in writing, develop reading ownership, etc.). Initially, we focused on one grade level, third grade, and used our discussions from the previous year to help us build a rubric. We worked back and forth from actual student portfolios to our vision of high-quality student performance. We tried using the rubric with portfolios, revised it, tried it again, and on and on. Eventually, after several years, we had developed four rubrics (grades K–2, 2–4, 4–6, and middle school) that we apply to our portfolios. The use of overlapping grade bands rather than a single grade level enables teachers to honor developmental ranges and a continuum of learning.

Table 10.1 is a section of the rubric we constructed for grades 2–4. To use the rubric, teachers read through the entire portfolio, gathering evidence across many pieces (9–36 per portfolio) to reach their decisions on each of the eight learner outcomes. The rubric shown includes descriptors for a score of 5, 3, or 1; however, teachers can assign a score of 1–5 or M for missing information for each outcome. A score of 3 is designed to represent typical performance for students at the designated grade level. M is designed to indicate that there is no evidence in the portfolio for a particular outcome; it allows teachers to distinguish between no evidence (M) and poor performance (1).

This could be considered a "high-inference" system because descriptors do not specify the form or type of information that must be found in the portfolio. Instead, general criteria are associated with each particular outcome and performance level. Teachers must read through all of the evidence looking for indicators of the outcomes in many different pieces. No individual portfolio pieces are scored. So, for example, when evaluating for "Constructs Meaning from Text," a teacher might find evidence in the Common Tools (reading logs and questions, reading summaries, and reading response journals) as well as in self-reports, running records, book reports, reading projects, or anecdotal records. After reading through all of the evidence, the teacher assigns a holistic score for each learner outcome (for more information on evaluation see Valencia & Au, 1997, and Valencia & Place, 1994).

Although the rubric and descriptors under each outcome may appear somewhat general, they are effective because of the process we built over time and because of the way we use the rubric. First, teachers have had several years of working with the outcomes and with portfolios, so they share an understanding of the outcomes, and have worked out many of the portfolio "kinks." Second, we spent time developing the rubric rather than using one developed elsewhere. As a result, teachers again had opportunities to clarify outcomes, and then they were able to add criteria for student performance to the discussion. Portfolio artifacts, actual examples of what students can do, grounded this work. Third, we use a two-step process on several practice portfolios before we begin scoring: (a) the moderation process in which we answer specific questions about the contents and the evidence (see chapter 8) and (b) actual practice scoring, discussion, and calibration of scores. Fourth, we created and use a scoring form on which teachers not only list scores, but also write out their conclusions and the

Table 10.1

Bellevue Evaluation System
(Grade 2–4)

Constructs Meaning from Text	Reading Ownership	Effective Writing	Self-Reflection & Self-Evaluation
(5) Personal response; synthesis; coherence; theme, major concepts; significant details; applies to prior knowledge; connections to other texts; draws conclusions and inferences; critical stance; grade level text or above	(5) Often/almost daily self-initiated reading; personal preferences; variety of interests and types; recommends or seeks book recommendations; comments with personal reactions; enthusiastic about reading and books	(5) Strength in narrative and expository; focus on ideas and communication; clear main focus/purpose/audience; organization; effective word choice and sentence fluency; voice; grade level conventions (spelling, grammar, usage; punctuation, capitalization); awareness of craft/style; flow and transitions; engaging/compelling communication	(5) Engages in self-reflection & self-evaluation (self-initiated and prompted); focus on meaning, ideas and personal reflections; understands and applies criteria for good work; sets appropriate goals; can identify strategies for goal attainment; generalizes across pieces about growth and areas for improvement
(3) Some personal response; attempt to synthesize; main idea or problem; some details; literal focus; logical sequence; draws some conclusions and inferences; connections and personal responses may be prompted; grade level text or above	(3) Moderate/average amount of reading; some personal preferences (may need encouragement); a few different types; self-selected books; personal reactions; enjoys reading and books	(3) Narrative and expository; focus on ideas and communication; clear main focus/purpose/audience; somewhat organized; acceptable word choice and sentence fluency; voice is beginning to emerge; grade level conventions (spelling, grammar, usage; punctuation, capitalization) most of the time	(3) Self-reflection & self-evaluation with prompting; some general and specific insights; some focus on surface features and meaning in reflections; goal setting usually realistic; recognition of growth
(1) Limited response; summaries are retellings; sketchy; main ideas missing; basic facts; may have misinformation or misunderstandings; few inferences; little/no connections or personal response; grade level text or below	(1) Little self-initiated reading; needs prompting to read; little interest in discussing or choosing books; doesn't enjoy	(1) Limited range of topics and genres; undeveloped ideas; sentences/word choice simple; inconsistent use of conventions; audience/voice undeveloped	(1) Limited response—focus on general/vague (I like) aspects or effort; little self-evaluation or understanding of criteria; little goal setting; may be able to see "change"
(M) No evidence in any of the artifacts; evidence missing	(M) No evidence in any of the artifacts; evidence missing	(M) No evidence in any of the artifacts; evidence missing	(M) No evidence in any of the artifacts; evidence missing

Source: Bellevue Public Schools.

evidence used to reach their decisions (see Figure 10.2). This puts the emphasis on understanding and judging evidence rather than simply on scoring. Fifth, the entire scoring process is conducted in a low-stakes environment where the emphasis is on determining what we can learn through the process. No individual students, teachers, or schools are at risk of being judged "unacceptable." In fact, on the scoring sheet, we encourage both "insider" (teacher of the student whose portfolio is being scored) and "outsider" (other teachers) perspectives on the student. We realize that insiders bring other valuable knowledge to understanding a student's performance, and we want to value that perspective as well as one based solely on the portfolio. So, for us, scoring is indeed a process that values deliberation and a focus on understanding.

The conversations and process of scoring are exhausting and intense; yet, remarkably, all of the participants come away saying that *all* teachers should have a chance to do this kind of thinking. We learn a great deal about our portfolios, our students, and ourselves. For example, the scoring process led us to be more committed to Common Tools—when they were in the portfolios teachers were more likely to have evidence on important district outcomes and more able to see students' growth over time. The scoring process also led to a need for teacher entry slips. We found that entry slips helped evaluators understand the context for a particular portfolio artifact, the kind of support that a student had in producing the work, and the teacher's goals. Scoring also led us to discussions about reading strategy instruction, difficulty level of reading texts, and the variety of types of texts that we want students to read and write. In the end, scoring discussions carry over to all other discussions we have about teaching and learning.

Analytic Evaluation of Specific Learner Outcomes: The Kamehameha Elementary Education Program and Hawaii Department of Education Rubric. This rubric, developed for third-grade Hawaiian children, provides a more detailed approach to standards than does the Bellevue rubric but a fairly similar approach to rubric development. It was designed to be used across two different literacy programs—the Kamehameha Elementary Education Program (KEEP), a privately funded educational program for native Hawaiian children, and the Hawaii Department of Education program, which serves all children in Hawaii's public schools (Paris, Calfee, Filby, Hiebert, Pearson, Valencia, & Wolf, 1992). Although the rubric was developed by outside consultants, it provides an interesting model that teachers could use to specify student performance.

The developers began their process of rubric development by spending several months examining curricula, observing in classrooms, and talking with teachers. Their goal was to identify dimensions, or outcomes, of both literacy programs. From there, they identified specific attributes and descriptors for each dimension. Table 10.2 is an example of the definitions and rubric developed for three of their seven dimensions: engagement with text through reading, engagement with text through writing, and knowledge about literacy. Under each dimension are listed two attributes that further

---

Table 10.2 *continued*

Performance indicators for each attribute and dimension of literacy

---

ENGAGEMENT WITH TEXT THROUGH READING

Low engagement	High engagement
Reading is constructive	
a. Fails to build on prior knowledge	a. Integrates new ideas with previous knowledge and experiences
b. Few inferences or elaborations; literal retelling of text	b. Exhibits within text and beyond text inferences
c. Focus is on isolated facts; does not connect text elements	c. Identifies and elaborates plots, themes, or concepts
Reading is evaluative	
a. Fails to use personal knowledge and experience as a framework for interpreting text	a. Fails to use personal knowledge and experience as a framework for interpreting text
b. Is insensitive to the author's style, assumptions, perspective, and claims	b. Is insensitive to the author's style, assumptions, perspective, and claims
c. Fails to examine or go beyond a literal account of the ideas in the text	c. Fails to examine or go beyond a literal account of the ideas in the text.

ENGAGEMENT WITH TEXT THROUGH WRITING

Low engagement	High engagement
Writing is constructive	
a. Writes disconnected words or phases with few identifiable features of any genre	a. Writes well-constructed, thematic, cohesive text that is appropriate to the genre
b. Fails to use personal knowledge as a base for composing text	b. Draws on personal knowledge and experiences in composing text
c. Little evidence of voice, personal style, or originality	c. Creative writing reveals a strong sense of voice, personal style, or originality
Writing is technically appropriate	
a. Writing includes numerous violations of the conventions of spelling, punctuation, and usage	a. Displays developmentally appropriate use of the conventions of spelling, punctuation, and usage
b. Inappropriate or inflexible use of grammatical structures	b. Writing exhibits grammatical structures appropriate to the purpose and genre
c. Limited and contextually inappropriate vocabulary	c. Rich, varied, and appropriate vocabulary

KNOWLEDGE ABOUT LITERACY

Low knowledge	High knowledge
Knowledge about literacy conventions and structures	
a. Aware of the functions of print conventions and punctuation in written communication	a. Understands the functions that print conventions and punctuation play in written communication
b. Aware of text structures and genres	b. Can identify and use several specific text structures and genres
c. Aware of the subtleties of language but does not understand or use multiple meaning, ambiguity, figurative language	c. Understands that words have multiple meanings; can use and understand ambiguity and figurative language
Writing is technically appropriate	
a. Unaware of the strategies that can be applied to reading and writing	a. Knows strategies that can be applied before, during, and after reading and writing
b. Limited understanding of how strategies can be used	b. Can explain how strategies are applied or might be used
c. Naive while reading or writing; does not value strategies; does not use selectively	c. Understands how and when strategies can be used and why they are helpful

---

Figure 10.2

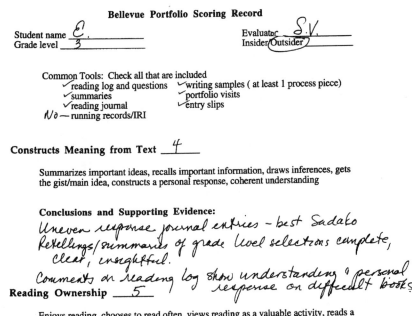

Bellevue Portfolio Scoring Record

Student name E.   Evaluator S.V.
Grade level 3   Insider/Outsider

Common Tools: Check all that are included
✓ reading log and questions   ✓ writing samples (at least 1 process piece)
✓ summaries   ✓ portfolio visits
✓ reading journal   ✓ entry slips
No — running records/IRI

Constructs Meaning from Text 4

Summarizes important ideas, recalls important information, draws inferences, gets the gist/main idea, constructs a personal response, coherent understanding

Conclusions and Supporting Evidence:

Uneven response journal entries – best Sadako
Retellings/summaries of grade level selections complete, clear, insightful.
Comments on reading log show understanding & personal response on difficult books

Reading Ownership 5

Enjoys reading, chooses to read often, views reading as a valuable activity, reads a variety of genres, reads for a variety of purposes

Conclusions and Supporting Evidence:

Reads variety (chpt. books, animal stories, fantasy, adventure)
Says enjoys reading in portfolio visits, reads at home
Teacher conference notes confirm frequency, enjoyment

---

break down, or explain, the dimension. For example, under "Engagement with text through reading" are listed "Reading is constructive" and "Reading is evaluative," which target specific areas within "engagement." Then, under each attribute are listed specific indicators that teachers would look for in student work. The indicators under "Engagement with text through reading" direct reviewers to look for evidence of students' ability to use prior knowledge, draw inferences, integrate ideas, reflect on meaning and style, and create personal responses. This analytic scheme encourages teachers to dig more deeply into their understanding of each of the dimensions or outcomes.

An interesting aspect of this project is that rather than require all teachers to keep portfolios, the consultants used a limited sample of student work and short individual student interviews to gather information. So, realizing

---

Figure 10.2 *continued*

Communicate Effectively in Writing __3__

Effective use of ideas, purpose, information, voice, organization, word choice, sentence fluency, conventions, presentation

Conclusions and Supporting Evidence:

Strong begin. & middle but ends trail off (see writing from 2/10 & 4/12)
Voice is beginning to develop - sporatic
Spelling / grammar moving toward conventional
Strong vocab & varied sentence structure (see Chinese Folk Tale)

Writing Process __3__

Evidence of planning, drafting, revision, editing, sharing

Conclusions and Supporting Evidence:

No evidence of planning
Revision includes insertions (mostly words)
Has edited for some spelling & capitalization
Mostly 1st draft writing

Concluding Comments:

Additional Evidence Needed:

More samples of writing taken beyond 1st draft.

Scoring form teachers use to put grades and comments on

Table 10.2

Critical dimensions and attributes of literacy

---

1. Engagement with text through reading
A critical aspect of literacy is the extent to which readers and writers interact with the ideas conveyed in text. They need to relate their background knowledge and experiences to new textual information and integrate the ideas. Thoughtful engagement with text implies that readers construct meaning sensibly, that they employ strategies as they read, and that they reflect on the meaning and style of the text. Comprehension is a key element of engagement, but the dimension also includes the demonstration of thinking strategies and personal responses to text that extend the basic interpretation of text.

2. Engagement with text through writing
Writing is a constructive expression of ideas that are communicated coherently and accurately. Students' involvement with writing and reading should provide mutual support for effective literacy strategies, habits, and motivation. Writing should be embedded in everyday activities and based on genuine communicative purposes. It should allow students to compose their ideas on a variety of topics with different genres and styles. Students' writing should include their personal opinions, reflections, and elaborations to texts they have read. The message and voice should be clear. The technical aspects of writing such as spelling, word choice, punctuation, grammar, and organization should be appropriate for the students' grade level.

3. Knowledge about literacy
Students should understand that language can be expressed through reading and writing according to literacy conventions and that adherence to these conventions helps people to understand each other through written communication. For example, effective readers and writers understand the different purposes and structures of various literary genres and know how strategies can be used while reading and writing. Their knowledge about literacy also includes their metalinguistic understanding of the nuances of language, such as ambiguity and figurative language, as well as their understanding about the connections among reading, writing, listening, and speaking.

Source: Paris, S. G., Calfee, R. C., Filby, N., Hiebert, E. H., Pearson, P. D., Valencia, W. Wolf, K. P. (1992). A framework for authentic literacy assessment. *The Reading* 46(2), 88-98.

---

that the work samples may not contain all of the needed information and that portfolio implementation takes time, they sought the kind of information that a classroom teacher might have about students from working with them on a daily basis. Taking all of the information together, student evidence can be assigned a score from 1 (low engagement) to 4 (high engagement) on each of the three layers of the rubric—broad dimension (e.g., engagement with reading), specific attribute (reading is constructive), or each specific descriptor (prior knowledge and experiences)—to meet the varying needs of administrators and teachers. Administrators would most likely want information about student performance at the dimension level; teachers would find information at the attribute and indicator levels more useful diagnostically and instructionally. So, this system can be as broad as

the Bellevue system (dimensions) or much more detailed (attributes indicators). Paris, et al. (1992) stress the importance of a cohesive framework that involves teachers and is responsive to local "We cannot emphasize too strongly the importance of their ating" what is important to assess (the dimensions) and the utes "because it allows local stake holders to create and concepts about literacy development."

Specific evidence for evaluation of learner outcomes mentary Education Program (KEEP) Benchmark

for evaluating portfolios comes from the Kamehameha Elementary Education Program (KEEP) itself. Unlike the preceding rubric, which was designed to be used across two different systems, the KEEP Benchmarks were designed to be used only by KEEP teachers and consultants working in KEEP classrooms. Therefore, the KEEP evaluation system was designed around its four major literacy outcomes: reading ownership, reading process, writing ownership, and writing process. Within each of these outcomes is a list of specific benchmarks that require specific evidence that should be found in the portfolios (Asam, Au, Blake, Carroll, Jacobson, & Scheu, 1993). There are between 7 and 21 benchmarks for each literacy outcome at the primary level; there are between 9 and 28 benchmarks for each at the intermediate level. The number of benchmarks increases by grade level. Table 10.3 is a sample of a portion (20 of 27) of the benchmarks for reading process at the fourth-grade level. A key element of the benchmarks is that they all are "susceptible" to instruction, that is, they are easy to see in student work. And, because portfolio evaluation at KEEP wasn't implemented until teachers had spent several years focused on instruction, the benchmarks were also easy for teachers to envision in terms of their classroom instruction.

This system could be considered "low inference" compared with the Bellevue and KEEP/Hawaii Department of Education systems because it is quite specific about what counts as evidence. For example, there must be copies from a student's literature log to count as evidence of "Writes personal responses to literature," and there must be written story summaries for evidence of "Comprehends and writes about theme/author's message." Some benchmarks can be covered by the same piece of evidence. For example, the summaries might also serve as evidence of students' knowledge of story elements. Using this very specific evidence, the evaluator of a fourth grader's portfolio must find evidence for all 27 benchmarks. On the basis of the evidence, the evaluator rates the student S (satisfactory, grade-level performance), D (developing, below grade-level performance), or M (missing, no evidence available) for each specific benchmark. Sometimes there are anchor pieces to help teachers determine what is grade level; at other times, teachers discuss expectations. If, after examining all of the evidence, the student receives an S on all benchmarks, the evaluator assigns an overall rating of "at grade level." If the student receives one or more Ds, the rating given is "below grade level."

Once again, the process for using these benchmarks has some striking similarities with the Bellevue process and the recommendations of Paris, et al. During the first two years of portfolio implementation at KEEP, teachers were most concerned with collecting evidence and focusing on instruction. Consultants who worked on a regular basis with classroom teachers therefore developed the benchmarks. However, in the third year of portfolio implementation, teachers began to work with the benchmarks to evaluate the portfolios of all of the students in their classes. Working with the consultants, they agreed that the benchmarks were good indicators of their curriculum and expectations for students. Then, they would get together at grade-level meetings and evaluate their own portfolios. As they had

---

Table 10.3

Kamehameha Elementary Education (KEEP) Benchmarks
(Grade 4)

READING/LISTENING COMPREHENSION

Small Group Discussions

Participates in small group reading discussions: teacher-led student-led
Shares written responses to literature in small groups: teacher-led student-led

Written Response: Aesthetic

Writes personal responses to literature
Comprehends and writes about theme/author's message
Applies/connects theme to own life/experiences
Makes connections among different works of literature
Applies/connects content text information to own life/experiences

Written Response: Efferent

Reads nonfiction and shows understanding of content
Writes summary that includes story elements
Reads different genres of fiction and shows understanding of genre characteristics

LANGUAGE & VOCABULARY KNOWLEDGE

Shows facility with language through quality responses during small group discussions
Notes and discusses new or interesting language in small groups
Uses clear, meaningful language to express ideas in written responses or summaries
Uses multiple vocabulary strategies
Responds in a variety of ways during small group discussions
Learns new or meaningful vocabulary from voluntary reading

Source: Asam, C., Au, K., Carroll, J., Jacobson, H., & Scheu, J. (1993). *Literacy curriculum guide: Kamehameha Elementary Education Program.* Honolulu: Kamehameha Schools/Bernice Pauhai Bishop Estate.

questions, they would share portfolios and talk about what they saw and how that fit with a particular benchmark. It took time for teachers to feel comfortable looking through all of the work and making judgments about student performance. The focus, however, was not on the ratings but rather on using the ratings to see patterns in student performance and in teaching. For example, one teacher noticed that the scores for all of her students were low in editing because she had done all of the editing for them. This helped her identify a new instructional strategy for engaging students in their own editing (Au, 1997). These conversations were "low risk," not aimed at identifying particular students or teachers in trouble. Instead, they were aimed at helping teachers think about students, curriculum, and instruction.

Developmental scale for evaluating one aspect of literacy: South Brunswick Early Literacy Scale. The South Brunswick schools have been using a districtwide Early Literacy Portfolio for more than seven years (Chittenden & Spicer, 1993; Salinger & Chittenden, 1994; South Brunswick Board of Education, 1992). It grew out of broader curricular changes in the early grades (K–2)—a move toward developmentally appropriate curriculum—that, teachers determined, required a corresponding change in assessment. The portfolio was developed primarily by teachers in collaboration with administrators and consultant researchers. Its purpose is to help teachers document students' literacy learning and to plan for instruction. So, this portfolio is more like the documentation and evaluation portfolios we described in Chapter 2; it is a teacher record-keeping system, documenting student growth during grades K–2. Specific portfolio components and procedures are required (e.g., writing samples, story retellings, oral reading records) and administered to students at designated times during kindergarten, grade one, and grade two.

In an effort to displace a districtwide standardized reading test in first grade and to answer questions about accountability, teachers and research consultants collaboratively developed a six-point scale for rating one aspect of literacy—students' "strategies for making sense of print" (see Table 10.4). No other aspects of literacy, such as interest or depth of understanding, are included in this scale or other scales. So the scale covers only a portion of the curriculum and a portion of the portfolio. It is referred to as a "theory-referenced" scale because it was developed based on research and practice in early literacy. Teachers spent considerable time researching and reviewing other early literacy scales, assessments, and research to determine what they wanted to include on their own scale. Each point on the scale describes what a child can do at various developmental phases of making sense of and with print from kindergarten through grade two. Nevertheless, even with these descriptions, it is obvious that teachers need a solid grounding in early literacy to be able to understand and apply the scale to children's work. Similarly, that same solid grounding is necessary for teachers to administer and interpret required portfolio pieces such as running records and writing samples. It is unlikely that this scale could be

---

Table 10.4

DRAFT 6

K-2 Reading/Writing Scale
Development of children's strategies for making sense of print

0 - N/A

1 - EARLY EMERGENT
Displays an awareness of some conventions of reading, such as front/back of books, distinctions between print and pictures. Sees the construction of meaning from text as "magical" or exterior to the print. While the child may be interested in the contents of books, there is as yet little apparent attention to turning written marks into language. Is beginning to notice environmental print.

2 - ADVANCED EMERGENT
Engages in pretend reading and writing. Uses reading-like ways that clearly approximate book language. Demonstrates a sense of the story being "read" using picture clues and recall of story line. May draw upon predictable language patterns in anticipating (and recalling) the story. Attempts to use letters in writing, sometimes in random or scribble fashion.

3 - EARLY BEGINNING READER
Attempts to "really read." Indicates beginning sense of one-to-one correspondence and concept of word. Predicts actively in new material, using syntax and story line. Small stable sight vocabulary is becoming established. Evidence of initial awareness of beginning and ending sounds, especially in invented spelling.

4 - ADVANCED BEGINNING READER
Starts to draw on major cue systems: self-corrects or identifies words through use of letter-sound patterns, sense of story, or syntax. Reading may be laborious especially with new material, requiring considerable effort and some support. Writing and spelling reveal awareness of letter patterns. Conventions of writing such as capitalization and full stops are beginning to appear.

5 - EARLY INDEPENDENT READER
Handles familiar material on own, but still needs some support with unfamiliar material. Figures out words and self-corrects by drawing on a combination of letter-sound relationships, word structure, story line and syntax. Strategies of re-reading or of guessing from larger chunks of texts are becoming well established. Has a large stable sight vocabulary. Conventions of writing are understood.

6 - ADVANCED INDEPENDENT READER
Reads independently, using multiple strategies flexibly. Monitors and self-corrects for meaning. Can read and understand most material when the content is appropriate. Conventions of writing and spelling are—for the most part—under control.

Source: South Brunswick/ETS Reading/Writing Scale. Making sense of print. Monmouth Junction, NJ: South Brunswick Public Schools.

used meaningfully without the in-depth curriculum discussions and study that preceded its development.

Teachers use this scale at the middle and end of each school year to rate their students' portfolios from 0 through 6, and they attend annual moderation meetings where they rate a sample of their colleagues' portfolios. The moderation experience provides teachers with additional scoring experiences and with a second, "blind," evaluation of some of their own students' portfolios. However, once again, the process of examining work and discussing interpretations with colleagues seems to be the key to the use of the scale. Salinger and Chittenden (1994) noted that the rating scale itself did not seem particularly salient to teachers but that the opportunity to discuss portfolios promoted a shared language and understanding of curriculum and expectations for children.

The four evaluation systems described in this chapter take different approaches to judging student performance. However, they have three important elements in common. First, all of the systems rely on a shared interpretive framework that was begun long before the rubrics were developed. The discussions were grounded in the curriculum first, then extended as participants developed their own evaluation rubrics. As a result, all of the evaluation systems are intimately linked to specific learner outcomes. Second, evaluation is seen more as a process than as a product. Participants must have ongoing opportunities to explore and anchor their understandings about teaching, learning, and standards with their colleagues. The emphasis is on understanding rather than on scoring even as teachers confront issues of making judgments about student performance. And third, the results of the evaluation process are meaningful for teachers—they learn something from the process that has immediate implications for their teaching. Scoring is a part of learning to understand student work, not a chore done to report to others.

Conclusion

Our approach to grading and to evaluating portfolios is based on the value of developing a shared understanding of learner outcomes and of standards for student performance. The more we discuss and deliberate these critical aspects of teaching and learning, the more comfortable we will become with judging student work and the more likely we will be to make good instructional decisions. That is why we believe that the *process* of evaluating portfolios must be part of portfolio implementation and why portfolios must be aligned with and support report card grades. Assigning grades and evaluating portfolios force issues of curriculum and standards to the fore, making them public and systematic rather than secretive and idiosyncratic. When we can talk confidently and knowledgeably about what we want students to learn and how well they are progressing toward specific standards, the public, administrators and parents will come to understand our expectations for their children, and they will come to trust our judgments as professionals. In the end, our students, of course, will be the winners.

References

Afflerbach, P. P., & Johnston, P. H. (1993). Writing language arts report cards: Eleven teachers' conflicts of knowing and communicating. *Elementary School Journal, 94*(1), 73–86.

Asam, C., Au, K., Carroll, J., Jacobson, H., & Scheu, J. (1993). *Literacy curriculum guide: Kamehameha Elementary Education Program.* Honolulu: Kamehameha Schools/Bernice Pauhai Bishop Estate.

Aschbacher, P. R. (1994). Helping educators to develop and use alternative assessments: Barriers and facilitators. *Educational Policy, 8*(2), 202–223.

Au, K. H. (1993). Personal Communication.

Au, K. H., Carroll, J. H., & Scheu, J. A. (1997). *Balanced literacy instruction: A teacher's resource book.* Norwood, MA: Christopher-Gordon Publishers.

Chittenden, E., & Spicer, W. (1993). *The South Brunswick literacy portfolio project.* Paper presented at the New Standards Project: English/Language Arts Portfolio Meeting, Minneapolis, MN

Delpit, L. (1995). *Other people's children: Cultural conflict in the classroom.* New York: The New Press.

Farr, R., & Tone, B. (1994). *Portfolio and performance assessment.* Fort Worth, TX: Harcourt Brace College Publishers.

Gearhart, M., Herman, J. L., Baker, E. L., & Whittaker, A. K. (1993). *Whose work is it? A question for the validity of large-scale portfolio assessment* (CSE Tech. Rep. No. 363). Los Angeles: Center for Research on Evaluation, Standards, and Student Testing.

Hansen, J. (1994). Literacy portfolios: Windows on potential. In S. W. Valencia, E. H. Hiebert, & P. P. Afflerbach (Eds.), *Authentic reading assessment: Practices and possibilities* (pp.26-40). Newark, DE: International Reading Association.

Hiebert, E. H., & Calfee, R. C. (1992). Assessing literacy: From standardized tests to portfolios and performances. In S. J. Samuels & A. E. Farstrup (Eds.), *What research has to say about reading instruction* (pp. 70–100). Newark, DE: International Reading Association.

Koretz, D., Stecher, B., Klein, S., & McCaffrey, D. (1994). The Vermont portfolio assessment program: Findings and implications. *Educational Measurement: Issues and Practice, 13*(3), 5–16.

LeMahieu, P. G., Gitomer, D. H., & Eresh, J. T. (1995). Portfolios in large-scale assessment: Difficult but not impossible. *Educational Assessment: Issues and Practice, 14*(3), 11–16, 25–28.

Mitchell, R. (1992). *Testing for learning.* New York: The Free Press.

Moss, P. A., Beck, J. S., Ebbs, C., Matson, B., Muchmore, J., Steele, D., Taylor, C., & Herter, R. (1992). Portfolios, accountability, and an interpretive approach to validity. *Educational Measurement: Issues and Practice, 11*(3), 12–21.

Paris, S. G., Calfee, R. C., Filby, N., Hiebert, E. H., Pearson, P. D., Valencia, S. W., & Wolf, K. P. (1992). A framework for authentic literacy assessment. *The Reading Teacher, 46*(2), 88–98.

Pearson, P. D., & Valencia, S. W. (1987). Assessment, accountability, and professional prerogative. In J. E. Readence & R. S. Baldwin (Eds.), *Research in literacy: Merging perspectives* (pp. 3–16). Rochester, NY: National Reading Conference.

Salinger, T., & Chittenden, E. (1994). Analysis of an early literacy portfolio: Consequences for instruction. *Language Arts, 71*(6), 446–452.

Shepard, L. (1989). Why we need better assessments. *Educational Leadership, 46*(7), 4–9.

South Brunswick/ETS Reading/Writing Scale: Making sense of print. Monmouth Junction, NJ: South Brunswick Public Schools.

Stiggins, R. J. (1991). Assessment literacy. *Phi Delta Kappan, 72*(7), 534–539.

Stiggins, R. J. (1997). *Student-centered classroom assessment* (2nd ed.). New York: Macmillan College Publishing Company.

Valencia, S. W., & Au, K. H. (1997). Portfolios across educational contexts: Issues of evaluation, professional development, and system validity. *Educational Assessment, 4*(1), 1–35.

Valencia, S. W., & Calfee, R. C. (1991). The development and use of literacy portfolios for students, classes, and teachers. *Applied Measurement in Education, 4*(4), 333–345.

Valencia, S.W. & Place, N. (1994). Literacy portfolios for teaching, learning, and accountability: The Bellevue Literacy Assessment Project. In S. W. Valencia, E. H. Hiebert, & P. P. Afflerbach (Eds.), Authentic reading assessment: Practices and possibilities (pp.134-156). Newark, DE: International Reading Association.

Wiggins, G. (1993). Assessment: Authenticity, context, and validity. *Phi Delta Kappan 75*(3), 200-208, 210.

Wixson, K. K., Valencia, S. W., & Lipson, M. Y. (1994). Issues in literacy assessment: Facing the realities of internal and external assessment. *Journal of Reading Behavior, 26*(3), 315–337.

Index